Beyond Old and New Perspectives on Paul

Beyond Old and New Perspectives on Paul

Reflections on the Work of Douglas Campbell

Edited by
CHRIS TILLING

With a Foreword by Edward Adams

CASCADE *Books* · Eugene, Oregon

BEYOND OLD AND NEW PERSPECTIVES ON PAUL
Reflections on the Work of Douglas Campbell

Cascade Books
An Imprint of Wipf and Stock Publishers
199 W. 8th Ave., Suite 3
Eugene, OR 97401

www.wipfandstock.com

ISBN 13: 978-1-62564-173-1

Cataloging-in-Publication data:

Beyond old and new perspectives on Paul : reflections on the work of Douglas Campbell / edited by Chris Tilling ; with a foreword by Edward Adams.

xvi + 342 p. ; 23 cm. Includes bibliographical references and indexes.

ISBN 13: 978-1-62564-173-1

1. Campbell, Douglas Atchison, 1961–. 2. Bible. Epistles of Paul—Theology. 3. Bible. Romans—Criticism, interpretation. I. Adams, Edward. II. Title.

BS2655.J8 T584 2014

Manufactured in the U.S.A.

Chapter 1: Torrance, Alan. "A Review of Douglas Campbell's *The Deliverance of God* from a Theological Perspective" © 2012 *Scottish Journal of Theology*. Originally published in *Scottish Journal of Theology* 65.1 (2012) 82–89. Reprinted with permission.

Appendix A: Torrance, James B. "Contribution of McLeod Campbell to Scottish Theology." © 1970 *Scottish Journal of Theology*. Originally published in *Scottish Journal of Theology* 23.1 (1970) 51–76. Reprinted with permission.

Appendix B: Torrance, James B. "Covenant or Contract: A Study of the Theological Background of Worship in Seventeenth-Century Scotland" © 1973 *Scottish Journal of Theology*. Originally published in *Scottish Journal of Theology* 26.3 (1973) 295–311. Reprinted with permission.

For my students and colleagues at
St. Mellitus College and King's College London

"Even more than the Reformers did, we must let God and His Word be one, with more emphasis, more joy, more consistency, and we must let Jesus Christ be even more self-evidently the one Mediator between God and humanity."

—KARL BARTH

Contents

Foreword

In December 2011, at King's College London, was convened a conference critically engaging with Douglas Campbell's monumental *The Deliverance of God*. A follow-up conference was held in November 2012 at Duke Divinity School. The present volume arises from papers presented at these gatherings. It is appropriate that the first conference took place at King's, where Douglas's work on the project that would lead to *Deliverance* began in earnest. I was a colleague of his during his time at King's and witnessed first hand the early birth pangs of the project. It was a great delight to welcome my old friend back to King's to celebrate and reflect critically on his achievement. And what an achievement! The breathtaking vision of the work, the immense learning that Douglas demonstrates, the depth of his conceptual penetration, the boldness and originality of his thinking, and his extraordinary ability to mount and sustain a highly complex yet sharply focused argument over the course of more than 1,200 pages make *Deliverance* a truly astonishing intellectual feat.

The Deliverance of God is one of the most significant books on Paul's theology ever written (as well as one of the longest!) and as such deserves very serious scholarly attention. The two conferences were structured to give Douglas an opportunity to recapitulate and clarify his main claims in the book and to enable invited biblical scholars, church historians, and theologians to offer their critical reactions to aspects of the work. Participants were generally in sympathy with a good deal of what Douglas says in the book, and where critical concerns were raised and (sometimes strong) disagreements were expressed, appreciative notes were also sounded. The friendly tenor of the conference proceedings is reflected in the volume contributions.

The title chosen for the first conference, retained for the second, and adopted as the title of the present book, reflects Douglas's concern to move beyond both "Lutheran" readings of Paul and the "New Perspective" on Paul (Michael Bird has helpfully labelled Douglas's work a "Post-New Perspective on Paul").

The length and complexity of *Deliverance* make it a formidable read! This collection of essays is designed in part to introduce the concerns of that book more accessibly. It is worth pointing out that Douglas has provided an overview of the argument of *Deliverance* in an article in *Expository Times* (Vol. 123 no. 8, pp. 382–93) and a summary of his take on Paul's theology in *Four Views on the Apostle Paul* (ed. Michael F. Bird, Zondervan, 2013).

In the preface, Chris Tilling, the editor of this volume, expresses various thanks. I would like to thank Chris himself not only for his work in editing the book but also for initiating the King's conference and thus setting in motion the whole endeavor. My role in the whole has been very minimal, but it has been a pleasure and privilege to be part of it.

Edward Adams

Preface

The book you are now holding grows out of two conferences focusing on the work of Douglas Campbell, particularly his exciting, brilliant, controversial, learned, and truly remarkable monograph, *The Deliverance of God*. The first conference was held at King's College, London, and the second, at Campbell's own Duke University, North Carolina. The title of this book is indeed the name chosen for the King's conference. Both drew on the wisdom and critical insights of classicists, systematic theologians, church historians, and (of course) New Testament scholars, a multidisciplinary response entirely appropriate to the subject matter of our discussions. The papers, the responses, the plenary debates, and the contributions from some exalted visitors all made the experience both an education and a delight, and we hope to have captured something of that vital dynamic in the following pages. A number of fortuitous meetings led to the richness of those meetings. I am particularly grateful for an entirely unplanned encounter and conversation with Dr. Robin Griffith-Jones on the London Underground, which led to his contribution in this volume.

The ethos of this book is detailed in the introduction, so let me get straight to some important "thank yous." We are very grateful for the team from Grace Communion International who filmed the main sessions of the London conference, making the live discussions available to a much wider audience (it can be found online at http://www.gci.org/media/paulconf2011). The book wouldn't have been possible without the help of a team of people who kindly volunteered aid at various stages. In this vein, thanks to a great team of proofreaders, namely Mia Smith, Doug Iverson, Dr. Jeffrey Gibson, Rhona Holliday, Jon Bennett, Tim Hall, Bryan Lewis, and Dr. Brian Tucker. Also thanks to Stephanie Gehring, Douglas's research assistant, for her help in formatting the manuscript, and to Dr. Carl Sweatman for his valuable work on Alan Torrance's article, and Appendix 2. Your helpfulness and kindness throughout this project was invaluable. Thanks to Mia Smith for final stage proofreading, to Dr. Rafael Rodriguez for his critical comments on a draft of a chapter, and to Shawn Wilhite for his work on Appendix 1. The rising star, William Glass, also generated a complete bibliography, for which I am immensely grateful. Joseph Longarino and Katie Law did a tremendous job with the indices. I am deeply indebted to Ashley Douglas for converting the appendices from old pdf files! My own precious wife, Anja Tilling, also kindly helped on this front—and on many others besides! While on the subject of wives, I ought to thank Rachel Campbell, Douglas's spouse, for providing vital impetus for the conferences. To have the wisdom and input of scholars such as Prof. Richard Bauckham, Prof. Jeremy Begbie, Dr. Willie Jennings, Prof. David Steinmetz, Prof. Richard Burridge, Dr. Edward Adams and others was a sincere privilege, so our thanks to you all for attending many of those early debates. I reserve a special mention for Dr. Andrew Perriman who flew to the London conference from Dubai! Finally, a warm thanks to the wonderful team at Wipf & Stock, all of whom I consider friends. In this respect, a special thanks to Robin Parry for his editorial skills.

It has been particularly gratifying as a faculty member at St. Mellitus College to work so closely with scholars from King's College London, St. Andrews University Scotland, and Duke University. I work with an astonishing team, and I must record my thanks and gratitude to all who make St. Mellitus such a rare and special place to work and thrive, to: Dr. Graham Tomlin, our Dean, Dr. Andrew Emerton and Ann Coleman, our Assistant Deans, Dr. Lincoln Harvey, Dr. Jane Williams, Dr. Stephen Backhouse, Dr. Sean Doherty, Dr. Mark Scarlata, Eileen Lockhart, Rob Merchant, Dr. Michael Lloyd (now the Principal at Wycliffe Hall), Hannah Kennedy, Philippa Bird, Jo Streat, Simone Odendaal, Rhona Holliday, Ricarda Baldock, Rosie Allard, and Sophie Francisco. A dream team. With much affection this book is dedicated to my students and colleagues at both King's College London and St. Mellitus College.

Contributors

KATE BOWLER is Assistant Professor of the History of Christianity in the United States at Divinity School, Duke University. She is the author of *Blessed: A History of the American Prosperity Gospel* (2013).

DOUGLAS A. CAMPBELL is Professor of New Testament at the Divinity School, Duke University. He is the author of *The Rhetoric of Righteousness in Romans 3:21–26* (1992), *The Quest for Paul's Gospel: A Suggested Strategy* (2005), and *The Deliverance of God: An Apocalyptic Rereading of Justification in Paul* (2009).

CURTIS W. FREEMAN is Research Professor of Theology at Divinity School, Duke University and Director of the Baptist House of Studies. His books include *Ties That Bind* (1994), *Baptist Roots* (1999), and *A Company of Women Preachers* (2011).

ROBIN GRIFFITH-JONES is Master of The Temple in London, and Senior Visiting Lecturer, King's College London. His books include *The Four Witnesses* (2000), *The Gospel according to Paul* (2004), *The Da Vinci Code and the Secrets of the Temple* (2006), and *Mary Magdalene* (2008).

SCOTT J. HAFEMANN is Reader in New Testament, School of Divinity, St. Mary's College, University of St. Andrews. His books include *Suffering and Ministry in the Spirit* (1990), *Paul, Moses & the History of Israel* (1994), *2 Corinthians* (2000), *The God of Promise and the Life of Faith* (2001).

DAVID HILBORN is Principal of St. John's College, Nottingham, and was Head of Theology for the Evangelical Alliance, UK. In this capacity he authored a number of EA reports, such as *The Nature of Hell* (2000) and *Evangelicalism and the Orthodox Church* (2001). He also authored *Picking Up the Pieces* (1997).

J. WARREN SMITH is Associate Professor of Historical Theology, Divinity School, Duke University, and author of *Passion and Paradise* (2004) and *Christian Grace and Pagan Virtue* (2010).

CHRIS TILLING is New Testament Studies Lecturer, St. Mellitus College and St. Paul's Theological Centre, and Visiting Lecturer, King's College London. He is the author of *Paul's Divine Christology* (2012).

GRAHAM TOMLIN is Dean of St. Mellitus College, London, and a Visiting Lecturer at King's College London, having formerly been Vice Principal of Wycliffe Hall, Oxford. His books include *The Power of the Cross* (1999), *Luther and His World* (2002), *Spiritual Fitness* (2006), *Provocative Church* (2008), *The Prodigal Spirit* (2011), and *Looking through the Cross: The Archbishop of Canterbury's Lent Book* (2014).

ALAN J. TORRANCE is Professor of Systematic Theology, St. Andrews University, Scotland. He is the author of *Persons in Communion* (1996) and *The Theological Grounds for Advocating Forgiveness and Reconciliation in the Sociopolitical Realm* (2006).

† **JAMES B. TORRANCE** (1923–2003) was Professor of Systematic Theology at the University of Aberdeen. He authored *Worship, Community and the Triune God of Grace* (1996).

BRITTANY E. WILSON is Assistant Professor of New Testament at Divinity School, Duke University. She is currently working on her first book, *Unmanly Men: Refigurations of Masculinity in Luke-Acts.*

Introduction

CHRIS TILLING

"*Beyond* old and new perspectives on Paul!" bemused students exclaim. "We are still trying to get our heads around the old and new ones! Now there is a *newer* one?" And then there are those students who know a bit more about phrases such as "old perspective" and "new perspective,"[1] and this elite group often already have a personal investment in one or the other. With narrowed eyes, they continue: "So, you're saying that both the Reformation and the New Perspective on Paul have it wrong? And you think you have it right?!"

Depending on how early in the day it is, and whether I have drunk enough coffee, my response often runs something like this: "The 'old perspective' is not simply wrong, it has much to offer and don't let anybody tell you otherwise! But it is not a portrayal of Pauline theology that is without its problems. And the 'new perspective,' which doesn't even exist in the singular, is really a group of very different scholarly positions united by a new perspective on Second Temple Judaism. And they are likewise helpful. They saw some very real problems associated with the so-called 'old perspective,' particularly its portrayal of 'the Jew.' Yet its diagnosis of the problem confronting readers of Paul is one-dimensional and its prescribed reinterpretation of Paul remains partly implicit in the real interpretative difficulties involved."

---

1. This is not the place to summarize the import of those phrases, a task that has been undertaken in summary form in a number of places. See, for example, useful student resources such as Beilby and Eddy, *Justification*; Westerholm, *Perspectives Old and New on Paul*; Yinger, *The New Perspective on Paul*.

After linking some of this with what we have covered in our classes on Galatians and Romans, I finally add: "At least this is what Douglas Campbell argues. He presents a complete rereading of Paul's letters that genuinely offers a way beyond problems associated with old and new perspectives. And his resultant picture of Paul's theology generally, and the Apostle's soteriology particularly, is beautiful, liberating, consistent, exegetically rigorous, theologically aware, and pastorally compelling. It captures, I think, the best of the old perspective, with its concern to speak energetically about the God who saves, and it takes seriously the concerns of the new perspective on Second Temple Judaism. But in remarkable and jarringly elegant ways, it moves beyond them both." At this point, more discussion (and hopefully coffee) ensues.

But also in the academy, Douglas Campbell's work, particularly his monograph, *The Deliverance of God* (hereafter *Deliverance*),[2] has many people engaging in heated debate. On the one hand, some have simply dismissed his numerous proposals without too much engagement, while others throw serious charges such as "incipient Marcionism" and "intellectual blackmail" in Campbell's direction![3] Barry Matlock, for example, accurately described his own review of *Deliverance* as "unrelentingly negative."[4] Yet on the other hand, others speak of Campbell's paradigm-shifting brilliance,[5] his being "terribly right when it matters,"[6] and write of his creative originality,[7] and so on. So it is fair to say that Campbell's work has generated a very mixed response! And though I would argue that much of the criticism has been less than helpful and has not always represented his position accurately, *Deliverance* is of such significance (not to mention sheer size!) that it *requires* the attention and sustained consideration of the scholarly community. Reason enough for publishing this book!

But indulge me a little personal aside in order to explain further my own motivations for helping to organize the King's College London conference on *Deliverance*, and my work as editor of this book. Of course, some will no doubt rightly note that the quality of contributors to this

---

2. Campbell, *Deliverance*.

3. Moo, "The Deliverance of God," 150; Matlock, "Zeal for Paul," 137.

4. Matlock, "Zeal for Paul," 146.

5. Tilling "The Deliverance of God, and of Paul?" 83, 98.

6. Gorman, "Douglas Campbell's *The Deliverance of God*," 99.

7. Jipp, "Douglas Campbell's Apocalyptic, Rhetorical Paul," 197.

volume is all the justification I would need for going to press! But for me there are also deeper reasons. Apart from a desire to seek clarity on the complex debates surrounding Paul, justification, and the "new perspective(s)," my concerns, when reading *Deliverance*, have revolved around my experiences as a New Testament lecturer at St. Mellitus College, where I help to train present and future church leaders how to read and handle Scripture. In this capacity, I have become keenly aware of, to use Tony Thiselton's language, the "deep chasm between the universe of discourse in which some New Testament specialists operate and that of many systematic theologians," and, I would add, that of pastors and ministers.[8] I found it sobering to remember that, despite training in the best theological and biblical scholarship of his age, the young Karl Barth likewise was at a loss during his pastoral experiences in Safenwil.[9] And as I sought in class to clarify certain key Pauline exegetical issues with recourse to, say, the most precise model for understanding soteriological themes in second Temple Judaism and its relationship to works of law, or the best salvation-historical models relating to the curse of exile, I began to realize that I was potentially making biblical historians the often confused priests through whom my students needed to go to gain, through the fog of historical reconstruction, a word of God from the Bible. And this hardly lent itself to the kind of confidence 1 Peter 4:11 speaks about, that preachers could orate as those "speaking the very words of God." Could my curriculum have been generating more Safenwils?, I anxiously wondered. Fueled by such concerns, and a desire to hold on tightly to the best historical-critical and grammatical-linguistic tools of biblical scholarship, I picked up *Deliverance*.

As a result of a close reading, tectonic theological and biblical plates started to slide into place. Of course, I was—and am—left with a host of questions, but, as I read and then reread *Deliverance*, theological and exegetical concerns, scattered across the divided mind of my Western European theological education, began to reconnect. If Douglas is right, I mused, then understanding Paul is about being more profoundly Christ-centered than I had ever anticipated. On top of this, I found that numerous murky discussions found profound conceptual clarity in *Deliverance*—here was a work that could take the debates relating to Paul forward.

8. Thiselton, *Hermeneutics of Doctrine*, 376.
9. See, e.g., Busch, *Karl Barth: His Life*, 61.

So you can perhaps imagine my disappointment when some key reviews started to come out, which not infrequently either ignored or sometimes quite seriously misunderstood Campbell's arguments, and then dismissed them. It goes without saying that though we may well end up disagreeing with Campbell for a host of reasons, it is better that they are *good* reasons that truly engage with his arguments, and not a caricature of them.

And so this book! It is based on the need to sit Douglas down, and think through his views carefully, making sure we understand him, and then we need together, with biblical scholars, church historians, systematicians, and classicists, to try to sift the wheat from the chaff. I am sure I speak for all of the contributors when I say we hope this book is an example of edifying sifting *and* listening.

To keep matters cohesive, and to make sure the central issues are covered, this book will roughly follow the structure of *Deliverance*. It is thus divided into two sections. Part One, chapters 1 through 8, analyzes key aspects of Campbell's account of the *problem* confronting readers of Paul. Part Two, chapters 9 through 15, analyzes key aspects of Campbell's proposed *solution* to understanding Paul aright. After each chapter—apart from his own, of course—Campbell writes a paragraph or two in response, what he has learned from each, or where disagreements remain. In this way, readers of this book will be drawn into a lively and important ongoing conversation. As the book goes to print, I will also release a video interview with Campbell, where we spend more time discussing some of the important critical issues.

In the first chapter, Alan Torrance focuses on the theological aspects of Campbell's proposal, particularly the contrast between Paul's apocalyptic and participatory theology, on the one hand, and contractual and foundationalist theology on the other. Torrance does not attempt to adjudicate on Pauline exegetical matters, but he does affirm the importance and appropriateness of the theological dynamics driving Campbell's project.

In chapter 2, Graham Tomlin focuses on Campbell's portrayal of Luther and a number of wider matters relating to Campbell's interpretation. If Campbell is right about Romans 1:18–32 being a position the Apostle apparently does not endorse, Tomlin asks, where does this leave the doctrine of the clarity of Scripture? Despite Tomlin's appreciation for Campbell's handling of Luther, he argues that Luther is not an example of a mix of contractual and unconditional theology, as Campbell suggests. The contractual contours of Justification Theory are simply never present in Luther. The reformer indeed fights them.

Campbell begins, in chapter 3, by outlining "contractual foundationalism," a methodological Arianism that wreaks theological havoc and interpretive mischief in readings of Paul. Over against this stands the Athanasian response to this foundationalism, an unconditional and covenantal theological vision that offers a very different account of God, atonement, humanity, and its freedom and ethical responsibility.

Campbell's strong distinction between the "Justification Theory" dynamics inherent in traditional readings of Romans 1–4, and the "alternative gospel" of Romans 5–8, has been rejected by most reviewers. To clarify his argument, Campbell claims that the apocalyptic or alternative gospel is Athanasian in its theological heart, while Romans 1–4, traditionally understood, involves Arian methodological commitments. These are not, in other words, readings "in tension" with one another, but ones with fundamentally irreconcilable accounts of theology. In chapter 4 I assess Campbell's claims by examining the nature of Paul's divine Christology. Although Campbell's position is endorsed in a number of ways, I raise questions about the appropriateness of Campbell's vectorial language ("forward"/"backward" thinking).

Smith's learned contribution, in chapter 5, examines the extent to which it is appropriate for Campbell to make use of the term "Arianism." Contra Campbell, he argues that one should not identify Arius's Logos theology with ahistorical foundationalism. That said, Smith is in overall sympathy with Campbell's concerns and suggests that, instead of speaking of Arian Foundationalism versus Athanasian Apocalypticism, "Campbell would be better served to speak of a Eunomian Rationalism vs. a Nicene Apocalypticism or a Nicene Economic Theology."

Campbell's second offering, in chapter 6, presents a way out of the problems outlined in chapter 3, by focusing on how one reads one particular text, namely Galatians 2:15–16. He maintains that if the antithesis between "works of the law" and "faith" is read forward, that is, from an account of the problem to the corresponding solution, then all manner of sinister ills are unleashed into our construal of Paul's argument. Campbell's solution is simply to present a reading of these verses in such a way that the antithesis Paul constructs is a straightforward "A is not the case but B," a contrast based on a revelational account of Paul's argument. Not only are all interpretative problems thereby solved, Campbell's argument here also offers a snapshot of his wider strategy and concerns.

In chapter 7, David Hilborn, while appreciative of Campbell's endeavors, raises a number of concerns in response to Campbell's chapter 6 essay. He questions Campbell's Barthian appropriation of Athanasius, and the strict distinction between forward and backward thinking. He also wonders to what extent Campbell has constructed another universalizing and mythologizing paradigm. Further, Hilborn asks whether Campbell's soteriology compels him towards universal salvation. This question involves a wider issue, namely concern about Campbell's use of the word "unconditional" as part of the "Athanasian" paradigm.

In chapter 8, Kate Bowler's short, yet lively, reflection draws Part One to a close. She draws lines of connection between Campbell's account of foundationalism, on the one hand, and various modern trends in American Christianity, on the other, particularly those aspects that tend to moralistic, therapeutic deism and America's "legal mind."

As noted above, Part Two of this book focuses on Campbell's proposed solution to the confused state of Pauline interpretation. A number of key exegetical issues are presented and examined. In chapter 9, Campbell shows why the problems he has already outlined in his previous chapters relate directly to how one reads Romans 1–3. He presents the case that a subtle misconstrual of Paul's argument has led to a massive distortion of Paul's theology. An analysis of Romans 1–3 paves the way for the claim that "any reader who holds that Paul is himself committed to the premises underlying 1:18–32 and 2:6 is endorsing forward thinking," a claim that is demonstrated via recourse to key scholarly contruals of this text. Picking up his argument from chapter 6, Campbell details one particular danger associated with this "forward thinking" reading, namely the (highly problematic) presentation of "the Jew." This leads to a summary of Campbell's "Socratic reading" of Romans 1–3, its justification and strengths, together with a number of responses to those who have challenged this crucial manoeuvre (including the arguments of Griffith-Jones in the next chapter).

In chapter 10, classicist Robin Griffith-Jones analyzes a number of texts that Campbell refers to as support for his claim that speech-in-character, *prosopopoeia*, would have been recognized in Romans 1:18–32 by Paul's original auditors. He examines Cicero, Quintilian, Seneca, and other relevant texts, and maintains that it is unlikely Paul would have deployed a long block-speech with no clear introduction, that is, without introducing and identifying the speaker. Despite sympathy with Campbell's project, Griffith-Jones thinks his reading is "a recipe for confusion," and in this light he also critically examines Campbell's exegesis and translation of key texts such as 1:18 and 3:1–3, 8.

In chapter 11, Brittany Wilson explains that she shares Campbell's rejection of prospective, foundationalist, and contractual readings of Paul. However, she seeks to show a different way of reading material in Romans 1–3. Instead of opting for—what she maintains is—Campbell's problematic Socratic rereading, she gestures towards an alternative apocalyptic construal of these chapters (drawing particularly on the scholarship of Beverly Gaventa). Romans 1–3 is, she argues, consistently apocalyptic even if we read it entirely in Paul's own voice.

Campbell's final offering, chapter 12, is based upon the conviction that contractual foundationalism can be reactivated—even after his rereading of Romans 1–3—by particular (mis)understandings of Paul's *dikaio-* terms. When they are informed by notions of "justice" understood in terms of a narrative of retribution, contractualism rears its ugly head once again. His analysis then turns to examine the noun phrase, the "the righteousness of God," and the cognate verb, δικαιόω. Drawing on his more extensive work in *Deliverance*, Campbell's methodologically nuanced approach leads him to understand the noun phrase as a singular, saving, liberating, life-giving, eschatological, and resurrecting event. His examination of the cognate verb leads to the conclusion that construals of Paul's language, in terms of a Western legal and conditional narrative, is wrongheaded. Paul, he argues, "is utterly opposed to any account of salvation or gospel couched in these terms."

In chapter 13, while agreeing with Campbell's concern to combat all "Western contractualism," Scott Hafemann pays attention to the intertextual dynamics in Campbell's argument to contend that he has underestimated the covenantal context of key terms. In particular, Hafemann focuses on Paul's understanding of divine kingship and, therefore, the righteousness of God. Putting the covenant relationship at the center instead leads to a reframing of notions that Campbell must problematically hold apart, such as unconditionality and conditionality, retributive and saving judgment, the supposed two meanings of δικαιόω in Romans 2:13 and 6:7, and so on. In so doing, Hafemann presents a rather different proposal for reading Paul.

In chapter 14, I summarize Campbell's handling of *pistis*-related matters by focusing on some of his wider theological concerns and his exegetical manoeuvres specifically in Galatians. I finish by reflecting on the claims of Francis Watson, concluding that although the so-called *pistis Christou* debate is far from over, Campbell's treatment of the data is compelling.

In chapter 15, Curtis Freeman energetically argues that rejections of Campbell's grammatical arguments for a subjective genitive reading of *pistis Christou* are based on theological missteps. In particular, he argues that evangelicals do not understand Campbell at this point because their theology is functionally unitarian rather than Trinitarian, and crucicentric rather than incarnational.

The appendices contain two articles that inspired the genesis of Campbell's work.[10] Appendix 1 is a reprint of James Torrance's 1970 article, "Covenant and Contract, a Study of the Theological Background of Worship in Seventeenth-Century Scotland." Appendix 2 is a reprint of James Torrance's 1973 article, "The Contribution of McLeod Campbell to Scottish Theology." The impact of these essays on Campbell's thinking is obvious, and indeed they both pay close reading not only as they lay the groundwork for a good grasp of the concerns that drive *Deliverance*, but also because of their own elegance and theological clarity.

In all of these essays our hope is better to discern whether Campbell's diagnosis of the problem is helpful, and whether his prescribed apocalyptic rereading of Paul really does deliver the goods, and manages to lead Paul away from a potentially very dark and complex problem towards maybe more than just a coherent reading, but also a very exciting and liberating one. The process of discernment will be facilitated as we all contribute in this debate, eschewing caricature, misunderstanding, and unhelpful polemics.

I finish with one final word of interpretative counsel. If we are to grasp Campbell's arguments aright, we must recognise that our discussions about Pauline theology are not ends in themselves. Our work on Paul needs to be *responsible*. Grasping this dynamic in Campbell's endeavors is essential. But behind this, and indeed grounding it, are the kind of issues with which I began—those I mentioned in terms of teaching Paul's theology to church leaders. Campbell leads us to recognize, once again, that Paul's language is to be interpreted ultimately in relation

---

10. Cf. Campbell, *Deliverance*, xxiv.

to its "object," namely God, a factor that involves certain theological conditions (as Alan Torrance brilliantly argues in his essay "Can the Truth Be Learned?").[11] Right at the heart of Campbell's project is, I believe, a sentiment more significant than the winds of exegetical or hermeneutical fashion, as important and indeed necessary as some of them may be. It is a concern that reading Paul be animated, given confidence, and nourished by the simplicity of disciplined and delighted focus on the revelation of God in Christ. As Karl Barth put it in an essay in the book, *God Here and Now*:

> Even more than the Reformers did, we must let God and His Word be one, with more emphasis, more joy, more consistency, and we must let Jesus Christ be even more self-evidently the one Mediator between God and humanity.[12]

If we understand this concern, I don't think we will be far away from comprehending the soul of the *Deliverance of God*, even when we choose to disagree. Such burdens, I suspect, will also lead us beyond both old and new perspectives on Paul.

11. Torrance, "Can the Truth Be Learned?," 143–63.
12. Barth, *God Here and Now*, 18.

PART ONE

Campbell and the Problem

A Review of Douglas Campbell's
The Deliverance of God
from a Theological Perspective[1]

ALAN J. TORRANCE

I have been invited to assess Douglas Campbell's door-stopper of a tome from a theological perspective. Given that this is a work in Pauline scholarship by a leading New Testament scholar, what is the justification for involving a theologian? Clearly, it is because the argumentation of this book is driven by a theological critique of certain key methodological, epistemological, and indeed, ontological suppositions that have functioned to sustain what Campbell calls "justification discourse"—an approach to Pauline interpretation that Campbell argues is outmoded, confused, and ultimately incoherent.

So, very briefly, what are the core concerns of this book? The first is to expose the fallacious reasoning underpinning justification theory as this has characterized Pauline scholarship since the Reformation. Justification theory or discourse, Campbell argues, has provided the Western church with an interpretive framework that has distorted the core

1. ©2012 *Scottish Journal of Theology*. Originally published in *Scottish Journal of Theology* 65.1 (2012) 82–89. Reprinted with permission.

of Paul's theology and notably its ethical, anthropological, theological, soteriological, and epistemological implications.

The second related aim is to solve the problem of the apparent tension between Romans 1:18–32, on the one hand, which underpins justification theory, and Romans 5–8 (anticipated in 3:21–26), which he sees as expounding the glorious heart of Pauline theology—his profound, apocalyptic, and participative vision of the gospel. What is presented here is nothing less than what Campbell describes as a divine "rescue mission" that liberates and reconstitutes a confused humanity, which is otherwise dysfunctional (ethically, epistemically, spiritually, and theologically), by giving it to participate *en Christo* and, thereby, in all-embracing and all-transforming communion with God—a communion that requires to be conceived in irreducibly Trinitarian terms with an essentially christological and pneumatological grammar. The associated interpretations of God, the character of the divine will, salvation, as also the role of Christ and the Spirit, constitute a profoundly coherent yet also a very different gospel from that presented in Romans 1–4. Although the tension here was already recognized by Deissmann, Schweitzer, Wrede, and others, none of the revisionist scholars who challenged the justification discourse offered a "satisfactory explanation of how the two discourses, forensic and mystical, might fit together either in Romans or in Paul's thinking about salvation as a whole."

Campbell's solution to this tension is to argue that the early chapters of Romans are a kind of rhetorical *exposé* of a legalistic "alternative gospel" that is not the gospel Paul himself is proclaiming. In short, in opposing this alternative soteriological program Paul uses various rhetorical devices (here Campbell utilizes the work of Stanley Stowers) which, as Campbell explains in chapter 14, would have made it clear to his contemporary audience that Paul was not *himself* endorsing the programme of Romans 1–4 and certainly not its building blocks as if they provided the route into the affirmations of 5–8. Although the rhetorical cues communicated to the performers are lost, we should not be misled by the naked text as it stands, given that there is much within it that serves to establish this reading.

Campbell goes on to draw parallels between Paul's concerns in Romans and those in Galatians, where he also opposed teachers who were presenting "*an alternative soteriological program.*" Just as Galatians is written in a context in which there were two gospels in play, two gospels were also in play in Romans, occasioned by "the spectre of the Teachers' arrival" (*DofG*, 522).

I am not qualified to assess Campbell's explanation of what is going on here. What I would like to do, however, is to consider Campbell's analysis of the methodological moves and theological suppositions that have supported the justification discourse and its utilization of Romans 1–4 for its specific ends. What must be clear to all is that justification discourse does not simply emerge in a spontaneous and unmediated way from Pauline texts. It is a theological doctrine, formulated on the basis of a series of theological premises, which addresses a particular problem, and is driven by a whole series of apologetic and other concerns. In other words, the genetic confusions here can be traced to doctrinal exposition rather than biblical scholarship *per se*. Lying behind the relevant theological moves is one of the tragedies of Western thought, namely, the manner in which theological and biblical interpretation has been driven by the mistranslation of Hebrew terms—let me mention three in particular. First, *berith*, as it is used in the Pentateuch to denote the Lord's relationship to Israel, denotes an unconditioned and unconditional covenant commitment to Israel grounded in love and characterized by *hesed*—God's sustained and unconditional covenant faithfulness. *Berith* in Hebrew and *diatheke* in Greek, were translated *foedus* in Latin, giving rise to federal theology. *Foedus* makes no distinction between covenant and contract and essentially means "contract." Subliminal within the Western tradition, not least the Calvinist tradition, as Campbell so rightly argues, was a contractual model of the relationship between God and Israel—contract of nature, contract of faith, etc.

The second concept, *Torah* (*nomos* in Greek), was translated *lex* in Latin, which was immediately interpreted in the light of categories of Roman or natural law. Whereas *Torah* articulated the unconditional, apodictic obligations that stem from God's covenant commitment to Israel, *lex* came to be interpreted in terms of a contract of nature—the contractual conditions of the divine acceptance of humanity. These legal conditions were perceived as being met by Jesus' death on the cross—the necessary condition of God's forgiveness of humanity.

Tsedaqah, dikaiosune in Greek, was interpreted *iustitia* in Latin. The righteousness that characterized God's covenant faithfulness toward an unfaithful people, and that placed them under unconditional obligations to be faithful (literally to image God's righteousness), was reinterpreted by means of a juridical concept of justice—initially distributive and, later, retributive justice, worked out in much Western theology in contractual terms.

In short, on the one side of this translation process we have God's purposes conceived as covenant, *Torah* (the obligations to be faithful), and righteousness. On the other side, we have God's essential purposes conceived through the categories of contract (conditional acceptance), *lex* (Stoic notions of natural law), and *iustitia* (justice). What takes place is nothing less than a *metabasis eis allo genos* of the very heart of Judaism. We have, in short, a foreign religion emerging—the re-schematization of a primarily *filial* relationship towards humanity as a fundamentally *legalistic* one, where divine acceptance is conceived as conditional upon our meeting legal requirements and the satisfaction of the demands of justice conceived in retributive terms. This, of course, led to the emergence of the various forms of the Western *ordo salutis*, together with juridical constructions of the atonement whereby the Son conditions the Father into having mercy on those who have offended his holy will by breaching the contractual conditions of his legal demands. The Father is conditioned into loving and forgiving sinners through the satisfaction of his wrath by the blood and innocent suffering of his Son.

For Campbell, when Romans 1–4 is taken as underwriting this kind of program, it is simply not possible to make it consistent with the thrust and implications of chapters 5–8. It is entirely unclear, that is, how the graft can be made to take—and no book I know of exposes this more effectively or more rigorously than this one!

So how precisely does Campbell conceive of the essential shape of the justification model?

First, it interprets human beings in essentially individualistic terms as rational, self-interested beings who possess immanent, epistemic access to God's ethical demands and, thereby, to the essential conditions of God's contractual acceptance of them. This is what Federal Calvinists referred to as the *foedus naturae* (contract of nature) or the *foedus operum* (contract of works). Contemplating the cosmos without provides veridical knowledge of God's nature and contemplating the conscience within provides knowledge of God's justice and just requirements. Whereas for Jews, therefore, God's ethical demands are revealed through written legislation, those same demands are revealed to everyone innately. Here we must note that, as Campbell rightly points out, this involves the de-historicization of the Torah, its divorce from its covenantal context, and its identification, in effect, with the dictates of natural law—and too often natural law is conceived in ways that bear little resemblance to the obligations of the Torah or, indeed, to the law as it is summarized by Jesus! The next step in the argument is the recognition that rewards/punishments are apportioned according to an individual's fulfilment or otherwise of God's ethical demands as these are apparent to our consciences.

This brings us to the next key moves in the reasoning of the justification discourse, namely, what Campbell describes as the introspective twist (*DofG*, 28) and the loop of despair (*DofG*, 29)—that is, self-perceived ethical incapacity (*DofG*, 34), the awareness that we violate God's ethical demands and that a negative divine judgement is unavoidable. On this basis, the gift of grace is then presented—the "compensatory mechanism of satisfaction, namely, Christ's atonement" (*DofG*, 34) whereby God redirects that *punishment which is our due to Christ* (who dies) and *his righteousness to us*, who are sinners but who are now viewed as if his righteousness were theirs. It is at precisely this point, however, that we are presented with a second contract, what the Calvinists referred to as the contract of faith (*foedus fidei*). God stipulates an alternative criterion or condition by which we may appropriate this redirection of divine punishment to Christ, namely, faith. If (if and only if) you have faith, you proceed to blessed eternal life because all the criteria or conditions are met by one means or another. Clearly, how the mechanisms by which these contractual conditions are met or conceived depends on whether you are Arminian or Reformed or hyper-Calvinist, but the same essentially contractual structure of the argument remains whichever position you adopt.

So where lay the problems?

First, it operates with an individualistic concept of the person driven not by love of God but ultimately by self-interest—fear of judgement, not least. Campbell writes, "Individuals are not disposed to act ethically because this is right or even because this is how they are constructed but largely because it is in their best interests so to act—an enduring conundrum for this approach to ethics" (*DofG*, 31).

Second, hand in hand with this go highly problematic epistemological assumptions. That is, our primary epistemic access to God is ahistorical—it is universal, innate, and *a priori* with respect to God's self-disclosure in the Old Testament and in Christ. Justification discourse,

Campbell argues, assumes a veridical natural theology. It is not irrelevant, therefore, that justification theory could be promulgated by the Lutheran *Deutsche Christen*, who believed that it is by this same ahistorical, universal knowledge of God's natural purposes that we know that Aryans shouldn't marry Jews, that Aryan culture is ordained by God to be distinctive and should not be polluted by interbreeding. Or that it could be promulgated by Afrikaner Calvinists in one of the most Christian countries in the world, who believed that God's purposes for the state, vis-à-vis race, should be determined in advance of any mediation of God's creative purposes in Christ by appeal to the cultural mandates delivered to natural reason—the theology that underpinned apartheid. Or that God's purposes for women should be interpreted accordingly by men, appealing to natural reason. There are many more examples! In short, justification discourse goes hand in hand with the notion of a *duplex cognitio*—a two-fold knowledge of God from creation by natural reason (that is, an ahistorical, non-christological revelation) and then salvific knowledge that is secondary and serves as an add-on for the faithful. In short, Campbell is absolutely right to point to the fact that there are immense sociopolitical and ethical implications and problems relating to the historical advocacy of this model!

As soon as one repudiates the *duplex cognitio*, and suggests that true, properly functional, reconciled knowledge of God's purposes for humanity *per se* are revealed *en Christo*, this key element in justification theory collapses! What is significant is that, as T. H. L. Parker shows in *Calvin's Doctrine of the Knowledge of God*, Calvin was arguably far closer to the mind of Paul—he repudiated any such veridical knowledge of God from creation. For Calvin, we would only have had veridical knowledge of God from creation *"si integer Adam stetisset"*—if Adam had remained true. Consequently, knowledge of creation is mediated to those who have that mind that was in Christ Jesus, whose apperceptions are reconciled or *metamorphosed* for the discernment of truth, where God's purposes for creation are interpreted therefore in and through the one for whom and through whom all things were created. . . .

Third, there are the assumptions vis-à-vis the doctrine of God. The underlying doctrine of God, Campbell argues, is a "strict authoritarian" God whose primary attribute is his justice—a Father who, in relation to humanity *per se*, "rules, judges, or parents in terms of retributive justice"—the counterpart to the essentially individual, rational, and self-interested subject.

Campbell then devotes an entire chapter to exposing the fundamental problems in the further concepts of revelation, law, theodicy, Christology, atonement, and faith that attend this confused construct.

Perhaps the most fundamental problem that underpins all the above is *methodological*. The justification construct echoes all the problems of the nature-grace model, namely, that we interpret nature, human nature, justice, and God by appeal to unredeemed, natural reason and *then* seek to interpret the gospel in that light. In short, we interpret the heart of Paul with recourse to a prior, foundational, worldview (one that is, for Paul, *echthros te dianoia*—alienated in its capacity to think through to the reality of God). What we see is that the direction of the pressure of interpretation, therefore, runs in precisely the opposite direction to God's self-disclosure in Christ with all that that involves for how we interpret creation, the world, humanity, the nature and character of God, and God's purposes for the world. The result, is that the gospel, as Paul would have it, finds itself presented with a Procrustean bed—molded to fit our prior (unreconciled) affirmations vis-à-vis God, humanity, law, the nature of the knowledge of God, ethics, justice, etc., rather than the other way round.

What Campbell applies in the interpretation of Paul are essentially the principles of theological hermeneutics that Eberhard Jüngel (author of *Paulus und Jesus: Eine Untersuchung zur Präzisierung der Frage nach dem Ursprung der Christologie.* Mohr Siebeck, 2004) argued for so profoundly in his classic *Gottes Sein ist im Werden*. In a devastating critique of all approaches that are driven by religious *Voraussetzungen*, *Vorverstaendnisse*, etc., he argues "das Sein Gottes geht und eben so allem menschlichen Fragen zuvorkommt"[2] ("the Being of God proceeds, and thus precedes all human questioning"[3]). Applied to the interpretation of Paul, it is our being *en Christo* which must precede and be presupposed by our questions and not our prior natural self-understandings or quasi-religious propensities. Romans 5–8 and, indeed, so much else in the Pauline corpus suggests that a reverent Pauline hermeneutic constitutes a form of *Nachdenken*—reflection after the event of God's self-disclosure in Christ and emphatically not an attempt to accommodate or *subject* the testimony to that self-disclosure within a series of pre-established vestibules that appeal to prior, unreconciled worldviews.

2. Jüngel, *Gottes Sein ist im Werden*, 10.
3. Jüngel, *The Doctrine of the Trinity*, xx.

In short, the direction of the pressure of interpretation must be *from* Paul's central affirmations vis-à-vis the nature of God, humanity, law, ethics, and the nature of epistemic access as these are given *en Christo* and not *to* these notions from conceptions dictated by our prior natural reasoning. This is the underlying concern in Campbell's repudiation of "foundationalism."

So what happens when (as Campbell suggests we should), we allow the solution of Romans 5–8 to determine our approach to the problem, when the hermeneutical direction of thought is reversed—or should I say redeemed? Well, things look very different!

We are obliged to consider our prior epistemic states, affiliations, and suppositions from an apocalyptic deliverance in which salvation is proclaimed as having arrived unconditionally, at the behest of the Father, through the Son, and bringing a spectrum of blessings, as Campbell puts it—"life, peace, glory, dominion, reconciliation, atonement, ethical capacity, and so on" (*DofG*, 72)—all of which require a radical re-evaluation of the human problem in its light. We find an event of atonement symbolized by metaphors signifying the death of the old and our rising with Christ—denoting genuine discontinuity with our prior states and orientation. The new situation, moreover, turns out to be an essentially koinonial, relational, and interpersonal form of existence rooted in the divine communion.

In stark contrast, the "natural" individualistic state is seen to be subject to hostile powers, enslaved by sinful passions—an old, unredeemed humanity that cannot comprehend the nature of the problem, let alone the solution. Old ways of thinking are hostile and erroneous, condemned to follow a confused trajectory that needs to be "metamorphozed" for the discernment of truth—emphatically not "securitized" with reference to the unredeemed, natural order (Rom 12:2).

What is recognized from within this reconciled state?

- that such perceptions are fundamentally discontinuous with our prior suppositions about the way God is, how we are created to be, the character of ethical existence, etc.

- that those prior suppositions reflect the alienated mind and do *not* constitute an appropriate vestibule for interpreting atonement, as the justification discourse appears to assume.

The ramifications of this move are immense, not only for epistemology, anthropology, and the doctrine of God (God is no longer conceived as essentially the God of retributive justice), but also Christology (no longer monopolized by his death to satisfy retributive requirements), soteriology, faith, assurance, sanctification, the sacraments, and so on. The danger of the nature-grace model is inevitably that a prior, alienated conception of the self serves as the foundation for Paul's vision of the new humanity, which then comes to be conceived in supererogatory terms and not as defining God's creative purposes for humanity *per se*! To understand Campbell's argument is to be persuaded that we must be consistent in our interpretation of Paul by conceiving of the pre-Christian state in the light of what it is to be human in truth—and not the other way round. In this respect, not least, this book is a profoundly cogent and refreshing rethink of Pauline interpretation—one that stands to generate a tectonic shift in Pauline scholarship. Viewing things purely theologically, that is, without judging the exegetical case, the Paul who emerges is emphatically more coherent than in the approach he critiques. Meanwhile, any countervailing claim that these issues are unimportant or marginal has to be treated with extreme skepticism.

Douglas Campbell's Response to Alan J. Torrance

I am grateful to Alan for introducing me to the seminal essays of his father, James, that are reprinted at the end of this volume. Those provided me with categories that enabled me to give a deeper and (hopefully) more plausible account of the debates swirling in Pauline studies around the interpretation of Judaism, the law, and so on, as well as to see a constructive way of resolving those. As we might expect, their key insights are summarized ably here. However, Alan does rather more than this. James's essays themselves presuppose a basic distinction between two modes of doing theology—one that is referred to frequently in this volume under the rubric of Athanasius versus Arius, a dichotomy scrutinized and improved shortly—that Alan has also summarized here with characteristic precision. That is, Alan explained to me long ago, and continues to explain to all who will listen today, the difference between two fundamentally different ways of understanding, learning about, and talking of the God acting in Jesus Christ. It is this distinction and these two fundamental modes of knowing and speaking that are ultimately at issue in the different ways of reading Paul that I am discussing, even as they are worked out in quite specific forms. And it will be vital to hold this in view in what follows since many of the responses to my work, both here and in other contexts, simply deny this difference and/or its importance. Alan suggests here quite clearly in my view that this difference remains both fundamental and critical, while any denials of its nature and/or importance risk being deeply confused and distressingly misleading, at least in ecclesial terms. Conversely, it will greatly enrich our future discussions of Paul's texts and thinking if Alan's observations can be appreciated and incorporated vitally into them.

2

Luther and the Deliverance of God

GRAHAM TOMLIN

D oug Campbell's book *The Deliverance of God* promises to be a mile-stone in Pauline exegesis and interpretation. The conference from which the papers in this book emerged was a lively, fast-moving, and valuable opportunity to scrutinize, examine, and question it from a range of perspectives. The particular aspect this chapter brings to bear is that of historical theology, particularly from the Reformation period. As primarily a student of the Reformation, I do not consider myself qualified to comment on the exegetical case Campbell makes in drawing such a sharp contrast between Paul's apparent teaching in the early chapters of Romans, some of which—especially 1:18–32—it is suggested the apostle does not endorse, and chapters 5–8. However I will try to give an impression of how Campbell's case seems when viewed through the lens of Reformation theology, as naturally, that case impinges on themes from the Reformation period a great deal. Much as I enjoyed the book and found it very illuminating and positive, two questions began to grow in my mind as I read it.

The Accessibility of Scripture?

One of the core convictions of the magisterial reformers was on the accessibility of Scripture to the ordinary reader. As we were forcefully reminded in 2011, the year of the 400th anniversary celebrations of the King James Version, from William Tyndale to Martin Luther through to the Authorized Version itself, perhaps the main legacy of the Reformation was a stream of translations of the Bible into vernacular European languages. All this was founded on the principle that Scripture could be read with profit by anyone, regardless of their level of theological education.[1] It was of course a controversial position. A strong and convincing case could be made, as it was by Cardinal Cajetan, Thomas More, and others, that the delicate unity of Christendom would be broken by allowing anyone to read and interpret the Bible for themselves, and consequently it had to be held back for interpretation by ecclesiastical and theological experts. Yet Tyndale, Coverdale, Luther, and many others continued with their vernacular translations. Not only that, but the Reformers chose to write sometimes complex theological treatises, not in the Latin of the theological professionals, but in English, German, or French, appealing above the heads of the scholars to the "ordinary Christian." Behind this lay the principle of the clarity of Scripture, yet also the conviction that the Bible was the book of the church, and that the church consisted not just of the clergy or the scholars but the "ordinary Christian" too.

From all this comes my first question. I recently found myself reading through the book of Romans as the Church of England's lectionary readings for Morning Prayer. Conscious of Campbell's approach, I found myself at something of a loss in reading chapters 1–4. Was this the voice of Paul? If so, which parts? Or was I reading an approach he disavowed? I was no longer so sure. As a non-specialist in Pauline studies I did not feel able to adjudicate the question thoroughly, and as a result, the text of Scripture felt a little distant, opaque, not something I was sure I could read rightly or trust.

The crucial issue here is the nature of a book such as the letter to the Romans. On one level it is a first-century text, to be read as any other first-century text, with all the expectations and conventions one would expect from such a document. On the other hand, we read it as

---

1. Of course this position was nuanced by guidance on how lay people were to read Scripture—see Evans, *The Language and Logic of the Bible*, especially 33–36, for a helpful discussion of medieval and Reformation approaches to biblical interpretation.

Christian *Scripture*, the book of the church, a means of grace that any reader can gain benefit from reading. Christians will presumably need to read it as both, but this distinction sets up a tension. NT scholars may wish to emphasize Romans as a first-century text, but as part of Scripture, we expect of it a quality which makes it possible to be read for profit by any Christian regardless of how versed they are in contemporary NT exegesis and the nature of ancient textual conventions. From a dogmatic point of view, we must admit a little nervousness about any approach that makes the Scriptures incomprehensible to the "ordinary reader"—in other words, one relatively unversed in the nuances of contemporary NT scholarship—and privileges the specialist exegete as the only one capable of seeing the true meaning of the text. Scholars and children of the Reformation will be wary of returning to the days when ordinary non-specialist readers had to wait on the opinions of experts and were deemed liable to seriously misread if left to themselves. It may be that Paul has left significant clues to tell us that we are not to take parts of Romans 1–4 as his own views, but it must be said that if he has, these are now virtually imperceptible to the ordinary reader, and presumably have been since very early readings of the text. On this reading, the ordinary reader, incapable of recognizing the clues, is resigned to either misunderstanding Paul or seeing him as inconsistent and confused. My first question then is how this reading can avoid rendering the text of Scripture opaque to the ordinary reader, and, it must be said, to most exegetes of the book of Romans for the past 2,000 years?

Inconsistent Soteriologies?

My second question concerns the wider implications of this reading in historical theology. Some readers of Campbell's book may be troubled by the idea that Paul deliberately presents two quite incompatible soteriologies in Romans. What are we to make then of the suggestion that Augustine, Luther, and Calvin also contain incompatible and self-contradictory understandings of salvation?[2] Can it really be the case that none of these three theological giants realized the incompatibility of these two soteriologies in their own work?

I do not have space to look at all three, but I do want to examine Luther's role in all this. I must confess that having read the first few chapters

2. See Campbell, *Deliverance*, 250–77.

of *The Deliverance of God*, I expected Luther to be the villain of the piece, as he has often been in various versions of the New Perspective on Paul. I was glad, and somewhat impressed, to find a more nuanced reading of him in chapter 8, where Campbell argues that Luther is not a straight-forward exponent of "Justification Theory," as he calls it, but that there are also traces of what Campbell sees as Paul's own alternative, participative understanding of salvation, especially in his later writings. Campbell refers to the Finnish school of Tuoma Mannermaa, which argues for "theosis" as a central idea in Luther, as evidence for this other reading. However, this may be something of a broken reed: the Finnish school has not gained much acceptance in wider Luther scholarship because most readers suspect they make too much of Luther's very occasional references to *Vergöttlichung* or divinization. Nonetheless, *The Deliverance of God* does present a Luther who is inconsistent in holding both Justification Theory and the alternative reading at the same time.[3]

I want to defend Luther against that charge of inconsistency, at least in this regard, by suggesting, not that he endorses "Justification Theory" as Campbell expounds it, but that his version of justification is significantly more nuanced and coherent than perhaps Campbell suggests. In fact, Luther's theology of justification has much more in common with Campbell's alternative, participative, non-contractual reading for a number of reasons.

As I understand, the presentation of Justification Theory in *DofG* focuses around at least four ideas:

1. That God's justice is essentially retributive justice.

2. That human beings are rational, ethical individuals, with a prior natural and objective knowledge of God as Judge.

3. That the answer to the dilemma of judgment is found in the death of Christ offered as atonement for sin.

4. That salvation is individual and conditional upon the prior exercise of faith.

I would suggest that Luther's move to a Reformation theology involves a questioning of much of this.

---

3. Ibid., 250–56 and 264–70.

1. God's Justice as Retributive Justice:

Our instinctive image of the early Luther is perhaps of the tormented, agonized personal soul, desperate to find forgiveness for his sins. Yet was this actually what troubled Luther? More recent Luther scholarship is not so sure. For example, David Yeago writes:

> There is a driving question in Luther's early theology, but it is not the question of the assurance of forgiveness. The troubling question that emerges from the preoccupations of the young Luther's thought is not "How can I get a gracious God?" but "Where can I find the real God?" All the evidence in the texts suggests that it was the threat of idolatry, not a craving for assurance of forgiveness that troubled Luther's conscience.[4]

In other words, it is a misunderstanding, fostered by later interpretations of Luther in Lutheran and pietistic circles (and perhaps some of Luther's own later reminiscences, shaped by his reading of Augustine), that focuses on his internal struggles of conscience. His writings at the time (between about 1510 and 1520) show little concern about assurance of forgiveness. Instead they are concerned with who the true God is.

We could describe Luther's move towards a Reformation theology as a move away from a juridical and retributive vision of God to a different fundamental understanding of God as a God of love and grace. Take the famous account of his Reformation discovery written in 1545. Here he describes his struggles with precisely the retributive God of judgment that Justification Theory presents: "I did not love, yes, I hated the righteous God who punishes sinners."[5]

The problem Luther struggles with here is not with his own conscience but with the God of retributive judgment, evident in much late medieval theology and spirituality, waiting to condemn his every thought, a God whom he could not love.

Luther's christocentric epistemology emphasizes this very point: we know God only through Christ, and we are not to look for him anywhere else. As he writes in "The Three Symbols or Creeds of the Christian Faith" of 1538, "in Jesus Christ the whole fullness of deity dwells bodily or personally, in such manner that whoever does not find or receive God in

---

4. Yeago, "The Catholic Luther," 17.

5. Luther, Martin et al., *Luther's Works*, Vol. 34, 336 (Henceforth referred to as LW).

Christ shall nevermore and nowhere have or find God outside of Christ, even though he should go beyond heaven, below hell, or outside of the world. For here I will dwell (says God), in this humanity, born of Mary the virgin, etc."[6] If we seek God outside of Christ he appears to us as condemnatory, wrathful, and our enemy. As Gerhard Forde points out: "Luther could even say that apart from Jesus, God is indistinguishable from the devil."[7] In Christ, he is a God of mercy, love, and grace. The God Luther finds is a new God altogether, a God of goodness, grace, and love, whose love elicits his own love and faith.

2. Humans with a Prior Natural Knowledge of God as Judge

Luther rejects the idea that we have a prior natural understanding of God that provides the framework for all further epistemology and soteriology. As Hans Schwarz puts it: "Because the natural knowledge of God is prone to so many misunderstandings, it cannot serve as the starting point of faith for Luther."[8] The rational, ethical, objective individual posited by Justification Theory simply cannot be found in Luther's understanding of the unredeemed self. Instead he explicitly describes the unredeemed state as "bondage." It was Erasmus, whom Luther took on in 1525, who posited the rational, ethical individual capable of both recognizing his or her own sin and responding with contrition and renewal of life. This was the humanist vision of the human soul, not that of the Reformers. And it was for that reason Luther insisted on the bondage of the will without Christ, and the unconditional nature of God's gift of Christ, received by faith.

The Deliverance of God mentions a number of passages in Luther, particularly in his early writings, where he stresses a knowledge of sin as an early stage of the journey to faith.[9] This is hardly surprising as it is a staple of late medieval theology—countless works of late fifteenth-century and early sixteenth-century writing did the same—Luther is not being particularly original here. If there is originality, it is in his idea that this is not a natural knowledge of sin, but something worked by God. It

6. LW 34:207.

7. Forde, *The Captivation of the Will*, 45

8. Schwarz, *True Faith in the True God*, 43.

9. Campbell, *Deliverance*, 250–56.

is a divine work, not a human one, to recognize how deeply sin entangles and binds.

Justification Theory, as Campbell explains it, suggests that outside of Christ, from our own natural powers, we have a prior ability to recognize God as Judge and ourselves as sinful. For Luther this is nonsense, even from his early days. The recognition of our bound, sinful, broken state is not something we can arrive at on our own. His early theology of the cross is an affirmation that contrition is God's work not ours. It also means we must re-think our natural understandings of God. If God is revealed in such an unlikely place as the cross, then that must question all our prior judgments ("prejudices") about God (our "theologies of glory") and start again at the cross of Christ. The recognition of our participation in an enslaved, broken humanity is something God alone can work by the Holy Spirit through the law (which of course is God's law, not a human construct). This is part of the work of redemption, not a prelude to it. Luther would have agreed with Stanley Hauerwas's observation, that "to be able to confess one's sin is a theological achievement."[10]

Luther insists that the law bringing about an awareness of sin is God's "alien," rather than his "proper" work (*opus alienum*, not *opus proprium*). The law is his work, and yet God's true purpose and nature is to bless out of his abundant goodness. However, in order to do that, he has to break our natural self-understanding, which is not so much a knowledge of sin and failure, an awareness that we are under the judgment of God, but a self-confidence that we are free to make our own way, that we are self-sufficient without God.

Law and gospel in Luther's thought are tightly bound together, not entirely separated entities. True, the work of God is twofold: the work of the law, which reveals our bound and helpless state outside of Christ, and the gospel, which announces our liberation through Christ. The point is not, however, that an awareness of sin always precedes a knowledge of the gospel. Law and gospel are not to be considered as inevitably sequential but dialectical in Luther's thought. The tension is an ongoing one in the entire Christian life, in that we are tempted to believe (law) that we are still under the bondage of sin, and refuse to believe (gospel) the word that says that Christ has brought freedom to those who are united with him by faith.

---

10. Hauerwas and Willimon, *Where Resident Aliens Live*, 77.

After Luther's death, the issue of the relationships between law and gospel was hotly debated between followers of Philipp Melanchthon, who broadly said that the law needed to be preached before the gospel, and Johann Agricola, who argued that the gospel alone is necessary and there is no place for the law in the Christian life.[11] Luther himself had written statements that could be quoted on each side of this debate, which explains much of why the "correct" Lutheran understanding was ambiguous. Luther could be claimed by both sides, but that is not so much because he is inconsistent, but that he sees the relationships between law and gospel as dialectical and not sequential. Although experientially at times law precedes gospel and at other times gospel precedes law, theologically they are correlative to each other: each needs the other for a true understanding. Suffice to say that for Luther, it is not that the preaching of the law produces repentance. As Bernhard Lohse puts it: "True repentance is effected not by the preaching of the law, but only by the preaching of the gospel. If only the law were preached, it would lead to despair, not to conversion."[12] It is ultimately only in the light of Christ and the gospel that true repentance (the kind that leads to faith) becomes possible.

3. Atonement through the Death of Christ

Reading Campbell's description of the apocalyptic, participative understanding of justification reminds this reader, at least, more of Luther's theology than does Campbell's description of Justification Theory. If Justification Theory places the emphasis on Christ's death, and the "participative" reading emphasizes the whole of the life and work of Christ, then Luther sides with participation. For Luther, justification is not an external, contractual transaction whereby we escape the consequences of divine judgment, it is the gift of the very righteousness of Christ that justifies us. Hence Luther's emphasis on Christ as gift. This is also why he insists on the real presence in the Eucharist. Christ in his full incarnate self—not just his death—must become ours if we are to participate in him. Campbell rightly draws attention positively to Luther's seminal work "The Freedom of a Christian" of 1520. However, this is not in conflict with a Justification Theory found elsewhere in Luther, but fully in harmony with his wider thought. "The Freedom of a Christian" is a work

11. See Wengert, *Law and Gospel*, for an account of this debate.

12. Lohse, *Martin Luther*, 182.

that describes the unredeemed state as bondage and the Christian state as freedom. Faith has three powers: the first is to lay hold of the Word of God that declares the promise of Christ. The second is to recognize God as he truly is and therefore to fulfill the first commandment. The third is to unite the soul with Christ, in which salvation consists. This is a fully participative understanding of salvation that focuses on the incarnation as the gift of Christ our righteousness—the death of Christ as atonement is hardly touched on in the treatise.

In this work Luther makes it clear that he has altogether left behind what Campbell describes as Justification Theory. The latter suggests we are unable to fulfill the "covenant of nature" (as Alan Torrance describes it in the previous chapter), and so God has introduced a "covenant of grace" that works around it. For Luther, this is not the way salvation works: "Though you were nothing but good works from the soles of your feet to the crown of your head, you would still not be righteous or worship God or fulfill the first commandment, since God cannot be worshipped unless you ascribe to him the glory of truthfulness and all goodness which is due to him." In other words, we were never meant to be justified by works, but instead are to be drawn into a relationship of trust, elicited by the good news of a God who is trustworthy.

If there is a culprit here in the exclusive focus on Christ's death as atonement, rather than a wider theology of salvation that includes incarnation, I would suggest it is Anselm and not Luther. It is Anselm's theology of atonement that explicitly assumes a feudal, contractual understanding of God's honor and the demands due to it. It is Anselm's not Luther's soteriology that focuses exclusively on the death of Christ. These however are ideas seldom found in Luther himself.

4. Salvation Conditional upon the Prior Exercise of Faith

Similarly, faith for Luther is emphatically not something we exercise in order to acquire the gift of salvation. It is not an independent prior capacity we have to fulfill our part of the contract of salvation. That is precisely the idea he is trying with all his might to counter. Luther's original theological struggles were compounded by the nominalist soteriology he had been taught, which told him that all he needed to do was to turn away from his sins and exercise a little love for God (*facere quod in se est*) and then God would give him grace to enable him to perform meritorious works. It is precisely this nominalist, contractual understanding of salvation that Luther rejects in his Reformation theology. He does not assume it, adopt it, and find another way round it; he firmly repudiates it.

In his "Disputation on Justification" of 1535, Luther writes: "Faith is a divine, not a human work."[13] Faith is not something we exercise, it is something elicited in us by the Word, which presents the true God, the God of love, not the God of judgment. We are simply unable to place faith in a God of judgment, because we cannot love such a God. By contrast, it is when we hear who the true God is, that good news, or gospel, evokes faith and love in us. As Robert Kolb puts it: "God creates the trust that constitutes the believer's very being by promising life in Christ, a promise unshakeable and therefore trust-creating."[14] Or in the words of Gerhard Forde: "Faith is the state of being grasped by the unconditional claim and promise of the God who calls into being that which is from that which is not."[15] Unbelief is sinful not because it is a failure to fulfill the human part of a contract, but because it is a sign of rejection of the first commandment: a refusal to acknowledge God for who he is, the God of faithfulness, mercy, and grace.

Fides for Luther is not the one-off mental act of saying a sinner's prayer at an evangelistic rally. It is the ongoing daily disposition towards God that refuses to believe he is full of wrath and anger, but instead he is what the gospel says he is: a God of goodness and love. Naturally, faith is pivotal for Luther, not as a human act that triggers God's grace, but rather a daily recognition of the true nature of God and what he has done and given in Christ.

To take an example: Campbell quotes Luther in "The Freedom of a Christian" as saying "if you believe, you shall have all things, if you do not believe you shall lack all things."[16] This looks on the surface like faith as a condition of salvation, however, in context it reads very differently. The full text is: "If you wish to fulfill the law and not covet, as the law demands, come, believe in Christ in whom grace, righteousness, peace, liberty, and all things are promised you. If you believe, you shall have all

---

13. LW 34:189
14. Kolb, "Contemporary Lutheran Understandings" 171.
15. Forde, *Justification by Faith*, 22f.
16. LW 31:34; Campbell, *Deliverance*, 254.

things; if you do not believe, you shall lack all things."[17] In other words, it is not a statement of an arbitrary contractual arrangement whereby God rewards faith with justification: it is a statement of what faith in the true God enables you to do: it liberates the heart not to covet because all things are already given in Christ. Faith is elicited by the proclamation of the gospel of the goodness of God in Christ, which in turn enables us to do what we have no power to do on our own: to love the law.

Having said all this, it is still true that Luther's vision of salvation is primarily individual rather than corporate. It was left to the Swiss Reformation under Zwingli, Calvin, and Bullinger to develop a more corporate understanding of salvation; Luther's focus does remain on how the individual can know he or she is safe in the hands of God. Faith as trust (and not just as correct belief or faithfulness) is still central to Luther's conception of salvation, but not as a mental action that triggers justification, but as the daily posture towards God that receives the gift of union with Christ by a firm grasp of the promise that God is as he is in Christ, a God of love and mercy, not anger and judgment.

Conclusion

The Deliverance of God offers us a fascinating and, at least in parts, compelling re-reading of Paul's soteriology. From a Reformation perspective, it is to be welcomed that it avoids some of the crude generalizations and assumptions about Luther's theology as found elsewhere in the "New Perspective on Paul" debate. Whether or not its case on the interpretation of Romans 1–4 is to hold, I leave it for others to judge. However, the doctrine of salvation it offers, of a God who is utterly good, full of love and mercy, who rescues broken people from the spiritual and intellectual bondage of sin to freedom in Christ, a gospel that is revelatory, unconditional, participative, and liberating is one that has a great deal more in common with Luther's own soteriology than might at first sight seem possible.

---

17. LW 31:348.

Douglas Campbell's Response to Graham Tomlin

Graham posed two basic questions to me—Does my reading undermine the perspicuity of Scripture for ordinary Christians? and Does it misrepresent Luther by suggesting that he periodically supports the discourse I am describing and criticizing as "the Justification discourse"? That is, Graham—in his main concern—plants Luther firmly on the good, participatory, essentially Trinitarian side of the distinction being articulated through much of the discussion—although Luther speaks there at times in terms of something called "justification."

Regarding the first question: a longer and a shorter answer—both still regrettably brief.

Graham is really raising here the relationship between historical critical interpretation of the Bible and the Reformation advocacy of lay reading, which presupposes sufficient clarity or perspicuity in Scripture for ordinary readers to "profit." My work is admittedly in conversation with historical critical professionals and those in related disciplines and hence will inevitably be difficult for ordinary readers to understand. Such, however, is simply the price that academic work must pay—and Graham himself pays it when he wrests the interpretation of Luther away from its popular pietistic but historically inaccurate appeals to justification theory to a more appropriate reading! However, his question is a good one, although this is not the place to discuss it. So I will simply note that I think it is entirely fair to ask how historical critical studies should relate to the reading of Scripture by the average Christian in the church. I suspect that it ought to, at the least, fit into a broader spectrum of approaches to Scripture that includes types of reading that do not disempower or marginalize non-academic readers. But in the mean time what are we to do about the identification of Paul's voice as against the voice of opponents in his texts when reading those texts in a historical mode?

Fortunately, there is a simple answer to this question: punctuation. After the scholars have had their deliberations, off-setting sentences and paragraphs with quotation marks identifies particular texts as the voices of others whom Paul is quoting as against his own speech—a technique used already in most of our Bibles to identify Paul's otherwise unmarked quotations of Corinthian statements in 1 Corinthians. (And the occasional explanatory footnote can help here as well.) So when teaching Romans 1–3 in class I offer my students a suitably punctuated text and this seems to deal with most of the confusion. Perhaps one day a published Bible will contain a Socratic punctuation of Romans 1–3 and thereby, at least from my point of view, avoid many nasty problems. (The Bible League International, concerned especially about African contexts, is currently working on the ERV—the easy-to-read version—and is considering punctuating Romans 1–3 in Socratic terms.) It is somewhat ironic to note that most of our difficulties here arose after Paul's day from the comparative lack of punctuation in ancient Greek texts. Once the original paralinguistic cues had been lost, Paul's original sense became much harder to reconstruct—a problem he probably did not himself envisage, but that was produced when his work was published later on in a letter collection and then incorporated into Christian Scripture.

Regarding the second question, concerning Luther: just as Graham has prescinded from judging the validity of my readings within the technical NT guild, I have prescinded in my book from asserting anything too strongly in relation to Luther, given the complexity and passion surrounding Luther scholarship and will continue to do so here. Graham, however, has not been so cautious, suggesting rather more forcefully than I did that Luther belongs on the good side of the debate, in principal if not nearly unalloyed support of a vigorous, gracious, and participatory account of the gospel. And as a Reformation scholar he is entitled to make this claim and more competent to do so than I.

I am of course quite happy to accept it since it strengthens the argument of *Deliverance* so much. That this critical Reformer would be so supportive of a covenantal account of the gospel and so consistently opposed to false contractual versions is only helpful to my main concerns. But accepting this bold position—bold because not many scholars are as confident as Graham is about Luther's consistency—has a couple of important entailments that must be grasped clearly.

It would follow, first, the Luther's weight falls strongly *against* the reading of Romans 1–4 currently being undertaken by so many modern Protestants. His testimony, rightly appreciated, would urge us still harder than it already does to find an alternative reading that does not release the contractual and conditional dynamics he recognized and abhorred into the wider church. *Moreover*, second, we must avoid a potential source of confusion here. If Luther characterizes his participatory account of the gospel occasionally in terms of "righteousness," "faith," "not law," and even "justification," this does not entail that we can rest from the labor of rereading Romans 1–3. The problematic reading of that text remains problematic—because the "justification" it speaks of in crassly conditional terms is, strictly speaking, a fundamentally different justification from the "justification" Luther speaks of in gracious and participatory terms. We might say then that Luther's commitment to a healthy type of justification, Justification Type A, does not eliminate but strengthens the need to find a rereading of Romans 1–4 that avoids the sinister type of justification, Justification Type B. Many of my critics have drawn the opposite and entirely false conclusion here so it is helpful to have the correct entailment emphasized so clearly by Graham.[18] In short, *Deliverance* is arguing, he avers, for a rereading of Paul's "justification" texts that Luther himself, properly understood, would have strongly and univocally advocated, and I am of course happy to accept this suggestion and hope that he is right about it.

18. That is, Luther is committed to a healthy view of justification, Type A, so we do not need to reread and eliminate "justification" from Paul as I do—thereby overlooking that Romans 1–4 releases a different version, Type B (!).

3

The Current Crisis

The Capture of Paul's Gospel by Methodological Arianism[1]

Douglas A. Campbell

W hat does all that has been said in this volume so far have to do with the reading of Paul and of Romans, most especially of Romans 1–3, and with my arguments in *Deliverance*? Much in every way.

It is my contention that Paul, rightly understood, is a clear-sighted and courageous advocate of a revelational gospel—of Athanasianism, so to speak. His advocates in these terms within specialized Pauline circles often denote their approach "apocalyptic" (from the Greek for "revelation").[2] But it is also my contention that large parts of Paul's theological description have been captured by Arianism, not at the explicitly theological level but largely unintentionally, so it is really a type

1. Parts of the following paper are gratefully reused by permission from my essay "What Is at Stake?" 109–32. In this paper (and that essay) I draw the terminology and constructions of "Athanasianism" and "Arianism" primarily from Heron, "*Homoousios* with the Father," 58–87; but see also T. F. Torrance, "*Spiritus Creator*," 209–28; T. F. Torrance, "Athanasius," 215–66, esp. 240; and T. F. Torrance, "The Doctrine of the Holy Trinity according to St. Athanasius," 395–405.

2. See (of course) J. L. (Lou) Martyn, and those persuaded by him, esp. Martyn's "Epistemology," 89–110.

of unwitting "methodological Arianism" that is in play. But it is in play nevertheless. And one of two things now tends to happen. Paul is still interpreted in many places in terms that theologians would recognize as fundamentally Athanasian but the (methodological) Arianism attributed to him in other places overrides his Athanasianism making Paul an Arian in effect. Or, less commonly, these two competing dynamics in his thought are both acknowledged candidly and neither is awarded primacy leading to a judgment that Paul is fundamentally confused.[3] Of course it is hardly ideal to have Paul the apostle, author of a quarter of the NT, either witnessing in practical terms in support of Arius or in a state of fundamental theological confusion. It is, rather, an interpretative crisis, if not for the academy then for the church, and hence the sense of urgency underpinning many of my suggestions. But in order to appreciate just how this has happened to Paul we need to explore a particular Arian variant in more detail.

Contractual Foundationalism

The relevant variant is best known in Pauline circles as the "Lutheran reading of Paul," in ultimate dependence on some classic essays by Krister Stendahl.[4] But *Deliverance* posited a deeper and broader explanation of the problem than Stendahl offered—an explanation that reached out to include much of the recent critique of Paul in relation to Judaism as well (and more besides), something Stendahl did not highlight.[5] The problem

3. Some scholars exercise good judgment and allow the Athanasian material primacy, but the price they pay for this compromise is that they are unable to rebuff the Arian interpreters of Paul decisively. Furthermore, elements of that system tend to leak into their own interpretations allowing Paul's Arian reading a partial endorsement and frequent reactivation. This is a risk that I fear Michael Gorman is running; see his generally insightful analysis, "Douglas Campbell's *The Deliverance of God*," 99–107; and his recent broader treatment of Paul, *Inhabiting the Cruciform God*.

4. See *Paul among Jews and Gentiles*. This moniker is not a particularly good one because it is not really fair to Luther. The problematic system is in Luther but much else is there as well, and this alternative material frequently contradicts and repudiates the problematic approach. Moreover, Stendahl's account of this "problem" within the interpretation of Paul is brilliantly creative and insightful but also rather scattered. I argue at length in *Deliverance* that his insights are coordinated, deepened, and widened when they are mapped onto a contractual framework (and I argue, of course, that this is a legitimate explanation *of* his intuitions); see 172–76, 247–83.

5. That is, at least in Stendahl's earlier critiques; his brief commentary on Romans, written thirty years later, has additional emphases: see his *Final Account*.

in many of these relations, *Deliverance* argued, is actually a particular form of foundationalism much at home in the Western theological tradition and in Western culture in general. (Note, by "foundationalism" I simply mean "Arianism" in the sense already intimated, namely, of an Arian methodology, with the initial human positing of an analogy for God in the pre- or non-Christian state. This analogy then functions as the foundation on which the rest of a putative theological system is constructed. In Athanasius's view, however, this is not proper theology at all, which should proceed strictly from God's provision of the correct analogy in Christ. Methodologically Arian systems were in his view not worthy of the name theology; they were, on the contrary, mere mythology; see note 1.)

Methodological Arianism or foundationalism takes many specific forms. But James Torrance saw with peculiar clarity that an especially popular way to introduce foundationalism into any modern account of the gospel in the West has been through the reinterpretation of salvation as a contract.[6]

A contract is a cultural practice known since antiquity but especially prevalent in modern Western and liberal societies since the rise of capitalism and the development of post-monarchical ("liberal") politics. It widely informs Western law, economics, politics, and broader culture.[7] But it supplies a fundamentally different account of the relationship between God and humanity mediated by Christ from an Athanasian one. Indeed, it is basically a classic Arian subversion of the orthodox gospel.

Like all foundationalisms it works forward from a particular understanding of the problem to its Christian solution, and hence, just because it works forward, its "Christian" solution is dictated before it arrives by

6. See his profoundly lucid and insightful essays, "Covenant or Contract," 51–76; and "The Contribution of McLeod Campbell to Scottish Theology," 295–311 (both are happily reprinted in this volume). To be clear, James Torrance articulated these issues with respect to Scottish Presbyterianism, and I argued at length in *Deliverance* that this narrative also explains a great deal that is going on in Pauline scholarship as well; the same categories—unsurprisingly, since we continue to speak of modern Western scholars—structure much of the apostle's interpretation today.

7. It is not absent from ancient and non-Western cultures but it is nowhere near as pervasive and dominant as it is in European and post-European societies. *Deliverance* provides further details and references: 284–309 (ch. 9). The extent to which it is present in the Bible is moot; Deuteronomy is a key text and is interpreted in different ways. To oversimplify: some scholars see consequences where others see contracts—and both systems tend to use conditional grammar!

assumptions derived within the problematic pre-Christian state. Hence contractualism builds the foundation for its truth claims in an account of the general problem facing humanity, and with natural theology.[8] It is in "the state of nature" that people learn all the key things about God, humanity, and broader reality, not to mention about Judaism: God is fundamentally just, this justice being conceived of in broadly Western terms as requiting things appropriately, good deeds with the appropriate rewards and bad deeds with the appropriate punishment.[9] And the content of those deeds is *prescribed* so reality is rule- or law-governed (and we have now created a permanent space for the modern state). It follows from all this, moreover, that people are individuals who can be held accountable for their deeds in some basic way, so they must possess moral and rational capacities that enable them to grasp God's rules and to choose either to obey them or not to—a fundamentally optimistic account of human nature. In short, reality for humanity is characterized in its most basic situation self-evidently by a rule-governed contract with a fundamentally just and judging God. If people obey God's rules then rewards will ensue; if they disobey them then the appropriate punishments will be visited upon them.[10]

The structure driving the entire scenario is the conditional agreement that *if* certain conditions are met *then* certain results will be provided ("If you do A then I will do X; but if you do B then I will do Y"; and so on). Contracts are binding in law so they are framed by an overarching legal system, and individuals can make them. Alternatively, individuals who have bound themselves into larger groups by an original contract or act of consent can undertake them in what we might call constitutional

8. Hence an important relationship here with the highly destructive development of Deism is apparent historically; see esp. Buckley, *At the Origins of Modern Atheism*; and Placher, *The Domestication of Transcendence*.

9. The actual content attached to the signifier "justice" varies widely from culture to culture and epoch to epoch. In this relation see esp. MacIntyre, *Whose Justice? Which Rationality?* MacIntyre does not merely demonstrate exhaustively how notions of the "right," ergo "just," have developed and changed but how they are irreducibly bound up with conceptions of "truth" and rationality. Hauerwas then makes the obvious application in "The Politics of Justice," 45–68 (ch. 2).

10. A future eschatology is an important component in the plausibility of this general schema. A strictly contractual approach is easier to doubt or falsify when it is assumed to be playing out strictly within history and within the lifetime of each individual—Job!

moments, and these are arguably the dominant European conception of legitimate sociopolitical organization.

But the genius of the Western contractual reading of Paul's gospel is that it develops its account by way of a second, softer, and specifically Christian contract; it is a tale of *two* contracts. This allows the system to assert that the first, essentially moralizing contract will fail, an outcome that seems to achieve a number of important results.

The first general contract ends negatively because individuals are held to sin without exception (a point where the reading seems to link up with an emphasis on depravity, although the resemblance is more apparent than real[11]). God's rules are flouted by everyone in some way, however subtle, and so all can expect only a fearful verdict on the Day of Judgment of unrighteousness and the appropriate punishment. But the breaking of this contract nevertheless seems to have several positive results.

First, rational individuals ought now to be predisposed to grasp salvation and to become Christians, and evangelism can now be conducted—and conversion understood—in these terms. Moreover, second, and as we have just seen, this story's dismal trajectory seems to affirm the Christian tradition's emphasis on sin, as well as, third, to provide an explanation of why Christianity is not Judaism—because Judaism, correctly understood, collapses at this point, being merely a particularly clear and rigorous rule-governed variation on the first contract that all fail. So this initial contract "levels the playing field" between Jews and pagans and seems to explain Paul's law-free mission. And where Jews stand in for other "religious" groups, like Catholics, then the reading can be even more useful.[12] Much seems then to have been either affirmed or explained.

But things cannot of course remain in this failed situation with all condemned. So salvation is offered by an alternative route—in the version found especially clearly in Melanchthon, *sola fide* or "by faith alone." In this variation those exercising Christian faith can grasp a second, easier,

11. That is, *complete* depravity cannot be acknowledged at this point without collapsing into incoherence. Even the failure of a contractual arrangement presupposes *some* capacity and accountability on the part of the contractor—to know that the contract is in place and its conditions, and to have some possibility of fulfilling them. Without these basic capacities the enforcement of any breach of contract would be deeply unfair; it would be like penalizing a one-year-old for not voting. So any contractual system is ultimately at odds with claims of total depravity.

12. Watson's *Paul, Judaism, and the Gentiles*, provides numerous helpful insights at this point.

and specifically Christian contract. They can thereby access a redirection of their coming punishment onto Christ on the cross. But they must of course hear about this new offer from God through preaching; it is not self-evident. Hence a missional imperative arises in a certain sense from this system; people within the first contract are doomed without preachers and their sending.

My suspicion is that the initial formulations of this particular foundationalism in terms of two contracts—a harsh condemning one followed by a softer arrangement—lay deep in the traditions of the Latin church where it is usefully known as the Western *ordo salutis* or "order of salvation." T. F. Torrance called it, rather more gingerly, "the Latin Heresy."[13] And it can be found, for example, in Augustine, as a fairly standard response to soteriologies that are simply moralizing (i.e., overly optimistic single contract systems) in figures like Pelagius and Julian of Eclanum, and arguably even in Origen.[14] But up to the time of the Reformation the second contract, although including faith, was fundamentally *ecclesial*. The conditions for its appropriation included some mix of catechesis, baptism, the Eucharist, and so on. Faith was one Christian activity among several.

A strong emphasis on the condition for the second contract as consisting of faith alone seems to have been a Reformation development, and it was Luther who opined that the word "alone" needed to be added to Paul's original text. I suggest that it is unwise to reduce the Reformation to this reformulation of the *ordo*![15] Nevertheless this particular variant, with its emphasis on *sola fide*, made sense in the sixteenth century given

13. T. F. Torrance, "Karl Barth and the Latin Heresy," 461–82.

14. Much more could of course be said at this point, but see Augustine (inter alia), *Propositions on the Epistle to the Romans, Miscellaneous Questions* 66 and 67, *On Nature and Grace, Sermons* 151–59, and *On the Spirit and the Letter*. There is an important relationship here with the catechized and often anxious approach of much Western tradition to baptism; the *ordo* arguably functioned most significantly in relation to those whom modern Protestants might very well view as effectively saved or converted, but who were not yet actually baptized, to move them through in the appropriate state of repentance to that critical act. Cf. esp. the elegant and insightful analysis by Smith of justification in Ambrose; (chapter 4) "Baptism: Sacrament of Justification," 69–123.

15. To make two very basic observations here: Calvin is seldom reducible to this system, and Luther is frequently not so and arguably not centrally so (see here the "Finnish" school of Lutheran interpretation). These claims are detailed in *Deliverance*, 247–83. Incidentally, their establishment was the principal argumentative burden of chapter 8, which has not been widely grasped by many of its readers.

the polemical posture of some of the Reformers against Catholicism (which was positioned in the first, rule-governed phase as something religiously conditional and so ostensibly akin to legalistic and recalcitrant Judaism). And this was all doubtless assisted by the rise of individualism in Europe at the time, the first whispers of which were heard in the Renaissance, but that accelerated so much in relation to the arrivals of both Humanism and capitalism. And this variant on the Western *ordo* has subsequently enjoyed the affirmation of increasingly individualistic settings in European and post-European contexts.[16] As we step back from this account a little, however, it is apparent that all the basic features of Arian foundationalism are present within it.

First, at the heart of this system is the initial projection of a set of cultural analogies into the key theological roles that then determine all that follows. The projection in this foundationalism is of course essentially *legal* and *political*. God functions like a Western monarch presiding over a law-governed reality. And note that this is not a tribal arrangement but an empire, so the arrangement is essentially Constantinian.[17] "His"[18] basic posture is "just," and the solution offered to infractions of justice is the meting out of an equivalent and proportional act, if necessary in violent terms, so the conception of justice is directly analogous to political justice.[19] We are basically speaking then in the *ordo* of a theological—but in reality mythological—projection of the state—although this is presumably one reason why people loyal to a state find this theological account congenial; any uncritical nationalism will reinforce the *ordo*. So when Christians are told that they can escape punishment in the future

16. So, rather regrettably, the approach has been exported to European colonies, whether actual or merely missional; see, e.g., Korea.

17. What I mean by this is that much of the legal architecture of the West was developed in the context of the Roman Empire, which sought in many respects to generate a moral framework that transcended tribalism (etc.). The Emperor needed to have the right to judge people from a multiplicity of ethnicities within the Empire, so an ethic ostensibly transcending such categories was necessary. An overarching ethical contract holding for all humanity couched in terms of universal laws derived from contemplation of the created cosmos consequently provided just what was needed. The church's complicity in this dynamic has long been lamented by some; see the discussion in *Deliverance*, 207–8 and notes. (This problem is perhaps most clearly appreciated now from a location in the U.S.A.)

18. The discourse is obviously "masculinist."

19. It is measured, so this is often presented as a superior arrangement to either anarchy or arbitrary tyranny (and it probably is). But its superiority does not entail its divine endorsement or (worse) its divine analogy.

it is because Christ and his activity have been configured in these essentially political terms on their behalf—largely into an act that absorbs their punishment for them. That is, this view of the atonement presupposes a law-governed society that punishes infractions with imprisonment and—if necessary—with execution. Moreover, in accordance with the rule of law, all individuals are held accountable; and all relationships are structured by way of contract and consent, so the church is basically a consenting arrangement analogous to a constitutional compact. Justice applies to all then, but mercy is accessed by and through the church, and the model betrays its Constantinian associations particularly directly at this point.[20] The church can contract out of its basic situation into a special privileged zone in soteriological terms but really never leaves its original legal and political obligations behind in doing so. The state will continue to enforce those. And I fear that this essentially Arian—and now privatized—construct will override the contributions of orthodox Christology to the gospel, to the church, and to politics.

An Athanasian Response to Contractual Foundationalism

An Athanasian account of all these things is subtly but significantly different. It assumes first that Christ reveals God as God, so there ought to be complete unity (although also distinction) between the Father and the Son. Moreover—as Paul puts it—"when we were still sinners [and indeed 'ungodly'] Christ died for us" (Rom 5:6, 8). That is, the Son reached out to and was executed for humanity while it was still sinful and actively hostile to that loving and gracious act. This divine act consequently took place when no condition had been or could be met. And we learn from this that God *does not conditionally act toward humanity at all*. God acts rather out of pure, overflowing benevolence that operates *prior* to all human actions (cf. Rom 8:29–30; Eph 1:3–14). But what applies here to the Son must apply also in full measure to the Father and the Spirit. Consequently *God's* relationship with humanity is fundamentally

---

20. It is also worth noting that critical identity issues consequently tend to arise for the church at explicitly foundationalist and contractual points—the defense of natural theology (creation; gender), and of the right and need for the politically conceived God to punish (the death penalty, and emphases on the equivalent theological loci of [a certain sort of] judgment and hell).

unconditional and benevolent. In more biblical parlance, it is covenantal.[21] In theological or dogmatic terms, it is elective, in the sense especially that Barth recovered so insightfully.[22] This christological insight then must (re)structure all our soteriological categories, if necessary purging them of their inappropriate contractual analogies.

The atonement is, moreover, clearly an act that *rescues*, rather like the exodus. It lifts a helpless and wretched humanity out of its awful condition and transforms it, so Christ's incarnation, life, death, resurrection, and ascension, are all vital aspects of salvation, and not just his death as tends to be the case in contractual schemas. In dying and rising, however, Christ also *judges* its sinful situation, terminating and executing it; indeed, the cross is where God's principal act of judgment against evil takes place (of course!). In Barthian parlance, God says a decisive "no" to our sin and complicity with evil in the cross.[23] The cross is, however, also the place where God shoulders this situation and deals with it directly and completely "himself."[24] And we learn immediately from this that we are, as Calvin so frequently emphasized, "depraved." The very unconditionality of God's act reveals that we can contribute *nothing* to our salvation; we are utterly fallen, judged irrevocably by grace.

We also learn at this point that the atoning death of Christ is not fundamentally a penal act. God is not *punishing* Christ in all this. This is not how sin and evil are dealt with. The Father and the Son (and the Spirit!) act in perfect concord. And in the cross sin and evil are judged as they are permanently extinguished from the cosmos through Christ's death. God thereby eliminates sin along with all its concomitants by carrying it

---

21. Gorman is absolutely right to integrate this motif into his account of Paul, but this covenant must be rightly understood—in Athanasian terms, hence christologically and unconditionally; see his *Inhabiting the Cruciform God.* The language of covenant has frequently been co-opted into contractual readings by being conditionalized. But, as James Torrance argued faithfully, a (biblical and theological) covenant is *not* a contract! They are qualitatively different arrangements. (See his "Covenant and Contract," cited in n. 6.) The use of covenantal language by Pauline scholars consequently needs careful scrutiny.

22. See especially his *Church Dogmatics* II/2 *The Doctrine of God.*

23. This is one of the principal suggestions of § 61.2, "The Judgment of God," in *Church Dogmatics* IV/1 *The Doctrine of Reconciliation,* 528–68; but Barth makes this point frequently, so *CD, passim.*

24. Quotation marks because it is a fundamentally Trinitarian action, not singular. Moreover, the introduction of the masculine pronoun also requires careful interpretation, and has a long history of abuse; cf. Tanner, "Kingdom Come," 129–45.

himself all the way to its agonized point of termination, and then creates new life beyond it as the Trinity affects the central life-giving moment within creation, the Father raising the Son through the Spirit. Hence, God does not provide an equivalent act himself to sin at this point *of violence and death* in essentially quantitative terms; rather, he bears and suffers these very things himself in order to extinguish them. So there is no endorsement of imperial politics or of retributive justice in the atonement but quite the converse. Indeed, those dynamics are arguably part of the evil God endures and bears away. And so, after pondering God's solution to wrongdoing in Christ, we see that when God and the Western state try to solve the deep problems facing humanity *they tend to act in fundamentally different ways*. (What a mistake it is to project Western politics into God's atoning act!)

Perhaps not surprisingly, in God's act in Christ we begin to understand what humanity is like as well. We learn about how freedom and agency, and ethics, are meant to work. And once again, in the light of these discoveries, we can see where our Western culture has often misled us.[25]

Much more could of course be said here, especially about the church. But hopefully enough has been noted for us to grasp that the interpretation of Paul at any point in an Athanasian sense must clash *fundamentally* and *programmatically* with his interpretation at any other point in terms of contractual foundationalism. Moreover, to deny this clash is ultimately to deny that there were any important differences between Athanasius and Arius, or between creedal orthodoxy and its heretical opponents. But I suspect that any such denials by Paul's interpreters simply rest on

---

25. Contractual advocates tend to think that only conditional arrangements can (1) preserve human freedom—by presupposing accountability in relation to some faculty of choice or will—*and* (2) generate ethics—by providing a suite of future threats and rewards that can elicit good behavior, essentially out of rational self-interest (so it is, strictly speaking, a rational*istic* account). But it needs to be appreciated that the Athanasian gospel is equally committed to freedom and ethics, although in very different terms. It suggests that human freedom cannot be presupposed—because people are sinful and depraved—but must be reconstituted. It must, moreover, be understood in fundamentally covenantal (i.e., biblical) terms, as obedience; it is the freedom to respond and *not* the freedom to choose, the latter being, we should recall, the mistake of the primordial couple in the garden of Eden. Hence, any contractual affirmations of freedom, and of ethics in those terms, turns out to be a disastrous corruption of the biblical notions, and ultimately allows sin a legitimate place within the created cosmos. See, inter alia, Bauckham, *God and the Crisis of Freedom*; and, in more general terms, Barth *Church Dogmatics* III/1 *The Doctrine of Creation*.

a failure to grasp the critical issues that are in play in relation to Paul's theological description in terms of foundationalism, especially in contractual variants, over against an authentically Athanasian account of his gospel rooted in the revelation of Christ (Gal 1:12b, 15–16). Once these differences and their implications have been clearly appreciated it seems unlikely that many Pauline interpreters would want to deny them. Similarly, I suspect that many interpreters would want to affirm with me that a fundamentally Athanasian approach supplies a true account of what is going on in Paul for most of the time—an apocalyptic account, suitably understood. More controversially, however, it should be apparent by now that any Athanasian or apocalyptic account of Paul's gospel exists in fundamental contradiction to any essentially Arian approach to Paul in "Lutheran" terms, the latter being merely another (rather inadequate) name for a construal of Paul's gospel in terms of contractual foundationalism following on from the more general dictates of the Western *ordo*.[26] Any compromises here will be fatal to Paul's theological integrity.

But of course *Deliverance* contends that this is exactly what has happened, and as much in conservative, and even "evangelical," circles as in liberal ones. Paul's interpretation has been captured by Arian foundationalism in the specific form of contractualism, notably by the double contract sequence of the Western *ordo* in its vulgar Protestant variation of *sola fide*. Hence many of the deleterious effects of foundationalism in general and of contractual foundationalism in particular can be traced through the apostle's *Wirkungsgeschichte* and modern description.

These last claims are to date rather an underappreciated aspect of *Deliverance*, so I will conclude this discussion by gesturing briefly toward them. And this should also help us to see how the rather abstract theological constructs that we have been talking about thus far have quite practical and recognizable effects; they reach into and shape many of the most important localized disputes within Paul's interpretation today, and many of the questions that the church is currently grappling with in this relation as well.

Chapters 3 through 6 in part one of *Deliverance* articulate many of the claims here, gathering up some of the major questions in current

---

26. The language of tension is really too weak to describe this. People can live with many tensions. Hence, the language of contradiction is better, but is not being used strictly in the logical sense of a violation of the law of non-contradiction; it denotes fundamental and irreconcilable differences within the relevant discourses "all the way down"—in ontology, epistemology, anthropology, and so on.

Pauline scholarship (*DofG*, 62–218). Chapter 3 introduces the long-standing question concerning the integration of Paul's apparently rather different forensic and participatory discourses. (The chapter illustrates this with particular emphasis on W. Wrede.) Chapter 4 introduces the standard question concerning how to position Paul in relation to Judaism (emphasizing the work of E. P. Sanders of course)—and we will return to this question in more detail shortly. Chapter 5 introduces the less prominent questions of evangelism and conversion, although these were identified for critical consideration by Krister Stendahl and have certainly occupied "Lutheran" scholars subsequently. (In fact, these questions arise in several more specific forms—in relation to Paul's own conversion, his approach to the conversion of others, both rhetorical and practical, and to conversion in general.) Chapter 6 then scans several other debates more briefly, not all of which need occupy us now. However, a standard concern of some Pauline scholars with revelation (i.e., "apocalyptic") is worth recalling here, along with the concern of some that Paul is simply contradictory or incoherent (a complaint associated especially with Räisänen). And other scholars are anxious about the harsh construction of the other or the Christian outsider that results, and especially if that figure has (purportedly) unusual gender or racial markings.[27]

One of the main suggestions of *Deliverance* is all this is, at bottom, a *single* problem, and so is rather larger than many people realize—the problem underneath it all is Paul's interpretation, at least at key points, in terms of contractual foundationalism. And there is, therefore, also only one way to solve them all satisfactorily, a suggestion I will elaborate further in chapter 6. For now it suffices to appreciate "the problem," and it is a serious one. Even if we are unaware of the gravity of the underlying situation, it is still grave. Paul's theological description today resembles an Arctic ice shelf—melting and rotting underneath, riven with fissures, and about to collapse into the sea. Either we do something about it, or we face real and terrible consequences for our inaction.

---

27. I have found this point put especially sharply and insightfully by my colleagues, Carter, in *Race: A Theological Account*; and Jennings, in *The Christian Imagination*; see esp. in the latter "Colenso's Heart" (119–68).

4

Campbell's Apocalyptic Gospel and Pauline Athanasianism

CHRIS TILLING

A. Introduction

In *The Deliverance of God* Douglas Campbell seeks to provide a vision of a revelatory, transformational, unconditional, and liberational Pauline theology, one that, he maintains, stands in stark contrast to readings of Paul influenced by contractual foundationalism.[1] In response to the reviews by me and Michael Gorman,[2] Campbell elucidates his understanding of the contrast involved by speaking of it in terms of the debate between Athanasianism and Arianism. The foundationalist reading is Arian in its basic theological dynamics, and cannot stand together with but is necessarily antagonistic towards Paul's essentially Athanasian gospel. In this chapter I will explore the basic rationale involved in this claim, and some of the corresponding key questions, by examining Paul's

1. In *Deliverance*, Campbell describes this form of foundationalism under the designation "Justification Theory" (JT), but in this book he tends to prefer to use the phrase "Forward Thinking" (FT). When I speak of JT in the following, I simply mean to label the contractual foundationalism described in the previous chapter.

2. Campbell, "What Is at Stake?" 109–32.

christological "Athanasianism." Ultimately, Campbell's strategy of aligning Paul with Athanasius boils down to the question: is Paul's gospel "all about Jesus," and thus the truly good news of the unconditional love of God? Campbell thinks it is, and his apocalyptic rereading seeks to demonstrate this.

B. Campbell's Argument Relating to (Methodological) Arianism and Athanasianism in Nuce

As part of a thought experiment in *Deliverance*, Campbell details the "alternative soteriological theory" of Romans 5–8, one that, he maintains, is representative of Paul's wider theological vision. I will now follow Campbell's basic argumentative strategy and summarize this "alternative theory" to contrast it with the apparently non-christologically grounded God-talk in Romans 1:18ff.

1. The "Alternative Theory" of Romans 5–8

The first point he notes is that Romans 5–8 clearly evidences a soteriology, albeit a complex one. For reasons of clarity, he begins with "the state from which humanity is rescued."[3] Humans are rescued from the powerful forces of sin and death that enslave them. Here humans are described as God's "enemies" and as "ungodly" (5:6, 10). "The mind set on the flesh," Paul says in 8:7–8, "is hostile to God" and "cannot please God," and so what is needed is not first and foremost forgiveness, but rather *deliverance*: "Who will rescue me from this body of death?" (7:24), Paul asks, "the law of the Spirit of life in Christ Jesus has set you free from the law of sin and of death" (8:2).

Romans 5–8 demonstrates that this rescue happens, to cite Campbell, as "the result of interlocking actions by God the Father; his only, beloved Son, whom he sends into the enslaved Adamic condition; and the Holy Spirit."[4] The Father, Christ the Lord, and the Spirit of God all work to deliver humanity from its slavery, an act described in fundamentally unconditional terms (it has to be, given humanity's enslaved nature). Out of sheer generosity and love, God acts and it is this event of redemption

---

3. Campbell, *Deliverance*, 62.
4. Ibid., 63.

that grounds Paul's God-talk: *God* proves his love for us in *Christ* (5:8). Paul's root metaphors about God are thus christological and grounded in unconditional love (which does not dispense with notions of wrath and anger, but locates them correctly in terms of divine love).

The nature of Christian salvation is derived from this picture, and is seen as *communal and interpersonal* (cf. 7:1; 8:12–17, 19, 21, 23, 29), *doxological* (7:25; 8:15. Cf also 8:26–27, 34), *transformational*, and thus also *ethical* (6:15, 23; 8:3–13). The text likewise evidences a retrospective soteriology; this salvation thinks "in light of Christ." Hence, humanity's dire situation becomes clear only *in light* of this salvation. This rescue is not completed but only *inaugurated*, as references to patience, persever-ance, character, and hope reveal (cf. 5:3–4). Moreover, this shows that the soteriology of Romans 5–8 is also fundamentally *pastoral* in that it secures Christian assurance in the face of trials, grounding it in God's unconditional love (5:6–11; 8:32). It follows that no "criteria for [salva-tion's] activation, appropriation, or reception by humans are apparent in this text, while what causality or agency is apparent is attributed to God."[5] Consequently, faith is not here understood as a condition for salvation.[6]

These chapters of Romans thus offer a coherent account of salva-tion, one rooted in the Trinitarian activity of God in which God, out of sheer unconditional love, reconstitutes an enslaved humanity after the image of the Son in the power of the Spirit.

2. God-talk in Romans 1:18–32

Contractual foundationalism, as Campbell's account in chapter 3 of this book claims, works like a computer virus, infecting the interpretation of Paul in powerfully counterproductive ways, unleashing contradic-tory theological implications in our readings.[7] This interpretative force,

---

5. Ibid., 65.

6. Faith is, rather, a theological journey into correct beliefs (reference can be made, here, to 6:8 and the struggle for this clarity of cognition suggested in 6:1a, 15a; 7:7a; 8:33a), and a life of "faithfulness" or "fidelity," a matter linked to our text via the themes of suffering and patience, endurance and hope (5:2–5; 8:9–25). Chapter 14 of this book will discuss these and other matters in more depth.

7. JT is, to be clear, certainly not a description of the proposed Pauline theology of any major academic sparring partners. It is not meant to describe a portrayal of Pauline thinking *in toto*. This is worth repeating, as not a few of Campbell's reviewers have misunderstood him at this point (see Tilling, "The Deliverance of God, and of

for the socioeconomic, philosophical, cultural, and historical reasons overviewed by Campbell in his chapter, has largely been activated by a construal of Romans 1–4 that reads the text in Paul's own voice. Because it does this, Paul's theo-logic runs forward—despite (well-intentioned) scholarly denials—from apparently universally self-evident God-truth, which in turn grounds an account of ethical accountability. And this is done without any explicit (or implicit) recourse to God-talk in terms of Christ. To cite Campbell, here we have "revelation generally available to all *prior* to the proclamation of the gospel,"[8] and its "articulation in positions established independently of and prior to them,"[9] and thus ultimately a "foundationalist argument rooted in non-christological analogies for God."[10] (Campbell will demonstrate these points in more detail himself in chapter 9 below.)

3. Contradiction or "Creative Tension"?

Campbell is clear about the import of these different theological discourses (this is the burden of chapter 3 of *Deliverance*). If all in Romans and beyond is to be read in Paul's own voice, then there is unavoidable and sheer contradiction in his theology at a deep level. However, precisely at this point, many of Campbell's reviewers protest. So Douglas Moo, in his *JETS* review, writing as "an unrepentant defender of the essence of what Campbell calls 'Justification Theory,'"[11] regularly resists Campbell's

---

Paul?" 85–86).

8. Campbell, "What Is at Stake?" 127, italics mine.

9. Campbell, *Deliverance*, 203.

10. Campbell, "What Is at Stake?" 128. Cf. his extended discussion in Campbell, *Deliverance*, 314–31.

11. Moo, "*The Deliverance of God*," 143. Moo's learned Romans commentary can be taken as evidence of this penchant for key aspects of JT: "We must consider 1:18—3:20 as a *preparation* for, rather than as part of, Paul's exposition of the gospel of God's righteousness. But it is a *necessary preparation* if what Paul wants to emphasize about this righteousness is to be accepted by the Romans. For *only* if sin is seen to be the dominating, ruling force that Paul presents it to be in this section . . . will it become clear why God's righteousness can be experienced only by humbly receiving it as a gift—in a word, by faith" (Moo, *The Epistle to the Romans*, 92, italics mine); "the knowledge of God rejected by those depicted in 1:18–32 comes solely through 'natural revelation'—the evidences of God in creation and, perhaps, the conscience" (ibid., 97); "the suppression of the knowledge of God available in creation, and the recognition that certain sins deserve God's judgment are constant aspects of human experience" (ibid., 98); in 1:19, Paul "is interested in the knowledge of God available to all people

claim that JT and the alternative theory (of Romans 5–8) contradict. For example, he claims that: "[t]he traditional understanding of justification can *easily* accommodate a 'from-solution-to-plight' reading of Pauline justification."[12] Beverly Gaventa writes that "Campbell's historical argument is not necessary for an apocalyptic reading of Romans, even of Romans 1–4,"[13] and Michael Gorman, too, claims that "[w]hile I strongly affirm Campbell's overall interpretation of Paul's gospel, I contend that his reading of 1:18—3:20 is wrong and that his analysis of Paul's gospel does not depend on his reading of 1:18—3:20."[14]

So, has Campbell simply overplayed what could perhaps better be called a "creative tension" in Paul's thought? Is the entire thesis of *Deliverance* based upon a delusion that there exists a fundamental theological contradiction in Romans, if it is all read in Paul's own voice? Is Barry Matlock correct, in light of Campbell's contrasts between contractual foundationalism and the "alternative theory," to charge Campbell with "intellectual blackmail," or is it rather, as Campbell opines, "a sad commentary on the state of theological description in relation to Paul that we tend to find these extraordinary tensions so easy to live with"?[15]

4. Enter Athanasius and Arianism in Campbell's JSPL article

In response to just these kinds of questions, Campbell has sought to clarify his position with recourse to the contrast between Athanasius and Arianism.[16] Campbell maintains that contractual foundationalism and the revelatory and Trinitarian "alternative theory" are not merely theological options that can be held in creative tension, despite the claims of some of his reviewers. What we are dealing with, he argues, is a divide as deep and fundamental to orthodox theology as that between Arianism and the greatest defender of orthodox Nicene faith, Athanasius. And this is not simply a historical example of an either/or situation, for Campbell.

---

through the nature of the world itself" (ibid., 104); etc.

12. Moo, "*The Deliverance of God*," 145, italics mine.

13. Gaventa, "Rescue Mission," 36–37. Wilson will present a similar position in chapter 11 of this book.

14. Gorman, "Douglas Campbell's *The Deliverance of God*," 102.

15. Matlock, "Zeal for Paul," 137; Campbell, *Deliverance*, 186.

16. See Campbell, "What Is at Stake?"

Contractual foundationalism theologically corresponds with Arianism and the "alternative theory" likewise with Athanasius.

To grasp these points, it is crucial to understand that, for Campbell, orthodox affirmations of the divine identity of Christ (to use Richard Bauckham's language), and their denial, involve epistemological correlates. Rather than beginning the theological task with Christ as "*homoousios* with the Father," Arianism must therefore begin its project *somewhere else*, and thus can be labeled, from an Athanasian perspective, as "foundationalist." Likewise, the argumentative structure of Romans 1:18–32 begins with an account of God from universally self-evident premises and moves to a description of ethical life without recourse to God's identification with Christ. For this reason it initiates an essentially Arian argument. Things are quite different according to an Athanasian account of theology, however. This fundamentally Trinitarian, revelational gospel, found in Romans 5–8, grounds its speech of God in God's activity in Christ and the Spirit, and, to use Lincoln Harvey's language in summary of Nicene faith, "it is only because *God* is truly present as Jesus Christ that God can be spoken of at all."[17] Because Christ is *homoousious* with the Father, we therefore begin our theology not somewhere else, but precisely with Christ. "*God demonstrates his love* for us in this," Paul writes, "while we were still sinners, *Christ* died for us" (5:8). This, of course, sets the stage for Campbell's rhetorical rereading, which then presents a coherent argument at the theoretical level and therefore also at the argumentative level in Romans, and thus can claim to be the "best fit" reading on offer.[18]

17. Harvey, "The Double *Homoousion*," 94.

18. Campbell's requirements for a successful reading of a Pauline text involve:
   1. A coherent account of the *lexical and syntactical* data.
   2. A reading that coheres with a text's immediately adjacent texts, the historical situation surrounding its production, and cultural and linguistic possibilities.
   3. A plausible construal of the *argumentative* dynamics in a given text. An exegetical proposal that presents the reader with a coherent argument ought to be preferred over a construction that suggests fundamental confusion.
   4. A coherent *theoretical* account of the "object" under discussion, something Campbell calls the "theoretical/explanatory level."

   Key is that a successful reading of Paul must possess integrity at all of these levels. But the result is that traditional readings of Romans 1–4 are left in great trouble. They not only lack integrity at the theoretical level (leaving us with a deeply confused and contradictory Paul), they therefore also fail to offer a smooth reading of the argumentative dynamic and rational coherence of Romans. And it is surely reasonable to assert that a coherent reading of a text is to be preferred over one that implies fundamental

What are we to make of all of this? Has Campbell's great learning "driven him mad," as Festus exclaimed about Paul? Has this impressive rhetorical hurricane swept him away to Wonderland, as some seem to think? Certainly, Campbell offers a provocative thesis, but is this instead because he has spotted problems others have overlooked, and is thus one step ahead of rival interpretations? To answer this question it makes sense to examine Paul in relation to the Athanasian theology of *homoousios* with the Father.

C. Paul's "Ontological Athanasianism"

Any recourse to Athanasius, with reference to Paul, must of course enter the debates surrounding Pauline Christology, particularly whether it is divine or not.[19] That is to say, if Paul's Christology corresponds at all with the Athanasian "*homoousios* with the Father," then, to use the words of Bauckham, Paul's Christ must be understood as "on the divine side of the line monotheism must draw between God and creatures."[20] Precisely this point, however, is disputed—or significantly qualified—by not just a few NT scholars, and given the necessary centrality of a divine-Christology for Campbell's reading of Paul, it is surprising that there was not more engagement with recent debate on this question.

While most these days would (quite rightly) not go as far as Earl Richard, in claiming that "Paul has a low Christology,"[21] many would not want to associate Paul and Athanasius too closely. One could mention the arguments of, for example, Anthony Harvey, Maurice Casey, James McGrath, James Crossley, and Pamela Eisenbaum,[22] and, most importantly,

---

confusion. In *Deliverance*, of course, Campbell lists fifty-six difficulties (!) relating to JT and its purchase on Paul's letters (that is, thirty-five exegetical under- and overdeterminations, plus twenty-one intrinsic, systematic, and empirical problems listed in part 1).

19. Campbell hints at his knowledge of this debate in Campbell, *Deliverance*, 695, and the related reference on p. 1117 n.50.

20. Bauckham, "The Worship of Jesus in Apocalyptic Christianity," 335.

21. Richard, *Jesus*, 328.

22. Harvey, *Jesus and the Constraints of History*, 154, 157–58; Casey, *From Jewish Prophet*; Casey, "Monotheism, Worship and Christological Developments in the Pauline Churches," 214–33; McGrath, *The Only True God*; Eisenbaum, *Paul Was not a Christian*; Bird and Crossley, *How Did Christianity Begin?*; Crossley, *Reading the New Testament*, 75–98.

James D. G. Dunn.[23] Although Dunn affirms a "high Christology," he tends to emphasize christological language and themes in Paul that seem to strongly qualify a divine-Christology. To this end, he focuses on the ways in which Paul's letters distinguish God and Christ,[24] and he emphasizes verses, such as 1 Corinthians 15:24–28,[25] that state Christ is, in one way or another, subordinate to God. In drawing christological conclusions from his exegesis, he lends particular weight to those verses where the Father is called Christ's "God" (see Rom 15:6; 2 Cor 1:3; 11:31), and he stresses the Adam-Christology of certain passages (e.g., Rom 15:6; 1 Cor 15:24–28; 2 Cor 1:3; 11:31).[26] And so on.

It is fair to say that most scholars engaged in this debate affirm, in different ways, a Pauline divine Christology.[27] But there remain problems with the most prominent arguments proffered by key scholars such as Bauckham,[28] Gordon Fee,[29] and Larry Hurtado.[30] My own published

23. Cf. esp. Dunn, *Christology in the Making*; Dunn, *The Christ and the Spirit*; Dunn, *Did the First Christians Worship Jesus?*

24. Dunn, "Was Christianity a Monotheistic Faith from the Beginning?" 337–38.

25. Indeed, he even goes as far as to claim that "Paul's fullest statement of Christ's lordship" is found in this verse (Dunn, *The Theology of Paul the Apostle*, 249).

26. Dunn, "Was Christianity a Monotheistic Faith from the Beginning?" 337–38. In reflecting on Romans 9:5, Dunn even argues that Paul could only refer to Christ as God if "Paul's own [christological] reserve . . . slipped at this point." It should thus not be taken "as a considered expression of his theology" (Dunn, *The Theology of Paul the Apostle*, 257)!

27. Cf., e.g., Fee, *Christology*; Richard J. Bauckham, *God of Israel*; Capes, *Old Testament Yahweh Texts in Paul's Christology*; Fatehi, *Relation*; Turner, "'Trinitarian' Pneumatology in the New Testament?" 167–86; Hurtado, *How on Earth Did Jesus Become a God?*; Moule, *The Origin of Christology*.

28. Cf. Andrew Chester's remarks that Bauckham's categories for identifying the unique divine identity are illegitimate (Chester, *Messiah and Exaltation*, 20–27). What is more, although Bauckham has insightfully drawn out the relational import of divine-identity in his approach to Christology, he has not made much of important (and more extensive) data in Paul which concerns Christ's relation to believers.

29. To be noted is his problematic equation of pre-existence and divinity, and his definition of Christology as concerning the person *in distinction to* the work of Christ. A number of other analytical problems in his *Pauline Christology* could be detailed, including his uneven usage of the language of "identity," and his reasoning relating to christological subordination texts in Paul. See Tilling, "Ephesians and Christology".

30. His emphasis on *cultic* devotion needs re-examination. Although worship, in the first-century world, gained greater significance if undertaken in a cultic and corporate context—as Hurtado tirelessly reminds critics such as Barker and Fletcher-Louis—it remains true that "God's praise does not only have its place in the church service [*Gottesdienst*] . . . , but the entire bodily existence should be for the glorification of God. . . .

work on Christology suggests another way forward, one that affirms a Pauline divine Christology, although in a very particular way. This is not the time or the place to elaborate my own views,[31] but I must, by way of summary, outline my wider thinking at this point in order to facilitate engagement with Campbell's proposals regarding Athanasius.

Despite alternatives (and cries of protest in some quarters[32]), I would affirm that one should still speak of a Pauline "monotheism," and an "exclusive monotheism" at that, one which, in Bauckham's brilliant advocacy of this view, speaks of "YHWH's transcendent uniqueness"[33] (God is not merely "the highest member of a class of beings to which he belongs"[34]). I would simply add, however, that this transcendent uniqueness was conceived in and expressed with *relational* language.[35] For ex-

True monolatry mobilizes and involves the whole" (Schrage, *Unterwegs zur Einzigkeit und Einheit Gottes*, 159, 163, translation mine). Jewish "worship" reached beyond the cultus into the life, habits, goals, and desires of the faithful. So the Psalms expressed a desire and longing for God precisely when absent from the cultus (Ps 84:1–2. Cf. also Ps 63:6). Indeed, worship that remained only in the cultus was often scorned by prophets (e.g., Isa 58:1–14 [cf. the commentary in Watts, *Isaiah 34–66*, 276–77.]; Amos 5:21–27; Zech 7–8). Now, if true Jewish faith in God was meant to embrace and invade all of life, to what extent has Hurtado captured this in Paul, *and thus grasped the best pattern of Pauline material?* Although Hurtado examines Christ's devotion to "do full justice to the way in which Jesus figures in early Christian circles" (Hurtado, *Lord Jesus Christ*, 4), his analysis of this devotion in Paul arguably lacks a certain appreciation of the richness and color of Paul's language. Noteworthy is that Dunn also, in his review of Hurtado's main work, *Lord Jesus Christ*, has questioned why "Hurtado did not give more explicit attention to what might be called the 'mystical' features of Paul's Christology, which seem to lie behind not simply his Christology but presumably also the devotional practices which he encouraged" (Dunn, "When Was Jesus First Worshipped?" 194)

31. For a detailed exposition of many of the following points, see Tilling, *Paul's Divine Christology*.

32. So Fredriksen, "Mandatory Retirement," 25–38. One could also mention Margaret Barker in this context, who has argued that YHWH was, in popular Jewish faith, the son of God Most High (see. e.g., Barker, *The Great Angel*; Barker, "The High Priest and the Worship of Jesus," 93–111).

33. Bauckham, "Biblical Theology and the Problems of Monotheism," 210–11.

34. Bauckham, *God of Israel*, 108.

35. Of course, "relational" is a slippery word, and here it means only to indicate "[t]he way in which one person or thing is related to another" (Pearsall and Trumble, *The Oxford English Reference Dictionary*, 1216). I do not mean necessarily to connote "personal relationship" with this language, nor any ordered narrative plot that would situate this relation in terms of a diachronic temporality. For this language, cf. Thiselton, "Human Being, Relationality, and Time," 78–79, who draws on the work of Paul Ricoeur. Simply put, I do not wish to over-define "relation," and so generate a foreign construct to impose on the letters.

ample, and apart from the many studies that would affirm this point with respect to "Old Testament" theology,[36] first-century Jewish monotheism,[37] and the expression of Paul's own faith in God,[38] one key monotheistic set of texts (the *Shema*), which Paul likely repeated twice daily in prayer,[39] evidences an affirmation of the oneness of God in such a way that included love and commitment to that one God over against capitulation to idolatry (see Deut 6:4–5).[40] It is not enough to claim, with Hurtado, that it is "in the area of worship that we find 'the decisive criterion' by which Jews maintained the uniqueness of God over against both idols and God's own deputies,"[41] nor are Bauckham's divine-identity categories unproblematic. Rather, to cite Nathan MacDonald, the "primary significance of the *Shema* is the *relationship* between YHWH and Israel. YHWH is to be

36. This is evident not only in the titles they give significant chapters, but even in the way some have arranged their presentations. So Eichrodt, in his two volume *Theology of the Old Testament*, has the following major subheadings: "The Covenant Relationship" (Vol. 1, chap. 2), "The Individual and the Community in the Old Testament God-man Relationship" (Vol 2, chap. 20), "The Fundamental Forms of Man's Personal Relationship with God" (Vol 2, chap. 21), "The Indestructibility of the Individual's Relationship with God (Immortality)" (Vol 2, chap. 24). As is well known, this covenant relationship was, for Eichrodt, "the central concept, by which to illuminate the structural unity and the unchanging basic tendency of the message of the OT" (ibid., 13). Th. C. Vriezen's relational emphasis is also strong, as chapter 6 of his Old Testament theology, "The nature of the knowledge of God in the O.T. as an intimate relationship between the Holy God and man," shows most clearly (Vriezen, *An Outline of Old Testament Theology*). Gerhard von Rad's section, "Israel before Yahweh" could also be noted (*Old Testament Theology. Vol. 1*, 355–459). Reference can also be made to more recent OT Theologies, especially the repeated discussions concerning Israel, the individual human person, the nations, etc., as "Yahweh's Partner" in Brueggemann, *Theology of the Old Testament*, Part 3.

37. Cf. various sections in Waaler, *Shema*; Woyke, *Götter*.

38. See, e.g., Waaler, *Shema*, 202; Dunn, *Theology of Paul the Apostle*, 46–49; Neyrey, *Render to God*, 107–211, and the appendix, "God-in-Relationship: Patron-Broker-Client" 249–55; Hurtado, *Lord Jesus Christ*, e.g., 48–50; Schnelle, *Paulus*, 441–61; Nicholson, *Dynamic Oneness*; Giblin, "Three Monotheistic Texts in Paul," 533–35, 537, 539, 542, 545–46; Schrage, *Unterwegs*, e.g., 185; Moxnes, *Theology in Conflict*, e.g., 28–29; etc. Indeed, according to Bassler the same emphasis is found in the NT generally (cf. Bassler, "God in the NT," II, 1049).

39. Cf. *m. Ber.* 1:1–9, and the discussion in Instone-Brewer, *Traditions of the Rabbis in the Era of the New Testament, Vol. 1*, 42–44, for evidence concerning the tradition's origin before AD 70. For a careful examination of the *Shema* in relation to *Tefillin, Mezuzot*, rituals and daily prayer in the first century AD, cf. Waaler, *Shema*, 124–33.

40. See the brilliant study of MacDonald, *Monotheism*.

41. Hurtado, *How on Earth Did Jesus Become a God?* 129.

Israel's one and only."[42] As Erik Waaler argues in a very helpful study of the *Shema* in 1 Corinthians, "to know that 'God is the only God' or that 'he is one' implies that one *relates* to one God only."[43]

And in 1 Corinthians 8 it is now well known that Paul makes recourse to the *Shema* as part of his argument against Christian participation in idolatry in Corinth.[44] Indeed, in 8:1–3, Paul frames his entire discussion (which will continue until 11:1) by distinguishing between the knowing of the "knowledgeable," and the necessary knowing associated with loving God and being known by him.[45] Over against what I will loosely speak of as Paul's positive relational monotheism, Volker Gäckle has argued that the negative "knowledgeable" were a group with a focus on a cognitive and an intellectualized perception of the world.[46]

What is remarkable, however, is how the rest of Paul's argument unfolds in relation to idol food. Instead of speaking in the main of the relation between Christians and *God* over against idolatry, Paul instead speaks of the relation between Christians and the *risen Lord* over against

42. MacDonald, *Monotheism*, 151, italics mine.

43. Waaler, *Shema*, 202, italics mine.

44. See, especially ibid.

45. There are variant readings in P46 and Clement of Alexandria, which omit τὸν θεόν as well as ὑπ' αὐτοῦ. ℵ* and thirty-three leave out only ὑπ' αὐτοῦ, which are probably best understood as the result of a copyist oversight (cf. Schnabel, *Korinther*, 435). This has been taken to refute the argument that Paul, in this context, is addressing love for God at all (see, e.g., Thiselton, *The First Epistle to the Corinthians*, 607, 625–26; Fee, *The First Epistle to the Corinthians*, 367). Johann Albrecht Bengel's textual critical dictum of *lectio brevior potior*, could be adduced in favor of this reading. However, the longer reading (including τὸν θεόν) is more likely. The context is concerned not with love generally, but rather with allegiance to God over against idols (see 8:6, 12; 10:14–21, and Wright, *The Climax of the Covenant*, 127). James Royse's important study of the scribal habits in early Greek New Testament papyri demonstrates that "the scribe of P46 displays a very clear tendency to omit" (Royse, *Scribal Habits*, 297). It is likely that the P46 shorter reading was an attempt to harmonize the love of 8:3 with the objectless knowing of 8:2a, thus generating an object free love. For a catalogue of further reasons to accept the longer reading as authentic, cf. Waaler, *Shema*, 306–7. It is worth noting at this point that there is some debate about the extent of the citation from the Corinthians in this passage. Some think that Paul cites his opponents at some length, from 8:4–6 in its entirety (!), on the basis of theoretical and argumentative level clues. Cf. the claims in Hofius, "Einer ist Gott—Einer ist Herr," 95–108; Woyke, *Götter*, 158–214; ibid., "Das Bekenntnis," 87–112.

46. Gäckle, *Die Starken und die Schwachen*, e.g., 108, 189–90, 200–204. Garland likewise maintains that Paul argues against a "mere propositional knowledge about God" (Garland, *1 Corinthians*, 391, cited approvingly also in Fitzmyer, *First Corinthians*, 337).

idolatry. What is more, Paul describes this Christ-relation with the themes and language traditionally used to describe the relation between Israel and YHWH. For example, in 8:6, the Deuteronomic κύριος is, for Paul, Christ, the risen Lord.[47] 8:12 speaks of "sin against the brothers," which is ultimately "sin against Christ." After what most commentators understand as the *digressio* of 1 Corinthians 9,[48] this Christ-relation finds more developed expression in 10:4, 9, and 14–22, where, drawing on scriptural YHWH-Israel relation themes, Paul speaks of "testing Christ" ("as some of them did"), faithful κοινωνία with the risen Lord over against the same with idols/demons, and of the (risen) Lord's jealousy in 10:22.[49] In other words, in a context in which Paul clearly understands monotheism as not intellectualized cognition, but the relational commitment of Christians to the one God over against idolatry, Paul speaks of the relation between Christians and the risen Lord.

Indeed, an analysis of the language in the Pauline corpus that describes, in one way another, this relation between the risen Christ and Christians, evidences a remarkable and rather familiar pattern. In ways that regularly overlap in theme and language with the YHWH-Israel relation, the Christ-relation involves and array of Christ-shaped goals and motivations[50] and expressions of devotion that extend into the whole of life.[51] The Christ-relation is all-consuming and involves great fervency[52]

47. Fee, *Christology*, 585. Certainly, McGrath has challenged this claim, but I see no reason to if the wider frame of the passage is remembered (see McGrath, *The Only True God*, 42). This is to say, he overlooks how Christ as Lord is spoken of in the rest of 1 Corinthians 8–10.

48. It is uncontroversial to claim that the argument in 1 Corinthians 8 is more directly continued in 1 Corinthians 10. See, e.g., Eriksson, *Traditions as Rhetorical Proof*, 146, 152 (and cf. also n.79); Fitzmyer, *First Corinthians*, 332; Schnabel, *Korinther*, 433; Fotopoulos, *Food Offered to Idols*, 223–27; Schrage, *Der erste Brief an die Korinther* (2), 213–14, 277–86; Thiselton, *The First Epistle to the Corinthians*, 661–63; Garland, *1 Corinthians*, 362; Waaler, *Shema*, 275–79; etc.

49. Incidentally, and given the variety of Pentateuchal narratives (and their Psalmic summaries) alluded to in 1 Corinthians 10, Campbell's case against Watson and the Numbers narratives seems justified (cf. Campbell, *Deliverance*, 422–23).

50. Rom 1:5; 14:9; 1 Cor 6:13; 7:35; 2 Cor 4:5, 8, 10–11; 5:9–10; 8:19; 12:7–10; Gal 2:20; Phil 1:20, 23; 2:9–11; 3:8; 1 Thess 4:17; 5:10; Phlm 6.

51. Rom 14:6–8; 16:5; 1 Cor 1:7 [cf. also Phil 3:20]; 1:31; 2:2; 6:16–17; 7:25–38; 11:23–26; 12:3; 15:19; 16:22; 2 Cor 3:16–18; 5:15; 8:5; 10:7; 10:17; 11:2–3; Gal 2:20; 3:29; Phil 2:6–11; 3:1, 8; 1 Thess 1:2–3; 3:8.

52. Rom 12:11; 1 Cor 1:7; 2:2; 7:32–35; 15:58; 2 Cor 11:2–3; Phil 1:20; 3:8; 4:4, 10; 1 Thess 3:11–13; 5:17.

and is contrasted with matters reminiscent of Jewish God-language.[53] As part of the Christ-relation, the risen Lord is also present and active in numerous ways,[54] and yet at the same time absent[55] and in heaven,[56] and so present *through the Spirit*.[57] To underscore the relational dynamic involved, Christians communicate[58] with this present-by-the-Spirit-yet-also-absent-Lord,[59] and the risen Lord likewise communicates with Christians.[60] And so Christ's character and the nature of his lordship are also described in God-language-analogous ways.[61]

This is all attested in multiple places throughout the Pauline corpus, and is best understood as a pattern of data that Paul would have recognized as such.[62] And when one examines the literature of Second Temple Judaism, it becomes obvious very quickly that this same relational pattern was consistently used, in a variety of ways, to describe the relation between Israel and YHWH (and remember, I would maintain that God's transcendent uniqueness was conceived in and expressed with *relational* language). This is also the case in those texts that are often deemed to be most troubling to advocates of a Pauline divine Christology. For example, the Similitudes of Enoch (1 *En*. 37–71) display this Christ-relation

---

53. See Rom 16:18; 1 Cor 6:13; 7:32–34; 8:12; 10:9; 10:20–22; 11:30–32; 2 Cor 4:4; 5:15; 11:2–3; Gal 1:10 (cf. 4:8); Phil 2:21.

54. Rom 1:7; 8:9–10; 14:4; 15:18–19, 29; 16:20; 1 Cor 1:3; 3:5; 4:19; 7:17, 25; 16:17, 23; 2 Cor 1:2; 2:10, 12; 3:3; 12:7–10; 13:3–5, 13; Gal 2:20; 4:6; 6:18; Phil 1:2, 19; 3:21; 1 Thess. 3:11–13; 5:28; Philem. 3, 25.

55. Cf. 1 Cor 11:26; 15:23; 2 Cor 5:6–8 (so Thrall writes on these verses that "life in this world means life in exile, life apart from the Lord" [Thrall, *The Second Epistle to the Corinthians Vol. 1*, 386]); Phil 1:20–24; 1 Thess 2:19; 3:13; 4:17; 5:10, 23.

56. Rom 8:34; 10:6; Phil 3:20; 1 Thess 1:9–10; 4:16. Cf. also 1 Cor 15:47–49; 2 Cor 12:2; Eph 6:9; Col 4:1; 2 Thess 1:7.

57. Rom 8:9–10; 15:18–19; Gal 4:6; Phil 1:19.

58. Following Ostmeyer's appropriate language (cf. Ostmeyer, *Kommunikation mit Gott und Christus*).

59. Rom 10:9–13; 15:11[?]; 1 Cor 16:22; 2 Cor 12:8; 1 Thess 3:11–13.

60. 2 Cor 10:18; 12:1[?]; 12:9; 13:3.

61. Rom 8:35; 10:12; 14:4, 9; 1 Cor 10:26[?]; 11:27–30; 15:45; 2 Cor 4:13; 5:14; 10:1; 13:5; Gal 1:1, 11–12; 2:20; Phil 1:8; 3:21; 1 Thess 4:6.

62. To be noted is that this Christ-relation was an *existential reality* in Paul's life; it was not merely a collection of loose ideas. The absence and desired presence of Christ was for Paul the force behind his most deeply expressed yearnings, and so on. What is more, the various points just listed are regularly found together in single arguments in Paul's letters.

shaped pattern in terms of the Lord-of-the-Spirits-relation, and not in terms of the Son of Man.

To bring this all together: as suggested by 1 Corinthians 8:1–3, the shape and overall pattern of Paul's monotheism and Christ-language, and recent studies in Pauline epistemology,[63] knowledge, for Paul, can be expressed as relationship.[64] Paul's way of knowing theology was relational (and not simply propositional).[65] This all leads, inexorably, to an affirmation of a fully divine Pauline Christology, but it does so in a particular way. Paul's divine-Christology (his equivalent to the Athanasian "*homoousios* with the Father") finds expression and conceptual shape as the Christ-relation. It is divine Christology expressed as relationship.[66] This further means that Christology was not just theoretical; it was the gift of

63. Here I note especially Scott, *Implicit Epistemology* and Parry and Healy, *The Bible and Epistemology*, though there is much to gain also from Munzinger, *Discerning the Spirits*.

64. Cf. the section title in Healy, "Knowledge of the Mystery: A Study of Pauline Epistemology," in *The Bible and Epistemology*, 142.

65. I am not sure why Scott divides his fifth chapter, "Paul's Theological Knowledge," from chapter 7, "Beyond Conceptual Knowledge," which involves (on his own terms) "Paul's Knowledge of God/Christ" (Scott, *Epistemology*, 146). If Paul's "knowledge of God" is not "theological," I don't know what is!
The contrast between "propositional" and "relational" is not meant to suggest that Paul is against propositions themselves, as is manifestly not the case. His letters are full of them, with "claims that things are such and such and so not their contradictories" (Gunton, *A Brief Theology of Revelation*, 13). Rather, the issue is how truth propositions were treated and understood. As Campbell himself writes, when drawing a distinction between personal and cognitive orientations in reading πιστ- words, a personal meaning "does not exclude beliefs but suggests certain beliefs appropriate to a personal relationship" (Campbell, *Deliverance*, 621).

66. It is difficult not to think of representatives of the older *Religionsgeschichtliche Schule* at this point: "The attempt is usually made under the heading, 'the Christology' of St. Paul. But it would be more accurate, because more historical, to inquire concerning the apostle's 'knowledge of Christ,' or 'experience of Christ,' or 'Christ as revealed to St. Paul.' Anything that tends to petrify the fellowship with Christ, which was felt as the beginning so vividly, into a doctrine about Christ, is mischievous" (Deissmann, *Saint Paul*, 124); "*The religion of the apostle is theological through and through: his theology is his religion.* The idea that we can find in him a cold doctrine, to be grasped by the understanding, a doctrine which soars more or less beyond the reach of mere piety, is false; and equally false is the idea that the piety of Paul can be described without mention of those *thoughts* in which he had apprehended Christ, his death and his resurrection" (Wrede, *Paul*, 76, italics his).

the transforming power of the Spirit, working at the center of the life of the Christian community.[67]

We must therefore confirm Campbell's major claim that a line of continuity must be drawn between Paul and Athanasius on the central matter of divine Christology. For Paul, *God* is in Christ. Certainly, care must be taken here. This is not to dispute that Paul and Athanasius expressed themselves quite differently. Indeed, "to suggest that the biblical writers were consciously thinking in later creedal terms is in fact," as Kavin Rowe notes, "a major anachronistic mistake."[68] But with Bauckham we can claim that though the "Fathers did not develop" the early fully divine Christology, they did "*transpose* it into a conceptual framework constructed more in terms of the Greek philosophical categories of essence and nature" (although, let it be remembered that the language of the creeds are largely drawn from Scripture, not Aristotle!).[69] With sensitivity to terminological questions (and here I think of the Heideggerian distinction between "ontic" and "ontological"), we must affirm Paul's "ontological" Athanasianism.[70]

D. Reflections on Campbell's Claims

A number of conclusions can now be reached regarding Campbell's wider argumentation in relation to Paul and Athanasius. We note, first, matters of agreement before turning to matters for discussion.

1. Matters of Agreement

First, not only was Paul's Christology Athanasian in that it was fully divine, the above analysis confirms that such a Christology was central to Paul. No longer does explication of a Pauline divine Christology depend

67. Paul would, I think, agree that "doing christology is a practice of disciples, not spectators" (Tilley, *The Disciples' Jesus*, 15).

68. Rowe, "Pressure" 297.

69. Bauckham, *God Crucified*, viii, italics mine.

70. Rowe maintains, in relation to the book of Revelation and Athanasius, that "the continuity for which I argue does not rest at the noetic level—the authors of Revelation and Athanasius obviously thought differently—*but at the ontic level*" (Rowe, "Pressure," 297, italics mine). But I think Heideggerian distinctions may suggest here use of "ontological" rather than "ontic" (Heidegger, *Being and Time*, 31 n. 3. Cf. also the helpful but short notes in Watts, *The Philosophy of Heidegger*, 26).

on the odd, isolated verse or passage (such as 1 Cor 8:6; Phil 2:6–11 or Rom 9:5). Understood in terms of the Christ-relation, material in some way constitutive of Paul's divine Christology is found in the majority of Romans, the large majority of 1 Corinthians, 2 Corinthians and 1 Thessalonians, and in all chapters of Galatians, Philippians, and Philemon. This foundation of Campbell's "alternative theory" indeed represents the heartbeat of Paul's letters.

Second, Campbell speaks in *Deliverance* of the "relational nature" of the redeemed existence, and of personhood and the ontology of the church as "relational."[71] He also, of course correctly, describes Athanasian theology in Trinitarian terms,[72] and maintains that, unlike JT, the "alternative theory" of Romans 5–8 is "inherently elective and Trinitarian."[73] This same theory is described as doxological and revelational.

Our analysis of Paul's extensive christological language confirms all of these points. Paul's divine Christology was expressed as the Christ-*relation*. What is more, whether in Paul's Christ-shaped aims, goals, and motivations, the variety of Christ-devotion expressions, or in the passionate nature of Christ-devotion, the mode of Paul's christological language was relational in a fundamentally doxological manner.[74] Paul gives us, to use Catherine LaCugna's language, *"theology in the mode of doxology"* (at least when doxology is understood in the broad terms I suggest).[75] His Christology was, further, one which involved at an integral level the work of the Spirit who mediated the presence of the (absent) risen Lord. The major monograph-length study of the Spirit's relation to the risen Lord in Paul, by Mehrdad Fatehi, correctly maintains that the "same Spirit that exclusively mediated and still mediates the active presence of *God,* comes to be experienced as mediating also the active presence of the risen and exalted Christ."[76] There is thus a "trinitarian grammar" in Paul's theology,[77]

71. Campbell, *Deliverance*, 69, 73, 84.

72. Campbell, "What Is at Stake?" 113, 124.

73. Campbell, *Deliverance*, 184.

74. Certainly, Dunn has argued, referring to the term δοξάζω, that "[f]or Paul, properly speaking, only God [not Christ] is to be glorified" (Dunn, *Theology of Paul the Apostle*, 258–59). But this forgets at least, 2 Cor 8:19.

75. LaCugna, *God for Us*, 15–16, italics hers.

76. Fatehi, *Relation*, 311, italics mine.

77. Cf. Schwöbel, *Gott in Beziehung*, 272, where, with reference to the NT, he correctly speaks of the "trinitarische Logik des christlichen Glaubens" ("the Trinitarian logic of the Christian faith"—my translation).

again conceived relationally, which "pressures" Paul's interpreters toward later Trinitarian doctrinal formulation.[78]

This also shows that the tendency of Paul's thinking was to work "backwards" (although I will momentarily examine the propensity of this language to oversimplify). In tandem with specific arguments in Paul's letters (e.g., Rom 5:12–21 [thus explaining Paul's pessimistic view of Torah]; 1 Cor 4:7; 10:11; 2 Cor 3:7–16; 5:16; 10:5; Gal 1:1, 11–12; Phil 3:7–8, etc.), it would be a bold person who made the claim that Paul's Trinitarian theological vision was grounded not in the unconditional revelation of God in Christ and the Spirit, but rather in non-christological analogies found in "the things God has made" (Rom 1:20). In this sense we can surely affirm that Paul's theological epistemology, right at its christological heart, was revelational and clearly not the *result* of any linear progression of thought grounded in an individual's exploration of the surrounding world. In other words, it would be difficult to assert a Pauline Athanasian ontology without also validating a key corresponding epistemological point: God in Christ, so central to Paul, means that Christ reveals God as God. Consequently, and this is important, any theological construal of even a part of Paul's letters that does not begin from this place will lead to significant internal contradiction.

Third, we agree that Campbell's theoretical-level clarification with respect to Arianism and Athanasius seems entirely justified as a strategy to clarify the debate. An impression one gets from the various reviews of *Deliverance* is that the key fundamental misunderstanding of Campbell's work boils down to a failure to grasp the nature and import of the theoretical-level of reading Paul. This explains, for example, why many have dismissed JT as a straw-man argument, a charge that misunderstands the said theoretical dimension in Campbell's thesis.[79] Given the long *Wirkungsgeschichte* of Johann Gabler's distinction between biblical and dogmatic theology, NT experts tend to be skilled in historical-critical methods but are not necessarily always conversant with—and sometimes no doubt even prefer to stay aloof from—the concerns of systematicians (for substantiation of this easily demonstrable claim, I can refer at the very least to Dale Martin's volume, *Pedagogy of the Bible*). Campbell's thesis is thus a powerful corrective to a situation in which, as Russell

---

78. For the employment of the language of "pressure" here, see Rowe's two remarkable articles: Rowe, "Pressure"; Rowe, "For Future Generations," 189–97.

79. See, e.g., Seifrid, "*The Deliverance of God*," 308; Watson, "*The Deliverance of God*," 181, 183.

Reno laments: "Theology has lost its competence in exegesis. Scripture scholars function with minimal theological training. Each decade finds new theories of preaching to cover the nakedness of seminary training that provides theology without exegesis and exegesis without theology."[80] Campbell's strategy, which forces NT experts to assess wider theological commitments inherent in proposed readings of Paul, is thus on the money.

Fourth, Campbell's recourse to Arianism also seems straightforward and fair (at least when Arianism is understood simply as a cipher for key christological distinctions in early Christianity. For more on this I refer to J. Warren Smith's helpful corrective in the next chapter).[81] Arian theology, like natural theology not controlled by Christology, ultimately leads "the creature to self-project onto a confused infinite, essentially domesticating God by replacing him with a constructed idol."[82] That Arianism leads to mythology is a picture confirmed by modern scholarship (and I think here especially of Rowan Williams' landmark study). Williams would no doubt object that Campbell speaks too hastily about "Arianism" (he would rather "relegate the term Arianism at least to inverted commas, and preferably to oblivion"[83]), and one must also take care, Williams insists, that Arianism not be used simply as "the radically 'Other,' projecting on to it whatever theological or ecclesiological tenets currently represent the opposition to a Christian mainstream in which the scholar and interpreter claims to stand."[84] That said, surely Campbell's concerns reflect a central theological impulse in the spirit of early Christian thought, in which the knowledge of God was possible only because of God.[85] (Reference could be made here to the theologies of Irenaeus,

---

80. In Jenson, *Ezekiel*, 13.

81. It is interesting to note that Athanasius could employ anti-Arian polemic despite the fact that he would acknowledge "that those who hold these views might not consider themselves to be Arians" (Anatolios, *Coherence*, 95, with reference to Athanasius' two letters, *Ad Adelphium* and *Ad Epictetum*). *It is possible to be an Arian without knowing it*, it seems, according to both Athanasius and Campbell!

82. Harvey, "Double *Homoousion*," 87. These words were written, in conversation with the (non-foundationalist) theology of Colin Gunton, in judgment against "natural theology," but the point applies to Arianism's distant God.

83. Cited in Leithart, *Athanasius*.

84. Williams, *Arius*, 2.

85. This phrasing, and much of what follows in this paragraph, is taken from Wilken's delightful introductory volume, Wilken, *Early Christian*.

Origen, and Augustine, to name just a few.[86]) As Robert Wilken notes with reference to Justin Martyr, Maximus the Confessor, and Ignatius of Antioch: they "reasoned from Christ to other things, not from other things to Christ."[87]

Fifth, and turning to Athanasius, we have already noted our agreement by maintaining that we should speak of Paul's "ontological Athanasianism." Yet some may object that Campbell's reading of the significance of Athanasius, largely in terms of epistemology, has relied too excessively on Barthian-influenced scholarship (Alasdair Heron, James and Alan Torrance, etc.).[88] Peter Leithart has recently argued that T. F. Torrance "imposes a Barthian framework on Athanasius," particularly in the shape of a disdain of natural revelation, "scruples that Athanasius," Leithart insists, "was far from sharing."[89] I look to my systematic theologian colleagues for rebuttal, but I have not found any scholarship that would dispute the basic Barthian epistemological point.[90] And even Leithart's account of Athanasius' theology of creation speak of it as "Christic," "Trinitarian" and "all about Christ."[91] I think the shape of *De Incarna-*

---

86. As early as Irenaeus, we find what later became called the "Irenaean principle that God can only be known through God" (see *Against Heresies* 4.6.4. Anatolios, *Coherence*, 210). As Robert Wilken writes about Augustine, his "thinking, like that of other Christians in antiquity, began with the facts of revelation" (Wilken, *Early Christian*, 168). The same must be said about Origen (see *Against Celsus* 3:47; 6:57; 7:33, 42; *Homily on Luke* 3:1, and the comments in ibid., 12, 19, 22.). What is more, Wilken shows that it was this confidence in the unconditioned movement of God in revelation to humans (grace), which early Christians such as the great Augustine and John of Damascus saw as the cure against speculation and abstraction (ibid., 23). In this respect, one must mention the—still influential—myth, perpetrated by Edward Gibbon, that the church and its dogmas "extinguished the brilliant flame of the intellect kindled by the ancient Greeks" [cited in ibid., 163]. This thesis has now been rather vigorously falsified in the Michael Ramsey prize-winning book, Hart, *Atheist Delusions*.

87. Wilken, *Early Christian*, 15.

88. Three key articles for Campbell, are Heron, "*Homoousios* with the Father," 58–87; J. B. Torrance, "The Contribution of McLeod Campbell to Scottish Theology," 295–311; J. B. Torrance, "Covenant and Contract," 51–76. These last two Torrance articles are reprinted in this volume. See also A. J. Torrance, "The Theological Grounds for Advocating Forgiveness and Reconciliation in the Sociopolitical Realm," 65–121.

89. Leithart, *Athanasius*, 182. Cf. also comments about the Athanasian conception of *analogia entis* in Anatolios, *Coherence*, 210–11.

90. Though some minor divergences are noted by Athanasius authority, Khaled Anatolios (see ibid., 210–12).

91. Cf. multiple similar references in the fourth chapter of Leithart, *Athanasius*, "Beginnings: Word and World."

tione speaks strongly for Campbell's basic point, even when the details of Athanasius' argument and his use of Romans 1 perhaps do not always fit perfectly.[92]

Finally, although I have focused mainly on the theoretical level in this paper, given Campbell's appreciation for the different levels involved in reading Paul, he is also able to develop a portrayal that is *responsible*.[93] There isn't space to discuss those wider issues now, but Campbell's account of "the Jewish question" in chapters 6 and 9 in this volume are examples of ethically aware readings, and both Kate Bowler and Curtis W. Freeman will mention other matters in chapters 8 and 15 respectively.

2. Matters for Discussion

Initially, two concerns may be in the mind of some, but I think they lack cogency and should be dismissed. Namely, 1) that asserting God is in Christ, for Paul, should not necessarily lead to a theological methodology: that Christ *reveals* God as God. 2) That because Chalcedonian christological orthodoxy also involves an insistence to maintain (not reconcile) theological tensions (so, the debates between Antiochian and Alexandrian christological concerns in relation to the two natures),[94] Campbell's either/or is discordant with such orthodox "inclusivity," which is an impulse to both/and.[95]

92. I particularly note §55 of this text: "[S]ince the Word of God has been manifested in a body, and has made known to us His own Father . . . [men] forsake the idols and come to know the true God. Now this is proof that Christ is God" (Athanasius, *On the Incarnation: De Incarnatione Verbi Dei*).

93. It is a theological vision of the apostle that attempts to elicit "life patterns that mirror God's own seeking of the creation," namely, the kind of responsible theology so eloquently portrayed by Jennings, Campbell's Duke University Divinity School colleague, in Jennings, *The Christian Imagination*, 291.

94. See, e.g., Sellers, *Two Ancient Christologies*; Grillmeier, *From the Apostolic Age to Chalcedon (451)*, vol. 1, etc.

95. On the first point, if divine Christology—so key throughout the Pauline corpus as we have seen—does not speak into Paul's theological methodology, then at the very least we have no basis for constructing an alternative. Further, it would run against the flow of Paul's theological concerns and argumentative strategies, making him incoherent. It would likewise underestimate the way Paul speaks of Christ in terms of "revelation," and this as part of his christological rhetoric. Of course, it would also unnaturally drive a wedge between Paul's relational Christology and relational epistemology. On the second point, at the risk of pointing out the obvious, the matter for Campbell concerns not Antioch and Alexandria, but Arianism and Athanasius.

Instead, I want to ask two different questions. First, I ask for clarity on a key issue. Campbell has placed much weight on the (vectorial) distinction between "forward" and "backward" thinking.[96] However, I argue that Paul's christological vision is divine precisely because the Christ-relation is, as a pattern, analogous to the YHWH-Israel relation. This is to say, Paul's "ontological Athanasianism" was itself shaped by and structured according to a pre-Christian analogy. I admit, to frame it like this is already to commit to certain theologically uninformed notions of time and history, ones that assume an Arian relationship between Christ and time. In this respect I refer to Douglas Harink's stellar essay, "Time and Politics in Four Commentaries on Romans."[97] I ask, simply, for clarification here.

This can be put in another way. In responding to Wright's potential salvation-history foundationalism,[98] he critiques "Wright's constant claim that Judaism was Paul's 'framework' . . . a metaphor suggesting the existence of a key prior structure within it," and so Campbell urges use of the language of "'encyclopaedia,' which would denote that Judaism was the critical semantic and narrative reservoir for Paul who nevertheless crafted something new under the impress of the revelation of Christ."[99] But it seems to me that Paul's Christology is divine precisely because of a recognizable "prior structure," the YHWH-relation. For different reasons, Watson seems to want to express a similar tension when he writes that "[i]n Paul, scripture is not overwhelmed by the light of an autonomous Christ-event needing no scriptural mediation [of course, this does not describe Campbell's position either!]. It is scripture that shapes the contours of the Christ-event."[100] If we continue to use vectorial language,

96. Indeed, he has raised the stakes high: to be delivered from all confusion with respect to our interpretation of Paul, we must "read Paul consistently 'backward' and *never* read him 'forward'" (Campbell, "An Attempt to Be Understood," 176). In that strong response to Matlock and Macaskill, he even suggests that greater clarity could be gained by speaking of Forward Thinking (FT) instead of JT.

97. Harink, "Time and Politics in Four Commentaries on Romans," 282–312. I also note Rae, *History and Hermeneutics*.

98. Campbell is certainly more nuanced in his appreciation of the significance of salvation-historical themes than, for example, J. Louis Martyn (and I refer to the exchanges between Martyn and Wright), and as Campbell notes in his JSNT response, Paul uses Scripture and rearranges his "encyclopaedia" according to revelation (and he is likewise correct to reject Macaskill's historicist objections in this way—n.19).

99. Campbell, "Is Tom Right?" 344.

100. Watson, *Paul and the Hermeneutics of Faith*, 17. I do wonder, however, if this

could Paul's Christology be evidence of a *dialectical relationship* between "forward" and "backward" thinking?

I suspect that Campbell's response may include reference to a distinction between psychological and epistemological retrospectivism, building on some of his comments in *Deliverance*, and his earlier engagement with Watson.[101] But in response to the terms he uses there, and to lead us to the second point, it could also be suggested that negotiating this "dialectic" (if that is the right word), something Campbell has referred to as Watson's "epistemological circularity,"[102] is better conceived with relational, rather than geometric (directional), metaphors, in a way that can still emphasize its revelational nature (as we shall now note).[103] Either way, I would still value further clarification on these matters.

So, and second, although the key epistemological point Campbell draws from Athanasianism is that it is retrospective, has this been stressed to the detriment of the specifically *relational* nature of the associated epistemology? This would be proper when speaking of either Paul (as

---

flattens the issue; it is not simply Scripture but a conglomeration of Scripture, symbol, practice, and existential priorities and habits that inform the way Christ was understood by Paul. But that is a point for another day.

101. Campbell, *Deliverance*, 1050 n63. He refers, there, to the following: "We need to know which criterion is more fundamental: Scripture or Christ (and we have already noted some difficulties endorsing the primacy of the former if we want ultimately to get to the latter)?" (Campbell, "An Evangelical Paul," 349).

102. He also speaks of Watson's "epistemological duality," which ends in "complete confusion" (ibid.).

103. Precisely this may help to reconceive the problem in other terms, not simply as a straightforward contradiction, as is the case when directional metaphors are used (one cannot travel forwards and backwards at the same time). Instead, there is a relationship, a conversation between two (albeit, with Christ dominant. Barth makes a similar point in *CD* I/2, 206–7). Perhaps in this way, Paul's relational epistemology works in a similar way to Jeremy Begbie's musical metaphors. Campbell, too, acknowledges: "I am particularly impressed at present by the capacity of musical and sonic metaphors to reconceive difficult theological issues helpfully" (Campbell, *Deliverance*, 942 n. 28; Begbie, *Theology, Music, and Time*). Perhaps one could suggest that relational metaphors could "reconceive" Paul's difficult theological issues, by exposing a bland propositional bias in previous attempts to understand them? (If we had space, we could test this thesis with respect to, for instance, human and divine agency. The language of my question of course uses Campbell's, but I also intend to reflect Begbie: "Music can provide virtually nothing in the way of propositions or assertions" [Begbie, *Theology, Music, and Time*, 11 and cf. the context of this claim, pp. 11–12]). Of course, this won't bring Arius back into the flock, nor does it—for reasons related to the argumentative level of reading—neatly reintegrate Romans 1:18–32 back into Paul's christological vision. But what impact could it have on Campbell's wider argumentation?

we maintained above) *or* Athanasius in terms of their divine-Christology (and for the latter I refer to the scholarship of John Zizioulas, Alwyn Pettersen, and particularly Khaled Anatolios).[104] A specifically relational "way of knowing" God in Christ in revelational terms also represents a key epistemological current in the spirit of early Christian thought generally (here I could note Origen, Gregory the Great, and Augustine, among others, and even the language of the creeds).[105] I do not wish to play a relational epistemology off *against* a retrospective one (they belong together, as I think also Barth knew full well.[106] He wrote, after all, that "[n]

104. So, a key modern authority on Athanasius, Khaled Anatolios, distinguishes the particular Barthian agenda from Athanasius, and agrees with Williams that the emphasis needs to move away from "the supposed Christological focus of the [Arian] heresy and towards the doctrines of God and creation" (cited in Anatolios, *Coherence*, 97). This is not to deny the importance of Christology (of course!), but to understand it in the wider context of Athanasian theology. That wider context, the "intrinsic center of coherence in Athanasius's theology" is, for Anatolios, "the distinction, and simultaneous relation, between God and the world" (ibid., 3. See also 211). "Athanasius," he argues, "was not interested so much in an analytical Christology . . . as he was in seeing the new *relation* between God and creation that is given in Christ" (ibid., 148). Athanasius' perspective, he adds, "is that of a relational ontology" (ibid., 211). John Zizioulas likewise maintains that "the being of God could only be known through personal relationships and personal love" on the basis that Athanasius "approached the being of God through the experience of the ecclesial community" (Zizioulas, *Being as Communion*, 16). Thus for Athanasius too, this "knowledge of God," to cite Alwyn Pettersen, is "more than mere knowledge about God. It is knowing God" (Pettersen, *Athanasius*, 37).

105. It is, further, precisely this relational dynamic that one also finds in the "spirit of early Christian thought" (to once again echo Wilken). So Origen noted that knowledge of God that brought no change in worship was imperfect, for "to know," for Origen, means to "'participate in something' or be 'joined to something'" (Wilken, *Early Christian*, 21. See also 12). Gregory the Great wrote that there "can be no knowledge of God without a relation between the knower and God" (cited in ibid., 21). Summarizing Augustine's theology, Wilken remarks that "[B]elieving in God . . . does not mean one believes that something is the case, but that one loves God" (ibid., 184). Jürgen Moltmann notes that for the church fathers "knowing" meant not power or domination, but *wonder* (Moltmann, *The Trinity and the Kingdom*, 9). The use of the language "I/We believe" in the creeds testifies to the relational emphasis. So Lash writes that the "threefold confession in the [Apostle's] Creed declares our *present* relationship with God" (Lash, *Believing Three Ways in One God*, 30, italics his). And so on.

106. To confidently rush in where NT scholars should rightly fear to tread, I would argue that a revelational relationality is coherent with Barth's (mature?) theology. Here I have learned much from Alan Torrance's book, *Persons in Communion*, and Gary Deddo's work on Barth's *Analogia Relationis* (Deddo, *Karl Barth's Theology of Relations*; Torrance, *Persons in Communion*). Here I must also acknowledge Lincoln Harvey's point, in dialogue with Colin Gunton, that the "doctrine of God and the doctrine of

ot God alone, but God and man together constitute the content of the Word of God attested in Scripture"[107]), and as noted above, Campbell's basic thesis affirms the "relational nature" of the redeemed existence, etc. I simply seek more balance in the presentation of an argument in terms of Athanasianism and Paul, for although relational and retrospective thinking profoundly overlap, they are not identifying *exactly* the same thing.

And this balance may prove helpful to Campbell. An emphasis on a relational epistemology may, to take one example, reveal further incongruences in conventional readings of Romans 1:18–32 (at the systematic frame). If, as noted above, Paul could distinguish between the theoretical and intellectualized theology of the Corinthians on the one hand (which needed to be corrected), and his relational loving "necessary knowing" on the other, I note Romans 1:21 and the oddly non-relational conception of the "knowledge of God" there voiced: "for though they *knew* God, they *did not* honour him as God or give thanks to him."

E. The Challenge of Campbell's Pauline Athanasianism

To come to a close, although I require some clarification and would counsel greater balance in his presentation of epistemological matters in terms of Paul and Athanasius, the thrust of my analysis suggests that Campbell has not only located but clearly elucidated some key problems in relation to reading Paul at the theoretical level that others have simply not taken seriously. He is, therefore, one step ahead of other prominent construals

---

creation are not to be confused: God is God and the creation is not. And so, given the ontological disparity between the two, a general ontology cannot serve epistemology because God would be rendered too close to be different. . . . It is only because the one Lord Jesus Christ is of one being with the Father *and* of one being with humanity (the double *homoousion*) that genuine identity exists between God and creation—but it exists precisely *as* this particular person, in him alone" [Lincoln Harvey, "Double *Homoousion*," 93]). I note Barth's fascinating discussion in CD I/2, and his later, 1956, essay, "The Humanity of God," in which he writes of "God's *togetherness* with man. Who God is and what He is in His deity He proves and reveals not in a vacuum as a divine being-for-Himself, but precisely and authentically in the fact that He exists, speaks, and acts as the *partner* of man" (Barth, *The Humanity of God*, 45). (For what it is worth, it is here I think that Anatolios misses the mark in contrasting Barth and Athanasius. I suspect that his comments [cf. Anatolios, *Coherence*, 211] relate better to an earlier Barth.) In other words, the relation *is* the revelation. (Again, I don't think Campbell will disagree here—this last phrase is how Campbell himself once put it to me over coffee!)

107. Barth, *Church Dogmatics*, I/2, 206–7.

of Paul. As we shall debate and explore in this book, I believe this further means that he is positioned to offer the most coherent reading of Romans at the argumentative level with his rhetorical and apocalyptic rereading (and in so doing clears up a host of tricky exegetical problems on the way). *Deliverance* is an inspired thesis, and if Campbell is right, Paul's Athanasian gospel is indeed consistently "all about Jesus" and thus the truly good news of the unconditional love of the Trinitarian God.

Douglas Campbell's Response to Chris Tilling

Chris has written a fundamentally supportive essay here in relation to my basic claims concerning current broad interpretative positions in relation to Paul. Specifically he affirms the accuracy and importance of distinguishing between fundamentally different theological modes when interpreting Paul. Not infrequently, when struggling to communicate clearly about such matters, I refer to these two modes and the distinction between them as the difference between Paul thinking "forward," at least in relation to a certain problem, as against thinking "backward" (utilizing here terminology originally developed by E. P. Sanders). The former mode, limiting it appropriately to epistemological dynamics, would then be foundationalist, is more specifically also often contractual, and would be methodologically Arian, and the latter would be non-foundationalist and (christologically) revelational, unconditional, and methodologically Athanasian. Hence the former, "forward" mode is an undesirable one from an orthodox theological point of view, the latter, "backward" one desirable, and the presence of both within Paul's thought—and especially within the same letter—evidence of distressing confusion in his thinking.

However, Chris goes on from his helpful characterizations to press me for some clarifications concerning how this terminology is being used more specifically and whether there are some dangers lurking in the way I have deployed it. In particular, he asks about the relationship between relational and retrospective dynamics within the supposedly desirable, orthodox, "backward" mode. And he places a set of questions to me concerning the utilization of important prior Jewish truths within the Christian gospel. Do these suggest abandoning language that is too rigorously retrospective? Hence in order to move forward to a higher level of clarity it is important to grasp just what work the language of thinking forward and backward in relation to Paul is—and is not—doing.

My concern in *Deliverance* is with what I take to be an unhealthy, not to mention inaccurate, construction of Paul's thinking that is rooted primarily in Romans 1–4. That construction is foundationalist and so thinks forward in a quite straightforward way; it begins with an account of "the problem" facing humanity, which is related especially to the problem facing Jews, constructing this from self-evident truths and their interrelationships (and this is where methodological Arianism is apparent). This problem is acute and eventually a specifically Christian solution is posited in relation to it—one that deals with the issues that have already been determined and so builds on its prior foundation. Hence the basic nature of humanity, of sin, of God's judgment, and of the law, have all been determined before the arrival of the Christian gospel and *must be*, moreover, precisely to prepare appropriately for that arrival. If the foundation has not been laid then the rest of the house cannot be built—an awful predicament for anyone favoring evangelism and thinking of it in these terms.

Backward thinking operates very differently. It recognizes that if the truths concerning God are fundamentally bound up with Christ then the revelation of this to someone will fundamentally restructure her thinking in relation to all other questions. The building blocks for answering those questions may well be present already but their arrangement must now be informed by the new realization that Christ is the truth at the center of both God and the universe. And this leads to what might seem at first to be some counter-intuitive dynamics that nevertheless turn out on reflection to be very necessary.

All the key positions that might have been in place prior to the disclosure of Christ must now be reevaluated. And it follows that any beliefs that non-Christians might hold about anything prior to the arrival of the truth about Christ must be reevaluated as well—including about their humanity, their own sin, their relationship to the law and to judgment, and their perceptions of God. So the arrival of the correct understanding of the fundamental truth about both God and the universe in relation to Christ does not build in any necessary way directly on truth claims present prior to its arrival; it *is* the foundation, now disclosed, on which all other truth claims must be built. Hence its arrival calls those prior truth claims into question and judges them. (Some questions tend to arise immediately at this point and they will be answered briefly momentarily.) Most importantly for our present purposes—scrutinizing the presence of forward thinking in Paul and in special relation to Romans 1–3—this means that any answers supplied concerning the nature of unredeemed humanity, of sin, of the law, and of the judgment of God achieved prior to the arrival of the correct understanding of God's activity in Christ, must now be stringently reevaluated in explicitly christological terms. Forward thinking is fundamentally unreliable. So such questions must be answered again, in the light of Christ, and the understanding of the pre-Christian existence appropriately reevaluated, hence thought through *retrospectively*.

This realization helps us immediately to grasp that, in turn, any accounts of forward thinking in Paul, which tend to be offered especially in relation to Romans 1–3, are offering definitive answers *inappropriately* from a *Christian* point of view. (They are indeed being offered in a way that is not overtly Christian at all.) Something very wrong is happening within any such approach. These questions are being answered in the wrong place and at the wrong time.

In sum then the distinction between forward and backward thinking helps interpreters to identify quickly—to name—when Paul is being presented as thinking in a way that is recognizably rooted in Christ and hence Christian, or not, even when the slightly deceptive optics of the situation are taken into account, namely, the presentation of his view of aspects of the pre-Christian situation. Paul's account of *that* situation must still be post-Christian, undertaken in the light of Christ, and hence fashioned in retrospect (which is how most accounts of the past are effected in any case).

Some anxieties can be raised by this insistence. But I suggest that they arise from certain confusions. This retrospective viewpoint is one to a large degree of perception, not ontology. God's activity *per se* is emphatically not being excluded from the pre-Christian situation, whether in relation to Jew or Greek! God's activity in the pre-Christian situation, drawing people to salvation, is clearly not being eliminated (as if it could be). It is merely being separated from a necessarily rationalistic missionary progression (this being undertaken in fact with little assistance from God). Moreover, the reshaping that takes place in the light of Christ tends to use prior constituents, in particular, the resources supplied by the Scriptures. So these treasured resources are not being excluded either. But the pressure of interpretation for the Christian in relation to pre-Christian realities is backward; Christ is the newly grasped key to what was previously going on—a dynamic the church fathers often spoke of with reference to "the divine cosmic secret" or *mystery* of Christ, now revealed to his fortunate community.[108]

Hopefully it is clear by this point from these expansions that Chris is quite right to ask me to clarify things. The retrospective or backward dynamic evident in Paul's thought is just one aspect of its ongoing clarification under pressure from Christ himself—and is one that his later

---

108. I owe this insight to T. J. Lang and anticipate his full treatment of the issue eagerly.

interpreters will hopefully echo. Hence his relationship with Christ is indeed more central than this particular epistemic result of its presence. Moreover, that relationship must be posited as existing prior to any Christian understanding that this is the case. It simply receives a marvellous clarification when someone bends the knee and exclaims "Jesus is Lord." Whatever her confusions up to this point, it is from this point on a matter of simple obedience that all thinking be done in the light of this central truth or, as Paul himself puts it, "that every thought [now] be led captive to Christ" (2 Cor 10:5). Claims of backward or retrospective thinking are nothing more—or less—than this.

5

"Arian" Foundationalism or "Athanasian" Apocalypticism

A Patristic Assessment

J. Warren Smith

When I am in the company of New Testament colleagues they ask what I, as a patrologist, think of Douglas Campbell's invocation of Athanasius and Arius to characterize the difference between his and previous readings of Romans. In their voice I detect a hint of skepticism. After all, they think of "Athanasian" and "Arian" as theological categories—markers for competing views of the Trinity or Christology. What do Arius and Athanasius have to do with issues of theological method or participatory soteriology that are at the heart of Campbell's assessment of Romans?

This skepticism is understandable given the way the theological controversies of the fourth century are often presented in church history classes. The "Arian Controversy" is presented as a dispute about the divinity of Christ, and the competing views are reduced to technical terms, such as *homoousios* or *hypostasis,* and slogans or formulae, such as, "there was once when he was not" or "three persons in one substance."[1] While

1. See Anatolios, *Retrieving Nicaea,* 7–8; Beeley, *Gregory of Nazianzus on the Trinity and the Knowledge of God,* viii–ix; Behr, *The Nicene Faith* 1, 3.

such terminology is an inescapable part of the Trinitarian *grammar* that emerged from the controversies, it does not reflect the richness of the Nicene faith any more than a high school grammar book can convey the richness of the English language expressed in Shakespeare's dramas or George Herbert's poetry.

Lewis Ayres, Khaled Anatolios, Christopher Beeley, John Behr, and others have sought to complicate the traditional narratives of the fourth century.[2] The disputes entailed disagreement about the nature of *theologia*, what claims could be made about God, and who could make them. In other words, at the root of the controversy was a difference of opinion as to man's access to the knowledge of God. Can God's essence or *ousia* be known by reason alone or is it entirely beyond our grasp? If the latter, can Christians make any positive claims about God's nature? Ultimately, Nicene Christianity distinguished between *theologia*, discussion of God's nature, from *oikonomia*, indirect knowledge of God's being through God's creative, redemptive, and divinizing activities or *energeia* revealed in the unfolding plan of salvation in the narrative of Scripture. Campbell, therefore, is correct that Arius and Athanasius represent not only competing Christologies but also competing theological methodologies—methodologies that resonate with competing nineteenth- and twentieth-century theological methods and epistemologies (e.g., Barth vs. Brunner) that have informed modern readings of Romans.

---

2. Although in late antiquity it was standard for defenders of Nicaea to refer to anti-Nicenes, including the Eusebians, Homoians, and Eunomians, as "Arians," in recent years it has been demonstrated that the term "Arian" really was a construction of Athanasius in his Orations against the Arians that tarred all his opponents with the errors of Arius, even if their theology is quite different than Arius's. See, for example, Ayres, *Nicaea and Its Legacy*, 105ff. While I appreciate the work of Ayres and others to complicate the picture of the fourth century and certainly recognize the profound difference between Arius's thought and that of later opponents of Nicaea, I do not think one can see the description of their enemies as "Arian" by Pro-Nicenes as purely *ad hominem*. Rather, I would suggest, it reflects their recognition that the Homoians and Eunomians fell into essentially the same error in their understanding of the Son's relationship to the Father and the creation.

Athanasius and Arius:
Historical Figures behind the Paradigm

The real question is whether "Arian" and "Athanasian" are the best fourth-century categories to describe Campbell's project. My answer is Yes and No.

First, the "Yes." The ultimate purpose of creedal formulae—whether 1 Corinthians 15:1–6 or the Nicene-Constantinopolitan Creed—is to guide the church in its interpretation of Scripture. The "Arian Controversy" began, after all, when Alexander, Bishop of Alexandria, required his presbyters to submit samples of exegesis to see that they presented Christ the Only-begotten Son as intrinsic to the Father's being. Nicene-Chalcedonian Christology should be, not only theologically normative for catholic Christianity, but also a guide for ecclesial interpretation of Scripture. Campbell's use of Arius and Athanasius draws the fields of modern biblical exegesis and the Nicene tradition into conversation.

But now for the "No." Arius and Athanasius do not work as cyphers for Brunner and Barth quite the way Campbell hopes because, as I will show below, Arius and Athanasius are closer in their epistemologies than Campbell presents them. This does not mean, however, that we must lose Campbell's incorporation of Nicene theology into contemporary studies of Pauline theology. On the contrary, there is a better way to capture Campbell's concern about theological method in other fourth-century terminology. The alternative is Nicene Apocalypticism and Eunomian Rationalism.

At the heart of the Campbell's analysis of the debate about the soteriology of Romans is the clash between Methodological Arianism and Athanasian Apocalypticism. Methodological Arianism is Campbell's term for the contractual foundationalism that imposes upon Romans a view of justice from social contract theory of the Western Liberal tradition, grounded in a theory of natural law and a natural knowledge of God's righteousness—knowledge universally available and thus outside the revelation of God's covenantal relationship with Israel and the church. This theory of natural law becomes the foundation of the Western *ordo salutis*. The alternative to Methodological Arianism is Athanasian Apocalypticism that roughly corresponds to the Pneumatologically Participatory Martyrological Eschatology (of the PPME Model) Campbell advanced in *The Quest for Paul's Gospel*.[3] God's redemptive work is not regulated or

---

3. See chapter 3 of Campbell, *Quest*.

conditioned by a system of justice that is external to God. Rather God's election of the saints by which they are incorporated into the covenantal relationship with God is purely gratuitous—the overflow of his benevolence. The righteousness of God, therefore, is entirely apocalyptic. It can be grasped, not by appealing to some natural law conception of justice, but solely in God's self-revelation in Christ. As Campbell nicely puts it, because God's unconditional love is the foundation of God's work of deliverance, "[no] criteria for [salvation's] activation, appropriation, or reception by humans are apparent, while what causality or agency is apparent is attributed to God."[4]

While Campbell's apocalyptic reading of Romans has certain affinities to Athanasius' understanding of the incarnation, the problem comes with his identification of Arius's Logos theology with an ahistorical foundationalism.[5] Far from maintaining that humanity has access to God through nature, Arius held as the first principle of his theology that God is radically transcendent and so completely unknowable *in se*. God is absolutely unique, Arius maintained. Consequently, God is beyond human analogical reasoning. Following the apophatic tradition of Middle Platonism, all human beings can say about God *in se* is how he is unlike us: immaterial, incorruptible, immutable, impassible, and most of all ingenerate (*agennētos*). Such negative terminology does not tell us what God is; it merely purifies our thinking about God by removing any erroneous comparisons between God and ourselves. Any claim of likeness between ourselves and God is, in Arius's thought, entirely Feuerbachian self-projection (if the reader can excuse the anachronism). It is precisely for this reason that we are dependent upon a mediator between creation and God. The mediator is the Logos, who, because he is begotten from the Father's will, is God's agent of creation, of revelation, and of redemption. One of Arius's more controversial claims is that God is so transcendent and unknowable that not even the Son knows him.[6] The Son's only knowledge of the Father is the knowledge he has of himself as the perfect

---

4. Campbell, *Deliverance*, 65.

5. For this analysis, I draw primarily on Rowan Williams's reconstruction of Arius's thought based on his Letter to Alexander, his creedal statement to the Emperor Constantine, and his *Thalia* that was addressed to the Eusebians in *Arius*, 95–116.

6. This claim appears in Athanasius's *De Synodis*, not in any of Arius's letters. Williams concludes, "The incomprehensibility of God in the *Thalia* is not therefore an isolated or arbitrary dogmatic affirmation; it is a necessary consequence of God's being what he is, *uniquely* self-subsistent," (Williams, *Arius*, 106).

reflection of the Father's will. Our only knowledge of God, therefore, comes through the historical revelation of the Logos in the life of Israel and in the incarnation. In other words, Arius is equally as insistent as Athanasius upon the apocalyptic nature of our knowledge of God. The chief difference is that for Athanasius the Logos cannot properly reveal God the Father or allow us to participate in the divine nature unless the Logos is equal in divinity with the Father.

An Alternative Paradigm

On this account of Arius's thought, it would appear that Campbell's contrast between Methodological Arianism and Athanasian Apocalypticism is not an appropriate model for thinking about the errant foundationalist reading of Romans. There is, however, another figure and school of thought in the fourth century that represents the error that Campbell attributes to Arius, namely Eunomius of Cyzicus and the Heterousians. The Heterousians—also called Neo-Arians or Anomoians or Eunomians—represent the third generation of Anti-Nicene subordinationists.[7] Eunomius, following his teacher Aetius, maintained that the task of theology (*theologia*) was "not to honor [God] in name alone by human conceptualization; rather we intend to repay him the most necessary debt of all, namely confessing that he is what he is."[8] Confessing "that he is what he is" meant naming the divine essence (*ousia*) itself, unbegotten (*agennētos*). Eunomius drew upon an argument in Plato's *Cratylus* that names give the essence; so things with different names have different essences.[9] For the essence is what is unique, setting it apart from all others. God's uniqueness, for Eunomius, lay in being unbegotten, that is, uncaused or conditioned by anything external to himself. From this position he rejected the Nicene claim that Father and Son are consubstantial (*homoousios*). If the Father's essence is his being unbegotten and the Son

7. Arius and his Eusebian allies (e.g., Eusebius of Caesarea, Eusebius of Nichomodia, Asterius) represent the first generation during the period between 313–36; while the second generation is the Homoians whose affirmed that the Father and Son were *homoios* or "like" but not of the same substance. The Homoian Creed crafted at the Councils of Ariminum and Selucia became the normative standard for the Imperial church under Constantius.

8. Eunomius, *Apology* 8.1–5 quoted in Basil of Caesarea, *Against Eunomius* 1.5, trans. DelCogliano and Radde-Gallwitz.

9. See Hanson, *The Search for the Christian Doctrine of God*, 630–32.

is called the "Only-begotten," then by definition the Unbegotten Father and Only-begotten Son are of different essences and so unlike each other. Since God is simple, he concludes, attributes such as incorruptible or impassible are not real, discrete properties of God, but only human conceptualizations (*epinoia*).[10]

Eunomius, like Arius, was concerned to maintain the uniqueness and majesty of the Father. Yet, where Eunomius differs radically from Arius and why it is misleading to call him a "Neo-Arian" is that Eunomius and Arius disagree about our ability to know God's essence. For Arius, God abides alone, enfolded in mystery, and so is known by human beings only indirectly in the Son's reflection of the Father's will. Thus God is completely unknowable, even by the Son. Eunomius, by contrast, held that the human intellect is able to penetrate the divine being and comprehend the divine essence.

The refutation of Aetius and Eunomius fell to the Cappadocians, Basil of Caesarea, Gregory of Nazianzus, and Gregory of Nyssa. The dispute between the Eunomians and the Cappadocians focused as much on assumptions about the nature of theology and the human capacity to know God as it did about competing interpretations of biblical claims about the person of Christ Jesus. Basil, in his *Against Eunomius*, deploys two arguments to counter Eunomius's claim that God's essence is his being unbegotten. First, he denies the foundational assumption that the essence of God is knowable. Divine attributes are not polyonyms. That is, they are not interchangeable, as are "Peter," "Simon," and "Cephas"; for the meaning of one term is not presupposed in the meaning of another. Saying that God is light is not the same as saying that God is omniscient and unbegotten.[11] Therefore, God's essence is fundamentally irreducible; all that God is cannot be subsumed under a single attribute, such as unbegotten. Moreover, Basil employs not a minimalist view of essence as a single distinguishing feature, but a maximalist view. God's essence is identical with God's being, that is, with everything that God is. Since God is infinite, his being cannot be comprehended by the finite human intellect. Consequently, since God's essence is unknowable, either reductively or comprehensively, Eunomius cannot claim that the Unbegotten Father and the Only-begotten Son are not consubstantial.

10. See Basil's analysis of the difference between Eunomius's view of *epinoia* and his own in *Against Eunomius* 1.6–7 (trans. DelCogliano and Radde-Gallwitz 118 and 152).

11. Basil, *Against Eunomius* 1.8.

Basil and the other Cappadocian Fathers formulated a strikingly different view of theology than that embraced by the Eunomians. Although God's *ousia* is incomprehensible and ineffable, God is not unknowable. He is known indirectly through his activities (*energeia*) manifest in the plan or economy of salvation (*oikonomia*). We know God's *energeia* through God's providential working in the history of Israel and the church as recorded in Scripture. For Scripture provides an account of the work of the Son and Spirit in revealing the Father who sent them to accomplish and bring to perfection his will for creation. The mediatorial work of the Son in revealing the Father is possible because the Son is the "living image" of the Father. "He is not a lifeless image, not handmade nor a product of art or conceptualization, but a living image, or rather self-existent life which always preserves the indistinguishability, not by likeness of shape, but his very substance. . . . [We] should conceive of 'the image of the invisible God' not as that which is produced later than the archetype like those images produced by human skill, but as that which is co-existent with and subsists alongside the one who brought him into subsistence. . . . [L]ike a teacher inculcating the full reality of an art in his disciples: the teacher loses nothing and the disciples attain the fullness of the art."[12] The Son is the image that reveals the Father because, like the radiance of light emanating from a flame, he as the Son has the same nature as the Father who begat him.[13] As eternally begotten from the Father, the Son bears the Father's wisdom and power and light to humanity in the incarnation. These terms—wisdom, power, and light—are the names Scripture gives to Christ. These biblical names, what Origen called *epinoia*, are the basis of Christian theology. That is, along with terms like "impassible," "immutable," "omniscient," the divine names are human conceptualizations of God's nature based on God's *energeia* recorded in Scripture.[14]

12. Basil, *Against Eunomius* 1.18 and 2.16 (trans. DelCogliano and Radde-Gallwitz 118 and 152).

13. For a discussion of how Basil links the notion of Christ as the "image of God" (Col 1:15 and 2 Cor 4:4) with the radiance of the flame (Heb 1:3), see *Against Eunomius* 2.17.

14. "There is not one name which encompasses the entire nature of God and suffices to express it adequately. Rather, there are many diverse names, and each one contributes, in accordance with its own meaning, to a notion that is altogether dim and trifling as regards the whole but that is at least sufficient for us. Now some of these names, applied to God, are indicative of what is present to God; others, on the contrary, of what is not present. From these two something like an impression of God is made in us, namely, from the denial of what is incongruous with him and from the

Here lies the critical difference between the Neo-Nicene understanding of theology developed by the Cappadocians and the view to
which the Eunomians subscribed. Whereas Eunomius was confident that
the human intellect was able to grasp the divine essence *directly*, the Cappadocians maintained that, while we cannot know God's essence *in se*, we
can still have knowledge of God *indirectly* through his *energeia*.[15] Unlike
Eunomius who dismissed conceptualizations (*epinoia*) as insubstantial
and presumptuously claimed to "confess that he is what he is,"[16] Basil's
view of theology as conceptualizations based on the revelation of God's
activities united *theologia* (i.e., knowledge of God's nature) and *oikonomia* (i.e., knowledge of God's self-revelatory actions in history), the
apophatic (i.e., a privative description that rules out what is alien to God's
nature) and the kataphatic (i.e., positive claims about qualities or characteristics proper to God's nature). The Triune God is his *ousia* (i.e., his
essence/being/substance/nature). God's *ousia* is who God is *in se*. God's
energeiai, from which our conceptions of God are derived, are expressions of God and thus of God's essence/nature. Thus when we say "God is
love," we have named an essential attribute of God. Kataphatic statements
or *epinoia*, therefore, are not insubstantial abstractions, but name real
properties or *propria* of the divine essence. So one cannot claim to know
the essence or substance of God either in the reductive sense, since God's
essence is irreducible, or in the maximal sense, since God is infinite and
knowing the essence in its totality is impossible. Since conceptualizations
about God are grounded in the *energeia* revealed in Scripture, theology
for the Cappadocians is not mere speculation or self-projection. Consequently, the truth of Christian theology lies in the dialectical relationship between the kataphatic and the apophatic. For Campbell's purpose,
therefore, the Eunomians represent the most egregious example of ahistorical theology while Nicene theology that includes Athanasius and the
Cappadocians draws an absolute line between Divine mystery and the
Divine revelation, between God's essence, which is absolutely unknowable, and God's *energeia* manifest in history. If Campbell wants to find a

---

affirmation of what belongs to him," Basil, *Against Eunomius* 1.10 (trans. DelCogliano
and Radde-Gallwitz, 105).

15. Gregory of Nazianzus, *Oration* 28.6 (SC 250, 110–12).

16. "Things said by way of conceptualization, you see, have an existence in name
alone and when they are being pronounced, by nature are dissolved together with the
sounds used to say them," Eunomius, *Apology* 8.1–5 quoted in trans. DelCogliano and
Radde-Gallwitz, 96.

patristic analogue to the division between Barth and Brunner, Eunomius, not Arius, is the paradigmatic villain and Nicene theology, represented by Athanasius together with the Cappadocians and their distinction between ineffable essence and knowable activities, is the precursor of a Barthian distinction between God *in se* and God *pro nobis*. The Nicenes are Campbell's theological allies. Instead of speaking of Arian Foundationalism and Athanasian Apocalypticism, Campbell would be better served to speak of a Eunomian Rationalism vs. a Nicene Apocalypticism or a Nicene Economic Theology.

This brings us to the harder question: Does the Nicene emphasis on the centrality of God's self-disclosure in Christ, which is foundational for the Cappadocian distinction between God's unknowable *ousia* and God's knowable *energeia*, give Campbell support for his understanding of the apocalyptic nature of the righteousness of God? In other words, it is one thing to say that the Nicene theology, which coalesced during the fourth century, denied that any rational creature has *immediate* access to the knowledge of God *in se*, but another thing altogether to say that they denied the possibility of *any* natural knowledge of God or of God's justice. Indeed, the Logos theology of Justin, which reaches its zenith in Athanasius's Christology, contends that even those outside of God's covenantal relationship with Israel and the church have received *some* knowledge of God and the moral law. What may be most helpful here is to describe the tension within the Nicene tradition between an allowance for some knowledge of God apart from special revelation, albeit insufficient for salvation, and the firm commitment that the highest knowledge of God that can be attained in this age comes through God's self-revelation in the incarnation of his Son.

Natural Law in the Nicene Tradition

The doctrine of creation put forward by the Nicene Fathers of the fourth century continued to be influenced by a strong anti-Gnostic and anti-Marcionite tradition arising from the second and third centuries that sought to avoid a dualistic presentation of creation and redemption. To put it in positive terms, the fashioning of the material world *ex nihilo* at the beginning and the redemption of humanity through the incarnation of the Word were but movements in a single process by which the divine economy unfolded over the course of history. Irenaeus's theory of the divine economy stands in contrast to a simplistic creation-fall-restoration paradigm; rather, God's *oikonomia* is a plan for bringing creation to perfection. Irenaeus conceives of the economy as a process of God's self-revelation whereby the human race grows into the likeness of God by being trained to see God and so becoming participants in the divine nature. God's self-disclosure was not confined to Old Testament theophanies, the covenants, and ultimately the incarnation. God revealed himself in material creation itself. This raises the question of the limits of natural theology, that is, what of God could rational creatures apprehend through reasoned reflection on the nature of the created world? Did patristic theologians maintain that humanity possessed a natural knowledge of God's righteousness and thus "were without excuse" for sin?

Origen of Alexandria wrote the first commentary on Romans—a text that exists only in an abridged Latin translation by Rufinus. The righteousness (*iustitia*) of God is manifest in God's inclusion of all people in salvation, Gentile as well as Jew. It came "from faith to faith" in that this revelation is passed to the Gentiles through the faith of the Jews in the law. The Jews also must come to faith in the gospel since belief in both Torah and the gospel are necessary for "complete life."[17] An unavoidable corollary of God's righteousness is God's wrath, which "is revealed from heaven against all ungodliness and wickedness" (Rom 1:18). Although the wrath is directed against *all* unrighteousness; it is, Origen says, *manifest* in those who "hold fast to the truth but suppress it by their wickedness." These people are the "wise of the world," "scholars," and "philosophers" who "[a]lthough they knew the truth and righteousness of God 'did not honor God or give him thanks, but they became bankrupt in their thinking,' having turned to idols."[18] Focusing on Paul's claim that the wrath of God is *revealed*, which Origen explicitly defines here as "brought forth from obscurity and hiddenness into the state of being known," he states that the wise of this age have some knowledge of God because God has revealed it to them.[19] How has God made known his truth and righteousness to the philosophers? Through the rational faculty with which God endowed the human soul, man is able to know the truth of God by way of

17. Origen, *Commentary on the Epistle to the Romans* I.15 (Scheck 103, 87).

18. Ibid., I.16.1 (PG 14:862; trans. Scheck, 88).

19. Ibid., I.16.2 (PG 14:862; trans. Scheck, 88). Origen makes a distinction between the wrath that is revealed from heaven and a self-inflicted wrath, "For in reality those who are totally devoid of the truth, as if they have nothing in common with heaven and with the light, are bearing the wrath of their own vices and sinful passions, or of the demons to which they have willingly subjected themselves," (I.16.4).

inference from creation. God's condemnation of the ungodly, who lived before Christ, is nevertheless just since they had the capacity to know and worship the Creator, but instead worshiped idols.[20] Yet Origen goes on to distinguish "what is known of God" through reasoned inferences from nature and the divine substance that remain unknown to all created beings.[21] This distinction anticipates the Cappadocian contention against Eunomius. The failure of the ungodly philosophers to move from their knowledge of God's power and eternal divinity through inference from creation to the worship of God has resulted in the corruption of the image of God in whom they were made. He writes, "through their own futile way of thinking, while they seek after forms and images for God, they have destroyed the image of God within themselves. Those who were openly boasting to be in the light of wisdom have fallen into the deep darkness of foolishness."[22] However extensive the destruction of the *imago Dei* may be, in Origen's thinking, it does not mean the complete loss of our reasoning faculty. For him, even embodied humanity retains the rational capacity inherent to its essential nature as *nous*. Abiding in the dark does not remove the faculty of reason; it merely means that we reason from errant assumptions to false conclusions. Origen does not trace this line of reasoning to the conclusion that the pagans, having "destroyed the image of God within themselves," have also lost the essential similarity to God that is the basis for our knowledge of God. Consequently, he never contends that we are unable to know God through nature and natural law. Origen may not have arrived at this conclusion but Athanasius certainly did.

Written between 328–33, Athanasius's double volume *Against the Gentiles* and *On the Incarnation of the Word* attacks the subordinationist Christology of Arius and his allies, the Eusebians, under the guise of an apologetic directed at Christianity's Jewish and pagan critics.[23] Athana-

---

20. Ibid., I.16.5 (PG 14:863; Scheck 90).

21. Ibid., I.16.6 (PG 14:863; Scheck 90–91). Based on Jesus words that "no one know the Father except the Son and anyone to whom the Son wants to reveal him," (Matt 11:27), Origen does leave open the possibility that human beings may eventually progress to the point of knowing God's nature; but this is know only to God.

22. Ibid., I.17.2 (PG 14:864; Scheck 92).

23. The apologetic form made his anti-subordinationist polemic acceptable to Constantine who was concerned that Athanasius's continuing conflict with the Eusebians threatened the unity of the church that the emperor had sought to achieve at Nicaea. See Anatolios, *Retrieving Nicaea*, 101–2.

sius offers a defense of the Son's full divinity grounded in a narrative of the loss of the *imago Dei* and with it the knowledge of God that was the result of the fall from paradise. In his goodness, God did not horde his goodness but sought to share his goodness with other beings. Through his Logos, God the Father created the cosmos so that in their created nature human beings might enjoy a share in God's goodness.[24] Since the Logos created the cosmos *ex nihilo*, creation has no life or existence in its nature. Rather its nature is inherently unstable, mutable, and inclined to fall back into the nothingness whence it was made. Into the nothingness of non-existence it would return were its existence not sustained by God who is life itself. In the case of humanity, the Logos fashioned man in his image. As the image of the Logos who is the wisdom of the Father, human nature bears a kinship with God's supremely rational nature so that we may know God and so be united with God through contemplative participation.[25] Here Athanasius is following the logic of the maxim that "like is known by like"; we are made capable of knowing God by being endowed with a certain affinity or likeness to the Divine that allows us to apprehend God. From this contemplative fellowship, man is able to partake of the divine nature and so, not only mirror God's moral virtues, but also gain a share in God's life that is free from corruption and decay. So, like the branches that draw life from the vine, inherently unstable humanity is able to receive the divine *stasis* by partaking of God's eternal life.

When humanity sinned and turned away from God, human existence became characterized by evil. Our likeness to God began to diminish. The rational image of God, in which we were made so that we might know God and participate in God's life-sustaining grace, was compromised. Consequently, our knowledge of God also waned.[26] Unable to know and participate in God, human nature became corrupt. Losing its ability to participate in God, humanity began to slide back into non-being. Christ, therefore, as the Son and Logos through whom the Father created the world and from whom humanity derived the divine image, became incarnate, not only to defeat Satan and death, but also to recreate human nature and restore the divine image with a proper knowledge of God.

24. Athanasius, *On the Incarnation*, 3.
25. Ibid., 4.
26. Ibid., 11.

What is important for the purpose of Campbell's argument is the effect of the fall upon humanity's ability to know God through creation. Athanasius allows that, although God is "by nature invisible and incomprehensible, having his being beyond all created existence," the Creator so ordered the universe that "one ought to perceive God its maker and artificer, even though [God] be not seen with the bodily eyes."[27] Not surprisingly, he supports this claim by quoting Romans 1:20. After the fall, however, humanity retained the knowledge *that* God existed but they lacked true knowledge of *what* or *who* God is. They developed a corrupt view of the Divine. Since in sin their minds were focused on the material world, they came to conceive of the incorporeal God in corporeal terms. So they crafted wooden or stone representations of God as nonrational animals. In other words, because of sin human beings were unable to know God rightly through nature. Instead of seeing God's power reflected in nature and so reasoning inductively from their knowledge of the creature to the Creator, humanity imputed to God the qualities of unstable and corruptible material creation. In the incarnation, therefore, the Logos, who is the "image of the invisible God" (Col 1:15) restores the *imago Dei* by revealing the image of the Father in bodily form. In revealing the Father, the Son gives humanity a proper knowledge of God that allows us to think about God properly. To put it another way, by revealing the Father in a way that enables us to reason rightly about God, the Divine Logos restores our ability to contemplate God. Through our contemplation of the Father in the face of the incarnate Logos, our mind receives the impress of his nature and we come to possess the *imago Dei*. We are able to participate in the divine nature by being conformed to the image of God revealed in Christ Jesus only because the Son is equal in divinity with the Father.

Here we see the difference between Origen and Athanasius. Origen allowed that some people, such as the philosophers, were able to gain right knowledge of God's power and righteousness from creation. For others, it was simply a failure to use their rational faculties. Therefore, the philosophers' participation in pagan idolatry reflects, not a failure *to see* God rightly, but a failure *to act* rightly upon their natural knowledge of God whose power and righteousness were revealed in creation. For Athanasius, by contrast, idolatry is a failure to act rightly that results from

27. Athanasius, *Against the Gentiles* III.35.1. I am grateful to Khaled Anatolios for pointing me to this passage.

a failure to see and know God rightly. He does not deny that creation reveals God's power and righteousness; rather sin has distorted human thinking, creating a carnal orientation of the mind and materialistic habits of thought that prevent us from receiving God's self-disclosure in the visible creation. The Logos sets our thinking about God aright and raises our thoughts above the visible creation to the invisible Creator by giving us a proper vision of the Father. This is possible only because the Logos abided with us, assuming a sensible form in the material creation upon which our carnal minds are fixated.

Ultimately, it is the incarnate Christ who makes theological reflection upon the divine attributes revealed in creation an object of theological reflection. Gregory of Nazianzus, writing around five decades after Athanasius' *On the Incarnation,* makes this point in the second of his famous Theological Orations preached in Constantinople in 380. Drawing on the Exodus narrative, Nazianzen used the story of Moses's encounter with God in Mt. Sinai to explain the work of *theologia*—which was narrowly understood as the study of "the great mystery," the Trinity and the nature of God, as opposed to *oikonomia* that would include topics of Christology, anthropology, biblical exegesis, eschatology, and ethics. Although he speaks of God's bidding him to enter the cloud and enjoy his divine company, *theologia* is not to be identified with an apophatic *experience.* Rather it leads to the apophatic conclusion that God in his essence is unknowable and that human speech, which is inescapably material and analogical, does not correspond to the divine nature. In the cloud of *theologia*, he describes his manner of reasoning, "detached from matter and material things, [I] concentrated, so far as might be, *in myself.* But when I directed my gaze I scarcely saw the averted figure of God, and this whilst sheltering in the rock, God the Word incarnate for us. Peering I saw not the nature prime, inviolate, self-apprehended[, i.e.,] the Trinity . . . [but] the majesty inherent in the created things he has brought forth and governed."[28] Fully consistent with Basil's arguments against Eunomius, Gregory denies that theological inquiry gives one knowledge of the Divine nature in its essence or of the inner workings of the Trinity (e.g., the manner of the Son's generation or the Spirit's procession). Rather one sees the Divine *energeia* as manifest in creation. The *energeia* that is visible in the material creation is, what he calls, the *averted figure of God*; i.e.,

---

28. Gregory of Nazianzus, *Oration* 28.3, trans. Wickham, in *On God and Christ,* 39 (SC 250, 104–6).

God's backside—that which God leaves in his wake. The critical point, however, is that the vantage point from which one is able to grasp the *energeia* revealed in creation is the incarnation of the Logos. Gregory does not here offer an opinion as to whether, as Origen, our reason allows us to discern God's power and righteousness in creation independent of the incarnation or whether, as Athanasius, we cannot see them because of sin. Rather, he simply allows that *theologia* reasons from the nature of creation to certain claims about its Creator, but one can rightly reason from creation to God's averted figure only through the apocalypse of the incarnate Son in the light of the Holy Spirit.

The contrasting models of Nicene Apocalypticism and Eunomian Rationalism that I offer as an alternative to the Athanasian Apocalypticism and Arian Foundationalism have a basic affinity with Douglas Campbell's larger theological project as it stands now while contributing additional strengths of its own. Eunomian Rationalism accurately represents the errors in theological method that have been attributed to Arius. Whether Eunomius's natural theology is precisely the foundationalism Campbell has in mind, I will leave to his judgment. Perhaps more importantly, Nicene Apocalypticism gives Campbell the christocentric foundation that he wants for making claims about the righteousness of God. At the same time, by grounding natural theology in the incarnation the Nicene tradition allows us to preserve continuity between the revelation of God's power and righteousness in creation at the beginning and in the history of Israel and the life of Jesus. It avoids a form of supercessionism that would deny that the shadowy knowledge of God contained in the book of nature can be abandoned now that we have the perfect revelation in Christ. Most of all, the Nicene Trinitarian theology gives Campbell the robust Pneumatology that is central for his reading of Paul's conception of how God enables believers to participate in God's life as Christ's body and so bear witness to the righteousness of God.

———

Douglas Campbell's Response to J. Warren Smith

Warren, like Chris, has written a fundamentally supportive paper and supplies helpful precision and depth to my brief invocation of the figures of Arius and Athanasius.

I invoked these figures in principal reliance on a study by Alasdair Heron,[29] and to make a single critical point. The first wave of responses to *Deliverance* suggested quite frequently that my concern with the presence of two modes of thinking in Paul, and with the very presence of the forward mode, was overblown. Hence, by implication, the pressure I built up on the reading undergirding this mode, in Romans 1–4, should be dramatically reduced, and it seemed thereby to become rather less important to find some alternative. Far too much fuss was being made about matters of small import; the things I was worried about were trivial.

My perception of the issues was of course rather different and so I appealed to Heron's treatment of Arius and Athanasius suggesting that nothing less was at stake than the orthodox account of the gospel. Things could not be more important. Moreover, the classic debate between Brunner and Barth lay in the background of this claim, along with Barth's reflections on the failure by most German Christians in the 1930s to confront the rise of Hitler—and I mention this because Warren's discussion of the patristic evidence (understandably) does not engage with the important sociopolitical correlates of "methodological Arianism," correlates seen in further historical episodes like the church's general insensitivity to the phenomena of colonialism and slavery as well as, more specifically and recently, the institution of Apartheid in South Africa. Barth's insight in relation to these dynamics was that Christian thinking that is not fundamentally committed to the disclosure of God in a real sense in Christ, and fundamentally and stringently disciplined by this central revelation, tends to lose its way in tragically practical as well as esoterically academic contexts.[30]

Warren has helpfully updated here my appeal to Arius and Athanasius. More recent scholarship than Heron's has softened the judgment of history on Arius. He is now not regarded as the quintessential heretic, and neither is his theological method regarded as so overtly suspect as it

29. Heron, "*Homoousios* with the Father," 58–87.

30. Some of these dynamics are usefully traced in Jennings, *The Christian Imagination*; Barth's journey is chronicled usefully by Busch in *Karl Barth: His life*, 216–53; also instructive is Koonz, *The Nazi Conscience*, esp. "Allies in the Academy," 46–68.

once was (given the correctness of the revisionists of course). Moreover, Warren rightly broadens the advocacy of orthodoxy from Athanasius to include the Cappadocians, and reorients it negatively toward the Eunomians, who remain overtly heretical and in the same basic methodological terms that I am concerned about. And I think all this is helpful—provided the initial rhetorical point is not lost by any readers that what is at stake in this discussion of Paul is a matter of fundamental Christian importance! Hence I suspect that something of a rhetorical progression will still have to take place.

That is, in face of any claim that the matters addressed by *Deliverance* are trivial, the figures of Athanasius and Arius might still need to be deployed to affirm, albeit in somewhat vulgar terms, that vital matters are at stake that reach back deep into the church's history. As discussion becomes deeper and more precise, however, especially in relation to patristic figures, the vulgar interpretation of Arius should be withdrawn and replaced by the Eunomians, and the concerns of Athanasius broadened to include all the Nicenes. New Testament scholars might find themselves traveling in this way up the divided line or, indeed, out of the cave of their own ignorance of patristic discussions (including myself in this journey). All of which is to say that Warren is quite right, but most New Testament scholars will not immediately know enough to appreciate why, and may, moreover, miss the initial point of the original patristic comparison if they jump to his articulation immediately. For those still in the cave, the shadows of the shapes around the fire must suffice. But beyond the shadows lie the shapes themselves, and beyond them, the dim perception of the realities they depict lying beyond the mouth of the cave. I am grateful then that Warren has taken the time to lead his New Testament colleagues from their gloomy ignorance toward this enlightenment. But Warren also gestures here toward another issue that requires a moment of further clarification—the question of natural theology.

As my response to the previous chapter, by Chris Tilling, already indicated, my concern in relation to the prevailing reading of Romans 1–3 is not with natural theology *per se* but with *foundationalist* natural theology that functions as the basis for all further theological reflection, and that thereby, as a Procrustean bed, trims subsequent Christology to fit. *This*, unfortunately, is what the current majority reading of Romans 1–3 commits the Pauline interpreter to, because the claims of Romans 1 are self-evidently true and then function at a basic level; everything that follows builds on them—the realization of innate sinfulness and God's pending judgment, the flawed nature of Judaism in relation to works, and so on. If these opening claims, generated by reasoning clearly (in a certain way) in relation to the cosmos, were to be renegotiated later on, in the light of Christ, the validity of the entire argument would be compromised and it would have to be abandoned. And clearly no one does this. ("Romans 1–4 seemed true until you became a Christian and then we learned that it was actually mostly wrong.") So my quarrel is only with natural theology functioning in this basic fashion. I, like Barth, have no quarrel at all with natural theology functioning vigorously in relation to non-Christians—or indeed in relation to Christians, provided that the christological *logos* is fully in play. Indeed, insights from nature and creation are to be welcomed in that location. I simply want to insist that any claims made in terms of natural theology be subject to christological revision. However, I suspect that neither Warren nor his beloved patristic forbears have any quibbles about this!

6

Connecting the Dots

One Problem, One Text, and the Way Ahead[1]

DOUGLAS A. CAMPBELL

The journey to a solution from the problems I outlined in chapter 3 can begin usefully by considering just one concern—Judaism—in relation to a limited text—Galatians 2:15–16.[2] This consideration can illustrate both why the presence of a fundamentally Arian type of Western contractualism in Paul is so problematic, however unnoticed, and what the basic strategy for resolving it is that *Deliverance* is proposing. In what follows, largely for the sake of convenience, I will call the problematic approach "forwardness."[3]

1. Permission from Sage Publications is here gratefully acknowledged to reproduce in what follows parts of my earlier study "An Attempt to be Understood: A Response to the Concerns of Matlock and Macaskill with *The Deliverance of God*," *JSNT* 34 (2011) 162–208.

2. I am following some sage advice here from Charles (Charlie) Cousar's review of (inter alia) *Deliverance*, 416.

3. I am drawing here on E. P. Sanders's important phrase and insight in much of *Paul and Palestinian Judaism* that Paul "thinks . . ." or is "thinking backward"; cf. esp. 434–35, 38–40, 42, 74–85. But I define this, unlike him, in rigorously epistemological terms, and in relation ultimately to the distinction between Athanasius and Arius argued for earlier. This is emphatically *not* a question of psychology and/or causality for me but of truth claims and their justification(s).

Galatians 2:15–16

In Galatians 2:15–16 Paul states, Ἡμεῖς φύσει Ἰουδαῖοι καὶ οὐκ ἐξ ἐθνῶν ἁμαρτωλοί· [16] εἰδότες δὲ ὅτι οὐ δικαιοῦται ἄνθρωπος ἐξ ἔργων νόμου ἐὰν μὴ διὰ πίστεως Ἰησοῦ Χριστοῦ, καὶ ἡμεῖς εἰς Χριστὸν Ἰησοῦν ἐπιστεύσαμεν, ἵνα δικαιωθῶμεν ἐκ πίστεως Χριστοῦ καὶ οὐκ ἐξ ἔργων νόμου, ὅτι ἐξ ἔργων νόμου οὐ δικαιωθήσεται πᾶσα σάρξ.[4]

Fortunately only one question in this abbreviated and controversial text concerns us at present: our basic construal of the antithesis between "works of the law" and "faith . . ." in relation to Jews. What is at stake for the Jewish question in Paul in whether we construe this antithesis "forward" or "backward" (forward being Arian and backward Athanasian)?

Almost everything.

The phrase "the Jewish question" really denotes a cluster of more specific questions springing from the apostle's relationship to Judaism that spans his past as a Jew, the roles of Scripture and the law in his apostolic thinking, the nature and status of Israel there, and so on—an important set of issues. But I suggest that if we construe Galatians 2:15–16 forward then this set of Jewish questions in Paul is *irresolvable*. Any solution to it that we derive from this moment on must lack integrity in a variety of ways. But most scholars probably do not realize this—that they are slipping into a form of Arianism in this way that renders their accounts of Judaism in Paul both odious and unsustainable. And this is one point where *Deliverance* is trying to supply a conceptuality to our debates that is helpful.

Forward constructions run—obviously—forward from some problem to a corresponding solution. They begin with a particular account of a problem, and the validity and integrity of the solution therefore depends on the validity and integrity of the construction of the problem; the solution builds directly on top of the problem, rather like a house made of bricks builds up from its foundations and first courses at ground level. But it follows from this that if the antithesis in Galatians 2:15–16 is read forward then Paul is speaking of some problem in terms of "works of law" to which "faith" is the corresponding solution. And faith is

4. "We ourselves are Jews by birth and not Gentile sinners; [16] yet we know that a person is justified not by the works of the law but through faith in Jesus Christ. And we have come to believe in Christ Jesus, so that we might be justified by faith in Christ, and not by doing the works of the law, because no one will be justified by the works of the law" (NRSV).

something to do with his gospel, so works of law must be something to do with the prior basis for that gospel, here presumably in some relation to Judaism. Moreover, given that both Paul and his later converts all seem remarkably free with respect to various Jewish practices prescribed by the law, it looks as though works of law in this antithesis is describing a problematic prior Jewish state to which faith is the Christian gospel's response, a response facilitating some freedom for both Paul and his converts *from* the law. Works of law are left behind here. But the later validity of that response will of course depend on the construction of the problem—of the Jewish works of law. The argument works forward. It follows then from these interlocking assumptions that works of law must *ground* a later position of faith, *and* must do so, moreover, in way that *collapses* on itself to *produce* faith and not works of law observance. Faith, after all, supersedes and displaces them; there are no more works of law on the right hand side of the antithesis. Paul's converts do not become Torah-loving Jews. In short, the assumption that this antithesis functions prospectively entails that works of law must be an *"objective," monolithic, and self-defeating description of Judaism precisely in terms of works.* And a number of important interpretative constraints are now operative that trap the Pauline interpreter. Indeed, this reading is nothing short of a historical and theological disaster.

It is a historical disaster on two (further) counts—because it places a preexisting grid onto all investigative scholarship concerning Judaism and because that grid is unworkably negative.

In the first instance it demands a unified account of Judaism from Paul (and in fact generally) and this looks unlikely given the way historical investigation usually proliferates and complicates description over time and space.[5] But, second, the argument needs not merely a universal description but an intrinsically negative one—the position that all right-thinking Jews should realize that their divinely-authorized way of life is self-evidently inadequate and flawed and so needs to be traded up for another system like faith at the earliest opportunity. Historical investigation

5. Imagine trying to build the Christian gospel on a prior "objective" historical analysis of the church! Do scholars even give an incontestably unified account of the Old Testament, which is a simpler matter?! Perhaps even more pointedly, imagine supplying an account of the Christian gospel that ended up concluding that its deepest truth was its own utter inadequacy and need to be abandoned as soon as something better comes along—perhaps like Islam, so the central truth of Christianity, considered on its own terms, would be that Christians acknowledge the collapse of Christianity and embrace Islam.

must therefore reveal an unwavering, uniform tradition that is continually collapsed in on itself as its fundamental identity—as its deepest truth. Things could be sharpened still further here if I introduced the extra negative twist contributed by the need to supply a conditional account of Judaism in relation the law, but we have enough at present to work with. Suffice it to say then that this just does not look anything like an accurate historical account of Judaism in Paul's day.[6] It is in fact very much an *outsider's* description of Judaism, from a later, superior viewpoint being offered as the definitive *insider's* reading.[7]

But the awkwardness of the forward approach becomes even more apparent when we turn from historical problems to consider some of the implicit theological difficulties (although not by any means all of them). God's covenant has now been bifurcated into Plan A and Plan B. Two fundamentally different modes of salvation are in play. Moreover, *the first one does not work properly*. Hence it will now be impossible to give a consistent covenantal account of God in Paul's thought (i.e., a unified one).[8] It will also be impossible to give a consistently benevolent and/or sover-

6. But it looks like it does describe a significant part of the Jewish question as many scholars currently struggle with it in relation to Paul's broader interpretation—the presence of an apparently monolithic and negative description of Judaism in his writings in terms of "works of law" that NT scholars often refer to as "legalism." (*Deliverance* orients this contention around Sanders's classic account in *Paul and Palestinian Judaism*, but adjusts it more precisely in relation to concerns with prospectivism and contractualism). Even more disturbingly, it overlaps neatly with a fair amount of the anti-Jewish polemic that Christians have traditionally directed toward Jews through history (and this connection becomes even clearer when Paul's putative argument is reconstructed in detail. That is, this description of Jews becomes even worse when we add in the ways in which non-Christian Jews [ostensibly] *resist* and *reject* it! See *Deliverance*, 85–87, 96–124, 205–6, and notes).

7. In this whole relation see the penetrating critiques of Carter, *Race: A Theological Account*, and Jennings, *The Christian Imagination*, already noted in my previous essay. Carter and Jennings address the unethical and self-serving construction of "nonwhite races" by Christian theology, Jennings in dialogue especially with post-colonial dynamics. But *exactly the same criticisms apply to the Christian construction in this relation of Jews*. An earlier classic treatment of these dynamics, not reliable in all its details now but still highly informative, is Ruether, *Faith and Fratricide*. Other scholars alert to these problems in relation to Paul include John Gager, Lloyd Gaston, Stanley Stowers, and Charles Cosgrove, although in *Deliverance* I pursue a different solution from theirs to try to resolve this conundrum.

8. I realize that certain advocates of the importance of the covenant in Paul's thought will reject this suggestion. But they still need to navigate past the historical and theological difficulties generated by Paul's "works of law" texts. And I am at present not convinced that Dunn does this (see ch. 12 in *Deliverance*, 440–59), and I raise similar concerns in relation to Wright in "Is Tom Right?" 323–45.

eign account of God.[9] God in his wisdom would have placed humanity in a system that does not work and yet go on to hold them accountable for its failure. Any benevolence is limited, moreover, to the recipients of Plan B, and even then it is only available if the right conditions are continually exercised. Alternatively, God did not anticipate that Plan A would fail so badly, or indeed expect Plan B to be so limited in its effects.

However, this is not just rather unappetizing theology. Note how the basis for theology has subtly been shifted into a historicizing exercise undertaken in relation to some universal problem. Everything depends on the definition of this problem, which is taking place from within the problem ("self-evidently"), so presumably by the people located there, prior to receiving anything recognizably christological through revelation. And this is clearly anachronistic (such a commitment to the historical basis of truth is distinctively modern); and it is also a further theological catastrophe.[10] The truths about God revealed in Christ will now depend on the truths about a group of people discovered by some of those people who know the sources well. And theology is now grounded in an essentially academic battle in terms of historicism and over history. Everything will turn on the definition of Judaism that is derived from history and its reconstruction.

Now scholars have their uses in my view but deriving and justifying the fundamental truths of the gospel is not one of them. None of these interpretative battles can ultimately be won in a constructive way and some of them will never actually end! We could put this a little more technically and speak of the triumph of Troeltsch and Bousset at this point—not good things! (Note, I am not advocating abandoning historical inquiry

---

9. Barth unleashes a devastating critique along these lines in *CD* IV/1, 54–66. I agree strongly with Barth both in relation to his concerns about improperly derived "covenants" and his claim that a proper account of the Christian gospel *must* be covenantal. But a true account of the covenant must be rightly derived—retrospectively of course, hence "one covenant valid from the foundation of the world to its end, providing for human sin with the determination of Jesus as Mediator and Redeemer" (57; cf. Rom 8:29–30). This is a theological construct and not a historical one in the sense of being a historically *derived* one. NT interpreters can be insensitive to the difference between a covenant that informs and runs within history but that is disclosed or revealed, and one that is grasped by historicizing. These are completely different things.

10. See Kerr, "Ernst Troeltsch," chapter 2 in his *Christ, History and Apocalyptic*, 23–62.

but it is essential to position this mode of inquiry in the correct location, which emphatically means not in first position.[11])

In short, the forward construal of the famous antithesis between works of law and faith in Galatians 2:15–16—which is done so easily—locks the Pauline scholar into an explanatory dead end in historical and theological terms. The Jewish question becomes irresolvable. And orthodox theology becomes impossible.

Now admittedly the Jewish question will not necessarily be resolved if we can avoid the difficulties caused by a prospective reading of this data in Paul, but it will never be resolved if we do not manage to avoid reading this text forward. Moreover, if we can relocate the reference of works of law away from Judaism *per se*, then we will simplify the relevant data in Paul concerning Judaism significantly, and might make a solution to the whole question more likely.

But before we consider whether we can do this we should recall quickly that the same explanatory dynamic as this is observable in relation to all the other problems in Pauline scholarship that were noted in chapter 3, and at more length in chapters 3 through 6 of *Deliverance*. This approach in terms of forwardness causes the basic set of clashes between Paul's forensic and participatory discourses, the former generally being held to run forward and the latter backward. It generates the Procrustean account of conversion, whether in relation to Paul, his converts, or modern converts. It causes alarm to apocalyptic readers of Paul, who work backward, and it constructs the generic outsider rather like the generic Jew and so in the intrinsically harsh terms that we have just noted. It is then a larger and more pervasive problem in Pauline scholarship than we might have hitherto thought—a quagmire we need rather desperately to escape. And it has serious consequences for the church as well.[12]

11. See the careful assertions of Yeago, "The New Testament and the Nicene Dogma," 152–64; and Rowe, "Pressure," 295–312.

12. It can legitimize a rather harsh politics revolving around matters of identity, and a consequent policing of perceived boundaries in punitive terms as the church tends to "contract out of" the dire problematic situation of broader humanity to form a special privileged group. There is a concomitant inability to subject matters of Christian identity to christological scrutiny, and a corresponding need to defend increasingly fragile truth claims in relation to "creation." In other words, forwardness underwrites a "church" constructed in terms of the powerful sociological dynamic of homophily, endorsing all the sinister aspects of that dynamic. Scholars are currently exploring some these dynamics, but often unaware of their sinister dimensions, in terms of Social Identity Theory; Philip Esler's work is a useful starting point for the

So the time is clearly right to consider the solution suggested by *Deliverance*—a way that can possibly chart the scholar out of this quagmire.

Charting a Solution through Galatians 2:15–16

This route will be clarified if we turn once again to the text we have just considered. How do we solve the problem generated in relation to Judaism by expectations of forwardness in the construal of Galatians 2:15–16? Clearly by avoiding reading the text forward. But can we do this? Actually, it is surprisingly easy to advocate an alternative, non-prospective construal.

When the text says "not by works of law but by faith" it might just be articulating the straightforward antithesis that "A is not the case but B" in the sense of "I am not a Communist but a Catholic" (i.e., "I am not a zebra but an elephant"). One is not necessarily a Catholic *because* one was formerly a Communist and then went through a process of deep theoretical disillusionment, the conceptual apparatus of Communism collapsing, although in doing so preparing the way for an embrace beyond it of Catholicism—thereby suggesting, moreover, that this is the *only* way in

---

former; cf. (inter alia) his *Conflict and Identity in Romans*. A more suspicious theoretical account of these dynamics is provided by Social Dominance Theory; cf. Sidanius and Pratto, *Social Dominance*.

This dynamic goes on to generate quite concrete problems. It has made significant contributions to two cataclysmic wars centered in Europe, to various smaller genocidal wars subsequently, as in former Yugoslavia, and to the endorsement of vicious political arrangements elsewhere in history ranging from chattel slavery to apartheid. The general insensitivity of the church to such problems, coupled with its frequent complicity in them, are not negligible matters. Moreover, exegesis is clearly involved and biblical scholars ought to try to map this, and not to avoid or deny it.

A lot of people think that Paul does not have very much to say to politics that is constructive *and this is why*, in large measure. A forward-oriented reading of Paul generates a Christian politics positioned somewhere between complicity and outright aggression. But this might simply be an incorrect reading of Paul.

An excellent primer on all these connections is Harink, *Paul among the Postliberals*, esp. 67–150 and 209–54. See also Rowe's superb *World Upside Down*. There has been a vigorous attempt in recent times to read Paul in more direct revolutionary terms using the Roman empire as a foil. This trajectory is refreshing but often struggles to find explicit evidence; see (inter alia) Elliott, *The Arrogance of Nations*. I suspect a christological account of Paul's politics ultimately offers more accuracy and radicality, although this is emphatically not to dismiss either the concerns or many of the insights of those engaged with the imperial discourse—see my "Paul's Apocalyptic Politics," 129–52.

which to become a Catholic. It is more likely that one was never a Communist and always a Catholic and that one dislikes Communism *because* one is a Catholic.[13] One is not A but B.

If we read Galatians 2:15–16 as a straightforward antithesis in these terms then the underlying epistemology of the gospel of faith, which is being spoken of on the right hand side of the antithesis so to speak, must be revelational. But this is not a difficult thing to argue in Galatians (see esp. 1:11–12, 15–16; and 3:23).[14] And if the text is presupposing a revealed gospel and articulating a straightforward antithesis between works of law and faith we are in much better shape in general interpretative terms.

If any shift to the gospel takes place because of revelation then the truth of the gospel is grounded in that revelation and no longer depends on the truth of some prior phase. Prior phases can still be present in psychological, rhetorical, or sociological terms, and probably will be, but they have no fundamental epistemological value. And although we would expect Paul to address prior salvation historical realities at some point, *these no longer need to be addressed here either, in a foundationalist manner,* and this is a very significant step forward for the whole cluster of Jewish interpretative questions that arise in relation to Paul.[15] It follows from this, moreover, that any motif in a Pauline text set in contrast to the gospel no longer needs to denote a prior causal phase or state. Hence the grounding of faith in revelation liberates the other half of the antithesis in Galatians 2:16 that speaks of works of law from the need to be anything. It can just be what it is. But can a responsible reading of the actual exegetical data be offered in these terms?

13. Obviously this example does not view Alasdair MacIntyre as paradigmatic.

14. J. L. (Lou) Martyn (1997) has of course offered us a sustained and powerful reading of the letter in such terms.

15. That is, any prior phase to the gospel can now be understood more clearly if not definitively in the light of the dazzling clarity and truth that has arrived with the gospel's disclosure, *retrospectively* (cf. 2 Cor 4:4–6; Phil 3:7–8). So, if we are considering Judaism, Paul will presumably supply a retrospective account of Judaism (i.e., of salvation history) *grounded in the revealed truths of the gospel* (cf. Rom 9:4–5). It will no longer be a historicizing account then, and we will be freed from the tyrannies and vagaries of scholars at this point (as we need to be). Neither will this Jewish construct be a vestibule through which everyone must pass en route to salvation. In fact, properly understood, it may not necessarily have to be left behind at all—a false understanding of Judaism, perhaps, but a *genuine* understanding?—possibly not at all (Cf. Rom 10:4; 15:8; 1 Cor 9:20; Gal 2:7–9). For a slightly longer articulation of this argument see my "Paul's Gospel, 'Apocalyptic,' and Salvation-History," chapter 3 in *Quest*, 56–68.

The good news—at least for this text—is that there are no obvious impediments to reading Galatians 2:15–16 in terms of a mere antithesis. This reading works perfectly well at the level of mere construal. We could go on to paraphrase Paul's text in verse 16 in such terms as "knowing that a [Jewish Christian] person is not delivered through works of Torah except (also) through the faithfulness of Jesus Christ, we also have become convinced with respect to Christ Jesus that we all are delivered through the gospel centered on Christ's fidelity and *not* through any gospel also involving works of Torah."[16]

But what is Paul talking about here when he references "works of Torah," and rather negatively? We need to supply a plausible answer to this question for our alternative, revelational reading to work. But fortunately, an obvious answer does not lie very far away.

In all his letters, with minor exceptions, Paul opposes false teachers who are troubling his communities with bad accounts of the gospel, alternatively seducing and tyrannizing his precious converts (and here we reach back to some foundational insights in the work of F. C. Baur),[17] and such figures are clearly present in Galatia. A useful name for their countervailing program that Paul is rightly reluctant to call a "gospel" is "religion." I mean by this any account of Christian salvation that undermines the gospel's unconditionality and grace—a "Jesus-and . . ." approach one might say—in other words, contractualism.[18] And

16. Personal faith understood in certain carefully qualified terms could be substituted in here for the references to Christ's fidelity, while the last reference, if present, evokes Christ's passion and resurrection. This text is treated in more detail, and the reading justified more closely, in *Deliverance*, 839–47.

17. Such third parties are clearly involved with the situations evoking 1 Cor, 2 Cor, Gal, Phil, and 1 Thess. I argue at length in *Deliverance* that this is the only explanation that makes sense of Romans (469–518), so this approach explains six of the seven letters in the "seven letter canon," excepting only the very short Philemon. If the Pauline "canon" is expanded to ten letters then third parties again lie clearly behind Colossians, and a specific type of external interference also probably explains 2 Thess (cf. 2:1–2). Ephesians then seems to be the only significant exception to this basic explanatory approach to Paul's texts, which draws on the founder of modern Pauline studies, F. C. Baur; see in particular his classic *Paul, the Apostle of Jesus Christ*. There are important methodological difficulties that have to be navigated when reconstructing any putative opponents precisely, but these do not detract from the basic insight that opponents are critical in explanatory terms; see esp. Barclay, "Mirror Reading"; and Sumney, *Identifying Paul's Opponents*.

18. James B. Torrance's analyses of contractualism over against authentic covenantalism are, of course, especially helpful at this point; see his "Covenant and Contract," and "The Contribution of McLeod Campbell to Scottish Theology" (both essays are reprinted in this volume in the appendices).

this observation points to a further important element in the solution articulated by *Deliverance*: a non-prospective reading of many of the key texts roots them more strongly in their practical circumstances, which is a significant advantage in any scholarly contest between construals.[19]

Good readings of Pauline letters are usually informed by robust accounts of their circumstances—of the factors that caused them to be written in the first place, and so written in a certain way—something *Deliverance*, borrowing a useful term from Derrida, discusses more precisely in terms of framing.[20] Prospective readings tend to lift their texts out of situational explanations by universalizing them into generic accounts of the gospel, and this can be a hard thing to justify in contextual terms. Non-prospective readers have plenty of gritty contingent information just to hand, however. They can consequently suggest that a strictly comparative argument is being signaled in Galatians 2:15–16 by Paul in which he will contrast his gospel with the religious system of certain troublesome opponents present in some sense at Galatia blow by blow and scriptural text by scriptural text. And such an account of the text in contextual terms needs no further explanation. It is entirely practical and understandable—the sort of situation that still arises frequently in Christian communities today (and not just in Christian communities of course). These texts arose out of conflict. This, indeed, is why they were written.

If non-prospective readers can support their readings with contingent framing explanations like these and prospective readers cannot, then the former turn out to enjoy a further advantage in any exegetical contest. But before moving on it is vital to note what has happened in broader interpretative terms.

Our difficulties with Jewish description in Paul in this relation—in terms of "works" and "legalism"—have disappeared because Paul is no longer describing Judaism in this text. Moreover, *all* the difficulties generated by *any* type of prospectivism in this text have evaporated—any clashes with retrospective thinking elsewhere in Paul, any crude rationalistic understanding of conversion, any grim construction of the non-Christian, and so on. And this very ease of interpretation—this problem-free quality at the levels of argumentation and broader theory

19. The importance of this sort of "contingent" explanation was articulated especially by Beker, *Paul the Apostle*, esp. 11–19; cf. 23–36; and xiii–xx in the 1984 edition.

20. See *Deliverance*, 225–28, 30, and endnotes.

and theology—functions as good evidence for the likelihood of this reading. Other readings generate these difficulties, but this merely antithetical approach does not. So which should be preferred? Obviously the reading that raises the fewest difficulties, hence the non-prospective, antithetical one.[21] And it is, in addition, the most responsible *contingent* reading.

But we have now not only navigated around any difficulties caused by prospectivism in this text, and done so in a responsible historical critical fashion; *we have mapped out what a solution to these particular difficulties through all of the rest of Paul will look like.*

Charting a Solution in General Terms

We have learned from our analysis of Galatians 2:15–16 that any successful account of a Pauline text in this relation will possess integrity in four different ways:

1. *contingent integrity*—a plausible account of the circumstances surrounding the composition and reception of the section of text in question, along with, presumably, of the letter as a whole;

2. *exegetical integrity*—an accurate account of the lexical and syntactical data in terms of sheer construal, that is, in basic lexical, grammatical, and phenomenological terms, insofar as modern scholars can reconstruct those;

3. *argumentative integrity*—a plausible account of the rhetoric and argument of the text in question, and this obviously ought to accord with criterion one above, but will be greatly eased by the presence of opponents, although to be successful in this relation any argumentation ought *not* to presuppose any form of prospectivism; rather, it ought to presuppose . . .

4. *theoretical integrity*—a fundamentally revelational account of the gospel, and hence a derivative, retrospective account of salvation history and of Judaism, as well as of any other analogous matters.

---

21. Note that some have not understood how these moves allow the traditional *content* of "works of law" in terms of legalism and the like to be retained, the exegetical dimension in my suggested construals thereby staying quite close to the traditional approach. But only the *reference* of the text has been shifted from Judaism to a false gospel, so no overarching theory or account of the gospel is now being launched in prospective terms with all its vicious consequences.

Two implications within this articulation now need to be accented.

First, it needs to be understood that *multiple interpretative dimensions are now operative in relation to any construal* and, furthermore, that the failure to satisfy *one* of these at any given moment *will cause the entire solution to founder.* My respondents have generally been insensitive to this so it needs to be emphasized here quite strongly.

As Tolstoy once famously put this, addressing a different issue, although the truth remains the same: "Happy families are all alike; every unhappy family is unhappy in its own way."[22] That is, readings, like marriages, are *complex* situations. Hence many things must work together at once if they are to work at all, but failure in any single subordinate system will cause the entire complex to malfunction.[23] So a happy construal is one in which everything is working well together, and that is clearly what we want. But in order to find it interpreters of Paul must learn to hold numerous, rather different interpretative dimensions together while reading him, and any failure to do so will lead ultimately to the payment of a hefty interpretative price.

The second critical implication that needs to be accented concerns the theoretical dimension. Needless to say, failure in this single dimension will lead to the failure of the whole—an unhappy construal will result—and this can happen in various ways.

The theoretical solution to the general problematic I chart in *Deliverance* was apparent in the sketch of the solution already evident in Galatians 2:15–16. We solved our localized problem there with respect to Judaism by reading that text at the argumentative level, (merely) antithetically and not forward, thereby presupposing a gospel rooted in revelation, that is, a retrospective theological epistemology. And we solve our problems generally in this relation in just the same way. If we read Paul consistently backward and *never* read him forward in underlying theological and epistemological terms, then this approach takes us out of our quagmire. But, conversely, if we read him forward anywhere in any

---

22. Tolstoy, *Anna Karenina*, 1.

23. So—to switch metaphors—it is rather like flying a plane. Everything needs to work at once if the plane is to take off and fly successfully. But failure in any one of several critical systems will lead to catastrophe. Hence, the engines, the landing gear, and the guidance system can all be working perfectly, but the loss of a wing will still doom the plane. The same holds for readings of Paul's texts, and especially for doctrinal or theological readings.

significant way then we are back in the swamp generated by foundational-ism. And several aspects of this basic insight now need to be appreciated.

Without the elimination of forwardness from Paul's interpretation, the widespread problems generated by it are permanent and intractable. They are precisely the problems of forwardness, and of forwardness operating juxtaposed with backwardness. Only if forwardness goes *in toto* then do these problems and tensions go. If it stays then they stay.[24] So there can be no compromise here. It is not a "both-and" situation but a strict "either-or."[25]

It is important to appreciate, moreover, that any forwardness will be particularly dangerous if it operates in relation to reconstructions of

24. It follows as well that if it has been eliminated at certain points, interpreters should also try to avoid *reactivating* it, whether overtly, or more subtly and sublimi-nally, e.g., as a traditioned association of key words and slogans like "justification." Space constraints preclude articulating this important dimension of things here as they deserve. I am particularly concerned about etymological reactivations, where sig-nifiers like "justification" can be especially problematic. And I am also concerned with reactivations caused by more general expectations of conditionality or soteriological contractualism—a major concern in *Deliverance*. These reactivate foundationalism or prospectivism automatically. Unfortunately, any construal of human agency or freedom in terms of "choice" leads almost inevitably to conditionality, to soteriologi-cal contractualism, and hence to "forwardism," as well, so the broader discussion of agency is involved at this point. But I do not have the space here to discuss these further critical issues as they deserve. And my respondents have not raised any of these important matters.

Conditionality and contractualism are identified and exposed helpfully by James B. Torrance in the studies already noted—"Covenant and Contract" and "The Contribution of McLeod Campbell." "Freedom" is analyzed helpfully by Bauckham in *God and the Crisis of Freedom*. Also informative in this relation are Gunton, *Enlight-enment and Alienation*; and Lakoff, *Whose Freedom?* A more thoroughly theological account of freedom is developed by Barth, especially in *CD* III/1 and IV/2.

25. Some of my respondents seem to think that this is overstating things and that some compromise is possible here. So Macaskill opines, "[w]hat is required . . . is a reading of Paul that can sustain such a theology [i.e., union with Christ] without dis-carding the forensic or contractual elements found in Romans 1:18—3:20" ("Review," 160); and Matlock asserts, "Campbell plays off against one another concepts that Paul holds together: the 'justice' and 'mercy' of God; 'justification' and 'participation.'" What is needed rather is "a satisfactory account of the interdependence of 'justifica-tion' and 'participation'" ("Zeal for Paul," 147).

But I am not so sure that the differences between Athanasius and Arius—or be-tween Barth and Bultmann—can be erased on this advice from two New Testament scholars. Neither Macaskill nor Matlock demonstrates how these differences can be negotiated in concrete terms—or supplies as much as a reference to someone who can show us how to do this—so I remain worried that they simply are not grasping the problems here properly, and are offering advice that amounts to mere appeasement.

Paul's soteriology because of its strategic importance for his thinking more broadly.[26] And any compromise in soteriology will be exacerbated by the fact that a foundationalist, forward-looking soteriology *will start first*; it will be the one that analysts begin with, in its account of the pre-Christian problem, so it will tend to override any later commitments to revelational and retrospective soteriology, should they be present in Paul as well. The forward-operating soteriology will frame and control the healthier version and Paul will, in soteriological terms, thereby be reduced in practice to a forward model. In other words, a prospective account of "justification" *will frame and dominate* any retrospective account in terms of "sanctification." (The alternative here is a picture of utter confusion, which most interpreters understandably avoid.)

It should be noted further that Paul's Christology will occupy a secondary explanatory position as well. The Christology in any forward account of soteriology is compromised by explanatory constraints introduced in its account of the problem, which dictate the shape of the solution; and the healthier, more central Christology in any alternative retrospective soteriology will be constrained by the prior presence of the forward system as just noted. To construe Paul forward then is to construe him inevitably in christologically constrained and fundamentally Arian terms. This is not to suggest that readings should be rejected simply because of their potentially unpalatable theological implications, but it is to note on which side of the debate any pressure from orthodoxy ought to be felt.

But it is apparent by this point in our discussion as well that any solution to our rather awful problems can be an *economic* one. Indeed a general solution to our difficulties will not add anything to Paul that is not already there; everyone agrees that for much of the time he thinks backward. So a solution needs only to eliminate any additional discourse

26. Part of the agenda of my *Quest*; see esp. "soteriologies have conceptions of 'the problem,' of 'the solution,' and of 'the transfer' between them. Within these broad categories they contain opinions of the nature of sin, of the atonement, of humanity, of Christ's nature and function, of God, of the role of the Spirit, and of the nature of the Christian condition, which may in particular have its ecclesial and ethical aspects usefully distinguished. There are important attendant claims about epistemology. So all the usual critical *loci* of theology intersect in these basic questions about salvation . . . [s]o the assumption that this soteriological focus overlaps directly with central matters in Paul's theological conceptuality seems prima facie justified. This focus almost certainly contains Paul's properly basic convictions that tend to give rise to his other commitments that are then, by definition, secondary" (33).

in terms of forwardness making Paul's overarching description simpler and more consistent. It will treat forwardness as a disturbing foreign interpretative accretion—which is quite possibly what it is. (We will return to this important possibility in chapter 9.)

Finally in this relation it is important to appreciate that the elimination of forwardness does not entail the elimination of all forensic terminology and rhetoric from Paul's theology. As we saw in Galatians 2:15-16, one half of this material—correctly interpreted, in revelational terms—continues to speak fairly directly of Paul's gospel: the faith side of the antithesis.[27] Only the opposing side concerning works of law was redeployed dogmatically as its concrete reference was shifted away from Judaism in general. All of this data might need to be subtly reinterpreted but 50 percent of it will continue to be applicable directly to Paul himself.

In closing then let us firm up our map of this path to a solution— and further clarify some treacherous byways to avoid that run away from it—by returning to consider Galatians 2:15-16 for one last time.

The Geographical Key

Earlier we found what we might call a merely antithetical and revelational construal of Galatians 2:15-16 resolved any difficulties with Jewish description and so by implication resolved any other problems associated with forwardness. In view of all its successes then we might ask why anyone would read Galatians 2:15-16 differently. And yet we frequently encounter an expectation of forwardness in the antithesis between works of law and faith in commentators on Galatians 2:15-16, while sometimes it seems as if there are no alternatives. But some might suggest I am making this up so here is a brief slate of instances, plucked almost randomly from a library shelf, demonstrating the presence of my concern.

This movement is clear in Luther's lectures on Galatians published in 1535: "Now the true way to Christianity is this, that a man do *first* acknowledge himself by the law, to be a sinner, and that it is impossible for him to do any good work. . . . When a man is thus taught and instructed by the law, then he is terrified and humbled, *then* he seeth indeed the

---

27. There is an important intertextual quality to Paul's argumentation here that I explore repeatedly in *Deliverance* in dependence on seminal work by Richard B. Hays and others (see especially Hays's *Echoes of Scripture*); see 610-16, 26-27, 688-702, 729-50, 86-87, 91-92, 797-809.

greatness of his sin. . . . The *first* part then of Christianity is the preaching of repentance, and the knowledge of ourselves."[28] Luther said a lot of other things, many in my view basically incompatible with this material (and this is the real import of chapter 8 in *Deliverance*), but he did say these things too. And he was a reasonably influential commentator. We would expect his views to recur in subsequent readings, and they do.

This forward argumentative movement is subtly apparent in Ernst de Witt Burton's classic ICC treatment: "[The phrase 'by Works of Law'] . . . is *causal*, giving the *reason* for the ἐπιστεύσαμεν of the principal clause" (*Commentary on Galatians*, 119, emphasis added). Burton is not reducible to this dynamic but it is present. And it is apparent as well in H. D. Betz's famous rhetorical commentary, where the frequent theoretical or doctrinal associations of the key terms are also apparent:

> The second part of the "self-definition" [in v. 16] contains what is traditionally called Paul's doctrine of justification by faith. . . . The first word of verse 16 states the *basis* for being a Christian in distinction from being a Jew . . . [which is a] theological conviction. . . . Next we are given the content of that conviction, again in the form of doctrinal principles. It is the denial of the orthodox Jewish (Pharisaic) doctrine of salvation . . . by doing and thus fulfilling the ordinances of Torah.[29]

The basis of the gospel is the failure then of Jewish works, and the argument works forward. And the same prospectivism is apparent in F. F. Bruce: "How can a man be just . . . before God? . . . [Paul] considers one answer ('By works of law')—the answer which he himself would previously have given—and dismisses it; he offers a new answer ('By faith in Christ')."[30] Not surprisingly, it is also apparent in Thomas R. Schreiner's recent analysis: "Paul *grounds* the claim that Jews, such as Peter and Paul, are only justified by faith in Christ with the proposition that no one anywhere can be righteous before God by doing the law."[31]

This movement is not equally apparent in all commentators interpreting Galatians 2:15–16. Neither are any of these commentators reducible to this dynamic. But it is certainly present in many, while alternative construals are not always as clear or cogent. So it remains a significant

28. Luther, *Commentary*, 131, emphases added.
29. Betz, *Galatians*, 115–16, emphasis added.
30. Bruce, *Epistle to the Galatians*, 138.
31. Schreiner, *Galatians*, 166, emphasis added.

problem. When it is present, *contradiction is unleashed and confusion ultimately reigns.* Paul oscillates between anticipating Athanasius and anticipating Arius.

There is no need to address here all the reasons for the widespread and complex advocacy of forwardness in Paul. *Deliverance* supplies a fuller account.[32] Given the fact that this destructive advocacy of Arianism in Paul exists we need to consider in closing this essay how exactly it makes its case. And our analysis can begin here with the important observation that Galatians 2:15-16 is too brief to launch a prospective argument definitively by itself. It simply does not say explicitly that it is summarizing an argumentative progression. It *might* be, but it might *not* be—and we have already met with some good reasons to think that it might not. So what we tend to find—admittedly oversimplifying a complex picture, but hopefully without too much distortion—is a set of appeals to a prospective soteriology embedded in the distinctive terminology of Galatians 2:16, which, as we have already seen, opposes works of law to faith in terms of justification, a process assumed to run forward, coupled with a broader general expectation that in relation to certain questions Paul just obviously thinks forward. ("What else would he be saying?!") In other words, we tend to encounter an expectation that a particular doctrinal construction must be operative at this point in relation to certain words and phrases. So something of an interlaced linguistic and conceptual trail now lies before us.

It leads to a family of distinctive texts in Paul. And consideration of these allows us to expand the specific terms involved appropriately from works, faith, and justification, to include things like "circumcision" and "uncircumcision," Abraham, and particular scriptural quotations, which further reinforces the identification of the distinctive texts because almost all these key terms and phrases occur in a well defined group. And these texts are, in the main, Romans 1:16—5:1 and 9:30—10:21 (the terminology fading through this last passage), Galatians 2:15—3:29 (although the terms also fade toward the end of this material) and 5:5-6, and Philippians 3:2-11 (especially vv. 6 and 9).[33]

32. Largely in ch. 9, 284-309.

33. *Deliverance* analyzes this material in 767-70. It also treats shorter passages that often use some of the key terms but possess more ambiguous relationships to the obvious texts—Rom 5:1-2; 6:7-8; 11:20-23; 12:1-8; 14:1, 2, 21, 23; 1 Cor 1:30; 2 Cor 4:13; 5:21; Gal 1:23, 6:10; 1 Thess 1:9b-10. Note that these texts, along with the slightly longer texts that *Deliverance* calls the "heartland," are too abbreviated and therefore

But we can cut a long story short here by recalling the set of explanatory criteria that we have just identified. At some point an advocate of forward thinking in Paul will need to find a text that speaks explicitly of a forward-oriented *theory* of salvation—that spells this theory out explicitly and fully—and that decisive text is obviously Romans 1:16—4:25. It is longer than all the other relevant texts put together and it apparently lays things out systematically and clearly for chapter after chapter. But another shortcut is possible at this point.

Because the theory being released is oriented forward the decisive argumentative and theoretical phase must be the account of the problem, to which a corresponding solution is supplied in 3:21—5:1, being anticipated in 1:16–17. And the problem is articulated in Romans 1:18—3:20. So *this* text will actually be the launching pad for the prospective understanding of much of Paul's thought and will therefore be the critical locus for the entire swamp that we have earlier described. Everything will stand or fall in relation to it. It is, indeed, either the heart of the problem or the heart of its solution. So it will repay us to consider this text very carefully indeed—the subject of chapter 9.

---

ambiguous to launch theoretical prospectivism if that reading is being contested.

7

A Response to Campbell's "Connecting the Dots"

DAVID HILBORN

Douglas Campbell has produced an ambitious interdisciplinary *tour de force* in *The Deliverance of God*. Those who, like me, are not New Testament specialists but who seek to ensure that their work in other theological fields is informed by contemporary biblical scholarship, will surely appreciate its rich synthesis of systematics, ethics, social theology, and church history with biblical exegesis and hermeneutics.

In relation to Campbell's second paper, chapter 6, I have a number of points to raise—most of them for clarification, but all, I hope, in a spirit of general admiration for what I am sure will be seen as a landmark publication in the study of Paul.

Campbell's second paper builds on the dichotomy drawn in his first paper, chapter 3, between Arian and Athanasian approaches to Paul—that is, between what he variously calls the "foundationalist," "individualistic," "conditional," "forensic," "contractual," and "mythological" model that has pertained in the Western, Latin tradition since at least the fourth century, and the "revelational" or "apocalyptic" reading that he expounds in *Deliverance*. The revelational and apocalyptic approach is cast as more authentically theological because in Campbell's view it is more properly christological and Trinitarian. On this reading it may be classified as "Athanasian" mainly, it appears, because it eschews Karl Barth's *bête noire*, the "analogy of being": that is, a domesticated, human-ly-constructed and even idolatrous procedure by which *we* seek to define God in relation to known natural phenomena, rather than allowing God to confront and define *us* in radical encounter with his self-disclosed and self-authenticating Word. Specifically, this baleful anthropocentric construct is associated with Arius on the basis that Arius' Christology is posited on an analogy for God constituting the foundation on which the rest of the system is constructed.[1] This same Arian foundationalism is then shown to pervade what Campbell terms "Justification Theory"— a theory with more overt roots in Augustine that intensified in the work of the Protestant Reformers, especially Luther, Melanchthon, and Calvin.

While I broadly concur with Campbell's appropriation of Athanasius and Arius as representative of the two very different theological methodologies he contrasts, I must say I am slightly less convinced than Chris Tilling of the propriety of reading Athanasius so clearly through the lens of Barth's polemic against the "Arianism" of *his* early twentieth-century context—namely, Emil Brunner's natural theology.[2] Tilling concludes that "the shape of *De Incarnatione* speaks strongly" for Campbell's dichotomy, but I would suggest with Peter Leithart that we must be rather more cautious about presenting Athanasius as a proto-Barthian in this respect.[3] Without doubt Athanasius is assiduous in keeping creation close to the Word of God, and thus christologically grounded. Yet in section 12 of *De Incarnatione* it is notable that he commends phrases from Romans 1:18–32 as positive statements of what humans might learn of God from "the works of creation" or the "harmony of creation."[4] Granted, the chief aspect of the created order that points us to God here is the image of God in us, which is itself "the Word of the Father." But in Athanasius' account this is far from being the *only* "means of the work of creation" by which we might know God. Of course, Athanasius recognizes those means as finally partial, inadequate, and corrupted by sin, which is why God "sojourns here as man, taking to Himself a body like others, and from things of earth, that is by the works of His body, [teaches them] who

---

1. Campbell, "The Current Crisis," chapter 3 page 39.

2. Tilling, "Campbell's Apocalyptic Gospel," chapter 4 page 67.

3. Ibid., chapter 67 page 89. Cf. Leithart, Peter J., *Athanasius*, 182.

4. Schaff and Wace, *Nicene and Post-Nicene Fathers, Second Series Vol. IV*, Section 12:1, 3, 42–43.

would not know Him from His Providence and rule over all things . . . [to] know the Word of God which is in the body."[5] Even so, the revelation of God through creation is in some, albeit attenuated, sense in *apocalyptic continuity* with the revelation of God in Christ, rather than in absolute *disjunction* from it.

Insofar as Campbell appropriates Athanasius for his own more thoroughly polarized construal of "apocalyptic" versus "foundationalist" models of Pauline epistemology, this is problematic, and it is problematic not least because Athanasius appears to read Romans 1:18–32 "straight," whereas Campbell crucially reinterprets it as prosopopoeic "speech-in-character" voiced by a teacher who is hostile to Paul's true intent. Others will be more competent to assess the exegetical coherence of this prosopopoeic reading. I merely suggest that attaching the apocalyptic paradigm it serves to Athanasius might need somewhat more qualification than Campbell has offered.

This point ties in with another fundamental distinction drawn by Campbell: that between "forward" or "prospective" readings of the antithesis of "works of the law" and "faith" as Paul relates it to the Jews, and "backward" or "retrospective" readings of the same antithesis. Campbell very clearly associates the authentic, "Athanasian" reading as "backwards" and the misconstrued "Arian" reading as "forwards." In chapter 6 of this volume, that association is expounded specifically with respect to Galatians 2:15–16, but it has general import for Pauline soteriology as a whole. So in Campbell's depiction of them "forward constructionists" move "forward from some problem to a corresponding solution," and in their reading of this text the problem is expressed in terms of "'works of the law' to which 'faith' is the corresponding solution."[6] Yet for Campbell this implies a "problematic prior Jewish state to which 'faith' is the Christian gospel's response, a response facilitating some freedom for both Paul and his converts *from* the law.[7] This prospective reading thus entails that works of the law "must be an objectively monolithic *and* self-defeating descriptive account of Judaism precisely in terms of 'works.'" However, Campbell goes on to describe this entailment as "nothing short of a historical and theological disaster"—one that not only distorts Paul's his-

---

5. Athanasius, "Of the Incarnation," Section 14:8, in Schaff and Wace, *Nicene and Post-Nicene Fathers Vol. IV,* 44.

6. Campbell, "Connecting the Dots," 96.

7. Ibid., 98.

torical context, but that has legitimized subsequent Christian collusion with militarism, colonialism, genocide, slavery, and apartheid.[8] Why? Because, he insists, "it generates a false account of conversion [that] constructs the generic outsider rather like the generic Jew . . . in . . . intrinsically harsh terms."[9]

In contradistinction to all this, Campbell proposes a "retrospective" reading that moves back to the perceived "problem" in light of the subsequent "solution," rather than vice versa. As he expresses it:

> When the text says "not by works of law" but "by faith" it might just be articulating the straightforward antithesis that "A is not the case but B" in the sense of "I am not a Communist but a Catholic." One is not necessarily a Catholic because one was formerly a Communist and then went through a process of deep theoretical disillusionment, the conceptual apparatus of Communism collapsing, although in doing so preparing the way for an embrace beyond it of Catholicism—thereby suggesting, moreover, that this is the only way in which to become a Catholic. *It is more likely that one was never a Communist and always a Catholic* and that one dislikes Communism because one is a Catholic. One is not A but B.[10]

On this construal, Campbell suggests that Galatians 2:16 can be paraphrased as "knowing that a [Jewish Christian] person is not delivered through works of Torah except also through the faithfulness of Jesus Christ, we also have become convinced with respect to Christ Jesus that we are all delivered through the gospel centred on Christ's fidelity and *not* through an gospel also involving works of Torah." On this account, the text "no longer" needs to be talking about Judaism; rather, it is talking far more generally about that brand of false teaching that replaces "Athanasian" apocalypticism with "Arian" or "religious" contractualism.[11]

Once again I claim no specialized exegetical expertise in relation to this interpretation, but as one who is more generally concerned with theological method I cannot help perceiving certain potential tensions and difficulties in it.

Firstly, I would want to ask whether Judaism in this and related Pauline texts is not more than merely the contingent "context of discourse"

8. Ibid., 93.

9. Ibid., 101.

10. Ibid., 102–3. Emphasis added.

11. Ibid., 105.

from which Paul moves on to construct his global soteriology. For all his concern that Judaism not be singled out as the "unique negative other" in opposition to the gospel, that it be not reified or mythologized as a part of an Arian ethnic polemic, is there not an equal and opposite danger that Campbell's universalizing exposition might underplay the quite specific and positive contribution made by the patriarchs, the law, and Israel itself to the divine "rescue mission"? Or as Tilling puts it in chapter 4, could it not in fact be that Paul's christological vision is divine *precisely because* the Christ-relation is, as a pattern, analogous to the YHWH-Israel relation?[12] After all, here in Galatians, the "Jerusalem above" is still recognizably Jerusalem (4:26); the ethnically diverse heirs of the promise are still "heirs of Isaac" (4:28); love, which otherwise dissolves distinctions between Jew and Greek, circumcised and uncircumcised, is still love as derived from and defined by the Torah (5:14).

In raising this question of old and new covenant continuities I do not, like Douglas Moo, charge Campbell with "incipient Marcionism"![13] Yet I do wonder how precisely the "faithfulness of Christ"—that reading of *pistis christou* in Galatians 2:16 and elsewhere that so underpins Campbell's Athanasian-apocalyptic paradigm—redounds to those who pre-dated the incarnation. What is the content of their *apocalypsis*, given that the incarnation is so central to Athanasian or revelational soteriology? My reading of *Deliverance* leads me to infer that this question is more fully addressed by Campbell's exposition of Romans 9–11 there,[14] but I would nonetheless appreciate clarification on how he understands it in relation to Galatians and other Pauline epistles.

My remaining concerns are more directly related to theological method, hermeneutics and argumentation. In his chapter 6 Campbell suggests that "prospective readings tend to lift their texts out of situational explanations by universalizing them into generic accounts of the gospel."[15] Yet as I have already hinted, Campbell himself might unwittingly have risked making just such a move in his otherwise admirable drive to shift the focus of Galatians from a Jewish to an essentially human problematic. Both in the previous chapter of this volume and in chapter 6 of *Deliverance*, Campbell commends poststructuralist approaches

12. Tilling, "Campbell's Apocalyptic Gospel," 60.

13. Moo, "The Deliverance of God," 150.

14. Campbell, *Deliverance*, 765–820.

15. Campbell, "Connecting the Dots," 105.

to texts for their critique of what Jean-François Lyotard calls "totalizing metanarratives" and what Jacques Derrida terms "logocentrism"—that is, the imposition of "uniform and universal patterns upon reality." As Campbell notes, these poststructuralist readings typically seek to expose the tendency of such grand, universalizing explanations to undermine and undercut themselves: "reality," he writes, "almost invariably squeezes out of the categories that are applied to it; it is a more complex, subtle, difficult thing than much theorizing admits."[16] Moreover, "such theorizing often masks unacknowledged ethical and political agendas. Reality in such templates is then not being explained so much as confirmed to what it should be like in view of the theorizer."[17]

As might be imagined, Campbell levels precisely this poststructuralist critique at the Arian or contractual paradigm. Justification Theory is a totalizing, logocentric metanarrative imposed artificially on a Pauline theology that in fact unfolds endogenously, "blow by blow and scriptural text by scriptural text."[18] Yet for all the "local" or "cumulative" exegetical criteria highlighted by Campbell as vital for understanding Paul, it could be argued that he himself goes on to totalize the dichotomy he has drawn between "forward" and "backward" theologizing with respect not only to Galatians 2:15–16, or Pauline theology, but to theology as such. Indeed, he asserts that "only if forwardness goes *in toto* . . . do these problems and tensions go. If it stays then they stay."[19] The binary opposition here then, in fact, becomes even more decisive: it becomes, at heart, a matter of orthodoxy versus heresy: "To construe Paul forward then is to construe him inevitably in christologically constrained and fundamentally Arian terms," a posture condemned by the church as heretical.[20]

By raising the stakes in this way—by making an antithesis in the reading which Paul *himself* has constructed tantamount to the antithesis between orthodoxy and heresy—Campbell stands either to gain or to lose significantly depending on whether exceptions or complications in that antithesis can be demonstrated, not least in his own work. I do not say definitively that such complications exist, but I will suggest two areas in which a poststructuralist approach *might*, ironically, reveal challenges

16. Campbell, *Deliverance*, 209. Cf. Lyotard, *The Post-Modern Condition*, 13–37; Derrida, *Of Grammatology*, ch. 3.

17. Campbell, *Deliverance*, 209.

18. Campbell, "Connecting the Dots," 105.

19. Ibid., 108.

20. Ibid., 109.

to his argument. I will do so again to invite clarification and disambiguation, rather than to make any conclusive judgment.

First, the hard question needs to be asked whether, in rejecting justification as an extrinsic imposition on the gospel, Campbell has not inadvertently replaced it with other extrinsically construed metanarratives that might, like justification, bear an apparent resonance with the semantic field of the New Testament, but that actually *function* in a more "Arian" way. If it is possible to construe "faith" in a mythological sense, is it not also possible to do the same with similarly benign yet culturally amenable concepts like "benevolence" and "nonviolence"—that is, with Campbell's favored ethical imperatives? No doubt it might be argued that these stem more palpably from the *apocalypsis*—that they are more demonstrable in the life, work, and redemptive acts of Jesus. And this is indeed how Campbell presented them in his chapter 3. Since Christ died for us "when we were still sinners" (Rom 5:8), he wrote we are saved unconditionally, through an act "of pure overflowing benevolence that operates prior to all human actions."[21] Benevolence is thus "fundamental" for Campbell, and because it absorbs punishment and bears it off in Christ, such benevolence is "primary" in a way that "wrath" and "penalty" are not. Yet what of other potentially "primary" attributes of God might function in a similarly fundamental way to "extinguish" sin?[22] What, for example, of holiness, which the Congregationalist theologian P. T. Forsyth insisted on as a corollary of divine benevolence and love at a time when they were threatening to subsume the doctrine of God at the expense of God's awesome otherness?[23] What of divine judgment or "judgliness," which is clearly to be distinguished from justification on Campbell's account, but which seems somehow less fundamental than benevolence? Could this very privileging of benevolence, if not its actual content, reveal a bias or predisposition that is *itself* prone to mythologizing? And inasmuch as Campbell links it inextricably to nonviolence, could it have led him to downplay not only the exercise of divine vengeance in the Hebrew Scriptures (e.g., Deut 7:1–2; 20:16–20; Josh 6:17–20; 1 Sam 15:1–8) but also the bloody conflicts depicted by Jesus, John, and indeed Paul in the various apocalyptic discourses of the New Testament (Mark

21. Campbell, "The Current Crisis," 44.

22. Ibid., 46.

23. Forsyth, *God the Holy Father*. For background and context see Hunter, *P. T. Forsyth: Per Crucem ad Lucem*.

13:5–19; Rev 14:14–20; 1 Thess 1:5—2:17)? To be fair, in chapter 3 of *Deliverance* Campbell does concede that Pauline eschatology is "mixed" in relation to punitive action by God, rather than uniformly opposed to it.[24] Yet it would still be helpful to know whether Campbell sees the possibility of over-determining even benevolence and nonviolence in the way I have outlined. As a further spur to his reflections on this question, I would suggest that the focus of Athanasius in *De Incarnatione* is not benevolence so much as *communication*—the communication of God to humanity through his Word spoken in creation and prophecy, and as enfleshed in Jesus. This communication is no doubt deeply relational, but it is not most obviously or most prominently agapeistic—at least not to the extent implied by Campbell in his "Athanasian" construal of Paul.

A second hard question concerns not so much soteriological uni-versalization as soteriological *universalism*. For Campbell, the very un-conditionality of divine benevolence in rescuing us from sin means that "we can contribute *nothing* to our salvation."[25] Since he goes on from here to invoke Barth's famous recasting of election in universalist terms in the *Church Dogmatics*,[26] it might appear for Campbell also that all humanity is elected, judged, and redeemed in the elected man Jesus Christ. Work-ing "backwards" from this fundamental solution might certainly suggest that all are saved, since universalism is the obvious concomitant of un-conditional salvation. Yet it is not entirely clear how far Barth himself understands this process of unconditional election to be decisive in *ac-complishing*, rather than merely *disclosing*, divine salvation for any *par-ticular* person. Barth is largely reluctant to envisage the possibility that *anyone* might either reject it or be rejected from it. At certain points, however, he does appear to countenance such rejection on the grounds that God's all-encompassing love must be a love that liberates people to isolate themselves from God's reach if they are insistent on so doing—that it might thus function as a "rejecting love." This is a scenario that Barth depicts in characteristically paradoxical fashion as an "impossible possibility."[27]

24. Campbell, *Deliverance*, 94.

25. Campbell, "The Current Crisis," 45.

26. Barth, *Church Dogmatics* II/1, 274, 373, 553; II/2, 2, 27, 92, 164, 265, 496; III/2, 562, 602–40.

27. Barth, *Church Dogmatics* III/2: *The Doctrine of Creation*. 186ff.; 602–40. For my own reflections on this topic see Hilborn, *The Nature of Hell*.

In the final main section of *Deliverance* Campbell allows that there is an apocalyptic construal of divine wrath that might legitimately cast it as "the reflex of benevolence or love"—as an expression of anger at "any situation that is sinful."[28] Earlier, at the end of chapter 3 of *Deliverance*, he notes that there is a "wrathful" strand in Paul's depictions of the final day which envisages the destruction or annihilation of non-believers (e.g., in Phil 1:28; 1 Thess 1:6–10). Yet even here benevolence, rather than punishment, is maintained as the "fundamental" paradigm. As Campbell suggests, "it might be more akin to a surgical action—the wrath of aggrieved love, not the anger of affronted justice."[29] My main question arising from all this is whether such "aggrieved divine love" is provoked by specific human actions, namely specific human choices to reject God's benevolence, such that final divine *condemnation* is conditional even if divine salvation is not. If so, how might that square, if it squares at all, with Campbell's more general link between unconditionality and the Athanasian paradigm of Pauline soteriology?

When I was preparing this response I watched a video featuring Campbell being interviewed about Paul's mission. It is available online and is produced by a network of churches and groups called Grace Communion International—formerly the Worldwide Church of God.[30] Although Campbell's appearance on this film might not tie him to every jot and tittle of Grace Communion International's statement of faith, I presume it indicates some broad sympathy with their approach. As it stands, that statement of faith offers a striking and unusual angle on final judgment for a member body of the U.S. National Association of Evangelicals:

> God judges all humans through Jesus Christ as those who belong to God through him. Therefore all humans are, *in spite of themselves*, loved, forgiven and included in Jesus Christ, who is their Lord and Saviour. God's love will never cease or diminish even for those who, denying the reality of who they are in him, refuse his love and *consign themselves to hell*; they will not enjoy the fruit of salvation but will experience his love as wrath.[31]

---

28. Campbell, *Deliverance*, 930.

29. Ibid., 93.

30. http://www.gci.org/yi/campbell97 Accessed 10th December 2011.

31. http://www.gci.org/aboutus/beliefs Emphases added. Accessed 10th December 2011.

My final question would be whether this essentially expresses Campbell's understanding and if not, how he might want to modify it in relation to Athanasian unconditionality?

Campbell ends his monumental exploration in *The Deliverance of God* by suggesting that it should help us to become more "presuppositionally self-aware," and more "hermeneutically sophisticated," yet confident in the "realization that this does not entail interpretative relativism." He then adds that "our interpretative traditions and communities will of course assist us at this point."[32] I want to thank him for succeeding masterfully in his stated aim, and as a relatively non-specialist member of the interpretative community to which he refers, I offer these reflections as a modest contribution to his ongoing and important project.

---

32. Campbell, *Deliverance*, 936.

Douglas Campbell's Response to David Hilborn

David's first concern resumes one already present in this volume and hence, to a degree, I would simply respond in the same way here. There is no implication in my suggested reading of Paul that God in Christ was not active prior to the time of the gospel; the pre-Christian Word is entirely real. However, human *perceptions* of this Word were constrained during this era by both an absence of information and a sinful resistance to divine activity. So it is entirely appropriate to view God as speaking through creation. But outside of the knowledge of Christ this speech is not entirely accurate, while it lacks accuracy at the most basic point, namely, concerning the identity of the one through whom and in relation to whom all things were created. So here David and I in fact are in close agreement. There is complete continuity between the voice speaking through creation and the revealed Word—in ontological terms we might say—even if that continuity is only fully recognized or grasped—in epistemological terms—after the revelation *of* that Word in Christ.

David's second concern has already come up as well, namely, in relation to the pre-Christian roles of Israel and Scripture. But this is a vital recurring set of questions that merits ongoing serious reflection.

I do not supply a very full account in *Deliverance* of what I take to be Paul's responses to these issues for the simple reason that I am involved in essentially negative work there. Certain Pauline texts have been misread as supplying answers to these questions as well as, most unfortunately, supplying conspicuously bad answers that then override and skew the important and constructive things he has to say elsewhere. And those positive contributions cannot be analyzed without a careful analysis of Romans, chapters 9–11, not to mention, of a number of other texts. Paul's view of the *Torah* needs to be grasped as well (!)—something necessitating some time in chapters 5–8. All of which is to say that I gesture toward what I take to be Paul's account of salvation history elsewhere, and I am hoping to address these questions in detail in future publications, some of which are well under way.[33] But the fact that I am resisting bad answers and readings here should not be taken to suggest that Paul does not himself ultimately possess good answers to these critical questions. It is just that while these bad answers hold sway it is difficult even to get to those

---

33. See "Paul's Gospel, 'Apocalyptic,' and Salvation-history," in *Quest*, 56–68; and my forthcoming theological analysis of Romans tentatively entitled *The End of Religion*. (About half the draft is completed.)

good responses; they seem to be difficult if not impossible to hear. With this plea for patience then I hope we can turn to David's further concerns.

David goes on to ask if I am hoist by my own petard. In particular, in accusing the Foundationalist, methodologically Arian readers of Romans 1–3 of engaging in a totalizing meta-narrative, am I counterposing my own with my advocacy of the universal truth of Athanasian or Nicene interpretation? I do not think so.

Methodological Arianism—more appropriately analyzed in due course as Eunomianism—is, I would suggest, committed to a prior, essentially unassisted act of cosmic description in universal terms, and hence necessarily to abstraction and thereby to a degree of oversimplification and self-ratification. So it remains, I would suggest, vulnerable to Lyotard's concern. It must be a totalizing meta-narrative. Methodolological Athanasianism—more appropriately analyzed in due course as Nicene orthodoxy—is, however, I would suggest, committed less to a description of all of reality in these terms (or, at least, of its key features) and more to a universal truth claim in quite specific personal terms, namely, the Lordship of Christ. This truth claim—and person—then reveals further truth in a methodologically disciplined but still incomplete and fragmentary rather than a totalizing fashion.

So, for example, it is worth noting that Barth's *Church Dogmatics* is profoundly attuned to this important issue that David raises. While this oeuvre could be accused initially of advocating a totalizing meta-narrative, a closer reading reveals that Barth maintains for its entirety an appropriate mode of Christian reflection that consistently eschews both abstraction and claims of completeness. And I hope that in a small and inferior way my own concerns reflect these dynamics. But I would want to go on to suggest, fully endorsing the substance of David's query, that any subsequent claims by me on behalf of an appropriate construal of Paul's gospel, hence in methodologically Nicene terms, should continue to be subject to the Lordship of Christ and hence purged of any inappropriate abstraction or universality.

In the slightly more specific terms noted by David, I would concede then that "nonviolence" cannot be elevated into a universal ethic. It can be discussed as a key feature of Jesus's life, and as an overtly integral part of an orthodox Christology. So we might expect instructions from the risen Lord in these terms quite frequently. But it is not more than this and I would not pretend otherwise. With regard to benevolence, however, the situation is slightly different.

This, it seems to me, does describe something fundamental about the character of God as revealed by a Son, sent by a Father, who dies for a hostile humanity (Rom 5:6, 8–10). It is then an appropriate description of the relationality evident in the heart of God, as revealed most directly by the cross (so I think Alan Torrance's essay in these terms is exactly right[34]). The description of God's character clearly cannot be reduced to this and we would all want to introduce other aspects and dimensions to try to describe a God who will always vastly exceed our capacity to describe. However, the introductions of holiness and judgment will have to run the christological gauntlet—so to speak—of incarnation and cross, and of resurrection and ascension. Without this, David's counterposed emphases lack narrative content, which is to say that they lack—as yet—overt theological warrant, whereas my emphasis on divine benevolence does not. Moreover, even if and when they receive affirmation, they must integrate with the fundamental narrative and relationality already in view; we will learn about the judgment and holiness *of love* and thereby possibly learn of our previous subversions and misrepresentations of these aspects of the divine character.

David asks finally if my alternative account of Paul's gospel is not merely universal in its claims but universal*ist* (a common concern expressed to those leaning on Barth). Like Barth, however, I tend to prescind from a definitive answer to this question, since it rests in the hands of a God who knows more than I do and will do a better job of finally unraveling history into its appropriate destinies. Beyond these observations, we do not really need to know the answer to this question. (We do of course if we are advocates of the Justification discourse! Non-Christians need to be threatened with the prospects of condemnation and hell. But fortunately it is no longer necessary to be quite so certain about distant eschatological events completely outside our appropriate jurisdiction.) However, I would want to emphasize in this relation that a God of benevolence is not "soft" in opposing or judging sin but is quite the converse.

There is no anger deeper or more implacable—or more appropriate—than the anger of a fundamentally loving God confronted with the evils of a humanity committed to hate instead of love, and to vicious relationships of exploitation and violence instead of relationships of fidelity, affirmation, and peace. (What parents are not unassuagably angry when their children engage in self-destructive and stupid

---

34. A. J. Torrance, "Is Love the Essence of God?," 114–37.

behavior—violence, abuse, and the like?!) The Paul—and the God—of my "alternative" account of the gospel is deeply opposed to sin, and committed to its judgment and termination—enough indeed to die in pursuit of these objectives. It is vital not to lose sight of these dynamics, and so I am grateful to David for prompting me here to emphasize them.

8

The Legal Mind
of American Christianity

KATE BOWLER

American Christians, contrary to popular opinion, have a soft spot for lawyers. When Charles Finney, the leading revivalist of the Second Great Awakening, described his career change from the law to the gospel as his "retainer from the Lord Jesus Christ to plead his cause" before God, the greater Judge, the crowd must have cooed.[1] Because what they loved about Finney they hated about another of God's lawyers, John Calvin, who would not have understood what Americans loved about themselves. Their reasonableness. Their self-confidence. Their ability to see a good bargain when they saw it, and what Jesus—through Finney—seemed to be offering was a very good bargain indeed. The cross offers believers a way out of a deal with their own righteousness gone wrong. And now Douglas Campbell wants to take it all away from them.

What Campbell calls foundationalism, many nineteenth-century American Protestants would have accepted as "orthodox rationalism," a heady view of the seamless integration of all knowledge, mundane and divine, as the fullest expression of God's revelation.[2] After having ejected the British, fortified their own constitution, and constructed their own political and religious language of liberty, Americans seemed to

1. Finney, *Memoirs of Rev. Charles G. Finney*, 24.

2. See Wacker, *Augustus H. Strong and the Dilemma of Historical Consciousness*, 9–15.

find something they could really believe in: themselves.[3] Their sky-high anthropology was infused with the rarefied air of the Enlightenment and the virtual helium of empiricism. And when their own late nineteenth-century crisis with modernity, religious pluralism, and German higher criticism let some of the air out, it did nothing to deflate their confidence in their own spiritual justifications—be they conservative, Pentecostal, fundamentalist, or liberal. Even at loggerheads, American Christians could be counted on to trust their own judgments and measure the results.

The cherished American notion that the good news of the Christian message is primarily juridical has been endlessly codified: in the short-list of non-negotiable creeds we find in the conservative manifesto, *The Fundamentals* (1910–15); in the mainline Protestant narration of social services as the checklist by which God's character and enduring presence is detected; in postwar evangelicalism's classic pamphlet, *The Four Spiritual Laws*; in metaphysical attempts to find the undergirding laws of the universe popularized most recently in churches as the prosperity gospel and on television as the Oprah-endorsed *The Secret*; in the moralistic therapeutic deism of today's youth that deems God to be the vague force that ensures that good things indeed happen to good people.[4]

Where can we look to find something untouched by what Campbell calls foundationalism? Perhaps we might have expected something a little more Athanasian from the religious upstarts that privilege the radical in-breaking of God. Surely we should look among the early Pentecostals who announced that signs and wonders had been returned as the Spirit was poured out on all flesh. Except that within the first generation, celebrity Pentecostal evangelists like F. F. Bosworth were touring the country under canvas cathedrals proclaiming Christianity as the search for the immutable spiritual laws that governed the universe in general and healed our bodies in particular.[5]

So, if Campbell is right, then Arianism is at the heart of America's soft spot for lawyers. Or perhaps our favorite New Zealander has been drinking the water here for too long, and everything is starting to taste like good old-fashioned American natural theology.

---

3. See, for example, Hatch, *The Democratization of American Christianity*.

4. Smith and Denton, *Soul Searching*.

5. Bowler, *Blessed*, 21–25.

Douglas Campbell's Response to Kate Bowler

Kate stands before the treasure chest that is American, primarily Protestant, Christianity and cracks the lid just sufficiently to indicate that cultural, intellectual, and political forces all combine to powerfully shape the posture of the modern American reader of Paul. In a way that my own work could only gesture toward (in *Deliverance* ch. 9), she indicates further that the tracing of the roots of what we might call American Pelagianism is a rich area for further exploration. I hope she or someone else writes the definitive work here in due course because I view it as a key component within the Pauline discourse that I am trying to displace. Why do modern American readers have no difficulty with a reading of Paul that privileges a person's unassisted contemplation of the cosmos and consequent derivation of firm and incontestable conclusions about rationality and punitive politics? Where is the sense of Augustinian fragility? Or the sense of a Martin Luther that human beings are unworthy of such speculations and incapable of such insights without the radical assistance of grace? Framed by *those* narratives the current majority reading of Romans, chapters 1–4, must strike its readers as shockingly and inappropriately overconfident—one destined in its hubris for a terrible fall. But framed by the *American* narrative, which overlaps significantly with the universally modern, liberal story, it is difficult even to hear the possibility that Paul in Romans 1–3 might be offering a critique, in sly parodic terms, of someone *characterized by just those pretentions*. Hence, we might say, were Paul's presuppositions American or was he fundamentally critical of the American project? Clearly it is easier for a New Zealander to supply an answer to this question than someone born in the USA.

PART TWO

Campbell's Solution
An Examination of Key Themes

9

Rereading Romans 1–3[1]

DOUGLAS A. CAMPBELL

We will begin, in this chapter, by seizing the bull by the horns on the assumptions that we are dealing with a bull and that chapters 1 through 3 of Romans are its horns. These badly need to be blunted by being construed differently or reread.[2]

Romans 1–3 and Forward Thinking

Despite what some have said, Romans 1–3 is generally read prospectively or forward, setting up a tacitly Arian or foundationalist variant within Paul's theology more broadly in the form of Western contractualism, so we need to engage with this text carefully if we are ever to rid Paul of this problem. Without a forward construal of Romans 1–3 I would suggest that this sort of dangerous prospectivism has no decisive claim on the apostle's thought. With this construal, however, it can lay claim

1. Permission from Sage Publications is here gratefully acknowledged to reproduce in what follows parts of my earlier study "An Attempt to be Understood," 162–208.

2. *Rereading* might suggest that this is a new account of Romans 1–3 and hence automatically somewhat suspicious, but it is supposed to be a retrieval of its original reading facilitated by close historical critical work. This important term and practice are particularly associated in relation to Romans with Stanley Stowers's brilliant but difficult *Rereading Romans*.

to a significant cluster of his texts. But has the largely unacknowledged enthusiasm of many Pauline interpreters *for* Western contractualism— generally on the mistaken assumption that this is the first phase of the gospel—led *to* this construal of Romans 1–3 in spite of what these texts are actually doing in detail? Has a subtle misconstrual of Paul's argumentation then unleashed a monstrous distortion into his dogmatics? The short answer in my view to both these questions is "yes."

But some of my interlocutors have challenged me immediately here, denying that such prospectivism is present in the broader interpretation of Romans 1–3. There is no such dynamic in play and my anxieties are mere paranoia, they assert.[3] So before I can suggest a reading that will solve our problems, I have to pause to consider if the problem I am trying to address is really there. (I would add that I do not think this is a very wise tactic on the part of my critics, but it is widespread so I need to try to clear it up a bit before moving on.) To switch metaphors, we need to ask first if the Titanic is happily sailing on intact and secure toward New York, or if, as I suggest, it has struck an iceberg and been deeply damaged. Here then is my account of the deadly iceberg, the bulk of which, it is worth remembering, lies concealed beneath the surface of the water. Nevertheless if it exists—departing a little from my metaphor—we will try to repair the damage and sail on with a new reading of Romans 1–3. But if we do not recognize its existence—that is, we have a problem in the first place—then we are doomed; our ship, heavily damaged but sailing blithely on, is going down.

We have discussed this problem already in my previous chapters, referring to it at different times as (methodological) Arianism, foundationalism, prospectivism, Western contractualism or conditionality, and even "the Latin Heresy." But I will refer to it here in the main as I did in chapter 6, as *forward thinking*, understanding this forwardness in the specific terms of epistemological foundationalism so it is not a mere rhetorical progression. We must ask here then first of all if Paul is generally held to be arguing forward in Romans 1–3, building from an account of a problem in the sense of *the* problem facing all humanity to a definitive account of the Christian solution offered in the gospel, thereby unleashing Arianism within the apostle's broader interpretation. And we must ask how this all happens in specific relation to the text. Many have apparently

---

3. This claim has been asserted almost bizarrely extensively by Barry Matlock in "Zeal for Paul."

not been able to see this, even after its theoretical description, exegetical demonstration, and extensive annotation, in *Deliverance*. So let me suggest here that forward thinking is present in the text and hence in anyone who reads this material in a certain fashion (and they usually do).

In its first paragraph Romans 1–3 offers its auditors an argument in terms of forward thinking, introducing the argument's key premises in the first few verses, while an appropriate conclusion rounds off the account in verse 32.

> [1:18] Ἀποκαλύπτεται γὰρ ὀργὴ θεοῦ ἀπ᾽ οὐρανοῦ ἐπὶ πᾶσαν ἀσέβειαν καὶ ἀδικίαν ἀνθρώπων τῶν τὴν ἀλήθειαν ἐν ἀδικίᾳ κατεχόντων,

> [19] διότι τὸ γνωστὸν τοῦ θεοῦ φανερόν ἐστιν ἐν αὐτοῖς· ὁ θεὸς γὰρ αὐτοῖς ἐφανέρωσεν.

> [20] τὰ γὰρ ἀόρατα αὐτοῦ ἀπὸ κτίσεως κόσμου τοῖς ποιήμασιν νοούμενα καθορᾶται, ἥ τε ἀΐδιος αὐτοῦ δύναμις καὶ θειότης, εἰς τὸ εἶναι αὐτοὺς ἀναπολογήτους [κ.τ.λ.].

> [1:18] For the wrath of God is revealed from heaven against all ungodliness and wickedness of those who by their wickedness suppress the truth.

> [19] For what can be known about God is plain to them, because God has shown it to them.

> [20] Ever since the creation of the world his eternal power and divine nature, invisible though they are, have been understood and seen through the things he has made. So they are without excuse;. . . . [NRSV]

Here a God is known universally, inferred from creation by the mind (τοῖς ποιήμασιν νοούμενα; "by means of those things that have been made, being understood"). "He" is transcendent, but also ethical, and is in fact poised to judge the sinfulness of humanity (Ἀποκαλύπτεται [γὰρ] ὀργὴ θεοῦ . . . ἐπὶ πᾶσαν ἀσέβειαν καὶ ἀδικίαν ἀνθρώπων; the wrath of God is revealed . . . against all ungodliness and wickedness of people who . . .).[4] That is, the natural knowledge of God is developed by the text immediately in more detailed ethical categories, which humanity goes on to violate (vv. 21–31). And the result is a descent into

---

4. I need to use a pronoun here but because of the limitations of English have to employ a potentially gendered reference when the argument suggests that this God transcends gender categories emphatically.

depravity, through three stages of idolatry, sexual immorality, and general viciousness, that God is held finally "to judge righteously with a sentence of death"; οἵτινες τὸ δικαίωμα τοῦ Θεοῦ ἐπιγνόντες ὅτι οἱ τὰ τοιαῦτα πράσσοντες ἄξιοι θανάτου εἰσίν (κ.τ.λ.; "They know God's decree, that those who practice such things deserve to die"). Indeed, so obvious is this entire arrangement that the brazen sinners mentioned climactically in verse 32 "acknowledge" it (ἐπιγνόντες). Certainly everyone is "without excuse" (ἀναπολογήτους). And this is a compact formulation of forward thinking.

Note how the conclusion of the argument—that brazen sinners obviously and appropriately merit a sentence of death from God—follows directly from the truth of the initial premises in verses 19–20. The universal culpability of the brazen sinners is indeed only appropriate if those premises are both ethical and universally obvious; however, the text states that they are. Hence this paragraph only makes sense if it is construed as an instance of forward thinking. It works prospectively as an argument in the full epistemological sense; something is being demonstrated here "forward" from universal self-evident premises.

But there is much more to Romans 1–3 than its opening paragraph. How does the entire text function prospectively? *By the assumption that the rest of the text—that is, through 3:20—functions in the same way as 1:18–32*; that is, as a continued argument from self-evident premises forward to a depressing universal conclusion about human sinfulness and pending divine judgment. However, clearly a set of further exegetical assumptions must be made in order for this to happen.

The premises underlying 1:18–32 are summarized again in the text in 2:6 in a brief but critical affirmation of divine judgment in accordance with desert, although this judgment is immediately oriented pointedly toward both "Greeks" or pagans, and Jews.

> [2:6] . . . ὃς ἀποδώσει ἑκάστῳ κατὰ τὰ ἔργα αὐτοῦ· [7] τοῖς μὲν καθ᾽ ὑπομονὴν ἔργου ἀγαθοῦ δόξαν καὶ τιμὴν καὶ ἀφθαρσίαν ζητοῦσιν [ἀποδώσει] ζωὴν αἰώνιον, [8] τοῖς δὲ ἐξ ἐριθείας καὶ ἀπειθοῦσι τῇ ἀληθείᾳ πειθομένοις δὲ τῇ ἀδικίᾳ [ἀποδωθήσονται] ὀργὴ καὶ θυμός. [9] θλῖψις καὶ στενοχωρία [ἀποδωθήσονται] ἐπὶ πᾶσαν ψυχὴν ἀνθρώπου τοῦ κατεργαζομένου τὸ κακόν, Ἰουδαίου τε πρῶτον καὶ Ἕλληνος.

[2:6] For he will repay according to each one's deeds: [7] to those who by patiently doing good seek for glory and honor and immortality, he will give eternal life; [8] while for those who are self-seeking and who obey not the truth but wickedness, there will be wrath and fury. [9] There will be anguish and distress for everyone who does evil, the Jew first and also the Greek.

This material summarizes the position delineated at more length in 1:18–32 just previously. It was grounded there explicitly on universal self-evident premises obvious to everyone from nature, as we have just seen, but this commitment to general revelation is reaffirmed shortly after this second, briefer statement of principle too, in 2:12–16. And the text signals the tight conceptual linkage between 1:18–32 and 2:6–11 overtly when it turns on an interlocutor in between these affirmations in 2:1–5 who does not practice what he preaches and is himself made subject *to* the theology *of* his preaching; his judgmental preaching is (at least) the content of 1:18–32, and the application *of* that preached judgment *to* him is summarized in 2:6–11. So these two texts are parallel affirmations and must be interpreted in alignment.

In view of this substantive correlation, the argument of Romans 2:1—3:20 will reproduce the forward thinking affirmed by 1:18–32 *if the premise of 2:6 is taken to ground the rest of the contentions in the text through to 3:20 in a universal self-evident demonstration* in a parallel way to the function of those premises within the argument of 1:18–32. And this is a reasonably plausible construal of the text.

The overarching argument through 3:20 can function as a demonstration from universal, self-evident premises of just universal condemnation, although, somewhat curiously, a series of arguments suggesting this conclusion self-evidently up to 3:9a seems to be corroborated in 3:9b–18, in the argument's final sub-section, by a massed scriptural assertion of the same (i.e., by an argument from special revelation).[5] An appropriate conclusion nevertheless seems to follow in 3:19: οἴδαμεν δὲ ὅτι ὅσα ὁ νόμος λέγει τοῖς ἐν τῷ νόμῳ λαλεῖ ἵνα πᾶν στόμα φραγῇ καὶ ὑπόδικος γένηται πᾶς ὁ κόσμος τῷ θεῷ. ("we know that whatever the law says, it speaks to those who are under the law, so that every mouth may be silenced, and the whole world may be held accountable to God.") But in the light of this broad function in terms of condemnation, that osten-

---

5. That is, the argument is affirmed by an appeal to revelation within a particular tradition, which is, strictly speaking, invalid in terms of the opening argument from nature, because this information is not universally self-evident.

sibly becomes so apparent in 3:9–20, we might ask why Paul's text does not simply jump from 1:32 straight through to 3:9b when Jews begin to be vacuumed up into its web of condemnation by the massed voice of Scripture. The extended tirade before this seems a little redundant (and, strictly speaking, 1:18–32 is redundant as well). And so here we come to a further critical assumption in the forward construal of Romans 1–3: the intervening material in 2:1—3:9a is understood to be *an attack on Jews in the same self-evident terms that were operative vis-à-vis pagans in 1:18–32.*

The text folds back from 2:1, as we have just seen, on a judgmental but hypocritical figure, who will eventually be marked explicitly with Jewish features (see 2:17–20). He is held to the standard of his own preaching. And the argument thereby supposedly begins to demonstrate how *the* Jew, considered in and of himself, independently and self-evidently, fails just as the pagans did. The Jew is a sinner too.

However, it is important to appreciate further that the premises of the argument dictate the configuration of Judaism apparent in this Jew as well; that is, the premises already derived from natural theology by pagans in 1:18–32. The Judaism that ostensibly implodes through 2:1—3:9 is consequently configured strictly and rather minimally in terms of desert (see 2:6), a straight reproduction of the premises already seen to be at work in relation to pagans in 1:18–32 (see esp. 1:32; and as the text goes on to argue explicitly in 2:1–6). So there is really no significant difference between the pagan and the Jew, and self-evidently so; the Jew is the quintessential "natural man" (as the argument in fact acknowledges explicitly in 2:29).

Both the generic Jew and the generic pagan, then, try to be perfectly righteous by works, both sin and fail, and both stand under the retributive judgment of God; they are all legalists (at which point you should hear the protests of Sanders and those like him rising in consternation and horror). And forward thinking now runs right through Romans 1–3, first for the Greek, and then for the Jew. But a further key concomitant of this construal should be noted before we turn to its critical evaluation.

The construal of Romans 1–3 in terms of universal condemnation must function in the context of a broader progression. Considered in and of itself it is a complete dead end; everyone ends up being condemned by God self-evidently, so everyone is damned and doomed—end of story. But if another arrangement lies beyond this one then this apparent dead end can be understood instead as placing a lot of pressure on anyone within it to reach out and open the single doorway that seems to lead out of it, albeit in a rather rationalistic sense (but the text construed in this way is an *argument* functioning *self-evidently* so the reading expects rational actors with some capacity or it is utterly incoherent, so this all seems to follow).[6] Consequently it is very important that the subsequent phase of Paul's argument in Romans can be construed in certain terms as well, that is, 3:21—4:25 be read as the offer of a new saving arrangement that can be appropriated by a more manageable act than perfect works like faith. But scholars can of course offer a plausible reading of the later arguments in such terms—although it is worth noting in passing that they have only done so in the last 25 percent or so of the text's interpretative history, that is, since the early 1500s.[7] (Earlier Catholic commentary to my knowledge never read the argument as culminating in salvation *sola fide*.) And an important preliminary conclusion in *my* argument in *Deliverance* is now apparent.

Any reader who holds that Paul is himself *committed to the premises underlying 1:18–32 and 2:6 is endorsing forward thinking,* because any commitment by Paul to these premises entails the function of the argument in the text forward, from universal self-evident propositions (perhaps corroborated by Scripture, but this is not strictly speaking necessary) to an unavoidable conclusion of self-confessed sinfulness and judgment. This is a foundationalist, prospective, and contractual argument and scenario—and, incidentally, it cannot be avoided by reframing it psychologically; that is, by supplying retrospective reasons that reduce it essentially to causes in Paul's head for its deployment. The argument is still in its actual workings a set of truth claims arranged in a foundationalist fashion. Their truth holds independently of their causality (and we know very little about the latter in any case).

6. The anthropocentric cast of the progression is consequently revealed in this. The key concern of the progression is that individuals learn something, and the key moment comes when they grasp the gospel by faith in order to leave their desperate situation under condemnation. This has to be, moreover, some sort of free decision or choice, although it has been arrived at for various reasons, so it must also be a voluntarist and rationalistic model.

7. And here in fact we see how interdependent foundationalism in relation to "works" and a construal of "faith" in Paul in terms of *sola fide* are. The collapse of works makes no sense without a following, easier saving contract revolving around faith alone. And the notion of salvation through faith alone makes no sense without the preceding collapse of an arrangement premised strictly in relation to works.

Some have asked me where my account of "justification" in Paul comes from, which is sometimes spoken of as "Justification Theory" or JT for short. So let me say in the interests of clarity that the problem in Pauline studies that I target in *Deliverance* as "the justification discourse," or JT, and that I am discussing here in terms of forward thinking is unleashed by anyone who reads Romans 1–4 in the usual way, forward, and who then reads anything else in Paul in this way. Moreover, this will happen if the argument of this passage is construed as functioning from universal self-evident premises to a conclusion of universal sinfulness, with Paul himself endorsing the premises stated in 1:19–20 and 2:6, and thereby endorsing forward thinking. In short, if Paul is held to believe himself in the information deployed in Romans in 1:19–20 and/or 2:6, and so views these claims as the basis for all that follows, then this unavoidably generates JT.

It is very important to appreciate immediately that I do not think that either Paul himself or any of his later interpreters is *reducible* to this position. But if interpreters commit to these premises *at any point* then they necessarily unleash a wave of destructive confusions and contradictions through the broader interpretation of Paul's gospel—whether they admit to this or not. And unfortunately I do not think commentators who enact this destructive practice are very hard to find, Douglas Moo being a nice example.[8] But there is no need to single out Moo for special

---

8. "We must consider 1:18—3:20 as a preparation for, rather than as part of, Paul's exposition of the gospel of God's righteousness. But it is a *necessary* preparation *if* what Paul wants to emphasize about this righteousness is to be accepted by the Romans. For *only if* sin is seen to be the dominating, ruling force that Paul presents it to be in this section (cf. 3:9) *will it become clear* that God's righteousness can be experienced only by humbly receiving it as a gift—in a word, by faith. 'Only those who are prepared to acknowledge that they are unworthy can put faith in the Giver of grace'" (*The Epistle to the Romans*, 92, emphases added). So 1:18—3:20 is an "indictment" (92, 93). Moreover, "[A]ll . . . stand under the awful reality of the wrath of God, and all are in desperate need of the justifying power of the gospel of Christ. We will *never* come to grips with the importance of the gospel, or be motivated as we should to proclaim it, *until* this sad truth has been fully integrated into our worldview" (98, emphases added). Note that when "all" or "everyone" is convinced and convicted of something—i.e, everyone in all of human history—and only a small group is subsequently introduced to Christian realities by way of special revelation, the argument must be working forward from everyone to the few. Further, "natural revelation leads not to salvation but to the demonstration that God's condemnation is just: people are 'without excuse.' That verdict stands over the people we meet every day just as much over the people Paul rubbed shoulders with in the first century . . ." (106). "Further, it is vitally important, if the passion of Paul's gospel is to be correctly appreciated and the argument

disapprobation (at least on this count). It is difficult to find those who do not endorse this basic approach.[9] Even famous revisionist interpreters of Paul in the modern period—like Dunn, Stowers, Wright, and Jewett—tend to retain a forward construal of the argument in Romans 1–3 overall, fiddling with its internal components and motifs, which means that they have not grasped the full extent of the problem and so gone on to resolve it satisfactorily. They are placing bandaids on a problem requiring major surgery. Prospectivism is still being unleashed within Pauline interpretation by all this so that such Pauline interpreters, no matter how revisionist their reputations, are still complicit in the propagation of

---

of this section correctly understood, to see that the knowledge of God that people possess outside special revelation is woefully inadequate, of itself, to save. Paul makes clear that . . . the evidence of nature and conscience (cf. 2:14–16) serves only to render them 'without excuse' before the wrathful God" (123). So "all humanity, stand[s] before God, accountable to him for willful and inexcusable violations of his will, awaiting the sentence of condemnation that their actions deserve" (205). However, "Paul's chief purpose throughout Rom 1:18—3:20 is not to *demonstrate* that Gentiles are guilty and in need of God's righteousness—for this could be assumed—but that *Jews* bear the same burden and have the same need" (206, emphases added).

Moo endorses other constructs as well, but the result is then just a conceptual mess. Paul thinks forward sometimes and backward at other times and so is simply confused on all the major soteriological issues.

Note further that Moo is an especially instructive instance of the quality of much of the interaction with my work in this relation because at times he stridently rejects my characterizations of the situation in terms of justification theory, but nevertheless seems frequently to turn around and endorse it vigorously; see his "Review Essay."

9. And it is especially interesting to consider Barth's views in this relation. Clearly Barth's views developed. His commentary on Romans (*The Epistle to the Romans*) was early in his career and although powerful and highly dialectical still construes the opening argument of Romans 1–3 forward. Of course, he frequently makes retrospective comments and applications as well. (The main edition read today derives from the second, completed in 1921, Barth later observing in the Preface to the largely unaltered sixth that "when . . . I look back at the book it seems to have been written by another man to meet a situation belonging to a past epoch. . . . [It is then] the *beginning* of a development" (vi, emphasis added). Barth later denied the theological implications of this reading strongly in his famous debate with Emil Brunner over natural theology in 1934 ("No!"). A little earlier than this he had made a critical transition, while working on Anselm, to a comprehensively christological and retrospective theological epistemology. This then informed the *Church Dogmatics*, begun in 1932. It is evident in IV/1, completed in 1953, where Romans 1–3 is treated again, however, that Barth never fully resolved the exegetical problem set for him by Romans 1 (although this material could derive in part from von Kirschbaum), but his broader theological agenda at this time is explicit and largely consistent: see *Church Dogmatics*, IV/1 *The Doctrine of Reconciliation*, 392–96; also 240. In this whole relation see Busch, *Karl Barth: His Life*, 92–109, 117–25, 199–262.

methodological Arianism.[10] That is, "the new perspective" on Paul leads us nowhere, at least in relation to these texts and concerns.[11]

But someone might say at this point, "So what?! The prospective reading isn't really that bad; after all, we have lived with it for some time. It hasn't done that much damage, and may even have done some good." However, the forward reading of Romans 1–3 *is* a destructive reading, and it is time to remind ourselves why. We will concentrate here on just one of its difficulties—the issue introduced in chapter 6 in relation to Galatians 2:15–16 in terms of the construction of Judaism.

Forward Thinking and Jews in Romans 1–3

What happens to Judaism in Romans 1–3 when these chapters are read forward? Exactly the same awful things as happened in Galatians 2:15–16 when that text was construed prospectively, except worse.

The Jewish figure apparent in the text must be characterized as *the* Jew because the argument is a foundational, universal one grounding the progression to a gospel beyond law-observant Judaism. And this construal is immediately committed to all the historical and theological difficulties that we noted in chapter 6 in relation to Galatians 2:15–16. But the Judaism addressed in Romans must also be defined as the more detailed text dictates—in terms of a judgmental person who is apparently a hypocrite as well (see 2:1–6, 21–22). His relationship with God is based on a strict moralizing contract revolving around works informed by the law (2:6–11) so it is highly conditional. In fact, he is really no better than a good pagan, if that (2:12–16). He can be accused of theft, adultery, and sacrilege, in addition to hypocrisy (2:21–23), and is so immoral that pagans slander his evidently false deity (2:24). There is even something superficial and dispensable about the bodily dimension of his Jewishness (2:25–29). Naturally, he complains about these implications (3:1–9). And he is roundly condemned in every respect by Scripture, that is, by his own sacred texts that apparently he does not remotely comprehend (3:10–18).[12]

10. See Dunn, *Romans 1–8*; Stowers, *Rereading Romans*; and R. Jewett, *Romans*.

11. Hence most of my difficulties with these proposals as articulated in ch. 12 of *Deliverance* (412–66).

12. Note that many important aspects of Judaism in Paul's day are also absent from this account—for example, the cultus, and other practices of atonement and forgiveness.

Now we need to be both honest and clear at this point. If this is the universal self-evident definition of the problem on which the solution by means of faith alone will build then the foundation of Paul's soteriology is intrinsically anti-Jewish. This is a *nasty* description, in addition to being merely *false,* which makes the gospel both nasty and false in turn. The entire arrangement is also somewhat unjust—asking people to fulfill demands that it turns out in their corruption they cannot possibly fulfill—which makes God (in something of an irony) unjust as well. It is also *historicizing, reductionist, bi-covenantal, non-christological,* and so on. But if we read Romans 1–3 forward then this is what Paul's gospel has to be all about; Paul is locked into this description, at least until other engagements with Jewish issues in his letters have been factored in, although the damage will have been done. We begin our analysis of Paul where he seems to begin, which is here, before the arrival of the gospel, in a universal and self-evident account of the human situation that revolves primarily around the generic Jew. This is the description of "Judaism" that frames all his subsequent suggestions, although it is, of course, not really a description of Judaism at all. (And it is, of course, deeply tragic that the church has taken so long to recognize that this description of one of its key "outsider" constituencies—and arguably its most important one—is so unfair.)

But this is just "the Jewish problem" in Romans 1–3, and a brief account of it at that. (It radiates through this text and then beyond into the rest of the letter in many directions.) All the other major problems noted briefly in chapter 6 are set in motion by this construal as well: the collision with retrospective, participatory thinking, which becomes apparent especially as the letter moves into chapters 5 through 8 (and where the forward and retributive conceptuality of Romans 1–4 effectively frames and overrides some of the key contributions from Romans 5–8); the distortions of conversion and of mission; the subversion of Paul's revealed truth claims, especially concerning Christ; and the harsh construction of other pagan outsiders, to name the main ones. But the exegesis of Romans 1–3 in these basic terms has its own direct exegetical difficulties as well, in particular, long puzzlement over what to do with a group of pagans who are apparently judged righteous by their deeds (see 2:13–16, 26–29)—a glaring anomaly if the argument is supposed to be demonstrating the universal sinfulness and culpability of all.[13]

13. These have been explained in three ways, all unsatisfactory: (1) as hypothetical—which makes them argumentatively pointless; (2) as a real option—which

So I agree with Sanders that we face an interpretative crisis at this point; however, unlike him, I view this crisis as deeper and broader than even his characterization—as basically destroying Paul's account of the gospel, and not merely his Jewish description.[14] In short, I take it that there is an iceberg, and that we have struck it and are foundering, although many seem either unaware of this or to deny it. But there is—to rearrange my narrative—a way to repair this ship so that it does not sink with great loss of life.

Just the solution that we already noted in relation to Galatians 2:15-16 could work in Romans 1-3 as well, namely, an understanding of the broader argument's concerns merely antithetically, presupposing a revealed gospel of faith (cf. 1:16-17 and 3:22!), that could then release Paul's engagement with something revolving around "works of law" from having to function either foundationally or as a description of Judaism and more in relation to "another gospel." But here as there we still have to ask if this argumentative possibility can be realized on the ground in rigorous exegetical terms. Can the argument of Romans 1-3 be read in a way that is not foundationally prospective? The answer is "yes."

---

destroys Paul's broader argument; and (3) as Christians—but a careful consideration of their constitution eviscerates all Christian particularity immediately *and* their location in the argument at this point is incoherent. Hence Richard N. Longenecker rightly notes recently that "[t]he interpretation of 1:18—3:20 has been notoriously difficult for almost every commentator" (*Introducing Romans*, 355). I would add two further nasty textual difficulties here (*Deliverance*, of course, supplying a more extensive tabulation), invariably overlooked: the provision of an option of repentance prior to conviction in 2:4; and the strange nature of the groups in 2:6-10, apparently containing either *entirely* righteous or *entirely* wicked people. In a broadly "transgression" oriented narrative, this distribution makes little sense.

14. And this is a point where the orientation of the problematic that *Deliverance* addresses in terms of Sanders is especially evident. Sanders himself intelligently pursues an editorial solution to the problem, essentially excising Romans 1-3 from Paul's corpus as a poorly integrated synagogue homily. And this certainly solves the problem. But it is an unpersuasive solution *and* Sanders still activates forward thinking in Paul frequently elsewhere. See his neglected but brilliant *Paul, the Law, and the Jewish People*, esp. 123-35, evaluated in *Deliverance*, 431-44. He also fails to distinguish between psychological and epistemological retrospectivism. These are the three major points then where I suggest going beyond his work on these questions.

A Socratic Reading

The text of Romans 1–3 actually works beautifully as a Socratic exercise or *elenchus*, which can be defined broadly as "any rigorous examination or refutation, any testing of the interlocutor's beliefs in which these beliefs are shown to be false or incoherent . . ." with the further critical proviso that this is achieved *strictly in their own terms* (Kahn, *Plato and the Socratic Dialogue*, 110). Another way of grasping this particular argumentative strategy is by realizing that it operates largely in terms of aggressive demonstrations of self-contradiction within an opponent's position (although the *style* of the argument need not be aggressive). And I suggest that Romans 1–3—specifically 1:18—3:20—is such a self-contained exercise in demonstrable self-contradiction and confusion within someone else's position. More specifically, I suggest that in Romans 1–3 Paul reduces another soteriological position that involves "works of law"—that is, a Jewish Christian gospel involving Torah observance—to absurdity in terms of its own commitments, and he does so ingeniously, and in several respects (so it is a complex *elenchus*).

In this construal all the vulgarities and excesses previously noted (i.e., in relation to a crass construction of Judaism, the presence of "righteous pagans," and so on) flip around to work in its favor; they are all aspects of an opposing position that Paul is seeking to embarrass and not conclusions that Paul himself is endorsing. They are then—as they should be—this Socratic argument's very dynamic.

The vulnerable opening of this alternative position is epitomized in 1:18–32 (since Paul's Roman auditors need to know what it is), rather as Cephalus, Polemarchus, and Thrasymachus, lay out their rival positions in the opening stages of Plato's *Republic*. But Paul's rival is of course fundamentally Jewish, and hence the resonances of this paragraph with the Wisdom of Solomon, that angry missive presumably being an important text within his rival's discourse.[15] The key premise in this opening is

15. As John Barclay noted some time ago, Wisdom is largely "a sea of polemic"— "an educated and deeply Hellenized exercise in cultural aggression" (*Jews in the Mediterranean Diaspora*, 184). And this does not sound to me like Paul's attitude to the pagan constituency to which he was called, although it does sound like a typical "religious" response to culture that divides reality sharply into an "in" and an "out" group, unleashing considerable hostility on the latter in order to promote the identity and cohesion of the former—the probable view of conservative Jewish Christians in the early church who were offended by Paul's ostensible libertinism. Galatians 2:4 and 12 are significant at this point. See also (inter alia) Riesebrodt, *The Promise of Salvation*.

isolated and then universalized in 2:1–6, that is, *applied to the preacher of this system* and not to the generic Jew or the letter's listeners. And a series of embarrassing reductions are then run through the remainder of chapter 2.

First, we learn that pagans will not actually need to embrace any "gospel" involving Jewish practices in order to be saved (2:12–16, 26); in terms of the argument's opening they need merely to act in accordance with the moral revelations of nature to be judged righteous—and the role of the righteous pagans in Paul's argument has now been explained. Their existence embarrasses the Jewish Christian preacher advocating Jewish customs like circumcision and Torah-observance on the universal and self-evident grounds for morality (and condemnation!) initially enunciated in the Wisdom of Solomon and echoed in 1:18–32. If you want to convert pagans to Jewish Christianity, we might say, you ought not to begin this way because—Paul is happy to point out—it is self-defeating. They can be saved by observing the dictates that nature has revealed to them, as you have already conceded.

But nothing in this gospel obviously saves Jews either, Paul continues in his second reduction, in 2:17–24, as we learn from the story of certain notorious rabbinic charlatans at Rome. In 19 AD, as every Jew, and possibly every Roman, knew, Tiberius had expelled the Jewish community from Rome because of a scam perpetrated on a Roman noblewoman. Ostensibly religious figures had apparently absconded with a large offering of silver intended for the Jerusalem temple. This narrative underlies Paul's lurid charges of theft, sacrilege, hypocrisy, and immorality in the text. Hence Paul is not attacking Jews universally in these terms. He is demonstrating that circumcision and training in the Torah do not *necessarily* lead to virtue and hence to salvation, as the story of these infamous "sages" demonstrated. Conversion to Jewish customs is therefore doubly useless, and Jews themselves may well find themselves in trouble on the Day of Judgment, as Paul's rival depicts it.

Indeed, these two possible reductive outcomes now generate a painful further possibility—that uncircumcised but righteous pagans will mock circumcised but sinful Jews on the Day of Judgment, at which point Paul's third reduction becomes apparent. The principle of desert, operative self-evidently in nature, actually defines anything specifically Jewish out of existence. "Jewishness" *per se* is now redundant—an inference so shocking that commentators have generally not known what to do with it, although it works beautifully as a Socratic reduction. Paul is not suggesting erasing his ancestral tradition; he is merely suggesting that the Teacher's aggressive rhetorical opening, grasped clearly, erases *his* ancestral tradition. In a world governed by self-evident morality within nature and desert there is just no point in being specifically Jewish, and it then follows, even more shockingly, that any identity claims in such specific terms are rendered dubious.

The reductive phase in Paul's *elenchus* is complete by this point. He has driven his rival's Jewish identity onto his initial rhetorical commitment to the premises of divine desert and impartiality, cashing this tension out in three separate subordinate moves (the salvation of the righteous pagan; the condemnation of the sinful Jew; and the elimination of Jewish particular identity). But Paul is not done yet.

He goes on to elicit in 3:1–9a a reaffirmation from the Teacher of the principle of divine judgment in relation to desert—which is, characteristically of many interlocutors in a broadly Socratic discussion, offered a little too confidently. But it is a great relief to have Paul now consistently asking the questions in this diatribal sub-section, as well as throughout the broader argument, as a Socratic figure should, and thereby offering views on Israel that are consistent with what he says later on in Romans, that is, God's relationship with his chosen people is fundamentally benevolent and merciful. Blithely unaware of the looming trap, however, the Teacher thunders against Paul's provocations that God must judge even sinful Jews, and the condemnation of those who differ from this opinion is deserved! With his final snare set, Paul springs it in the sub-section's last argumentative phase.

"But if you [i.e., this alternative 'gospel's' preacher] insist on maintaining your commitment to divine judgment of transgressors (3:1–9a), then you will find *yourself* in deep trouble, because the Scriptures that we all endorse define *everyone* as being so thoroughly sinful (3:9b–18). Your gospel cannot deal with sin, as we have already established, so in the light of this new premise—of total human depravity—your gospel just ends up with everyone being sentenced by God to death, including you! And your 'proclamation' has been reduced thereby to a dumbfounded silence (3:19–20). It is useless." That is, the existence of human depravity, which the Scriptures attest to widely, must lead in the Teacher's terms to *universal* condemnation. So, far from being an announcement of good news, the Teacher's "gospel" is now actually an exercise in futility, in numerous respects, and self-evidently so. *It cannot even save its proclaimer,* whom the Scriptures declare is a sinner too, and hence liable to condemnation! And with this final realization the Teacher is of course reduced to silence (so 3:19).

It is hard to know whether this last refutation is, strictly speaking, another argument in terms of self-contradiction pursued on the broader grounds that both Paul and the Teacher submit to Scriptural authority. Possibly the Teacher did deploy harshly condemning Scriptural texts within his preaching to the pagans—and perhaps even *this* catena—in which case Paul is still moving within the argumentative orbit of strict self-contradiction. But this cannot really be proved, although neither does it need to be. Irrespective of the premise's exact origin and argumentative definition, it functions theologically and argumentatively to put the last nail in the Teacher's own soteriological coffin. Having conceded that his gospel of circumcision and Torah-observance offers no advantages in the critical struggle against sin, and hence also against the consequent risk of judgment, the Teacher is still technically able to fulfill his own program. There may be no point in converting, but some righteous pagans and Jews, including him, might still be saved on grounds of adequate performance. However, the Scriptural catena's emphatic insistence on universal and thoroughgoing sin puts paid to these last hopes. "No one is righteous" it declares repeatedly, at which point the Teacher's program is rendered *entirely* useless, even for him. He too will be liable to condemnation, along with everyone else. In true Socratic fashion then, the foolish interlocutor, largely on grounds of self-contradiction, but perhaps assisted by appeal to a mutual authority, has ended up utterly humiliated, his position in complete ruins.

The key realization within this alternative Socratic construal of Romans 1–3, which solves so many problems, is that Paul does not need to be committed himself to the initial premises of the text for the argument to work; indeed, it works *better* if he is not so committed and the argument consequently folds back on itself, inexorably exposing the difficulties of any advocate of its initial premises in sequential steps, and ultimately humiliating that advocacy.[16] The puzzling redundancies and

---

16. So, a little ironically, although I am often accused of bringing unwarranted assumptions to the text in my reading, it is those who construe it forward who must bring that critical assumption to the text without any explicit support. Where does the text ever state that Paul himself endorses the premises of 1:18–20 and 2:6? It does not. And I know of no evidence or good arguments from elsewhere that suggest he would.

concessions of chapter 2 noted briefly earlier on now function as powerful argumentative moves on Paul's part. Conversion to Jewish practices is pointless, Jewish superiority (in these terms) is ephemeral, and ultimately the entire arrangement is futile.[17] And the text's broader collisions between the concerns of retributive justice and desert in relation to transgressions over against the constraints of sinful depravity, are also now explicable.

There is insufficient space to note the many advantages of the Socratic reading here, although *Deliverance* documents them (arguably a little overzealously). However, observe what has happened to the acute problem in the usual forward construal of Romans 1–3 with "the Jew" and Judaism. As for Galatians 2:15–16, this problem has now evaporated. Chapters 1 through 3 of Romans are simply not talking about Judaism *per se*, and the sigh of interpretative relief should be audible. (The entire argument is actually a devastating subversion of *religion*, that is, of soteriological conditionality or contractualism—a subversion that is still rather useful.) This is a *huge* advantage in my alternative reading that my critics seem oblivious to. Sanders's problem with respect to Jewish description in Paul has at this point been resolved. Why fight it, I ask myself? But many have and it is time now to consider the principal objection.

Is My Alternative Socratic Reading Possible?

Some have been unhappy that more sources contemporary to Paul have not been cited by me supporting the phenomenon in the ancient world of what we moderns would call "block quotation" (i.e., use of up to a paragraph of someone else's material), which my reading suggests is the case for 1:18–32, where the argument begins with—I suggest—a

17. And it does so, moreover, in a way that certain theologians and philosophers have often recognized. A foundational commitment to desert is very destructive to particular revealed traditions; they are essentially incompatible. Paul, moreover, seems well aware of this and so is using an initial concession to desert by his opponent to embarrass his commitments elsewhere to particularity and revelation, not to mention, to sinfulness. The result is a master class in Socratic subversion pursued here by way of the collision between desert and Judaism. I learned about this dynamic first when studying Islamic mediaeval philosophy and the travails, in particular, of the Mu'tazilites, Islam's first philosophical school. They ran into deep difficulties with orthopractic Moslems by pressing the premise of God's justice too far. Wolfson's account, *The Philosophy of the Kalam*, is dated but a useful starting point.

repristination of the opening position of the Teacher. One of my *JSNT* reviewers, Grant Macaskill, even goes on to suggest that my reading is *therefore* an implausible one ("The Deliverance of God," 158–59). Rapid reflection suggests that this is not an especially powerful rebuttal, but it has been so widespread that I am going to devote some time in what follows to its refutation. That is, the principal "reason" cited in my experience for the rejection of my suggested construal of Romans 1–3 is along the lines of "the Roman readers of Paul's letter would never have realized that he was arguing Socratically in 1:18—3:20; therefore your construal ought to be rejected as untenable"; "Romans simply could not have been understood this way"; "there is not enough explicit evidence for your reading"; or some such.

However, there are a number of serious problems with this line of objection.

(1) It overlooks the positive evidence I supply for the cogency of my reading, which is primarily argumentative, as we have just seen in specific relation to Judaism, although it is important to appreciate that I am not suggesting analyzing Romans 1:18–32 in isolation and making a snap judgment of "speech-in-character" in relation to this text alone. This role is only apparent when all of 1:18—3:20 is in view. With this extended purview, I suggest there are good reasons for construing Romans 1–3 in Socratic terms as a whole as against prospectively. It is a better argument, and more responsible in theoretical terms in relation to the rest of Paul's thinking about important topics, and so on. These broader advantages then make the assignment of a "dramatized" role to 1:18–32, the first paragraph in the argument, likely. And this positive evidence adduced by me at some length in *Deliverance* cannot just be ignored. Put slightly differently: the objection that "the Romans just would not have heard this text in this fashion" leaves all this positive, essentially argumentative evidence for my proposal intact. If the original Roman readers could distinguish a good argument from a bad argument, then they did hear the text in a Socratic fashion.

But (2) there is sufficient data in the sources explicitly attesting to the presence of Socratic argumentation, along with its intrinsic dramatized sub-sections, in the ancient world to confirm its possibility for Paul and his auditors. There is even a letter genre that affirms it: the "ironic" ('Εἰρωνική). Pseudo-Libanius describes a type of letter "in which at the beginning we praise someone by means of acting, but in the end reveal our goal—that what was spoken was acted." This is an apt description in general terms of what I suggest is taking place in the opening chapters of Romans, namely, an opening argument in a letter that subsequent developments reveal is not in the letter-writer's own voice.

(3) Even more significantly, children in Paul's day were taught to recognize this technique. It is described in ancient school teaching manuals, the *Progymnasmata*, usually as "character-making" or *ethopoiia* (ἠθοποιία; another useful translation alternative is "speech-in-character").[18] Children were taught how to read and to compose fictitious speeches in character—and sometimes even in letter form—in the ancient equivalent of a modern high school education. So, far from being a rarified rhetorical technique, it was an interpretative staple in Paul's day. Dramatizations in texts seem to have been standard. Expansions on Hermogenes' classic textbook attributed to John of Sardis state that this technique "often occurs in narratives *and refutations* . . ."[19] Later he then says "practice in ethopoeia is most useful everywhere; for it does not contribute to only one species of rhetoric but to all. Everywhere, as it happens, we form characters and attribute speeches to persons. . . . We shall have need of it in any speech."[20] But the *Progymnasmata* are helpful in a further important respect.

(4) Every extant treatise trains its students in argumentation, and so devotes considerable attention to refutation, going on to speak explicitly in this relation of refutation through the (Socratic) demonstration of internal contradiction. Theon says "contradiction (*antirrhêsis*) is

18. The earliest recorded teacher, Aelius Theon, discusses it as *prosôpopoiia* (προσωποποιία), but this becomes a more specialized designation in the later material referring the personification of entities as against character-making in the sense of speeches composed for historical or past figures. See Malherbe, *Ancient Epistolary Theorists*, letter 68, 17–19; see also the manuals by Aelius Theon, Hermogenes, Aphthonius, Nicolaus the Sophist, and John of Sardis's and/or Sopatris's comments on Aphthonius; references and further discussion in *Deliverance*, 533. See Klauck and Bailey, *Ancient Letters*, 203: Ps-Dem 20 has become Ps-Libanius 5. See also Pitts, "Philosophical and Epistolary Contexts." Note, the Papyrus Anastasi I[15] (late second millennium BC) contains a satirical letter which first praises the qualities of its recipient, but then mocks his limited knowledge and achievements; see Gardiner 1911 (British Museum, papyrus no. 10247). Paul's letters have consistently defied exact parallels, but ancient letters were supposedly close to conversation: Cic. *Fam.*, 9.21.1. Moreover, Paul says he wants to "teach and admonish" (etc.) if he is present, so presumably this is what happens in his letters too. How would he deal with opponents then?

19. Kennedy, ed., *Progymnasmata*, 214, emphasis added.

20. Ibid., 217.

discourse that attacks the credibility of another discourse. Try to show
... [inter alia] that the speaker spoke as much against as for himself—
what some call turning his argument against himself..." (72). One of the
techniques used for rebuttal then was the demonstration of inconsistency
in the opposing position. Students were also trained to undermine opposing positions because of unclearness, incredibility and impossibility,
inappropriateness, inexpedience, and other circumstantial factors, says
Nicolaus the Sophist (145). He goes on to opine, however, that "the most
contentious heading, and the one most useful to us, is what is called 'inconsistency' (*makhomenon*), where we show that the opponent is speaking in contradiction of himself and in opposition to his own proposition"
(146). (John of Sardis comments helpfully, further, that "there is no need
to use intemperate rudeness; one should suit the words to the quality of
the supposed persons. . . . One ought to compose the argument in a way
that is restrained and indicative of character" [200]). So the Socratic argumentative strategy that I am suggesting is operative in Romans 1:18—
3:20 is explicitly identified in what we might loosely call the high school
textbooks of Paul's day, in particular relation to the students' training in
refutation.[21] Not surprisingly then we find this argumentative style present in various contemporary Jewish and Roman, and in later Christian
sources.[22]

21. The rest of his argument is susceptible to this type of analysis as well, in particular, the introduction of an extended *synkrisis* in 3:27—4:25; the last part of this
comparison, 4:16b–22, arguably employing *ecphrasis* or vivid description—as Hermogenes puts it, "bringing what is shown clearly before the eyes" (117). Confirmations of
Paul's own positions then begin from 5:1.

22. Cf. Kahn, *Plato and the Socratic Dialogue*; Clay, *Platonic Questions*; and more
generally Genette, *Palimpsests*. Cicero attests to the presence of this form in Paul's day,
and there are frequent, more fragmentary utilizations in Philo. The mode then recurs
in church tradition—for example, in Justin's *Dialogue with Trypho*; in the *Adamantius
Dialogue* (probably fourth century); in Gregory of Nyssa's *On the Body* and *Dialogue
on the Soul and Resurrection*; and perhaps more distantly in Origen's *Against Celsus*.
It is likely that Paul would have been quite familiar with the phenomenon of debate,
being a member of the one of the Jewish "parties," the Pharisees, that was constantly
in both internal and external debate, as the Gemaras especially attest. Jewish debate
has its own distinctive practices, obviously quoting Jewish Scripture extensively, but
it also shared many features with wider Hellenistic rhetorical practice. See in this
relation esp. David Daube, "Socratic Interrogation," in *The New Testament and Rabbinic Judaism*, 151–57; see also 158–69. I am also encouraged here by the fact that
at a relatively recent presentation at Duke on purity issues, Christine Hayes quoted a
Talmudic text that contained some nice examples of Rabbinic speech-in-character; cf.
M. Yad 4:6–7. See also Zellentin for wider documentation of Rabbinic sensitivity to

(5) We turn now to the question of explicit evidence in Paul. And here we need to recall that all scholars accept that Paul does quote from an interlocutor at times in the early argumentative stages of Romans, and as close by 1:18–32 as 3:1–9a. (This figure is even addressed directly, in apostrophe, from 2:1.) Many scholars accept, further, that Paul uses another distinctive voice in what we would call paragraphs as well, especially through much of Romans 7:7–25, a text rather longer than 1:18–32.[23] And the use of this strategy here has even been recognized since ancient times, Origen, for example, reading much of this passage in terms of προσωποποιία. Some have objected that the relevant ancient sources generally mark the beginnings of such speeches overtly, a cue absent from the vicinity of Romans 1:18; however, this ancillary objection collapses on closer examination.[24] Suffice it to say then that quite a

---

irony (etc.), *Rabbinic Parodies*. An interesting discussion over the importance of the oral, performed dimension within Rabbinic textual interpretation is also relevant here; see Jaffee, *Torah in the Mouth*.

23. An even longer instance of speech-in-character in Paul is "the fool's speech" in 2 Cor 11:16—12:10. This speech is marked explicitly; however, it is the assumption on Paul's part of a stereotypical comic role and not of a particular person known both to him and the Corinthians. On Paul's important appeals to this discourse see esp. L. L. Welborn, *Paul, the Fool of Christ*. That Paul quotes repeatedly from the Corinthians in 1 Corinthians is also widely acknowledged, although many of these quotations are unmarked, leading to something of a cottage industry in relation to their reconstruction; cf. esp. 1:12; 3:4; 6:12–13; 7:1; 8:1, 4, 8; and 10:23; and possibly also 4:6b; 8:5a; 12:3; 15:12; and 15:35. It is, in short, established incontrovertibly that Paul quotes or voices positions from other figures within the broader epistolary situation in an unmarked fashion, *and* that he "speaks" in the voice of another person or role at times for extended periods, sometimes rather longer than Rom 1:18–32. What is not so clear is that he speaks in another voice for an extended time in an unmarked text, but it would seem to be obtuse to exclude this possibility categorically. However, Rom 7:11–25 may well be such a parallel instance, *and in Romans*.

24. That is, the ancient authors of some of the explicit theoretical discussions—and some of its most famous ancient examples—say that they are about to make such a speech-in-character. But I am not impressed by this argument, on three principal grounds.

(1) It is not surprising that elite published texts by people like Cicero or Quintilian mark examples or instances of speech-in-character explicitly. These markings would be necessary for audiences reading such generalized texts who were far removed from any concrete circumstances. However, *contingent* texts needed no such signals (which are often clumsy in those locations), and Romans was contingent.

(2) This argument involves a false entailment and a false inference. The argument goes: "theoretical texts discussing 'speech-in-character' contain explicit markings. *Therefore,* unmarked texts contain no 'speech-in-character.'" This is

body of evidence in Paul himself, and in Romans, attests directly to the presence of this dialogical strategy.

(6) We should recall as well that texts functioned very differently in the ancient world from our modern one within a fundamentally different culture of production and reception. Hence we must resist the tendency for anachronism to intrude into subtle interpretative judgments that we are not actually competent to make; readers of Paul are operating in an emphatically cross-cultural situation and must make due allowance for this (and even in modern geographically and socially dispersed situations these differences are often underestimated). Duke classicist William Johnson drew my attention to the following passage in Quintilian that describes ancient reading culture:

> (20) . . .[O]ur reading must be almost as thorough as if we were actually transcribing what we read. Nor must we study it merely in parts, but must read through the whole work from cover to cover and then read it afresh, a precept which applies more especially to speeches, whose merits are often deliberately disguised. (21) For the orator frequently prepares his audience for what is to come, dissembles and sets a trap for them and makes remarks at the opening of his speech which will not have their full force till the conclusion. Consequently what he says will often seem comparatively ineffective where it actually occurs, since we do not realise his motive and it will be necessary to re-read the speech after we have acquainted ourselves with all that it contains. (*Institutes of Oratory* 10.1.19–21)[25]

a false entailment. But it is also a false claim. This argument must, if taken seriously, *exclude all unmarked parodic and ironic textual functions from the Greco-Roman encyclopaedia*, which is self-evidently absurd (see esp. the comments related to Juvenal below). The Greco-Roman world was replete with texts speaking unmarked, often for comic effect, in voices other than those of the author.

(3) The evidence of Origen just noted is especially instructive, who appeals to *prosôpopoiia* extensively in relation to Romans 7 but without overt textual markings. (Other patristic evidence corroborates Origen's basic manoeuvre extensively.) Origen's comments simply falsify this contention.

25. That is, some of my critics seem to suppose that Paul's letter to the Romans was meant to be comprehensible on one reading, like many modern English texts. So they ask "when" Paul's auditors were supposed to detect that 1:18–32 was a block quotation denoting the preaching of some other preacher, at the front end of a Socratic argument. But this concern betrays an anachronism. Ancient texts were syllabic documents lacking a vast amount of interpretative assistance delivered to modern readers by way of punctuation. (So Stephen Saenger goes so far as to suggest that non-spaced texts

I have no doubt in view of this that Quintilian, after repeated readings and ongoing reflection, would have been able to detect a Socratic strategy on Paul's part, and presumably been delighted by it. Conversely, modern scholars, located within a fundamentally different reading discourse, should be cautious of snap judgments based on their own interpretative intuitions.

(7) A further deep problem for this objection is its oversight of the role of performative cues in relation to any ancient text's public presentation, cues that were in play for a letter's reception by way of the letter bearers. Scholars have begun to realize relatively recently that communication in any contingent or "live" context depends to a surprisingly large extent on performed verbal and bodily non-verbal cues, estimates of the contributions of these to the actual communication taking place ranging as high as 70 percent. Given that the letter bearers of Romans, Phoebe and her entourage (cf. 16:1–2), would have heard the performance of this letter in Paul's presence at Corinth and been instructed by him in various ways, it seems positively absurd then to suggest that a Socratic opening could not have been communicated to the original Roman auditors utilizing such cues by the original letters bearers. The opening would have been performed in this way, both verbally and non-verbally, and repeatedly. And then, if necessary, it would also have been explained.[26]

(8) It should be added, finally, that ancient Roman readers were probably rather more sensitive to such performative cues than modern

functioning in the first instance syllabically require a fundamentally different reading process from modern spaced texts, including preparatory, oral, and repeated readings: see his *Space Between Words*; this claim is greatly exaggerated, however.) They also participated in a very different reading culture. So they were often read repeatedly, and practically memorized, before being read out loud more definitively. And then they were often reread and pressed for further insights. Johnson's work is now definitive in this relation; see "Toward a Sociology of Reading in Classical Antiquity," 593–627; and *Readers and Reading Culture*.

26. Helpful here are Head, "Letter Carriers"; "Named Letter-Carriers"; see also Boegehold, *When a Gesture Was Expected*. Modern readers have of course lost these, but performed in the right way—perhaps assisted by people bearing the letter and so originally instructed by Paul—there is no doubt that the apostle's ancient auditors could have grasped that someone else was talking in 1:18–32. This would have been as easy to signal as shifting voices in a rehearsal of a Shakespeare play. A different performance of a text means different characters are involved. It is pretty obvious. The literature on performative and non-verbal cues is vast but cf. esp. Bauman, "Verbal Art as Performance." An instructive reminder of the importance of Corinth in relation to the composition and performance of Romans is Hartwig and Theissen, "Die Korinthische Gemeinde als Nebenadressat des Romerbriefs."

post-European interpreters.[27] It is worth recalling that the Romans loved pointed comic drama and virtually invented satire.[28] Moreover, their culture was generally more attuned than ours is to the inflections of irony, perhaps as modern British (and New Zealand) culture is still more attuned to this subtle form of humor than modern American culture. Even more importantly but in like manner, ancient hierarchical societies tended to generate a web of discourses that were considerably more sensitive to sub-texts than those operative within modern "open" societies. As James Scott's classic analysis has shown (*Domination and the Arts of Resistance*), a person's life often depended on her ability to detect these nuances, so these skills were highly developed. In addition, however, nuanced oral performances by the lower classes provided subtle means of resistance to oppressors, the broader situation requiring that such acts of resistance nevertheless be temporary and completely deniable, hence oral and nuanced—a situation barely comprehensible to most modern academic interpreters. (And the original recipients of Romans were poor.[29]) In short, it seems likely that members of ancient Roman society were more attuned to subtle performative signals, and to those operating in a fundamentally ironic mode, than interpreters located in modern post-European culture within open societies less structured in terms of

27. See (inter alia) Susanna M. Braund's analysis of Roman satire, *The Roman Satirists*, particularly her comments on 56; and Susan Braund's published doctorate *Beyond Anger*. Juvenal has recently been reevaluated as classicists have detected his unsignaled and near-universal use of προσωποποιία—for him more likely *fictiones personarum*—to sustained comic effect. And this reinforces the extent to which philosophical dialogues, especially when well done, were merely *dramatizations* of arguments, and so could be recognized with the standard dramatic cues, i.e., by *acting* at the appropriate moments. That is, the sense of a text often depends on performed and non-verbal cues (which are different and reinforce one another), which would have been present in an epistolary situation.

28. Putting things a little more bluntly (although there should really be no need to state the following): modern interpretative intuitions are not an automatic guide to ancient textual dynamics but, on the converse, will often be misleading. That a reading of a text composed two thousand years ago by an author located in a different culture speaking and writing a different language "does not feel right" is clearly not an argument for its implausibility unless evidence can be martialed from the ancient interpretative encyclopaedia that explicitly supports such an intuition. Without such evidence we may simply be suffering from a case of modern interpretative hubris. And when the intuition in question *is* explicable in terms of deeply-rooted modern theological commitments and ecclesiastic locations, scholars should be doubly wary of any such pronouncements.

29. See definitively Lampe, *From Paul to Valentinus*.

class. Modern interpreters could easily be as insensitive to certain subtle signals as ancient overlords were, recalling that this was entirely deliberate, and resulted in mockery and derision.

With this realization I suspect that more than enough has been said to refute the principal objection offered to date against my suggested construal of Romans 1:18—3:20 in Socratic terms.[30] My "refutation of the refutation" does not establish the truth of my Socratic suggestion. But it does establish that is a real possibility, and hence affirms in the same breath the need for a candid comparison of respective readings as well.

30. I have detected two other types of substantive objections:

(1) That various pieces of text in Romans 1–3 are incompatible with this reading. This really ought to be the principal line of objection (i.e., the construal cannot explain all the overt extant data), but to date it is largely limited to one suitably annotated paragraph in Matlock's extensive critique ("Zeal for Paul," 141–43; cf. 115–49)—a sign I take it of the difficulty of actually finding such problem texts for the reading. (Presumably if they lay obviously to hand then Matlock would certainly have found and exploited them extensively.) But all the "problem texts" that he names were clearly anticipated and addressed in *Deliverance* (see 1:18 in an obvious parallel to 1:17 [?!]; the presence of a doxology in 1:25; the citation of Scripture in 2:6 [?!]; the phrase "my gospel" in 2:16; the assignment of voice in 3:1–8 [?!]; and the middle or passive aorist in 3:9; discussed in *Deliverance*, 542–81 and notes). Suffice it to say then that my critics need more than problematic and possible readings of textual data to refute my construal; they need problematic and necessary readings, which as yet they have not produced.

(2) An appeal to tradition is often made—an especially curious objection because it is generally asserted by *Protestants*. But the basic Protestant *and* historical critical postures are that reconstruction of the original (Scriptural) text overrides and informs tradition, not vice versa. So probably a different sort of objection really underlies this protest, namely, that it is implausible that the correct but very different approach to Romans 1–3 I am suggesting lay undiscovered for so long. However, this is again a weak objection to make in a historical critical arena. If valid, it must consign the vast majority of historical critical work to invalidity and oblivion, which seems wrong. Equally significantly, good reasons can be supplied in explanation of the insensitivity of the bulk of the tradition to a Socratic reading. This tradition has been predominantly ecclesial. And ecclesial tradition has generally been insensitive until very recently to the stereotypical and insensitive description of Jews. It has also treated Romans (in Beker's terms) coherently, rather than contingently. The current insensitivity of "tradition" to a Socratic reading is then actually a relic of its pre-critical reading, a situation facilitated by the struggles scholars have had explaining Romans' contingency. These are both powerful explanations of past reading(s) but utterly illegitimate interpretative postures today. A historical critical retrieval of the original reception of Romans is therefore both legitimate and salutary.

My approach cannot simply be dismissed out of hand and this concrete comparison thereby just avoided. But it will be profitable to pursue this broad line of objection by some of my detractors for just a little longer.

Some of my critics, in a related attack, have suggested that my construal of Romans 1–3 lacks an explicit declaration of its strategy. ("Where does Paul ever tell us that he is running a reduction from 1:18?" or some such.)[31] This is, of course, on one level just a false claim. The interlocutor I orient Paul's Socratic refutation around is quite overt in the text (see 2:1–5, 17–24; 3:1–9a); he is indeed the most detailed character ever constructed explicitly in a Pauline text, with the possible exception of Abraham. The presence of this figure in this text surrounded on both sides by dialogical exchanges is a clear direct signal—at least to ancient readers—that a Socratic text is present. (It has been masked through much of Romans' interpretative history on the assumption that this figure represents Judaism.) But a further rejoinder to this charge is possible.

It seldom seems to be noticed that my critics tend to fail their own challenge at this point; that is, they seldom offer any explicit positive support for their own reading. ("Justify your own reading you judger," I am tempted to say.) Scholars tend to read Romans 1–3 as an argument, as we have earlier seen, from self-evident premises to a particular conclusion—that God will condemn everyone, Jew and Gentile, if the gospel of faith is not embraced. They read it forward. And an enormous amount flows from this decision: a quagmire of interlaced problems that may render the broader theological description of Paul's gospel incoherent. This is therefore an absolutely critical interpretative decision. Indeed, it is arguably one of the most important that we ever make in relation to a Pauline text. But such readers apparently do not seem to feel the need to offer much explicit justification for the initial interpretative judgment on their part that generates this swamp (apart, that is, from an odd appeal to "tradition"). So I ask them here and now: *where is the explicit*

---

31. See (inter alia) Schreiner: "[C]lear contextual evidence for an interpretation of this sort is lacking . . ." ("The Deliverance of God," 290). Matlock makes the same complaint: "[t]he problem again is that none of this is explicitly marked. Could Paul's audience have picked up on what he was doing?" ("Zeal for Paul," 141). So too Gorman: "Campbell is unable to provide credible formal evidence for this thesis from the immediate context or from Paul's letters more generally," "Douglas Campbell's *The Deliverance of God*," 106). He adds on p. 107: "Appeals to a knowledgeable first-century audience that will detect what we miss will not suffice." But presumably the original audience *did* detect a lot of things that we modern interpreters miss. And we can only detect such omissions by reconstructing their encyclopaedia, in explicit resistance to our own interpretative prejudices.

evidence that in Romans 1–3 Paul is arguing forward? Where does he say this in Romans—"I am about to prepare the ground for the gospel's reception," or some such? The short answer is that he does not. Indeed, Paul never tells us explicitly how the argument in Romans 1–3 is to function. We must therefore reach a judgment about this passage after reading it through repeatedly as Quintilian recommended, and considering it both as a whole and in its broader epistolary context—whether it reads appropriately as a *praeparatio evangelica* that spends a great deal of time crushing Jews in rather jaundiced terms, or, rather better, as a cunning Socratic embarrassment of a Jewish Christian missionary rival. In short, the observation that there are no explicit signals of an argumentative strategy in the text settles nothing. It merely poses the key question. But my critics have opened themselves up by way of this objection to a further nasty problem for their own prospective approach.

In the absence of explicit textual indicators in Romans, we should bring in comparative evidence from Paul's other letters to evaluate the claim that Paul is beginning to preach his own gospel from 1:18. The usual approach to Romans 1–3 has been on the assumption that Paul is laying out his gospel—articulating his basic evangelistic stump speech, so to speak—so we are entitled to ask for evidence supporting this claim. What evidence do we have from elsewhere in Paul that when he preaches his gospel he preaches it in *this* way, forward, as Romans 1–3 ostensibly argues? And at this point we encounter a profound problem for advocates of the conventional, forward reading.

The short answer is that, outside of Romans 1–3 read forward, there is no decisive, explicit evidence that Paul presented his gospel in a foundational way, arguing from a primary and definitive account of a problem on self-evident grounds to a particular solution comprehensible on that basis.[32] What evidence we do have suggests instead that the gospel was *not* presented by Paul in an epistemologically progressive fashion. As the word εὐαγγέλιον itself suggests, it was *announced!*[33] Moreover, there are good reasons for reading the rest of Paul's texts apocalyptically or in terms of revelation—an unconditional divine action not merely

---

32. Any appeal at this point to "the Areopagus speech" should now be informed especially by the recent definitive study by Rowe ("The Grammar of Life"). He has shown how, correctly understood, this speech by Paul—which I take to have some historical veracity, although its degree is very difficult to establish—is further evidence of his practice of Socratic engagement with opposition and therefore corroborates my suggested reading of Romans 1–3.

33. See *Deliverance*, 158–64 and endnotes.

dispensing with any philosophical preamble but explicitly overruling it. Hence every such apocalyptic emphasis elsewhere in Paul stands against the suggested reading of Romans 1–3 forward. The matter can be put crisply by observing that if an interpreter takes the theological epistemology articulated in 1 Corinthians 1:18—2:16 seriously, then the conventional forward approach to Romans 1–3 *must be excluded*. Paul's famous theology of the cross necessitates it.

So we have ended up at a supremely appropriate end point in this essay: an objection by some of my critics—that I provide demonstrable evidence from Romans for a Socratic construal of Romans 1:18—3:20— has turned out to rebound onto their own heads. Their *own* reading fails this challenge and its implications, and quite spectacularly, generating a not inappropriate point at which to draw a discussion to a close that contends that in Romans 1:18—3:20 Paul himself is demonstrating with some skill that the gospel of his Jewish Christian opponents, soon (in his view) to arrive at Rome, collapses on closer examination into self-contradictory futility.

10

Beyond Reasonable Hope of Recognition?

Prosōpopoeia *in Romans 1:18—3:8*

ROBIN GRIFFITH-JONES

By June 1845 Dr. Wiseman was anxious to know whether John Henry Newman would really convert to Rome. Wiseman sent Father Smith, a former pupil of Newman's who had converted, to Littlemore, "under cover of a simple visit of friendship," to discover how the land lay. In a cool conversation that never reached matters of substance, Father Smith found no clues. So the afternoon ended. But when they re-assembled for dinner, Smith noticed that Newman had changed his trousers. It was all that Smith needed. He returned post-haste to Wiseman. He reported that all was well: Newman clearly no longer regarded himself as an Anglican clergyman; he had worn *grey* trousers for dinner; it could not be long before he would submit to Rome.[1]

I feel rather like that visitor. Faced with the vast and intricate machinery of Campbell's argument, I will be drawing attention just to a single squeaky cog. My point is surely pedantic, and is perhaps answered

---

1. Strachey, "Cardinal Manning," 37.

in some measure by Campbell's own refinement of *Deliverance* in this book. But there remains, I think, some (serious) repair to be undertaken.[2]

Campbell's claim for Romans 1:32—3:20 is now familiar. At 1:18 Paul introduces a new *persona*: an opponent of his own views, who speaks until 1:32. The figure is not announced in the written text, of course; the new speaker will have been flagged up in the letter's declamation by gesture, expression, and tone—even perhaps by pitch and character—of voice. Paul starts his reply at 2:1 with a clear apostrophe, ὦ ἄνθρωπε πᾶς ὁ κρίνων. This dialogic form continues, with one clear and brisk exchange at 3:1–9, in Socratic, elenchic style through to 3:20, by which time the opponent's view has been driven to its inescapable and absurd conclusion.

The most striking element in the argument is the first: that 1:18–32 is a block-speech in character. Elsewhere in this volume exegetes and theologians discuss the substance of this claim. Here I ask only the formal question: whether Paul's text suggests that he is likely to be using this rhetorical device here in this way. The challenge might be bluntly phrased: would Paul—and *why* would Paul—have launched into speech-in-character without introducing and identifying the speaker? If Campbell is right, every other reader in nearly two thousand years has missed the whole point of the passage; and Paul, by the unannounced change of "speaker," has only himself to blame for the confusion.

Such speech-in-character, *prosōpopoeia*, pervades ancient literature; and Campbell is in his current work emphasizing, to good effect, the *Socratic* character of the device. Plato, however, may not offer Campbell the precedent that would strengthen his case. The dialogues were—very famously—*dialogues*.[3] At the start of the *Theaetatus* Euclid explains to

2. Similar concerns have been raised by Macaskill, "*The Deliverance of God*," 158–59, and Matlock, "Zeal for Paul," 141–43.

3. Douglas values a comparison with Socratic dialogues. We have some slender evidence for at least some types of their performance. The host in *Deipnosophistae* 9 tells of a man who had his cooks learn the dialogues of Plato and to recite them—one slave to a part—as they brought in the dishes, nicely starting with (for example) that part of the *Timaeus* where the setting is established (Athen. *Deipn.* 9:381–2). Plutarch has a dialogue that tells of such performances reaching Rome: slaves were taught the most lively of the dramatic dialogues, to say them by rote, in a *hupokrisis* suited to the personalities of the characters in the text, with modulations of voice and gestures and delivery suited to the meaning. (It is unclear whether a single slave played more than one part.) The innovation had met with mixed reactions: some thought that even the great lyric poets such as Sappho should be listened to only in silence and with great respect, others that new comedy was suitable for a party, whereas old comedy—with its outspokenness and buffoonery—was not (Plut. *Mor.* 711C–712A). So in elite circles,

Terpsion, "I have written the account in this way: not Socrates describing things as he described them to me, but Socrates in dialogue with those with whom he was in dialogue. He was speaking to Theodorus the geometrician and Theaetetus. So I have omitted the interlocutory explanations both about Socrates himself (when he said such things as 'I spoke,' or 'I remarked') and about his interlocutors (such as 'he agreed,' or 'disagreed'), to prevent them being a nuisance" (142b–c). The listener or reader is being warned: there are none of the familiar markers in the following dialogue.[4]

Would the audience hearing Paul's letter to the Romans have expected or spotted such an unannounced dialogue in any forensic or deliberative speech, or in any narrative? Stowers and then Campbell invoke a sentence of Quintilian's: "words [in *prosōpopoeia*] may be inserted without the introduction of any speaker at all" (Quint. *Inst.* 9.2.37).[5] As an example, Quintilian quotes one line (*Aen.* 2:29) from Virgil's account of the Trojans' exploration of the deserted Greek camp. Here is its context:

> . . . Iuvat ire et Dorica castra
> desertosque videre locos litusque relictum.
> hic Dolopum manus, hic saevus tendebat Achilles;
> classibus hic locus; hic acie certare solebant. (*Aen.* 2.27–30)[6]

No speaker is specified because no one speaker (if any speaker at all) is in mind; Virgil is simply making the scene vivid. Whatever this is, it is not an extended block of "speech-in-character."

Campbell adduces some further examples of the device that he understands Paul to be deploying in Romans 1:18–32. But Campbell's examples have this particular difference: *the speech is clearly introduced and the speaker is clearly identified.* Why does this matter? At issue here is

---

at least, it was natural to enjoy the drama of the dialogues.

4. The *Symposium* has, among the dialogues, the most elaborate setting: Apollodorus is telling a companion how he was stopped by Glaucon only two days before and was asked to tell Glaucon just what his present companion wants: an account of Socrates' discussion (when he and Aristodemus had been invited into by Agathon) of love, about which Aristodemus had told him and whose details he (Apollodorus) had checked with Socrates.

5. Stowers, *Rereading Romans*, 20, and now Campbell, *Deliverance*, 533.

6. . . . It was a joy to go and see the Greek camp,
the deserted sites and the abandoned shore.
Here stayed the troops of Thessaly, here cruel Achilles,
here lay the fleet, here they would meet us in battle.

no grand principle, just practicality: how did Paul expect his letter to be *effective* if he did not make unambiguously clear that he was relaying the words of his opponents? Here are three of Campbell's examples:

Cicero, Pro Caelio 14:34—17:39: Cicero's attack on Clodia.[7] Cicero invokes with fanfare Appius Claudius the Blind.

> If he appears, this is how he will plead, this is how he will speak: "Woman, what have you to do with Caelius? . . . Did I build the Via Appia so that you might process along it with a train of other women's husbands?" But why, judges, have I introduced so stern a person? . . . But as for you, woman (for now I speak with you myself, with no other person brought in). . . . If you prefer me to take a more urbane tone, . . . I will take your youngest brother. . . . Imagine him speaking with you: "Why are you making such an uproar, sister? . . . Why do you trouble this man who rejects your advances?" Now I return to you, Caelius, and myself assume the authority and severity of a father. . . . Such a father would say, "Why have you taken yourself into that company of prostitution? . . ." To this glum and outspoken old man, Caelius would reply that he had not been led by any greed to stray from the right path. . . . But if I take a mild and indulgent father, . . . then Caelius' case is without difficulty. . . . But someone else will say, "Is this then your self-restraint? . . ."

All the protagonists, so unambiguously introduced, can speak forcefully and clearly.

Seneca, Ad Neronem Caesarem De Clementia, 1:1–4. Seneca is addressing the Emperor. He imagines the Emperor speaking with himself. The Emperor's words are, as we would expect, clearly introduced. Seneca opens: "I have undertaken, Nero Caesar, to write on the subject of mercy, in order to serve in a way the purpose of a mirror, and thus reveal you to yourself. . . . It is a pleasure to inspect and go round a good conscience . . . and thus to speak with oneself: 'Have I from all mortals been chosen to serve on earth as regent of the gods?'"

And so in turn when the speech imagined for Nero ends, Seneca marks its conclusion: "You can, Caesar, boldly make this pronouncement."

---

7. Such clearly signaled speeches are commonplace. The Fatherland can speak (Cic. *In Cat.* 1:18: quae tecum, Catilina, sic agit et quodam modo tacita loquitur; ibid., 27, si mecum patria . . . si cuncta Italia, si omnis res publica loquatur). So can Death and Life (Quint. *Inst.* 9.2.32, 36), and the sea (Aristeides, according to Hermogenes, *Progymnasmata* 9); see *Ad Herenn.* 4.52–53 for further examples. In the translations that follow I have benefited gratefully from the LCL editions.

Quintilian, Institutes 10.1.16–17, 22: Campbell quotes Quintilian for the insight he offers into "ancient reading culture": "our reading," writes Quintilian, "must be almost as thorough as if we were actually transcribing what we read . . ." But Quintilian is making a particular point.

> Some things profit the listener, other things the reader. . . .
> [When we listen] everything is alive and stirring[;] . . . we are
> affected not only by the fortune of the trial but by the risk run
> by those who speak. Besides this, voice, appropriate gesture,
> the form of delivery adapted to the demands of every passage
> (the most powerful factor of all in speaking)—in a word, all
> are equally instructive. . . . Reading is independent; it does not
> hurtle past with the speed of performance, and you can go back
> over it again and again if you have any doubts or if you want to
> fix it firmly in your memory.

Next follows the passage quoted by Campbell. Then Quintilian instructs: "This is the most useful course: to know the cases . . . and wherever possible to read the pleadings on both sides." This, then, is not an example of general "ancient reading culture." It is what *students of forensic oratory* were to do, and what they still do today. Quintilian had in mind the speeches that were "in circulation," which should be "sought out" by the student; this would suggest the collection of texts for private study. Cicero edited and circulated his own speeches, and was no doubt pleased to have his speeches studied by students in the years following their delivery.[8] But first he had to win his case, there and then. Paul too, as Campbell himself rightly insists, was confronting a particular situation to which he sends a particular response. It is perhaps ironic that, as we shall see, Campbell's own construction of *prosōpopoeia* at Romans 3:1–9 occludes the best clue we have, in 3:8, to the immediate crisis that Paul was facing in the Romans' misapprehension of his gospel.

Pseudo-Libanius, Epistolary Styles 9: the ironic (εἰρωνική) letter.[9] Is the first part of such a letter, praising the recipients who will then be mocked, a neat example—as Campbell claims—of speech-in-character? No. The letter worked because the recipients believed that the praise

---

8. Cicero, unsurprisingly frightened by the Clodian claque disrupting the court, failed to win the acquittal of his client Titus Annius Milo. What Cicero published was not what he had said—however stumblingly—at the time. Milo remarked, from his exile, that if only Cicero had delivered the published speech, Milo himself would "not now be enjoying the delicious red mullet of Massilia," Dio *Hist.* 40.54.3.

9. Malherbe, *Ancient Epistolary Theorists*, 68, lines 17–19.

was serious; and for this, they must believe that the writer was speaking sincerely in his own voice.

We might round off this analysis by a return to Plato's dialogues themselves. Plato's Socrates uses such a block-speech in the *Crito*: the laws speak to Socrates at length; and just as we would expect, they are introduced, three times, to make sure we know they are still speaking (*Crito* 50C—54E).[10]

We can more quickly do justice to the form of short and snappy dialogue in which the speakers are indeed unannounced. Arrian's *Discourses* of Epictetus are peppered with such exchanges. (Dialogue may in many cases overstate the case; the thinking subject is just articulating the course of his or her thought. This is a simple trick, open to no misunderstanding.) Here is just one example:

> So-and-so is dead. Answer (ἀπόκριναι, flagging up the fact that an exchange has started), That is beyond the control of the reasoning will (ἀποαίρετον); not an evil. So-and-so's father has disinherited him. Beyond the control of the reasoning will; not an evil. Caesar has condemned him. Beyond the control of the reasoning will; not an evil. He was grieved at all this. Within the power of the reasoning will; an evil. . . . His son is dead. What happened? His son is dead. Nothing else? Nothing . . . (Epict. *Disc.* 3.8.2–5)

There is nothing surprising in either of these techniques. The difficulty lies in our imagining *how and why an orator would deploy a long block-speech with no clear introduction.* We must make a judgment here about likelihoods, a judgment based on a reading as wide and alert as possible in ancient literature.[11] My own reading is neither wide nor alert

10. Such speech-in-character was indeed a part of basic rhetorical education: Quintilian complains that teachers of *literature* were teaching boys *prosopopoeias ac suasarias*, which should clearly be taught in the schools of *rhetoric* to which the boys would move on next (Quint. *Inst.* 2.1.2). The "Jew" whom Celsus introduced at length (προσωποποιεῖ, εἰσάγει, Origen *Contra Celsum* 1:28) into *The True Doctrine* is among the most famous of such characters. At times he addressed Jesus, at times the Jews who believed in Jesus (*Contra Celsum*, Praef. 1:6, 1:28 and then books 1 and 2 *passim*). Origen is scornful about the character: Celsus "also introduces an imaginary character, somehow imitating a child having his first lessons with an orator, and brings in a Jew who addresses childish remarks to Jesus and says nothing worthy of a philosopher's grey hairs" (*Contra Celsum* 1:28). (Origen invites his readers to deride the rhetoric—and with it the more general intellectual standing—of a Celsus who composes speeches that so ill suit their speaker.) We cannot now tell how the Jew was introduced.

11. Stowers, *Rereading Romans*, 18, adduces Homeric speeches: "sometimes one

enough to be the basis for such judgment; but it is striking to find that the supposed examples of such speeches, adduced by those who have good reason to look for them, are in fact not examples at all.

To broaden our own horizons, it must suffice here to glance at just two of the church fathers. (I do so with some caution; we know, from the history of English-language rhetoric, that styles and fashions vary widely at different periods and in different places.) We will look briefly at Origen (because he has been invoked in support of Campbell's thesis) and at Cyril of Alexandria (because he made lavish use of block speech-in-character).

In Origen the argument for *prosōpopoeia* in Romans surely has its most powerful witness. Origen saw the device at 7:14–25; and Origen had an ear for Greek and for its rhetoric far better than any of us.

Origen is, however, a dangerous witness for Campbell to call here.[12]

1. At 7:14–25 Origen does not glide readily and relaxedly into an exposition of Paul's speech-in-character. On the contrary, he is driven to it by necessity. He has just elaborated his argument, sustained throughout the commentary, that Paul uses "law" in two quite different senses, of the Mosaic and of natural law; and that at 7:7–25 the "law" is—for to make sense of the passage it *must* be—the natural law. And now he must explain how the spiritual Paul, speaking with apostolic authority, could have spoken of his *spiritual* self as he speaks of the "I" in 7:14–25: "Let us conclude from these things that it is the custom of Holy Scripture to imperceptibly change the personae and the subject matter and the reasons about which it seems to speak, and the designations. Or rather, it uses the same designations at times for some subjects and at other times for others."[13] Paul, then, is adopting here the persona of a fleshly person (except at 7:25a) who is making the first efforts towards conversion. To

---

character or another speaks but often without the poet specifically indicating that such and such has begun to speak except by keeping the words in character with the speaker." But the speaker is always the character on whom the immediately preceding lines have focused, almost always as the subject of a verb of address and often with opening vocatives to signal the addressees. An indicative sample: in *Iliad* 1 there are thirty-five speeches; before every one the speaker is unambiguously identified *as the speaker*.

12. Text: Origen, *Comm. in Ep. B. Pauli ad Romanos*, PG 14:838–1292; and now Bammel, *Der Römerbriefkommentar*. Translation: Origen, *Commentary* (adapted).

13. Colligamus ex his quomodo moris est scripturae divinae et personas latenter et res et causas de quibus dicere videtur et nomina commutare, imo potius eisdem nominibus in aliis atque aliis rebus uti. Sheck draws attention to the argument that Origen "made homonymity the key of his interpretation" (Origen, *Commentary*, 2, 37 n. 211, citing R. Roukema, *The Diversity of Laws in Origen's Commentary on Romans*).

vindicate the reading, Origen adduces other examples of saints taking on the personae of sinners (Ps 38:3–6; Dan 9:5–7). As "law," so "I": Paul uses them both—as Origen explains in his long justificatory argument—with varying reference. Origen, faced with the obscurity of Paul's text, offers the best solution he can find.

2. This same Origen does *not* see *prosōpopoeia* at Romans 1:18–32. On the contrary: here he sees Paul expound the failings and destiny of the fleshly person who lacks all insight and all will to reformation. Far from seeing a change of voice or direction at 1:32, Origen breaks the section not at 1:32/2:1, but at 2:1/2:2; and he ends Book 1 of his commentary after his comments on 2:1.[14]

Cyril of Alexandria was clearly fond of *prosōpopoeia*. His usage reinforces all that we have said so far. Here are just two examples of extended block-speeches, both from his commentary on John.[15]

First: on John 5:23 (*Comm.* 2:8: 226d–229a) Cyril, interrupting his own exposition, flags up the impending objection from his opponents. I abbreviate the substance of the two positions to A and B. "What do they say to this, those who distort everything as Isaiah says? You suppose A, but you are stepping far from the truth. We will not grant B. Why do you (sing., as if addressed to Cyril himself) multiply words . . . ?" Cyril starts his own long reply: Τί οὖν πρὸς ταῦτα καὶ παρ' ἡμῶν; κτλ. After Cyril has spoken up for his own position, he reverts to the opponent: ἀλλὰ ναί, φησὶν ὁ δι' ἐναντίας, κτλ. Twice in the opponent's following speech Cyril adds φησίν, once before and once after the opponent quotes Genesis 9:6; Cyril wants to make clear at the start and end of the quotation that the opponent is still speaking.

And so to our second example. On John 6:38–39 (*Comm.* 4:39: 332d–337e) Cyril again alerts us to the opponents' looming interruption.

14. There are moments where Origen or Cyril was so vividly evoking the story's characters that it seemed quite natural and proper to expand those characters' speech in the commentator's own words. Even here, the technique is in general unambiguously clear. So Origen expands on the speech of the priests and levites at John 1:20–23; *Comm. in Joh.* 6:59; of the Baptist at Matt 3:11, *Comm.* 6:162–3 (with the Baptist speaking at length in the first person singular); and of Jesus himself at John 4:13–14, *Comm.* 13:14–16 (with a resumptive "I" after several lines); at John 13:6–11, *Comm.* 32:87–8 (on "my" washing your feet); at John 13:16–18, *Comm.* 32:156; at John 13:19, *Comm.* 32:169. Cyril expands the words of Jesus at, for example, *Comm. in Joh.* 4:1 ad 6:38–9 (331d–332a, with φησὶ three times), 4:5 ad 7:21 (418d–419a).

15. Text: Cyril, *In D. Joannis Evangelium*. Translation: Cyril, *Commentary*.

"But I perceive that I am saying what does not please the enemy of the truth. For he will by no means agree to the things which we have just said; but will cry out loudly, and will come with his shrill cry, 'Whither are you (sing.) leading astray, you sir (ὦ οὗτος), our line of thought. . . . You blush I suppose,' he says (φησί), 'to confess the involuntary subjection of the Son.'" A second φησί, several lines later, keeps the speaker's identity clear. Then Cyril counters: "With dreadful and extremely well-wheeled words, good sir (ὦ γεννᾶιε), as you surely think, you are riding us down." Some pages later we hear a formula used twice, once by each speaker, in quick succession and in opposition to each other. No reader could be in any doubt about the crispness of the exchange: Cyril's opponent interrupts Cyril, ἀλλ' αὐτὸ δὴ τοῦτο, φησί, τοῖς παρ' ἡμῶν λόγοις ἐπαγωνιεῖται, κτλ; Cyril snaps back: ἀλλ' αὐτὸ δὴ τοῦτο κατὰ τὴν σὴν φωνήν, ὦ οὗτος— "you will find to be nothing other than the fruit of your own ignorance."

The feature we should notice here above all else is how *natural*, how clear and conversational Cyril's usage is. It is everything that Paul's *prosōpopoeia*, in Campbell's argument, is not.

Campbell's argument depends on a performance of Paul's letter in which it was clear not only when the speaker changed but who at any moment the speaker was. We can of course suggest a setting for the letter's first performances that satisfies this need. Phoebe, perhaps, brought the letter to Rome (16:1–2). She knew Paul's thought well; she was well equipped—and perhaps as the person delivering the letter would have been invited?—to read out the letter to a closed meeting of the leaders in the Roman church or churches, with all the gestures and changes of tone, and perhaps with even the glosses too, which will have prevented any misunderstanding. This could have been a session of careful discussion and assessment. It will have been up to local leaders to decide whether and when such a letter was to be recited to the congregations (1 Thess 5:27). We might then envision the letter's declamation to the congregations—once more by Phoebe?—in the setting of one or of several weeks' liturgy. Such a reconstruction is speculative; but it is probably better to speculate than to blind ourselves *tout court* to the likelihood of a performance and to the surrounding circumstances.

Let us then imagine the first pages of Romans as they would have been heard, on Campbell's interpretation, in their first public delivery. We are to envision an assembly whose members had never heard Paul speak or received a letter from him before.

Immediately after the prefatory paragraphs, just two minutes or so into the letter's declamation to a church-assembly (allowing two minutes per page of NA26), the lector started speaking in a second "voice," of a character who in elegant parallelism followed at 1:18 what Paul had said in 1:17, only gradually over the next two minutes revealed his own distinctive non-Pauline style and thought, was answered by a second character, engaged this second character in dialogue for another four minutes, and—only after some six minutes of this unheralded and un-identified personification—was finally revealed, by the absurdity of his conclusion, to have been throughout an *opponent* of Paul and to have pursued his own non-Pauline argument to the point of ridicule. It now turned out that Paul disagreed with all the arguments, well-known to the audience, which the audience has, perhaps with warm approval, just heard. This will surely have been a recipe for confusion.

Why, we will ask, did Paul not do what one would expect any orator to do? He could simply introduce the change of direction and tone with an adversative ἀλλά (instead of the quite misleading γάρ), flag up the change of speaker and place ὀργὴ θεοῦ emphatically.

> δικαιοσύνη γὰρ θεοῦ ἐν αὐτῷ ἀποκαλύπτεται ἐκ πίστεως εἰς πίστιν, καθὼς γέγραπται, Ὁ δὲ δίκαιος ἐκ πίστεως ζήσεται. ἀλλὰ ὀργὴν δὴ θεοῦ λέγει τις ὅτι ἀπ᾽ οὐρανοῦ ἀποκαλύπτεται ἐπὶ πᾶσαν ἀσέβειαν καὶ ἀδικίαν ἀνθρώπων τῶν τὴν ἀλήθειαν ἐν ἀδικίᾳ κατεχόντων.

Then Paul would surely have marked the end of the speech too. The text as it stands does not support Campbell's reading. At 2:1 διὸ suggests the steady, onwards pursuit of the argument that the same inferential conjunction has driven on at 1:24 (cf. διὰ τοῦτο, 1:26); and πᾶς steers the audience away from Paul's opponent as the specific objects of his attack. Nothing suggests that Paul is now turning the tables on a previous speaker. With a different conjunction and a deft emphasis on the change of target (καὶ σύ) Paul could have made the point, briskly and clearly, that Campbell ascribes to him:

> ἀλλὰ οὖν καὶ σὺ ἀναπολόγητος εἶ, ὦ ἄνθρωπε ὁ κρίνων.

Tellingly, Campbell himself (*Deliverance*, 140) disputes one reading of Romans 7:7–25 because the listeners could not have understood who the "I" was supposed to be without "some explicit markers" to make that identity clear. (Stowers makes a similar admission: "I find the identity of the speaker at 7:7a unclear: perhaps it is Paul, perhaps the person characterized in what follows, perhaps an anonymous objector," *Rereading*, 270.) It is just such markers that are lacking at 1:18.

What was the danger in failing to give such markers? That nobody would recognize what Paul was doing. And indeed for nearly two millennia, if Campbell is right, nobody has.

Similar concerns weaken more of Campbell's analysis. He sees the climax of the exchange between Paul and his opponent at 3:1–9a, which Campbell breaks down into dialogue between speakers A and B. Campbell translates 3:1–3 as follows:[16]

> A: What [then] is the advantage of the Jew? Or what is the benefit of circumcision?
>
> B: Much in many respects! First (πρῶτον μὲν [γάρ]), is it not that they have been entrusted with the very utterances of God?
>
> A: So what (τί γάρ)? If some were untrustworthy, will not their untrustworthiness (μὴ ἡ ἀπιστία αὐτῶν) nullify the trust of God?
>
> B: Absolutely not! Let God be true though every person is false (γινέσθω δὲ ὁ θεὸς ἀληθής, πᾶς δὲ ἄνθρωπος ψεύστης).

This translation calls for refinement. There is no reason to think 3:2b is a question; Campbell has introduced the interrogative, to get a dialogue under way. At 3:3 "so what" translates τί οὖν not Paul's τί γάρ. At 3:3 Campbell, in an important slip, mistranslates μή (Latin, "num"; English, "surely . . . not": expecting the answer No) as οὐ (Latin, "nonne"; English, "surely": expecting the answer Yes). At 3:4 Campbell's translation calls for γάρ and not for δέ. (The δὲ may be answering the μὲν at 3:2.) In 3.4 πᾶς is emphatically placed by Paul: all, not just *some*. So the text of 3:2–4a would be better rendered:

> First, they were entrusted with the utterances of God. Is there a problem here? If some were untrustworthy, surely their untrustworthiness will not nullify the trust of God? No, certainly not. Indeed let God be true, and *every* person false.

The search for a dialogue between opponents has seriously distorted a paragraph more readily comparable to the exchange in Epictetus that we heard above: the vivid exploration of a line of thought.

16. Campbell, *Deliverance*, 573.

So, on to 3.8. Campbell translates:

> A: And even as we are slandered, and as some report us as saying, should we not do evil so that good can come!?

> B: . . . whose judgment is positively deserved!

Here Campbell breaks up Paul's indignant rebuttal of *a claim that was being made in Rome about his own gospel*, a claim which (if well founded) would have given Paul good reason to be ashamed of that gospel (1:16). To this claim and to the crisis facing Paul's gospel in Rome, I turn in these last pages of the chapter. Here is the answer to Campbell's own demand, that we root Romans in the soil of a particular place and time.

I claimed, at this paper's outset, to be addressing merely formal concerns. But real substance is at stake. Campbell is over and again having to twist Paul's text into a meaning it does not bear. So what shall we say? It may be that this paper has loosened a block—even quite a large block—near ground-level in the load-bearing wall of Campbell's argument. Does this block need replacing? Yes, I think so. But my deeper concern will by now be clear: that this block, as it stands, is indispensible to Campbell's whole building. The cracks may spread through the whole wall, and may—before we even rise to the substance of Campbell's argument—bring the building down.

Campbell is consistently gracious to his critics; it is a pleasure to be in discussion with him. He issues a final challenge to those of us who are wary of his argument: what's to lose by accepting it? Here is one response. Scholars are at last, in our own generation, giving due attention to Paul's rhetoric. But this can "blind-side" New Testament scholars. We are not at home among the volumes—indeed, the bookshelves—of Greek and Roman speeches and letters that it seems we must now carefully read. (We hope it will suffice to read the ancient theorists; it won't.) If a scholar constructs an Olympian argument in which, as we trudge through its foothills, we find serious attention paid to Paul's rhetoric, we are re-assured. We accept his or her analysis of the rhetoric with gratitude and relief, and climb the mountain towards the substantive topics that *matter* to us.

But we might be moving on and upwards too soon. We should keep our eyes wider open for the specifically *rhetorical* signals that Paul himself gave to his audience to steer them through the letter and to mark their progress. Let's start with his repeated, emphatic evocation of the νοῦς.

Campbell challenges us to advance an alternative to his own construction that will do justice both to Paul's rhetoric and his thought. I am glad to pick up the gauntlet that Campbell has thrown down; here, to round off this chapter, is one such alternative.

The opening attack on idolaters climaxes at 1:28: καθὼς οὐκ ἐδοκίμασαν τὸν θεὸν ἔχειν ἐν ἐπιγνώσει, παρέδωκεν αὐτοὺς ὁ θεὸς εἰς ἀδόκιμον νοῦν. Paul located the origin of the Romans' divisions in just such an unreckoning mind (2:1). By Romans 7 the listeners were to recognize within themselves the incapacity to which the persona of 7:7–25 was still subject: ἄρα οὖν αὐτὸς ἐγὼ τῷ μὲν νοῒ δουλεύω νόμῳ θεοῦ, τῇ δὲ σαρκὶ νόμῳ ἁμαρτίας (7:25). By 12:2 Paul expected his listeners to be able to reckon aright, δοκιμάζειν: μεταμορφοῦσθε τῇ ἀνακαινώσει τοῦ νοός, εἰς τὸ δοκιμάζειν ὑμᾶς τί τὸ θέλημα τοῦ θεοῦ. The recipients were now ready to hear Paul's guidance, 12:1—15:33, for the healing of the divided body of Christ of which they were members. The letter to the Romans was therapeutic; Paul set out to heal the νοῦς of the letter's recipients through and during its reception.

Let's listen too to the letter's pattern of diatribal questions. Paul was defending himself through much of the letter against claims that his gospel was libertine. "I am not ashamed of the gospel" (1:16). Paul himself reveals what could be shameful about it: "it is certainly not— as we are slandered and as some say that we claim—that we should do evil so that good shall come; the judgment on them is just!" (3:8). In Rome this misreading had gained traction not only among those who opposed him, but also—and far more dangerously—among those who claimed his endorsement of their own libertinism. Paul was not yet ready at 3:8 to address the slander. He must return to the topic of 3:8 at 6:1 (Τί οὖν ἐροῦμεν; ἐπιμένωμεν τῇ ἁμαρτίᾳ, ἵνα ἡ χάρις πλεονάσῃ;) and 6:15 (Τί οὖν; ἁμαρτήσωμεν ὅτι οὐκ ἐσμὲν ὑπὸ νόμον ἀλλὰ ὑπὸ χάριν;) and to the theme of 3:5–7 at 9:14 Τί οὖν ἐροῦμεν; μὴ ἀδικία παρὰ τῷ θεῷ; μὴ γένοιτο) and 9:19 (Ἐρεῖς μοι οὖν, Τί [οὖν] ἔτι μέμφεται;). The Romans must be well on the way to being healed before Paul can effectively correct their errors about Paul's own preaching. Paul was mounting a sustained response to a credible misreading of his good news.[17]

The Romans were to re-envision their own identity by the sustained engagement of their imagination on a typological re-working of their own selves. This was to affect the healing of their νοῦς; and only when healed

---

17. I advance this reading in detail in Griffith-Jones, "Keep Up Your Transformation."

would the addressees be able genuinely to appropriate the knowledge to which at the letter's start they had been blind. Paul believed the gospel to be the power of God for deliverance (1:16); and the letter itself was to be that power in action as the listeners heard. Paul wrote to heal and transform his listeners in ways and terms alien to modern self-understanding. Romans was a therapeutic, even a *maieutic* letter. It is precisely the letter's rhetoric, invoked (but, I suggest, misunderstood) by Campbell, which reveals it to be far more deeply Socratic than Campbell allows.

Douglas Campbell's Response to Robin Griffith-Jones

In his essay Robin has attacked a key claim within my broader position—with panache!—and in doing so I suspect represents the doubts of many concerning my proposals at just this point, namely, a fundamentally ironic reading of Romans 1:18–32. So it will be useful to respond here to his argument at a little more length.

Robin makes a quick but learned case in terms of a single principal claim that he then buttresses with some further evidential flourishes. Engaging with the evidence cited by Stowers and myself in relation to the phenomenon of ancient *prosōpopoeia*, he argues that in the key texts in Cicero, Quintilian, Seneca, and Plato, a change in speaker is always explicitly signaled with a written cue, or at least clearly implied in the context with such a cue. He goes on to point out that no such explicit written cue is present at the start of Romans 1:18–32, therefore no change in speaker is really plausible at this point within the text of the letter. As he puts it at one point, the change in speaker is "unannounced." The inability of the Christian tradition and (most!) modern interpreters prior to me to detect such a change in voice then reinforces this case; all these later readers have not detected a change in voice because there wasn't one. Restating things slightly differently: the ancient auditors of Romans must have been as puzzled as Robin is now with my suggested reading of the letter at this point. What would remove their doubts?—an explicit announcement of a change in voice of course. Without this explicit announcement, however, such a change seems implausible. Putting things at their simplest then: if Paul wanted to change argumentative voice in 1:18–32 he should have explicitly told us this was what he was doing. Centuries of misunderstanding would thereby have been avoided.

There are of course some elements of truth in this argument. Some of our ancient sources do announce a change of voice explicitly. And detecting a change of voice in Romans 1:18–32 is no easy matter. People have missed this for a long time and so are entitled to ask for an appropriate level of proof, if not to complain that Paul did not signal this for them explicitly. I quite understand this posture. Moreover, my case for a broadly Socratic construal of Romans 1–3 beginning with another person's tirade in 1:18–32 is a delicate and cumulative one. Indeed, I do not expect *any* modern reader simply to realize this on a first reading of Romans 1:18–32 itself, without reference to the broader argument and a lot of further reflection. Only an explicitly written cue could deliver this degree of clarity up front, so to speak, as Robin suggests. So I appreciate these difficulties fully. Let me suggest some corrections and rejoinders, however, as we try to move forward, beginning with a clarification.

I suspect that discussion of this entire interpretative situation will be eased considerably if we shift the stated technique at issue from *prosōpopoeia* to *parody*. *Prosōpopoeia* is a rather forbidding technical Greek term that most modern readers instinctively recoil from. They (we) are not trained to detect this textual technique intuitively as ancient readers were. I have found, however, that if we speak of parody instead, modern readers have a much better instinctive grasp of what I am suggesting, and more cultural analogies lie readily at hand that allow a constructive discussion. I do not think this change in terminology will blunt the force of Robin's attempted critique, although I do apologize for switching terms on him; but I only received this suggested clarification after he and I had our exchange in London and have since decided that it should be adopted.[18]

My thesis then, suitably clarified, is that Romans 1:18—3:20 is best construed as a broadly Socratic argument that refutes an opponent in terms of his demonstrable self-contradictions. And it begins by presenting a particular position occupied by that person, which will be the basis for the contradictions demonstrated later on, this process beginning with a turn in 2:1. The presentation takes place in a moment appropriately described as parody, in Romans 1:18–32, while ancient parody, it should be recalled, did not necessarily intend to ridicule and was not necessarily even aggressive, although it was generally comic or humorous.

With this clarification in place, what should we make of Robin's argument against it?

Unfortunately, it should now be apparent that this rests on an argumentative fallacy—specifically, on a *non sequitur*. That is, Robin has pointed out quite fairly that many of the ancient sources currently in play within this debate signal a change in speaker with an explicit written cue. This is true. But it does not follow from this evidence—that

18. It was made by Michelle Fletcher in conversation. A useful introduction to parody that she referred me to is Rose, *Parody*. Rose observes helpfully that "[t]he 'simulation' of other styles, where the parodist pretends to be sharing the words and meaning of the object of parody, has been a technique used by many parodists to elicit the expectations of their audience for a text, before presenting another version or view of it" (30).

some ancient changes in voice employ a written cue—that *all* changes in voice in ancient texts *had* to employ a written cue. Robin has not proved this broader claim, although this is what he needs to be true in order to exclude a parodic reading of 1:18–32. Putting things the other way around again for the sake of clarity: we know that when a text introduces a change in speaker explicitly, the speaker changes. (Even much later, modern readers cannot argue with this.) But it does not follow from this that whenever a text does not explicitly change the speaker, the text does not change its voice. Indeed, *this* supposition is obviously false.

We know already from a cursory reading of 1 Corinthians that Paul frequently changes voice in a text without announcing it. This letter is filled with Corinthian quotations—statements that scholars now confidently hold to be allusions to if not verbatim reproductions of the words of the Corinthians and not of Paul himself. But the reason for the scholarly debates over the extent of these quotations is that Paul never announces them![19] Moreover, a quick consideration of the Greco-Roman corpus suggests that Robin's inference is wrong in broader terms as well. If he is right—that all changes in ancient textual voice *must* be explicitly signaled by explicit textual cues—then ancient Greek and Roman parody did not exist (except, that is, when it was explicitly signaled by a written cue). And we might suspect immediately that this was not the case, while the recall of just two names falsifies it immediately—Juvenal and Lucian. Both these authors do nothing *except* write in the voices of others and both *never* signal explicitly that they are doing so. So Robin's broader inference is clearly wrong. It is true that when a text explicitly signals a change in voice it changes voice; however, it is not true that when a text does not explicitly signal a change in voice it does not and cannot change voice, this false inference being the *non sequitur*. But the recognition of this fallacy brings us to the verge of a critical realization.

Ancient parody, like modern parody, when "live," that is, performed in immediate circumstantial humor, if not mockery, did not generally employ explicit written cues. This would have been clumsy and unnecessary, would have detracted from the parody's comic force, and for lower classes might even have been dangerous. Lower class parody of upper class foibles was a standard "means of resistance" but was necessarily

19. See 1:12; 3:4; 6:12–13; 7:1; 8:1, 4, 8; 10:23, and perhaps also 4:6b; 8:5a; 12:3; 15:12, 35; these are briefly discussed in *Deliverance* 540–41.

anonymous and transient, to avoid reprisals.[20] And it is consequently significant to note that Robin's attempted critique entirely overlooks the extent to which the sources he cites, emphasizing explicit written cues, were later published works that had long lost their live settings. (They were elite too, hence lacking any fear of reprisal.) In those situations, written cues were understandable—although even then, as the examples of Juvenal and Lucian show, they were not always thought necessary.[21] But Paul's letter to the Romans was not intended for publication. It was a typical "live" parody, which rested heavily, like all live parody, on prosodic and paralinguistic cues (i.e., performance, including inflexion and body language)—and the amount that these activities contribute to communication should not be underestimated; in some situations non-verbal cues may supply as much as 70 percent of the information. And all these realizations, concerning the important differences between the sources in play, lead us to a further response to Robin's concerns.

It is now apparent that the difficulties modern readers like Robin are experiencing with my proposal stem from their modern location reading a published and Scriptural text that has long lost its original "live" setting. This means that all the typical cues surrounding the instance of parody in 1:18–32 have fallen away, making the detection of parody here extremely difficult. Moreover, modern readers no longer share the sense of humor originally presupposed by the text's comic touches—its jokes in terms of the ancient Greco-Roman comic encyclopedia.[22] But these difficulties did not exist for the ancient Roman auditors of the letter, who could have detected parody here immediately given the text's appropriate performance and interpretation, along with its subtle comic extensions of its target discourse. So it is apparent now that what has happened

20. See Scott's classic treatment in *Domination and the Arts of Resistance.*

21. And in fact Robin has to try to marginalize the evidence of Origen in this relation since Origen detected "speech-in-character" so confidently in Rom 7, but without any explicit verbal cue for a change in speaker. It is true that Origen did not go on to detect such a change in Rom 1:18–32, but I am not sure that this is fatal to my proposal. Historical critical reconstructions are not reducible to patristic readings. The latter inform the former helpfully at times but do not control them.

22. That is, Rose suggests that the key marker for parody is comic incongruity or discrepancy suggested in the main by extension, a practice relying on a spectrum of subtle stylistic clues (*Parody*, 36–38). Hence, unless readers of the text share the sense of humor of the author, something rooted in his or her originally cultural location, it will be difficult to detect parody. Modern readers consequently need to be able to detect Greek and Roman jokes in order to read Rom 1:18–32 parodically with ease.

is that modern readers like Robin have projected their *own* difficulties caused by their modern reading locations back into the original historical situation surrounding the reception of the letter. But although this is an understandable mental operation it is, of course, entirely artificial and invalid.[23] Paul never expected his letter to the Romans to be published, and then to circulate as Christian Scripture for two thousand years, the fate that rendered his parodic moment at the outset of Romans extremely difficult to detect. And it is odd to expect him to have recognized this in advance. So Robin argues at one point: "What was the danger in failing to give such markers? That nobody would recognise what Paul was doing. And indeed for nearly two millennia, if Campbell is right, nobody has." But these expectations are of course overtly—and somewhat hilariously—anachronistic. And modern historical critics must of course resist them, learning instead to recover the radically cross-cultural nature of any reconstruction of Paul's meaning. Historical critical exegesis is a voyage into a far country and must be undertaken with the appropriate interpretative humility. Consequently modern readers are not in a position to say what Paul ought in their view to have done, and especially in order to alleviate *their* interpretative difficulties arising a millennia or two later. So in this instance in particular, when contemplating the possibility that 1:18–32 is an instance of ancient parody, they must resist the temptation of projecting their own insensitivity to the dynamics of ancient parody, compounded by the loss of its original contextual clues, back into the situation of the original ancient Greco-Roman auditors, who might have thoroughly enjoyed Paul's comic performance. That possibility should not be erased by modern interpretative pique.

But, as Robin might be quick to point out, with the collapse of his negative case, I still have to demonstrate that 1:18–32 is best interpreted as parody. We have merely kept that possibility open for the time being.

23. Kahneman might suggest that it is a nice example of the substitution fallacy, that is, the answering of a difficult question with an easy answer to a similar looking but easier question; see his seminal *Thinking, Fast and Slow*. Hence, instead of asking whether ancient Greco-Roman auditors could have detected parody in Rom 1:18–32—a very difficult question that involves reconstructing the ancient comic encyclopedia and hence the reading of large numbers of ancient Greek and Roman texts in a way that few modern NT scholars want or have the time to do—modern critics of my suggestion have often asked instead whether *they* themselves can detect parody in Rom 1:18–32 and, not surprisingly, the answer is "no." When parody has lost its comic encyclopedia *and* its original immediate performative cues, its detection is very difficult indeed—not to mention, impossible if its assessors do not really want to detect it!

However, I will not, of course, attempt any such proof here, within a response to Robin's argument, but will merely point out that I have made that case elsewhere, and add that in my view it is yet to be decisively refuted. Most responses to it have been along the lines of Robin's critique and hence from my point of view rely on anachronistic concerns with explicit textual cues. In order to disprove my suggestion of parody two different arguments need to be advanced that have not yet been made: (1) the broader argumentative construal of Romans 1–3 needs to be engaged, since I suggest both that my Socratic reading is currently the best available construal and that the usual construal is demonstrably flawed;[24] and (2) the cues involved in ancient parody need to be reconstructed and assessed and a proof offered of how 1:18–32 does not fit that nuanced account. However, I am confident—having pushed a little further down this path since the publication of *Deliverance*—that it is arguably parodic. The subtle shift in stylistic texture and the comic incongruity and extensions that are the hallmarks of parody are evident in this text; think just of Paul's eye-watering account of sexual activity in 1:27 and bombastic vice list in 1:29–31, not to mention, his labored word plays.[25]

24. Most of my critics have adopted a rather curious response here too, namely, the denial that my account of their standard argument is accurate. It is a straw man, and hence warrants no further engagement. However, the lie is given to this procedure both by the way that they never go on to supply a correct account that I could then engage with, and the way that this straw man, which should really just be ignored, nevertheless elicits long and agonized responses—a sign rather that something has in fact hit home.

25. I am grateful to William Johnson, a colleague from the Classics department at Duke and renowned expert in ancient reading, for his ongoing help in this relation. Admittedly, he detects parodic style only from around verse 20 in Rom 1. However, he suggests that 13:1–7 is laughably parodic and in a similar style to 1:18–32. Hence, I am quite happy for parodic markers to become apparent from around 1:20; 1:18 is, in my reading, a counter thesis to 1:17. It is reprised in 1:32 and 2:6, while 1:17 is resumed (obviously) from 3:21. And the voice of the Teacher is parodically resumed, entirely appropriately, in 13:1–17. See also in this relation Baldwin, *Studies in Lucian.*

Paul's use of γάρ to connect verse 18 with what precedes is often cited as a further impediment to a change of voice around this point. This sense of this conjunction could, however, as Cranfield suggests, be adversative, or even indicative of the introduction of a thesis, as in Gal 5:5. Alternatively, as arguably over forty times in Isaiah (LXX), *it introduces a change in voice.* See esp. Isa 1:27; 5:7; 26:21; 45:15; 55:8, 12; 58:3, 14; 59:21; 60:10, 20; 61:8. (My thanks to the Bible League International translation group at Stellenbosch, and especially to Daniel Rodriguez, for this data, and also to Ross Wagner for its further learned discussion.)

I would add in closing that the recovery of this understanding of Romans 1:18–32 has proved largely impossible until a widespread awareness arose tragically recently within the Academy that the construction of "the Jew" being offered by previous ecclesial and academic readers of this text in its broader setting was fundamentally problematic. Wrestling with this conundrum has opened up the text's argument in constructive new ways. But all this has only unfolded since the work of Sanders in 1977 made this challenge unavoidable, while even now—incredible to think—"many oppose him," making forward progress difficult. So the newness of my suggested reading has a plausible, if painful, explanation rather than its sheer unlikelihood, as Robin opines cheekily.

I would of course like to say much more in response to Robin's lively critique, but things must come to a close for the moment.[26] It remains only to express my thanks for his direct and learned engagement. It has prompted me to try to express myself more clearly in what is hopefully a broadly plausible response to his legitimate concerns even as I have suggested that his key argument rests on a fallacy. Doubtless these rejoinders will not end matters but they should at least move the conversation forward.

26. Robin debates some detailed points of translation and suggests that his alternative readings—inter alia, of 2:1 and 3:3—undermine the cogency of a Socratic construal of the argument. I am happy to concede these instances where he has caught my translation out but fail to see how any of these adjustments are fatal to a Socratic construal in general.

11

Rereading Romans 1–3 Apocalyptically

A Response to Douglas Campbell's "Rereading Romans 1–3"[1]

BRITTANY E. WILSON

In my response to Douglas Campbell's essay "Rereading Romans 1–3," I want to begin by way of disclaimer. Overall, I am very sympathetic to Campbell's reading of Paul. Like Campbell, I read Paul apocalyptically, and I agree that Romans 5–8 lies at the heart of Paul's apocalyptic soteriology.[2] Moreover, I also reject what Campbell calls a "prospective" reading of Paul, or what he elsewhere terms "Arianism," foundationalism,

1. I originally presented this response at the conference "Beyond Old and New Perspectives on Paul" held in Durham, NC. I have since expanded and revised the piece, but, overall, it retains the style of oral delivery. I thank Douglas Campbell and T. J. Lang for their invitation to respond at the conference, and I also thank Douglas Campbell and Chris Tilling for their subsequent invitation to publish it in this volume.

2. Like Ernst Käsemann, J. Louis Martyn, and other proponents of an apocalyptic Paul, I use the term "apocalyptic" to reference the radical disclosure of God's salvific righteousness in Jesus Christ. See de Boer, "Paul, Theologian of God's Apocalypse," 21–33; Gaventa, "Maternal Imagery in Its Cosmic and Apocalyptic Context," in *Our Mother Saint Paul*, 79–84.

contractualism, and justification discourse. Such readings lead, *inter alia*, to an individualistic view of salvation in which the gospel is not freely given, but necessitated because of human sinfulness. I applaud Campbell for highlighting the numerous problems with this traditional Western interpretation of Paul, and I agree that Paul himself does not advocate a forensic soteriology.

In my response, however, I will don the role of Campbell's "opponent." I will begin by "speaking in character" as a critic of Campbell's exegetical argument. Here I will identify the main critique New Testament scholars have leveled against Campbell's exegesis of Romans 1–3 and contend that "Rereading Romans 1–3" does not resolve this critique. I will then speak more specifically as Campbell's "apocalyptic opponent," assuming the voice of an apocalyptic interpreter of Paul who is, in my opinion, Campbell's most formidable adversary: Beverly Roberts Gaventa. Although Gaventa has written a number of important articles on Romans and Paul's apocalyptic soteriology, Campbell does not engage her work at any length.[3] Like Campbell, Gaventa notes the problem of reading Romans 1–3 forensically. Unlike Campbell, Gaventa's solution to this "problem" is to read Romans 1–3 *apocalyptically*.[4] In other words, Gaventa maintains that Paul is consistently apocalyptic in Romans 1–3 itself and that he speaks in his own voice throughout these opening chapters. I will thus suggest that Gaventa's work not only addresses the problem of Paul's so-called forensic soteriology in Romans 1–3, but that it also solves the "problem" of Campbell's own "solution": namely that Romans 1:18—3:20 represents the perspective of Paul's "opponent," not Paul himself.

Yet before turning to Gaventa's solution, let us start first with Campbell's solution and the resulting problems. According to Campbell, Romans 1:18—3:20 represents "the opponent's" forensic soteriology, whereas Romans 5–8 represents Paul's apocalyptic soteriology. More specifically, Romans 1:18–32 reflects Paul's usage of "speech-in-character"

---

3. Even though Gaventa has been publishing on the topic of Paul's apocalyptic theology since at least 2002, Campbell only mentions her work in a smattering of footnotes in *Deliverance*, and he does not mention her at all in the article at hand. Gaventa's work will be referenced throughout my response, and a number of her essays on this topic are conveniently compiled in her book *Our Mother Saint Paul*.

4. The title of this response in fact alludes to Gaventa's article "God Handed Them Over," 42–53. This article has been reprinted in *Our Mother Saint Paul*, 113–23, and I will cite this latter edition throughout the response.

through which he presents his opponent's soteriological position. In Romans 2:1—3:20, Paul then universalizes this position and exposes its logical absurdities. Romans 3:21–26 finally unveils Paul's own perspective on soteriology, which Romans 5–8 discloses in full. Two interrelated issues, however, emerge with Campbell's claim that Romans 1:18—3:20 does not in its entirety represent Paul's own perspective.

The first issue concerns Paul's employment of "speech-in-character" in Romans 1:18-32 (and thus Paul's employment of Socratic argumentation in Romans 1:18—3:20 as a whole). "Speech-in-character," or *prosōpopoeia*, is a well-known rhetorical device in the ancient world, but the question is whether Paul is in fact employing this device here and whether his audience would have recognized this device if he is. If this is an instance of *prosōpopoeia*, why is it unmarked? Why does Paul not clarify that the opening soteriological position is "incorrect"? Does he dare leave such a key point to those performing the letter (i.e., Phoebe and her entourage)? Why not ensure that the Roman Christians understand Paul's satirical role-playing from the very beginning?

The second related issue involves Paul speaking in the voice of the Jewish Christian teachers (or "the Teacher," to adopt Campbell's and J. Louis Martyn's turn of phrase).[5] Campbell's argument that Paul adopts the voice of "the Teacher" in Romans 1:18-32 primarily relies on a historical reconstruction. Campbell must read "behind" the text by turning to Galatians where Paul explicitly engages these opponents throughout. But Paul makes no mention of these opponents in Romans aside from a (potential) reference in 16:17-20. If Romans 1:18—3:20 is in fact a "preemptive strike" against these heretical teachers, why does he only mention them at the end of the letter?[6] Why does Paul not mention them earlier? Or even better, why does Paul not mention them directly before assuming "the Teacher's" voice in 1:18? Once again, we return to the question of why Paul would have left such an important point unmarked. Certainly it is possible that Paul is using *prosōpopoeia* in Romans 1:18-32, but in light of the paucity of internal evidence, is it the most plausible explanation?

In "Rereading Romans 1–3," Campbell responds to this pervasive critique and provides additional evidence to support his claims. I will not

5. On Martyn's use of the title "the Teacher," see his *Galatians*. Note that Martyn only uses this title in reference to the opponents who appear in Paul's letter to the Galatians. Martyn makes no reference to "the Teacher" in Romans.

6. See also Gaventa's comments in her review of Campbell's *Deliverance*, "Rescue Mission," 36–37.

rehearse all eight of his main rebuttals, but I want to highlight a number of his more persuasive points and propose in brief that even these points do not fully "refute the refutations."

(1) Campbell appeals to Pseudo-Libanius, who describes a letter genre known as Εἰρωνική (the "ironic") and later (in a footnote) to Juvenal, who incorporates unmarked instances of *prosōpopoeia* in his satires. Campbell makes these appeals to provide precedent for Paul's usage of *prosōpopoeia*. In terms of genre, however, Paul's letter to the Romans does not fall into either of these above categories. Romans does not qualify as Εἰρωνική nor does it qualify as satire, two genres that condition the audience to expect tongue-in-cheek *prosōpopoeia*. The genre of Romans, on the other hand, has not prepared the audience to hear such satirical instances of *prosōpopoeia*.

(2) Campbell marshals the *Progymnasmata*, in which children would learn to recognize *prosōpopoeia* and "Socratic" argumentative strategies, in order to argue for the ubiquity of these rhetorical devices. *Prosōpopoeia* and Socratic argumentation, Campbell maintains, are not "rarefied" techniques only known to the elite. Yet it is far from clear that non-elites in the ancient world would have had access to the *Progymnasmata* or would have even been literate.[7] Paul's recipients may include both elites and non-elites, but Campbell himself situates Paul's audience among the "poor" and "lower classes."[8]

(3) Campbell points to other instances of unmarked "speech-in-character" in Paul, including Romans 7:7–25 and (in a footnote) 1 Corinthians 1:12; 3:4; 6:12–13; 7:1; 8:1, 4, 8; 10:23. But in Romans 7:7–25, Paul consistently uses the first person singular "I" (ἐγώ), and thus incorporates a traditional marker of *prosōpopoeia* throughout the passage. In Romans 1:18–32 by contrast, Paul does not use the first person singular once; he instead speaks consistently in the third person. Furthermore, Paul's incorporation of unmarked quotations in 1 Corinthians forms a discernible pattern throughout the letter. These quotations do not even technically qualify as *prosōpopoeia* since Paul is referencing remarks made by the Corinthians in their previous correspondence.

(4) Campbell underscores the importance of Origen, who reads portions of Romans 7 in terms of *prosōpopoeia*. Yet many scholars agree

---

7. On literacy in the ancient world, see Harris's landmark book, *Ancient Literacy*. For a more recent nuancing of this argument, see Watson, ed., *Speaking Volumes*; Woolf, "Literacy," 875–97.

8. See Campbell's argument in his eighth refutation, p. 156.

that Paul is using *prosōpopoeia* in Romans 7, and Campbell has not found evidence that Origen (or other early Christian authors) identify *prosōpopoeia* in Romans 1.

(5) Campbell claims (in a footnote) that elites such as Cicero or Quintilian explicitly mark their examples of *prosōpopoeia* because they were writing generalized texts far removed from concrete circumstances. Paul did not need to mark his use of *prosōpopoeia* because Romans is a "contingent" text. Of course, Campbell is correct that Romans is a situational letter written to a specific community in concrete circumstances. However, Paul does not *know* this community and vice versa. Unlike the recipients of his other letters, Paul has not visited the Roman Christians and this lack of a prior relationship suggests that Paul would have erred towards clarity (i.e., marked *prosōpopoeia*) in order to avoid miscommunication.

All of these points could use further elaboration and Campbell no doubt has more rebuttals in response. But I would like to move now to my proposed "solution" by beginning with the following question: Is it the case—as Campbell maintains—that Romans 1–3 provides a forensic account of soteriology and Romans 5–8 an apocalyptic account? Or is Paul (in Paul's own voice) consistently apocalyptic throughout? Can Romans 1–3 *itself* be read apocalyptically? Of course, Campbell is in good company when he maintains that Romans 1–3 (or more specifically 1:18—3:20) reflects a forensic soteriology. Among New Testament scholars in particular, Campbell is also typical when he distinguishes between Paul's respective discussions of sin and salvation in Romans 1–3 and Romans 5–8.[9] To Campbell's credit, his overarching project aims to reconcile this ostensible disconnect within Romans 1–8. My solution, however, reconciles this disconnect by maintaining that Paul is consistently apocalyptic throughout Romans 1–8. Romans 1–3, I will argue, does not in fact reflect a forensic soteriology in the first place.

If we are to argue this latter position, we must begin by noting Paul's style of argumentation. Contra Campbell, Paul does not appear to unfold his argument in a linear fashion, moving from incorrect to correct

9. Since Martin Dibelius, New Testament scholars have typically distinguished between Paul's discussion of sin as an individual transgression (often associated with Rom 1–3) and sin as an external force (often associated with Rom 5–7). See Gaventa, "God Handed Them Over," 120, citing Dibelius, *Geisterwelt im Glauben des Paulus*, 119–24. New Testament scholars also traditionally identify Rom 1:18—3:20 and Rom 5–8 as two distinct sections of the letter that conflict with one another.

soteriology in Romans 1–8 (or from "the Teacher's" position [1:18–32] to Paul's universalization and *reductio ad absurdum* of this position [2:1—3:20] to Paul's own position [3:21-26; 5:1—8:39]). Paul instead writes his letter in a manner more akin to a symphony: Paul introduces a theme that disappears but then reappears later on in a different key.[10] For example, Paul introduces the topic of God's righteousness in 1:16–17, but he then immediately drops this topic and does not return to it again until 3:21. Paul does the same thing with respect to his narration of sin. Paul alludes to sin in 1:18–32, specifically mentions "sin" (ἁμαρτία) in 3:9–20, and then continues to develop his understanding of sin throughout chapters 5–8. In this "spiral" discussion of sin, Paul continually circles back to this important topic, gradually fleshing it out until he climatically reveals the full picture.[11] At the conclusion of Romans 8, Paul's spiral account of the powers of sin and death reaches a crescendo when he proclaims: "neither death, nor life, nor angels, nor rulers, nor things present, nor things to come, nor powers, nor height, nor depth, nor anything else in all creation, will be able to separate us from the love of God in Christ Jesus our Lord" (vv. 38–39). As the rhetorical climax of the first half of the letter, Paul finally discloses the full cosmic scope (and ultimate failure) of sin. It takes Paul eight chapters, however, to make this full disclosure. Thus it is not necessarily the case that Paul's discussion of sin and salvation is "incorrect" in Romans 1–3; it is simply—at this point in the letter—incomplete.

But what in Romans 1:18—3:20 itself might point to Paul's consistently apocalyptic perspective? Let us start with Romans 1:18. Campbell identifies 1:18 as the point at which Paul's "opponent" starts to speak, and 1:18 does in fact begin a new section of the letter. Yet at the very outset of Romans 1:18, Paul writes ἀποκαλύπτεται ("it is revealed"), a cognate of the word "apocalypse" itself. The same verb appears in the verse directly beforehand and forms a striking parallel. In verse 17, Paul writes that "the righteousness of God is revealed" (δικαιοσύνη γὰρ θεοῦ . . . ἀποκαλύπτεται), and in verse 18 he writes that "the wrath of God is revealed" (ἀποκαλύπτεται γὰρ ὀργὴ θεοῦ). Campbell claims in *Deliverance of God* that the verbal parallel denotes a deliberate contrast between verse 17 and verse 18 (i.e., verse 17 represents Paul's conception of a compassionate God and verse 18 represents "the Teacher's" conception of a

10. Gaventa, "Paul and the Roman Believers," 93–107, here 101.
11. See Gaventa, "To Preach the Gospel," 179–95, esp. 180–82.

wrathful God).[12] The verbal parallel, however, may just as easily suggest continuity. Paul has just discussed God's power and God's apocalypse of righteousness in 1:16–17 (the so-called "thesis" of the letter). He then continues this discussion of God's apocalypse—now with respect to wrath—in 1:18—3:20 until he returns again to God's disclosure of righteousness in 3:21.

In addition to the verb ἀποκαλύπτω in 1:18, the threefold repetition of the phrase "God handed them over" in 1:24–28 also points to the apocalyptic orientation of Romans 1:18—3:20.[13] Paul's repetition here is striking, and with this repetition, he names God as the agent who "hands over" (παρέδωκεν) humanity "to" (εἰς) something else (vv. 24, 26, 28): respectively "uncleanness" (v. 24), "dishonorable passions" (v. 26), and a "deformed mind" (v. 28).[14] According to the typical forensic reading, God hands over humanity to judgment since humans exhibit these "bad behaviors." Yet later in Romans, "uncleanness," "passions," and a "deformed mind" do not signify human transgressions, but the cosmic anti-God powers (to use Martyn's expression).[15] In Romans 5–8, Sin is not an individual action, but an external force that holds humanity in its grasp.[16] Sin is a power, an agent with a capital "S," who is in league with Satan and the other powers that actively fight against God. Given Paul's overarching apocalyptic worldview, it makes sense that Paul would view Sin operating in this same way throughout Romans (including Romans 1–3).

What is more, Paul's use of the verb "hand over" (παραδίδωμι) furthers this sense that God hands over humanity to the anti-God powers in Romans 1:24–28. Both biblical and non-biblical authors overwhelmingly apply the verb παραδίδωμι to reference the surrendering of a person or a group of people to another agent within the context of war or some other

---

12. Campbell, *Deliverance*, 542–43.

13. On this point, see Gaventa, "God Handed Them Over," 113–23.

14. Verse 24: διὸ παρέδωκεν αὐτοὺς ὁ θεὸς . . . εἰς ἀκαθαρσίαν
Verse 26: διὰ τοῦτο παρέδωκεν αὐτοὺς ὁ θεὸς εἰς πάθη ἀτιμίας
Verse 28: παρέδωκεν αὐτοὺς ὁ θεὸς εἰς ἀδόκιμον νοῦν

15. On these terms as instances of synecdoche that reference the anti-God powers, see Gaventa, "God Handed Them Over," 118–19. On Martyn's expression "the anti-God powers," see *Galatians*, 370–73. See also de Boer, *The Defeat of Death*; de Boer, "Paul and Apocalyptic Eschatology," 345–83.

16. See Gaventa, "The Cosmic Power of Sin in Paul's Letter to the Romans," in *Our Mother Saint Paul*, 125–36.

conflict.[17] Paul himself explicitly uses παραδίδωμι in this sense elsewhere, as when he tells the Corinthian community that a man who lives with his father's wife should be "handed over" to Satan (1 Cor 5:5).[18] If Romans 1:24–28 is read in this same light, humans are not handed over to God's judgment because of their individual transgressions (i.e., the traditional forensic account). Humans are instead handed over to a third party who is actively fighting against God: namely, the power of Sin. Because humans refused to recognize God (1:18–23), God "handed over," or "surrendered," humanity to the anti-God powers for a time (1:24–28). God then freely liberates humanity, according to Paul, when Jesus himself is "handed over" to the anti-God powers and defeats those powers on the cross (4:25; 8:32).[19] Of course, Sin and Death are only defeated and not yet completely destroyed, but Paul promises their ultimate destruction with Christ's second coming (e.g., Rom 16:20; 1 Cor 15:24–26). Thus interpreting Paul's emphatic "handing over" language in Romans 1:24–28 as God's surrendering of humanity to the anti-God powers not only undermines forensic interpretations of Romans 1:18–32, but provides greater continuity to Paul's argument in the letter as a whole.

Finally, Paul's use of the word "Sin" (ἁμαρτία) itself in 3:9–20 suggests that Paul is consistently apocalyptic throughout Romans 1:18—3:20. Indeed, the word ἁμαρτία—which plays such a prominent role in Paul's discussion of the anti-God powers in Romans 5–8—appears for the first time in this key section. At the start of 3:9–20, Paul writes that "all"— both Jews and Greeks—are under the power of Sin (v. 9).[20] With rhetorical flair, Paul next demonstrates the depth of this captivity by describing

---

17. E.g., Herodotus, *Historiae* 1.45.1; 3.13.3; Pausanias, *Graeciae description* 1.2.1; Xenophon, *Cyropaedia* 5.1.28; 5.4.51; Deut 2:24, 31; 20:13; Josh 2:14, 24; Jer 21:10; Ezek 7:21. For more on this point, see Gaventa, "God Handed Them Over," esp. 114–18; 195 n. 11.

18. On Paul's other usages of παραδίδωμι, see Gaventa, "God Handed Them Over," 116–17. On Paul's use of conflict language, see Gaventa, "Neither Height nor Depth," 185–201; Gaventa, "The Rhetoric of Violence and the God of Peace in Paul's Letter to the Romans," in *The Armor of Light*.

19. See also 1 Cor 11:23; 15:24; Gal 2:20; Isa 53:12. On Jesus' apocalyptic "handing over" in Romans, see Gaventa, "Interpreting the Death of Jesus Apocalyptically," 125–45.

20. Although the word "power" (δύναμις) does not occur in the Greek, Gaventa is surely right that this meaning is conveyed since Paul writes that "all are under sin" (πάντας ὑφ' ἁμαρτίαν εἶναι). Gaventa, "Cosmic Power of Sin," 129.

in hymnic fashion how "all" lack God's righteousness (vv. 10–18).[21] Paul then concludes that the "entire cosmos" (πᾶς ὁ κόσμος) falls short of God's righteous decree (v. 19) and that knowledge of Sin comes through the law (v. 20).[22] Paul's discussion of humanity's captivity in 3:9–20 is consonant with his later explanation that "God has imprisoned all in disobedience so that he may be merciful to all" (11:32).[23] Moreover, Paul's mention of the law revealing Sin in verse 20 is also consonant with his later argument that Sin has ensnared the law for its own evil purposes (7:1–25).[24] Overall, consistently reading Sin as a power throughout Romans problematizes forensic interpretations of Romans 1–3 itself.

In sum, when we read Romans 1–3 apocalyptically alongside Romans 5–8, we find that all of us—both Jew and Greek—need to understand the depth of our subjection to the anti-God powers. As Campbell rightly notes, God saves us by delivering us. For Paul, it is all about the deliverance of God.[25] But without Romans 1–3, from what are we being delivered?[26] When we read Romans 1–3 alongside Romans 5–8, we find in fact that God in Jesus delivers us from Sin and Death, for—as Paul writes in 3:9—both Jews and Greeks are under the power of Sin. Humanity's enslavement to the anti-God powers is cosmic in scope, and God's defeat of those powers is likewise cosmic in scope. Rereading Romans 1–3 and Romans 5–8 (and indeed the entirety of Romans) apocalyptically captures the cosmic nature of both our enslavement and our deliverance.

Although this apocalyptic rereading of Romans 1–3 barely scratches the surface, I want to suggest that reading Romans 1–8 as consistently apocalyptic provides a more plausible "solution" to the problem that Campbell rightly identifies. Such a reading undermines forensic interpretations of Romans 1:18—3:20 and at the same time allows Paul to speak in his own voice throughout this same passage. This reading still requires further exegetical exploration, and many proponents of an apocalyptic

21. On humanity's captivity in this hymn, see Gaventa, "From Toxic Speech to the Redemption of Doxology in Paul's Letter to the Romans," 392–408.

22. On Paul's use of the term κόσμος throughout Romans, see Gaventa, "Neither Height nor Depth," 185–201.

23. Gaventa, "God Handed Them Over," 121.

24. For a discussion of how Sin has ensnared the law in Romans 7, see Meyer's ground-breaking article, "The Worm at the Core of the Apple," 62–84.

25. Hence the title of Campbell's book that initiated the two conferences this book is based upon: *The Deliverance of God*.

26. Gaventa makes this point in her review of *Deliverance*, "Rescue Mission", 36–37.

Paul have begun to take up this mantle.[27] This reading, to be clear, also does not erase all of the "problems" in Romans 1–3. Paul's discussion of the law in 2:12–29 looms large among these problems, as well as, *inter alia*, the uncomfortable notion that God would "hand over" humanity to the anti-God powers in the first place. Overall, however, I still believe that this proposal provides a more fruitful way forward, and I am eager to hear how Campbell responds to this apocalyptic opponent.

---

27. Gaventa is among those leading the way. In addition to the works listed in this response, see also her discussion of God's "glory" within Paul's apocalyptic worldview: "For the Glory of God," 6–14.

Douglas Campbell's Response to Brittany E. Wilson

Brittany begins her lively response like many others—with criticisms suggesting the rejection of my proposal that Romans 1:18–32 is an instance of *prosōpopoeia*. But I have just suggested rephrasing this proposal in terms of ancient parody, when responding to Robin in the previous chapter, and it is interesting to see how much of her critique lapses from this point as well. Like Robin, she demands specific verbal cues and so, like Robin, tends to overlook the parodic clues that *are* and *could have been* supplied in context. So I would maintain that it is important to approach Romans 1 reconstructing the perceptions of an ancient auditor and to discipline the intrusion of modern interpretative needs and expectations. But Brittany's concerns are really rather different from Robin's.

Deliverance is admittedly too long and complex and so some of its key claims tend to get lost. However, my main case for parody in 1:18–32 is an *argumentative* one that is, because it concerns ultimately the construal of Romans 1–4, a *theological* one as well. And Brittany does not engage very directly with this aspect of things, so it might be useful to clarify it here since this will speak directly to her main critique.

Both Brittany and I follow to a significant degree the interpretative lead established in relation to Paul by J. Louis (Lou) Martyn. Whether or not it is helpful to call this tradition "apocalyptic" is an interesting question that we will unfortunately not be able to pursue here. But it will save time to use that moniker for the moment *in this specific sense*—to denote someone basically following in Lou's footsteps, as it were. And some of the key contours of this interpretative pathway were already apparent in his famous essay, "Epistemology at the Turn of the Ages," which analyzed 2 Corinthians 5:16–17 and was first published in 1967.[28]

Lou argues there with matchless precision and clarity that Paul distinguishes between two rather different realities and modes of knowing. He begins with the observation that "Paul defends his apostleship [in 2 Cor 2:14—6:10] by various arguments, all of which refer to the turn of the ages. . . . [O]nly at that juncture is a person granted the new means of perception which enable one to distinguish true from false apostles. . . . Paul's statements establish an inextricable connexion between

---

28. In Farmer et al., *Christian History and Interpretation*, 269–87; it was subsequent republished in Martyn's collection of essays *Theological Issues*, 89–110. Page numbers are cited from the 1997 edition.

eschatology and epistemology."[29] The result of this discovery is the articulation of "*two* ways of knowing, and . . . what separates the two is the turn of the ages, the apocalyptic event of Christ's death/resurrection. There is a way of knowing which is characteristic of the old age. In the past Paul himself knew in that way. And, since Paul now knows Christ (Phil 3:8), there must be a new way of knowing that is proper either to the new age or to that point at which the ages meet."[30] Lou consequently goes on to argue in relation to the correct interpretation of 2 Corinthians 5:16–17 that "[t]he essential failure of the Corinthians consists in their inflexible determination to live somewhere other than in the cross. So also the essential flaw in their epistemology lies in their failure to view the cross as *the absolute epistemological watershed*. On a real cross in this world hangs God's own Messiah, the Lord of glory (1 Cor 2:8)!"[31] Hence "in [the] community the veil is taken away, the creation is new, the old has passed away, look!, the new has come (2 Cor 5:17; 6:2). Yet all of this can be seen only by the new eyes granted at the *juncture* of the ages."[32] "For, as the second half of 2 Cor 5:16 and the first half of v. 17 show, the epistemology characteristic of this community is thoroughly and without remainder Christological. . . . [A]t the juncture of the ages the marks of the resurrection are hidden and revealed in the cross of the disciple's daily death, and *only* there."[33]

Lou and those who follow him here would argue that these insights, developed in relation to 2 Corinthians 5:16–17, are characteristic ultimately of Paul's gospel as a whole; some of his deepest convictions have been identified. However, if this is the case then the customary approach to Romans 1–4, and especially to 1:18—3:20, *creates a crisis for this approach*. The crisis is inaugurated—as both Barth and Brunner well knew—as early in the text as 1:19–20, when the text commits irrevocably to natural theology. This is the only place in Paul where such an overt commitment takes place (and this is not to be confused with commitments elsewhere to the value or even the disclosures of creation). In Romans 1:19–20 it is presupposed that humanity as a whole has access to fundamental truths about the divine nature and activity by unaided

29. Martyn, "Epistemology at the Turn of the Ages," 92.
30. Ibid., 95, emphasis added.
31. Ibid., 108, emphasis added.
32. Ibid., 109.
33. Ibid., 110.

contemplation of the cosmos, prior to any involvement with Christ; indeed, they will be held firmly accountable for this general knowledge. The very things then that the powerful statements of 2 Corinthians 5:16–17 exclude—perception by means of the flesh and unassisted by the cross—*are affirmed here by Paul's text in a presuppositional argumentative location.*

One immediate result of this is a disruption of the way that an apocalyptic approach should develop its account of human sin.

The apocalyptic articulation of what the Christian community is saved or delivered from can only be undertaken fully in retrospect, in the light of its deliverance. A community still decisively in the grip of sin cannot articulate its own location accurately; its very articulations will be distorted and untrue. Only after the clarifications of grace have arrived can it turn and provide an accurate account of the problem—a point where apocalyptic readers should join hands with Augustine. (Stanley Hauerwas gives a superb account of these dynamics in his essay "Seeing Darkness, Hearing Silence."[34]) Hence it is interesting to note that Paul seems to do just this for much of Romans 5–8 (see esp. 5:12–14; 7:7–25; 8:31–39). There the solution defines the problem (i.e., epistemologically). However, this is exactly the opposite way around from the argument of Romans 1, where the problem sets the stage for the solution. So what is the apocalyptic reader of Paul to do?

My response to this conundrum was argued at some length in *Deliverance*. In particular, I tried to point out there that the initial starting point of natural theology in Romans 1—that readers of this volume will now recognize as fundamentally foundationalist and Eunomian—went on to create localized textual difficulties *and* broader difficulties for the construction of Judaism as the rest of the argument was interpreted through 3:20 on this basis (i.e., assuming that 1:19–20 were Paul's own presuppositions). Indeed, an entire raft of difficulties is discernible once the usual hermeneutic of generosity in relation to this reading is replaced by a hermeneutic of suspicion. These difficulties then create a certain amount of interpretative pressure justifying the move in turn to an alternative reading that resolves them. A Socratic construal, in which someone has their own presuppositions turned against them, works rather better. And surprisingly few direct problems are apparent with such a reading, at which point the basic problem for the apocalyptic reader

---

34. Hauerwas, "Seeing Darkness, Hearing Silence," 8–32.

of Paul seems to have been resolved. Paul does *not* commit *himself* in Romans 1:19–20 to epistemology that is not located at the turn of the ages but is thoroughly rooted in the perceptions of the age of the flesh. Rather, he masterfully deconstructs *an opponent* who thinks in these terms—and my argument links hands again here with an aspect of Lou's work, since he read Galatians very much in these terms.

Let me simply say then that I am surprised that Brittany continues to offer a reading of Romans 1–3 that essentially reproduces all the problems that the apocalyptic reader of Paul should be striving to eliminate. She is entitled of course to be unpersuaded by my particular exegetical proposal. But what I would like to see is some analogous exegetical attempt to pluck this infamous text from the hands of its anti-apocalyptic interpreters. And suggesting that Romans 1–3 somehow "sets the scene" for the gospel, articulating what it is that Christians have been delivered from *before they have been delivered from it*, and hence *arguing still in the age of the flesh and in a location prior to the cross* is *not* an apocalyptic reading of this text as much as the undoing of that approach. It is not an articulation of an epistemology located at the turn of the ages. So, at the end of the day, as an apocalyptic reader of Paul and a tradent of Lou's basic approach, I have to pronounce myself unpersuaded by her reading.[35]

However, I suspect that this impasse has been created more by a failure in communication—for which I take much responsibility—than by any disagreement over substantive matters, and so I look forward to a future rapprochement. What holds us together is considerably more important than anything evident here that might pull our readings apart. Furthermore, I appreciate her bold and articulate development of concerns that I know many others share, while I hope that my brief observations here also indicate my concerns with those concerns. Let the conversation continue. . . .

---

35. An "apocalyptic" reading is pursued in part by claims based on a suitable reading of two verbs—ἀποκαλύπτω in 1:18 and παραδίδωμι in 1:24, 26, and 28. However, Brittany fails to take into account the syntactical developments of these verbs in their context that preclude the more acceptable reading she urges. The text does not, in short, say, when read carefully and in full, what she says it says at the critical points. And this is not to note the arguments that have been omitted—although in a short response clearly some things had to be.

12

Rereading Paul's ΔIKAIO-Language

DOUGLAS A. CAMPBELL

Introduction

We considered in chapter 9 one way that a destructive foundationalism can be unleashed into our broader accounts of Paul's thinking about salvation—through a forward construal of the argument in Romans 1–3. This construal will release foundationalism in its own right, in the specific form of course of Western contractualism, although it may form an alliance with a more general commitment on the part of Paul's interpreter to a fundamentally rationalistic and moralistic, and invariably quite individualizing, anthropology—a conception of the human person that primarily governs itself, which is deeply congenial to modern thought and culture (repeated critiques notwithstanding). This type of anthropology will lead Paul's interpreter to read him "forward" as well, as an essentially autonomous individual sets off on a quest for salvation, driven and governed by her own conceptions. These two moves, perhaps operating in tandem, will unleash a virulent conditionality and contractualism within Paul, although an alternative reading of Romans 1–3 in non-foundationalist, Socratic terms will counter this eventuality, thereby closing down one important point of access for Paul's distortion in ultimately Arian, or more precisely Eunomian (and Pelagian) terms.

However, winning this battle will unfortunately not win the war. Contractual foundationalism in my experience can corrupt Paul's thought in two other principal ways—through a correlative conditional account of Paul's discussions of faith (which then retrojects conditionality back into the account of the problem, elaborated with reference to "works"), and through a particular construal of the apostle's *dikaio-* (δικαιο-) terms. These may be viewed as informed fundamentally—like Western society—by a notion of "justice" that is itself understood in terms of a narrative of retribution (as well as with the appropriate correlative metaphors, Lakoff would remind us, of things likes equivalence and straightness, and a broader "quantified" approach to morality), thereby releasing Western conditionality within Paul's thinking again.[1] Both these Arian interpretative projects must be countered if the Athanasian gospel is ever to emerge from Paul clearly—the proverbial war then, at this point, on two fronts.

We will address the struggle surrounding Paul's faith terminology in chapter 14. For now we will concentrate on the struggle surrounding the interpretation of his δικαιο-language. And here I really need to achieve two subordinate results.

I need to offer a suitable account of the relatively rare but strategic noun phrase δικαιοσύνη Θεοῦ, usually rendered as "the righteousness of God"; and I need to provide a suitable account of the important cognate verb δικαιόω, usually translated "[I] justify." After these two moves the rest of the δικαιο- data in Paul will basically take care of itself. More specifically, I need to provide accounts of these two data points that do not introduce inappropriate Western notions of justice into Paul's texts at the lexicographical level, and I made detailed suggestions in *Deliverance* about just how to do this. So I will first summarize here my suggestions concerning δικαιοσύνη Θεοῦ, and then, second, my suggestions concerning the verb.[2]

1. Alasdair MacIntyre is supremely helpful at this point; see esp. his magisterial *Whose Justice? Which Rationality?*; but see also, rather more compactly, Stanley Hauerwas's essay "The Politics of Justice," 45–68.

2. But be warned from the outset that these are difficult discussions not because of their complexity as much as because we struggle at these moments against some of our deepest presuppositions and commitments. These must be exposed and scrutinized in a way that feels thoroughly unnatural; although, having said this, I would point out that this is what a lot of Christians, and especially Protestants, say that they ought to do with the Scriptures.

1. The meaning of ΔΙΚΑΙΟΣΥΝΗ ΘΕΟΥ

As perhaps Gadamer has emphasized most clearly, we all approach texts with a network of presuppositions or pre-understandings (*Vorverständnisse*), without which we simply cannot make sense of them (*Philosophical Hermeneutics*). And this certainly holds for our convictions about ontology or being. So may I suggest at the outset that—informed ultimately by the Trinity—we assume that being, and especially divine being, is fundamentally active and dynamic, and so we should vigilantly resist any dichotomy in our thinking between being and act or activity (see, inter alia, Gunton, *Brief Theology*). These realizations will help us straightaway when we try to understand what Paul was getting at when he used the phrase δικαιοσύνη Θεοῦ. Many scholars in the past have worried at the outset about the genitive used here, considering especially subjective, authorial, and "objective" possibilities (and the definitive Cranfield actually discusses five in his *Romans*, 95–99). But given a dynamic understanding of ontology any reference to a divine attribute or aspect of being *must* be a reference simultaneously to divine activity and hence to something both inherent in and proceeding from God, at which point emphasizing distinctions between the foregoing genitive construals could fail to capture Paul's meaning. A dynamic being breaks through these categorizations, we might say. And the same applies to human δικαιοσύνη or "righteousness." This *must* be an ongoing, dynamic state of right behavior and activity—something that presumably both God and humanity are ultimately interested in affecting.

Alert to this ontological dynamism, and to the treachery of certain Western interpretative distinctions, I suggest we turn first to the internal evidence of Paul's actual texts. I make this suggestion for two reasons, one again involving possible treachery.

In the past scholars have often approached the meaning of δικαιοσύνη Θεοῦ by way of long histories of scholarship and of the broader lexical data. Vast surveys of OT usage are not uncommon. But such surveys need to be handled carefully. Strictly speaking, such analyses establish a spectrum of semantic possibilities for Paul's phrase—different options at the level of the signified when we try to interpret the Greek signifiers. Such surveys also provide information about contextual activators—what Eco in his *Theory of Semiotics* calls denotations and connotations—that can lead us to affirm particular semantic options if those activators are present. Properly used then, such data is invaluable, but it is also fundamentally incomplete. We must still attend carefully to Paul's texts to try to discern which meaning from within the available spectrum provided by our survey is in play, if we can, in relation to which activators, if they are present. Moreover, the internal evidence is always decisive (or, at least, methodologically superior; we might not have enough data to reach decisive judgments). But we should attend to the internal evidence for another reason.

Unfortunately, much of this survey material is gripped by a methodological fallacy James Barr exposed some time ago in *The Semantics of Biblical Language*, "etymologism," in which "words" are supplied with some kernel or essence of meaning that supposedly holds over time (in fact, a mistaken ontology). This semantic essence can be ostensibly detected in a survey of a sign's historical antecedents and introduced after this into its current textual location, although fundamentally illegitimately. Unfortunately, a theological agenda is often thereby introduced, perhaps subliminally, into the selections and commentary that inevitably inform a vast survey, and can subsequently be insinuated into the Pauline data.[3] And this is a particularly egregious imposition because it takes place before the syntax and broader grammar of the Pauline texts have been processed, which this distorting prior decision tends to shape. It is consequently very difficult to correct this sort of lexicographical mistake once it has been made in the light of what Paul is actually saying with his phrases and sentences.

The right safeguard against this distortion is, once more, a rigorous emphasis on the internal evidence that can detect and resist any such illegitimate etymologizing decisions introduced from further afield. So now we should turn to this internal evidence, although it will have to be in summary form here.

I suggest that Paul provides enough information in context, and especially in certain revealing argumentative parallels, for us to construct a basic map of the signification of δικαιοσύνη Θεοῦ, and one that falls well within the possibilities established by earlier surveys of the broader data. *Deliverance* scans certain Pauline texts concluding that the δικαιοσύνη Θεοῦ is an event; it is singular; it is saving, it is liberating; it is life giving;

---

3. One aspect of Polanyi's important work: see *Personal Knowledge* and *The Tacit Dimension*.

and it is eschatological or resurrecting.[4] And nothing here is very controversial. Indeed, this account basically corroborates the famous judgment of Ernst Käsemann's classic study, *Paulinische Perspektiven*, that the δικαιοσύνη Θεοῦ is "God's sovereignty over the world revealing itself eschatologically in Jesus" leading to a saving gift with the characteristics also of a power—this last being his careful modification of important claims within prior Lutheran tradition. And at this point, I suggest that we have enough to go on with; my broader apocalyptic construal of Paul's δικαιο- texts remains on track simply by endorsing Käsemann's position. But it will enrich our construal if we explore things a little more deeply—in this instance, by recognizing the scriptural intertextuality in play.

When writing *Deliverance* up through the end of 2007, I returned to consider a suggestion made by Richard Hays in his seminal book *Echoes of Scripture*. Hays observed there, almost in passing, that elements of Psalm 98 (97 LXX) informed Paul's language in Romans 1:17. And I was lead in 2007 to repent of my earlier churlish rejection of this proposal when writing my doctoral thesis back in 1989. With a new sensitivity to such intertextual suggestions—possibly assisted by the fact that the suggester now had an office just down the corridor from mine—I realized that Hays was right, although his proposal had yet to be argued for in detail. So I proceeded to try to do this. I will not reproduce that argument in full here; it is the heart of chapter 18 in *Deliverance* (688–702; see also "An Echo of Scripture"). Suffice it to say that multiple allusions to Psalm 98 in and around Romans 1:17 suggest this linkage. The clauses are unequalled in proximity in extant Greek; salvation occurs in the immediate context in both texts; and various other themes occur in common as well—God's activity in relation to an antithesis between Jews and pagans, God's disclosure of something, etc. So I concluded that it can be fairly firmly established that, as Hays suggested, Romans 1:17 echoes the opening verses of Psalm 98, which read:

97:2 LXX: ἐγνώρισεν κύριος τὸ σωτήριον αὐτοῦ,
ἐναντίον τῶν ἐθνῶν ἀπεκάλυψεν τὴν δικαιοσύνην αὐτοῦ.

97:3 ἐμνήσθη τοῦ ἐλέους αὐτοῦ τῷ Ιακωβ
καὶ τῆς ἀληθείας αὐτοῦ τῷ οἴκῳ Ισραηλ·
εἴδοσαν πάντα τὰ πέρατα τῆς γῆς τὸ σωτήριον τοῦ θεοῦ ἡμῶν.

[98:2] The LORD has made known his victory;

4. Campbell, *Deliverance*, 683–88.

he has revealed his vindication in the sight of the nations.
[3] He has remembered his steadfast love and faithfulness to the
house of Israel.
All the ends of the earth have seen the victory of our God.
[NRSV]

But we should now advance beyond Hays's important observation by recognizing that Psalm 98 is a psalm of divine kingship; it rejoices as God draws near to rule the earth by his strong right arm. And consequently Paul's use in Romans of phraseology drawn from this psalm—as well as from other related texts, as we will see momentarily—subtly evokes the discourse of divine kingship that runs through much of the OT. Moreover, a quick reprise of that material reveals that much of it overlaps with the raw data of "righteousness," although it tends to do so in a distinctive way. God is often described as a King when appeal is being made to "him" to save his people. He is frequently being asked to rescue them from some extremity, or thanked and praised when he has done so. Hence when δικαιο- language occurs in these contexts it seems very much to confirm the classic study of δικαιοσύνη Θεοῦ by Hermann Cremer (*Paulinische Rechtfertigungslehre*), which detected this saving dimension in a lot of the δικαιο- language in the OT and in Paul (although he did not explain it in precisely these terms). He called this *iustitia salutifera*, recognizing its differences from other customary—arguably more Western—ways of conceiving of *iustitia* in terms of retribution.[5] So, once again, a classic German study of the question seems to have been right. But in the light of the surrounding discourse of kingship that informs this usage we can now perhaps grasp a little more clearly than we did before how Paul (like the OT) can speak in these saving terms in Romans 1:16–17 of something "right" happening, hence using the word δικαιοσύνη especially appropriately, a signifier that often seems to have a connotation of "rightness."[6]

---

5. Cf. the RSV translations, mostly reproduced in the ESV, of Judg 5:11 ("the triumphs of the Lord"); 1 Sam 12:7 ("the saving deeds of the Lord"); Ps 40:9–10 ("deliverance" 2x); Isa 41:2 ("victory"); 56:1 ("deliverance"); Mic 6:5 ("saving acts"); cf. also Dan 9:16—generally renderings of the Hebrew *tsidqot YHWH*. *Tsdq* words occur 276x in the OT.

6. This is often denoted in the relevant lexicographical studies as a "norm" and is frequently associated with Hellenistic culture. But I suggest resisting the introduction of "norm" into an ancient discussion of "rightness" as a probable introduction—anachronistically—of what amounts to Kantianism. MacIntyre is once again instructive (*Whose Justice? Which Rationality?*).

It is "right" for a king to save his people when they are in extremity; this is the appropriate ethical action for a ruler in relation to the ruled that we sometimes hear spoken of today in an aristocratic vestige as *noblesse oblige* (although, strictly speaking, the precise equivalent here is *royaume oblige*). The nature of the underlying relationship even demands this. A king *qua* king has responsibilities (as does a queen), and when he (or she) acts accordingly, this is "right." And the same applies to the divine monarch. In situations of duress something right is happening precisely in and as something saving happens. These two notions in that situation framed by this discourse are coterminous. So Paul's phraseology is not conforming to some other standard of rightness at this point, and there is really no need to make such a claim. The story of divine kingship that he evokes establishes the rightness of God's saving action in its own terms. Indeed, this divine act is arguably now *the* definition *of* rightness above all others, as Barth articulates so clearly in IV/1 of the *Church Dogmatics*.

It is now worth grasping in this relation that God's saving act in this sense resonates more in contemporary terms with an executive than with a judicial or forensic activity. We tend to forget that the separation of the executive and the judiciary in modern nation-states is a function of modernity—of its vast productivity, its creation of bureaucracies, and its distribution of executive and forensic functions between them (and these can, of course, have a distinctively modern political rationale as well). But in the world of the Bible these functions were concentrated in a single institution that converged in a single figure: the monarchy and its presiding monarch. Ultimately, the king made executive *and* judicial decisions—hopefully wisely—and so the biblical terminology used to describe both these distinguishable acts interwove (and, after all, both sets of judgments were supposed to be ethical). Hence it is worth grasping that God's δικαιοσύνη for Paul, by way of Psalm 98, harks back to ancient *executive* actions. It belongs to the same family of acts as the exodus, the conquest, the successful campaigns of the judges, the delivery of Jerusalem from the hand of the Assyrians, and so on—the *saving acts* of Israel's divine king. It is misleading for modern readers then to suggest that God's δικαιοσύνη in Paul suggests a judge unless that notion is carefully contextualized; God is acting in this phrase like an ancient king visiting *executive* "judgment" on his enemies and liberating his oppressed people, and not like some modern presider over a court of appeals upholding due process. And in the light of all these realizations we can perhaps grasp an interesting dimension in Paul's broader argument a little more precisely than is often the case—one that will also be useful when we turn shortly to consider the meaning of the verb.

Precisely because of this compassionate and obligated sense of rightness inhering in the identity of the divine king *qua* king, people in the OT often appeal to this when they are in extremity. At times they even make this appeal in the full knowledge that they have no other basis for an appeal, that is, in terms of their own uprightness. Because God is their King *sinners* can still appeal to him for help—a scenario that comes up quite a lot. He should still at least hear their petition because it is right for him to do so, just as, strictly speaking, it is right for him to act and to save them. So it is especially intriguing that Paul quotes a text from *this* tradition in Romans as well (recalling it from Galatians 2:16)—Psalm 143:2 (142:2 LXX): καὶ μὴ εἰσέλθῃς εἰς κρίσιν μετὰ τοῦ δούλου σου, ὅτι οὐ δικαιωθήσεται ἐνώπιόν σου πᾶς ζῶν ("Do not enter into judgment with your servant, for no one living is righteous before you"). This quotation and psalm are part of the tradition that recognizes the sinfulness of the supplicant. The petition to God for help is therefore rooted in an appeal to God's obligated "righteousness" (v. 1): Κύριε, εἰσάκουσον τῆς προσευχῆς μου, ἐνώτισαι τὴν δέησίν μου ἐν τῇ ἀληθείᾳ σου, ἐπάκουσόν μου ἐν τῇ δικαιοσύνῃ σου ("Hear my prayer, O LORD; give ear to my supplications in your faithfulness; answer me in your righteousness").[7] And that this further appeal to God's *iustitia salutifera* is in play by way of an echo in Romans 3:20 (and Gal 2:16) seems pretty likely in view of the fact that the next verses in the letter—21 and 22—foreground a δικαιοσύνη of God as attested by the Torah and the prophets explicitly (see also vv. 25 and 26). In short, Paul's echo of Psalm 98 (2–3) and citation of Psalm 143 (2–3) seem to be linked together, and informed fundamentally by the OT discourse of divine kingship.

However, in order to grasp the full significance of this connection for Paul's unfolding argument we should take another explanatory step and (re)introduce the circumstances of Romans into our discussion.

No one denies that Paul is opposing someone in Galatians. And I have argued in *Deliverance* that Romans is best explained in these terms as well (and, indeed, in precisely these terms in that the same opposition is in view[8]). Paul objects deeply and strongly to the "gospel" proclaimed

7. See also v. 11: ἕνεκα τοῦ ὀνόματός σου, κύριε, ζήσεις με, ἐν τῇ δικαιοσύνῃ σου ἐξάξεις ἐκ θλίψεως τὴν ψυχήν μου.

8. See ch. 13, "Rereading the Frame," 469–518; of course, I draw heavily on Martyn's analysis of Galatians at this point as well: cf. his "Epistemology at the Turn of the Ages" and *Galatians, passim.*

by these opponents, who were probably messianic Jews unhappy with his abandonment of the Torah. They (as we have already seen) seem to have urged the importance of the Torah rather in the manner of *4 Maccabees* and Philo. Only the cutting off of the sinful passions through circumcision, and subsequent control over the passions exerted by a mind instructed by the Torah, in their view, facilitated righteous behavior. And yet this ethic could and did affect righteousness, they thought, presumably and especially when transgressions were cleansed by the blood of the dying Messiah. The result of a disciplined pursuit of all this would then be an appearance before the throne of God on Judgment Day and a firmly anticipated judgment of "righteous," at which point those so affirmed could enter into the blessings and life of the age to come. (Not so the wicked, of course, and most especially, the foully wicked pagans.)

But Paul is skeptical about the value of any of this, and on numerous grounds. His principal problem seems to have been this alternative gospel's abandonment of the ethic supplied by God in Christ, seen, on the one hand, in its emphasis on a decisive future event—the verdict of the Day of Judgment—as against a decisive past event centered on Jesus with present effect, and, on the other hand, in its conditional, and hence inevitably insecure and anxious, saving arrangement as against an unconditional salvation grounded in God's loving election as evidenced by Christ. This alternative gospel, in other words, does not do very much with Christ, and provides precious little assurance, in Paul's view. Things must apparently be *added* to Christ before anyone is saved or can behave properly, and at this point the loving character of God is called into question and salvation is opened up to considerable insecurity.

But God's gracious and radically saving provision in Christ has also revealed for Paul a hitherto unsuspected depth of human depravity, which he narrates in terms of an Adamic story of demonic invasion and oppression. And in the light of this unpleasant disclosure Paul seems to feel that not only has his opposition foolishly abandoned God's appointed mode of salvation and ethical behavior—found in the arrival of God in person—but they have turned back confidently to the efforts of a fundamentally twisted human nature, thereby entering a double bind. And these countervailing concerns of Paul are apparent in the scriptural texts that we just noted, which subtly compete through the argument of Romans, as well as through much of Galatians and Philippians.

The opposition to Paul centered on the Teacher is banking on salvation through its *own* righteous activity, arising from a human nature ostensibly trimmed by circumcision and tutored by the Torah. So Paul opposes to this optimistic nomistic proto-Pelagianism, a devastating set of correlative objections. *He* will rely on *God's* righteousness, not on his own, which in context means the divine monarch's salvation of his people from their extremity by way of Christ. Moreover, *this* salvation will save *sinners*—a group Paul is very skeptical will produce righteousness, even after a wholehearted embrace of the Teacher's pedagogy. Paul's protest is framed then by *God's* saving act and human *depravity*, both of which counter the Teacher's reliance on his own rectitude. All of which is to say that something of a battle for the Bible is going on in Romans between two opposing and very different positions—a battle that anticipates in many key respects (although not all) the later struggles between Augustine and Pelagius, and between some of Calvin's interpreters and certain followers of Arminius. Scriptural texts are flashing across this battlefield, unleashed by both sides. And the saving righteousness of God, the compassionate divine King, who delivers his struggling and sinful subjects from their oppression, is Paul's scriptural discourse that opposes a Jewish Christian teacher overly confident in his *own* righteousness, as one of the Teacher's probable key texts indicates reasonably clearly, Leviticus 18:5: ὁ ποιήσας αὐτὰ ζήσεται ἐν αὐτοῖς ("You shall keep my statutes and ordinances; by doing so one shall live . . .").[9] One final thing is now important to recall in relation to this data.

I suggest in *Deliverance* that Paul is especially assertive and confident about all this *because it has happened*; the OT appeals for God's intervention have been definitively answered. Moreover, the semantic space that they map out has been filled with quite specific, concrete content. And that fulfillment is, of course, the resurrection, ascension, and heavenly enthronement of Jesus Christ at the right hand of the Father. *This is the decisive saving life-giving act of the divine monarch—the resurrection and enthronement of his chosen and appointed Son as Anointed One and King*, along with all that followed.

---

9. Among other things, Paul replied to this: Οὐκ ἀθετῶ τὴν χάριν τοῦ θεοῦ· εἰ γὰρ διὰ νόμου δικαιοσύνη, ἄρα Χριστὸς δωρεὰν ἀπέθανεν. Moreover, ἐξ ἔργων νόμου οὐ δικαιωθήσεται πᾶσα σὰρξ ἐνώπιον αὐτοῦ, διὰ γὰρ νόμου ἐπίγνωσις ἁμαρτίας. "That is, the Torah will only reveal to you how sinful you really are, after which you will cry Ταλαίπωρος ἐγὼ ἄνθρωπος· τίς με ῥύσεται ἐκ τοῦ σώματος τοῦ θανάτου τούτου?!" (and so on; i.e., Gal 2:21; Rom 3:20/Gal 2:16c; Rom 7:24).

Now it should not be too controversial to suggest that δικαιοσύνη Θεοῦ in Paul (and much else besides) has explicit christological content—put a little more colloquially, that this phrase is infused with a sense of resurrection; that its meaning really *is* eschatological; that Christ's rising from the dead is the actual point in space and time where God's definitive salvation is revealed and effected. But scholars have been slow to grasp this, and the failure to do so has led to an unfortunate christological understatement in some accounts of Paul's subsequent argument. Hence I suggest that we reverse this negative spiral if it is operative and recover the degree to which Christ informs all of Paul's language and argumentation in his δικαιο- texts. Christ is not playing a bit part in a broader drama here—a Rosencrantz or even a Polonius; Christ infuses this phrase with its very meaning and rationale; he is the prince of Denmark in this play. And if we fail to grasp this I worry that we fail to grasp Paul's argument at a fundamental level, and, moreover, we might commit his interpretation ultimately to incoherence.[10] (The prices paid for any christological understatement, in other words, are high.)[11]

Once we grasp that the announcement that is the gospel in 1:16–17, far from being shameful, indicates an act of royal divine power to save centered in Jesus Christ, and hence that it can be conveyed by a story of his faithful suffering followed by his dramatic resurrection, we can see that Paul has introduced some of his most important contentions (probably while simultaneously affirming the deepest convictions of the Romans Christians) in the letter's opening syllables. In verses 2 through 4, somewhat incredibly, even before scripting the second element in an ancient letter's address, Paul has already announced the good news: God has fulfilled promises made long ago in the Scriptures by sending his Son as a royal figure, and—rather more importantly—by establishing him as the Son of God by his resurrection, which is to say, by his resurrection from the dead and enthronement on high. Jesus is therefore Messiah, Son, and Lord, something 1:16–17 (construed christocentrically) reiterates almost exactly. Indeed, 1:2–4, 16–17, 3:21–26 (and so on), speak with

10. We might do this by introducing a non-christological but fundamental notion of rightness and justice into Paul's thought that later clashes with fundamentally christological commitments.

11. I have not used the πίστις Χριστοῦ texts to exert leverage on Paul's δικαιο- texts here (or in *Deliverance*), but have let the internal evidence in other respects nudge us toward a christocentric reading. However, I would want to suggest that that debate *does* supply important evidence for the christocentric approach to Paul's δικαιο- material.

one voice—christocentrically—in a way that simply continues through the rest of the letter's argument (and it is something of a relief to be able to speak constantly of Christ in Romans "from the get go").[12] Moreover, we also see here that Christ's resurrection has been infused not just into Paul's δικαιο- terminology but into his terminology of *life* as well, language that parallels a great deal of his δικαιο- material elsewhere. And so this is an appropriate point at which to turn to consider the argument of *Deliverance* with respect to the verb.

2. The Meaning of ΔΙΚΑΙΟΩ

Our realizations in relation to the noun phrase lead us to suspect that similar considerations are in play in relation to the cognate verb—that it is dynamic (which is not hard to imagine for a verb), in a saving sense, and that its content can be articulated most decisively by a consideration of the internal evidence. Perhaps more controversially, we are also invited to consider it in relation to Christ himself. The result of these considerations, I would suggest, is a recognition of the importance of Romans 6:7 in context—something E. P. Sanders saw very clearly in *Paul and Palestinian Judaism* and *Paul, the Law, and the Jewish People*. In 6:7 Paul states ὁ γὰρ ἀποθανὼν δεδικαίωται ἀπὸ τῆς ἁμαρτίας ["For whoever has died *is freed* from sin" NRSV].

Scholars have often struggled with this verse but I suggest that fairly strong arguments exist in favor of the suggestion of Robin Scroggs (and a few others[13]) that "the one who has died," ὁ . . . ἀποθανών, is Christ, and that *he* has therefore δεδικαίωται ἀπὸ τῆς ἁμαρτίας by his resurrection from the dead. Hence, we must translate the verb δικαιόω here with a fundamentally and univocally liberative sense such as "set free," "liberated," or "delivered." Indeed, *this reading is unavoidable.* Christ has not been "justified," or "pronounced righteous," or even "vindicated." As the context makes clear, his resurrection has delivered him from death and

---

12. Clearly here I link hands with some of the recent work on Romans undertaken by scholars like N. T. Wright ("Coming Home to St. Paul?," *Resurrection, Justification*) and J. Daniel Kirk (*Unlocking Romans*), but with the important caveat that for me the discourse of kingship is primary, dictating the shape of any covenant in play, and not the reverse. (Kirk's book is based, incidentally, on a doctoral thesis supervised at Duke by Richard Hays.)

13. Schreiner (*Romans*, 319) refers to Kearns, "The Interpretation"; Thyen, *Studien*, 204–5; and Frankemölle, *Taufverständnis*, 79.

from a state preceding that death oppressed by the evil force of Sin. It is this and only this that allows Paul to make the extraordinary claim that those "in" Christ no longer sin in a way that is also emphatically beyond any nomistic pedagogy. So the verb is participating here in—as Lou Martyn would put it—a three-figure drama. God is delivering us in Christ from *an opposing power*, here Sin. The verb δικαιόω denotes the all-important transfer of Christ beyond death to the new, resurrected realm, and it is this that opens up the possibility of our transfer as well, as symbolized by our baptism. And we can now see how Paul's christological use of the verb links up with the language of resurrection and life that we have already noted are operative in relation to the cognate noun phrase. Conversely, a strictly forensic sense—to which we shall return—makes very little sense; that is, a two-figure drama in which God presides as judge over a transgressing individual, sin being an act of the individual and death an act of God. I conclude then—at least for the moment—that when Paul is informed directly by his Christology he uses the verb δικαιόω in an overtly liberative and even resurrecting sense, and it would not be unfair to call this, in deference to Martyn's categories, an "apocalyptic" usage. But how do we explain this in the broader context of Paul's writings and arguments?

I ask this question because of the apparent problem that in Romans 2 the verb seems to have a somewhat different sense from 6:7. Perhaps most clearly in 2:13 the context suggests as directly as 6:7 that δικαιόω denotes that someone is being "declared righteous" in the full ethical sense, meaning that God is judging this person to *be* righteous and therefore pronouncing a judgment in relation to her of this, certain important consequences following upon this pronouncement. οὐ γὰρ οἱ ἀκροαταὶ νόμου δίκαιοι παρὰ τῷ θεῷ, ἀλλ᾿ οἱ ποιηταὶ νόμου δικαιωθήσονται. (The NRSV is far too weak here: "For it is not the hearers of the law who are righteous in God's sight, but the doers of the law who will be justified"; these "doers" are "being pronounced righteous"!) What is going on?

It seems at the least that two quite distinguishable referents exist for the same signifier in Paul—although this is hardly a big problem, at least in linguistic terms. Signifiers activate different meanings all the time; they are—with due apology to Plato on this point—not immutable, simple entities, but part of complex, shifting sign systems. But does Paul's double usage press argumentative, theological, even linguistic boundaries too far, or can we explain it? I think we can and, not a little ironically, largely because of Romans 2.

If we pay careful attention to the verses just preceding verse 13 we see that the process of judgment being described has *two* distinguishable components. As Paul says in verse 6, God ἀποδώσει ἑκάστῳ κατὰ τὰ ἔργα αὐτοῦ (i.e., "he will repay according to each one's deeds"), indicating a process of evaluation, specifically of "works," followed by a process of "giving," which actually dominates the discussion. Those who have evil works will be given some rather awful things— ὀργὴ [Θεοῦ] καὶ θυμός, θλῖψις καὶ στενοχωρία/"wrath and fury . . . anguish and distress"—while those who persist faithfully in good works will receive things like δόξα . . . καὶ τιμὴ καὶ εἰρήνη/"glory . . . and honor and immorality" and indeed ζωὴν αἰώνιον/"eternal life." And at this point we can see that existing Western ontological assumptions have perhaps tripped us up again. Commentators have generally ignored the way in which this divine word of judgment is not merely an indicative action, indicating a state—here either evil or righteous—but a *performative*. This divine act of judgment does not merely *evaluate* things but in so doing also *effects* things—very important things! It is a speech *act* (and, strictly speaking, of a certain sort)—although one could just as usefully recall Luther's account of divine and evangelical *thettelwörter* at this point; that is, his emphasis on *doing* words.[14] When a particular word is uttered by the relevant authority figure, someone is either condemned or set free. And when this is taken into account we can begin to see a way forward in relation to Paul's double usage, although we will have to revisit some presuppositional issues if we are to fill out the broader picture more completely.

Modern Western readers tend to assume that any forensic speech act is situated within a process of discovery, evaluation, and impartial judgment—within something like a modern courtroom and court case. And this is probably because, broadly speaking, what we might call a modern Western politics assumes that any such forensic activity will be fundamentally indicative, and in terms largely of Western justice, which is generally proportional and retributive. But narratives of justice interweave inextricably with accounts of rationality as well as with related accounts of politics, history, and ethics, as perhaps MacIntyre has shown most famously. So the forensic speech act that is a verdict will

14. Pauline scholars have not used speech act theory much. I have found limited uses in Brown (*The Cross*), Watson (*Text and Truth*), and Seifrid ("The Narrative of Scripture and Justification by Faith"); and extensive use only in Thiselton (*The First Epistle to the Corinthians*; *First Corinthians*)—detailed references in *Deliverance*, 1109, n. 63. The classic accounts are Austin, *Words*; and Searle, *Speech Acts*.

almost certainly suggest for a modern Western reader an indicative as well as a performative act, and it will be indicative, moreover, in terms of a Western notion of justice. It will operate therefore in a fundamentally legal sense, which is as a result utterly and thoroughly conditional, and it might even be difficult to think of it in any other way.

Now this discourse is not alien to ancient contexts. However, it cannot be presupposed there universally in the way that it can more readily—although arguably still unwisely—be assumed within Western modernity. But its underlying metaphors and narrative were present (which time constraints unfortunately forbid us from studying here in more detail). And Romans 2 participates largely within this particular discourse, as does its construal of the verb δικαιόω. In this setting—that is, within this broader story, including its accounts of justice, human capacity, and morality—δικαιόω denotes a forensic speech act that is both indicative and performative. The indication indeed generates the appropriate correlated effect, whether an estimation of good deeds leads to eternal life or of wicked deeds leads to anger and destruction.

But of course we well know by now that Paul is utterly opposed to any account of salvation or gospel couched in these terms. Such a gospel is simply wrong all the way across and all the way down. Paul's christologically mediated narrative supplies a fundamentally different account of salvation at every point: a different account of God, of Christ, of Christ's unconditional saving activity, of justice and rightness (so to speak), of sin, of humanity, and so; but then we have already spoken much about this. So suffice it here to say that any account of the gospel in the terms just described—a largely forensic account with God functioning as a judge on analogy to modern Western courtroom procedures—is a foundationalist projection of a particular human analogy into the being of God, and hence a fundamentally Arian project. It will be attractive precisely because it is a projection of a certain justice and politics into the being of God, and especially for those unaware that projection is taking place and/or those benefitting from Western juridical and political arrangements. But it will be a projection nevertheless and hence an idolatry. And we have also just answered our preceding question about two distinguishable senses for the verb.

It seems that the verb δικαιόω played an important role in the proto-Pelagian system of the Teacher where, in accordance with that discourse's broader dynamics, it is a particular speech act in the specific sense of a divine verdict with indicative and performative dimensions. Indeed, the Teacher's discourse largely converges on this future moment of evaluation before God on the Day of Judgment. Doubtless he hopes that contemplation of the two basic possibilities of that Day will lead to strenuous ethical activity to try to lay hold of one of them and to avoid the other. A little anxiety often leads to increased effort, he might say, even if (Paul would doubtless reply) the price paid for this is radical soteriological insecurity along with ethical self-deception. I can argue for the function of the verb in this sense in an opposing system to Paul's because of my Socratic construal of Romans 1–3; this is the sense there that he *opposes*.

But Paul has not of course left things at this pass. One of his specific counter-moves seems to have been a reclamation of the verb δικαιόω for his own system. And it is precisely its performative dimension that allows him to do this, along with the failure of most ancient forensic systems to be based on anything that approached what modern Western secularists would call justice.

A verdict is (and was) a speech act spoken by one authority figure in relation to another. But numerous situations existed in which this speech act was not made with reference to the accused's own ethical standing. A particular command by a figure in power could simply lead either to the accused's death or to her release. John the Baptist was languishing in the fortress of Machaira when Herod Antipas was foolishly cornered at a symposium into giving a command, and so he was executed. A judgment was carried out then, but it was not based on John's righteousness. It was rooted in Herod's turpitude. Analogously, but rather differently, Paul holds that humanity has been set free from its imprisonment within Sin because of the character and resulting command of God. The divine King has had compassion on his people in their suffering and oppression and has delivered them *and this is all to the good*, because they cannot deliver themselves or appeal for deliverance on any grounds of their own. Given their oppression, they are unrighteous and incapacitated; they are in prison! They must simply be set free, and God does so. And *this* seems to be where the verb δικαιόω functions within Paul's broader account of the gospel as seen especially in Romans 6:7.

When Paul uses the verb *dedikaiotai* (i.e., δικαιόω in the perfect passive) in verse 7 he seems to be indicating some pronouncement or command that affects a release from captivity in the way a verdict affects the release of a prisoner from jail—a meaning that fits the broader context perfectly. Jesus died and was resurrected and has thereby been "set free" or "released" from the evil grip of Sin. He has left the prison of fleshly captivity and been set free into resurrection life. And we can see now why δικαιόω is such a useful verb for Paul. Read in this liberative way, it speaks of *both* aspects of the journey of Christ—and therefore of the baptized Christian—*away from Sin*, stretching across and speaking of both his death and resurrection. It indicates where that journey began, in a captivity to Sin and Death, within an Adamic body, which is appropriately likened to life in captivity or in a prison. But it also indicates release from that captivity through a liberating event into a positive state. As verse 6 (b) puts it, the "body characterized by Sin" is left behind, and "a new life" (so v. 4) is entered, in which the old confinements no longer apply—in which it is "no longer necessary to serve Sin." And at this moment we join hands with another key motif for Paul, namely, baptism.

We can perhaps now see rather more clearly than we did before that *Paul's* use of δικαιόω is fundamentally *baptismal*, speaking of two key aspects in the narrative that critical ritual describes and enacts. This is suggested rather directly in 1 Corinthians 6:11 (although it is always vital to recall that this liberative and baptismal meaning is grounded in Christ's life, death, and resurrection): ἀπελούσασθε, ... ἡγιάσθητε, ... ἐδικαιώθητε ἐν τῷ ὀνόματι τοῦ κυρίου Ἰησοῦ Χριστοῦ καὶ ἐν τῷ πνεύματι τοῦ θεοῦ ἡμῶν ("you were washed, you were sanctified, you were justified in the name of our Lord Jesus Christ and in the Spirit of our God," although the NRSV is again too pallid; in this context of transfer and cleansing the verb would be better rendered "set free" or "released"). How much changes if we carry this liberative, "baptismal," and basically "resurrectional" meaning of the verb δικαιόω into the other texts where it occurs in Paul![15] It is worth noting in this relation that Charles Wesley has captured Paul's meaning *exactly* in the famous Methodist hymn "And Can It Be That I Should Gain?" (specifically in verse four):

> Long my imprisoned spirit lay,
> fast bound in sin and nature's night;
> thine eye diffused a quickening ray;
> I woke, the dungeon flamed with light;
> my chains fell off, my heart was free,
> I rose, went forth, and followed thee.

15. See also esp. Gal 3:24 in the broader context of vv. 22–24, where the metaphor of forensic confinement overlaps with a narrative of infantile confinement under a pedagogue.

My chains fell off, my heart was free,
I rose, went forth, and followed thee.

This is as good an account of the meaning of δικαιόω and of the event of "justification" in Paul as one could wish for.

In closing, it might be helpful to ask just where we have ended up after tracing through all these scriptural echoes and performative distinctions.

May I suggest that we have given a rigorously apocalyptic account of Paul's phrase δικαιοσύνη Θεοῦ and cognate verb in the best sense of that descriptor, that is also positioned tightly with respect to the texts. And, equally importantly, in doing so we have *not* endorsed key elements within the Arian reading of this material that is so widespread among Pauline interpreters; so we have not opened the door to Paul's later corruption or confusion. And we have done this by resisting the introduction into Paul's language and thinking of inappropriate notions of judgment and justice that depend on broad cultural analogies—and often on largely unexamined resonances with cultural practices in Western modernity, in particular—as against explicitly christological content. The sense of "rightness" being deployed by Paul was not assumed in this paper to be a "self-evident" sense of "justness," and certainly not an essentially quantitative sense of justice in terms of "retribution." It is this last notion that unleashes conditionality through Paul's thinking, and not infrequently a Western politics to boot. The notion of rightness operative in Paul in relation to these important words is, however, informed primarily by Christology, and then, secondarily, by a use of Scripture that is nevertheless under that primary control. It speaks of God's benevolent and unconditional deliverance of his struggling people through and in Christ, and of the way that deliverance functions, on one level, like a release from the incarceration of sin and mortality into a new liberty. This discourse stands in sharp relief over against the foolish conditionality of the Teacher that views salvation, righteousness, and—at the end of the day—the nature of God, very differently (and in terms rather closer to our Western notions of justice, with all their problematic potential associations). It is not, of course, entirely fair to label the Teacher's views Pelagian, not to mention Arian, but that is the direction in which they were headed; hence Paul was right to oppose them. And it is a great tragedy that he has often been presented subsequently to the church as if some of those views that he so perceptively and trenchantly opposed were his own.

13

Reading Paul's ΔΙΚΑΙΟ-Language

A Response to Douglas Campbell's "Rereading Paul's ΔΙΚΑΙΟ-Language"

SCOTT HAFEMANN

Theologically, we ought to agree with Campbell's concern to combat all "Western contractualism," which is so "congenial to modern thought and culture."[1] Contrary to Paul's perspective, such a worldview entails "a fundamentally rationalistic and moralistic, and invariably quite individualizing, anthropology" based on "a conception of the human person that primarily governs itself."[2] Campbell is right to reject any anthropology in which "an essentially autonomous individual sets off on a quest for salvation driven and governed by her own conceptions."[3]

Campbell's own resistance to such a construct is based on his conviction that this "Western contractualism" can be countered once we reject "a forward construal of the argument in Romans 1–3" and resist its "virulent conditionality . . . within Paul."[4] This rejection of Romans 1–3 as the

1. Chapter 12, p. 196.
2. Ibid.
3. Ibid.
4. Ibid.

foundation to Paul's own thought must include a corresponding rejection of any "conditional account of Paul's discussions of faith"[5] and its corresponding retributive-justice reading of Paul's δικαιο- terms.[6] Concerning the latter, Campbell rightly points out that inasmuch as δικαιοσύνη θεοῦ is a subset of all descriptions of being, it too is "fundamentally active and dynamic," since we should resist any dichotomy between "being and act or activity,"[7] following Gunton). A "dynamic understanding of ontology" further underscores an essentially subjective reading of the genitive θεοῦ, since "any reference to a divine attribute or aspect of being must be a reference simultaneously to divine activity and hence to something both inherent in and proceeding from God."[8] The same holds true for the "ontological dynamism" of human δικαιοσύνη, which "*must* be an ongoing, dynamic state of right behavior and activity."[9]

In turning to the texts themselves, a proper emphasis on the decisive role of internal, contextual evidence in order to overcome the lexical fallacy of etymologizing[10] leads Campbell to conclude that "δικαιοσύνη θεοῦ is an event; it is singular; it is saving, it is liberating; it is life giving; and it is eschatological or resurrecting."[11] This description aligns with Käsemann's conclusion in *Paulinische Perspektiven* that the righteousness of God is "'God's sovereignty over the world revealing itself eschatologically in Jesus,' leading to a saving gift with the characteristics also of a power."[12]

The Activity of Being

At this point, a small but eventually significant observation needs to be made about Campbell's adaptation of Käsemann's work: given Campbell's own emphasis on "ontological dynamism," it is equally important not to collapse being *into* activity (e.g., indicating that the righteousness of God *is* an event or power) lest the dynamism itself be destroyed or replaced

5. Chapter 12, p. 197.

6. Ibid.

7. Chapter 12, p. 198.

8. Ibid.

9. Ibid.

10. Chapter 12, p. 199.

11. See his *Deliverance*, 683–88.

12. Chapter 12, p. 200.

with a being-less monism. Käsemann's definition exhibits this danger. The righteousness of God is not the activity *per se*, but an inextricable, organic *expression* of God's character in saving, life-giving, eschatological acts of deliverance that express both God's sovereignty and his power, which in turn can be evaluated or described as a characteristic of God in view of God's right actions (i.e., in the abstraction, δικαιοσύνη θεοῦ). As Campbell himself points out, the use of δικαιοσύνη in reference to God "often seems to have a connotation of 'rightness.'"[13] God is righteous because, as the expression of his being, he does what is right. This becomes significant in view of the scriptural contexts of the Pauline affirmations dealing with the righteousness of God, to which Campbell then turns.

Paul's use of Psalm 98/97:2–3 (LXX) in Romans 1:17 points to the significance of the organic unity, but distinction between being and activity. For as Campbell helpfully points out, Paul is relying on this psalm of divine kingship for his understanding of God's righteousness, in which God displays his sovereignty as king by delivering his people. The distinction *between*, albeit *unity* of God's character as King and the expression thereof also makes it possible to do justice to the expressions of God's righteous kingship in terms of his judgement of the wicked as well as his rescue of the righteous. Cremer's classic study pointed in the right direction, but it failed to incorporate the entire scope of God's being-action. This led to the one-sided interpretation of God's righteousness only in terms of its salvific action that is typical of German scholarship.[14] Indeed, as Campbell observes, it is "'right' for the king to save his people when they are in extremity"; but there is a strong, albeit secondary emphasis in the biblical tradition that it is also right for the king to judge those in rebellion against his rightful authority.[15] Both are equally "ethical action," and both are demanded by the "underlying relationship" with his people that exists in accord with the king's responsibilities (quotes from chapter 12, page 202; the point is mine). This dual focus is reflected in Psalm 98/97 itself. There the *inclusio* to the revelation of God's righteousness in saving his people in Psalm 98/97:2–3 is the affirmation in Psalm 98/97:9

---

13. Chapter 12, p. 201.

14. For the German tradition and its subsequent adaptation to include God's *Richtergerechtigkeit*, see my "The 'Righteousness of God,'" xv–xli.

15. Cf. Isa 5:16; 10:22; Lam 1:18; Neh 9:33; Dan 9:14; cf. Rev 19:11; and in relationship to God's "righteousness," see Deut 33:21; Judg 5:11; 1 Sam 12:7; Pss 31:1–3; 51:14; 89:15–17; 103:16; 143:1–2, 11–12; Isa 26:8–10; Dan 9:7, 13–19.

that the Lord comes to judge (κρίνω) the inhabited world ἐν δικαιοσύνῃ and the peoples "in justice" (ἐν εὐθύτητι).

It does not seem possible to limit the divine judgment in view in Psalm 98/97 only to his salvific actions on behalf of his people; rather, in order to deliver his people, God must judge the nations, an action that is equally righteous and just. In view of the unity of God's righteous character and the entirety of his actions in general, and against this scriptural backdrop in particular, no wedge need be driven between Romans 1:17 and 18. Instead, it is possible to take the γάρ of Romans 1:18 seriously as grounds for the argument of the revelation of God's righteousness in 1:16–17 (is Paul following the flow of the argument from Psalm 98/97:2 to 97:9 in his own move from Romans 1:16–17 to 1:18?).

Kingship and Covenant

Campbell derives God's right action from God's underlying identity as a king "*qua* king" and from the "nature of the underlying relationship" with God's people that this entails, which he can then parallel in part with the role of a contemporary business executive.[16] As he summarizes it, "The story of divine kingship that [Paul] evokes establishes the rightness of God's saving action *in its own terms*."[17] It must be asked, however, whether biblically, and especially in Psalm 98/97LXX as a backdrop to Romans 1:17, this relationship between God as king and his people is presented as intrinsic to God as a divine King or whether it is established with Israel as a contingent consequence of God's particular covenant actions on her behalf.[18] In *Deliverance*, Campbell could affirm in regard to divine kingship in general that covenantal associations of divine faithfulness "are clearly not far away, and any such reading is not far from the truth," so that "covenantal associations" are also "*possibly*" found in relation to the "righteousness of God"; nevertheless, such "covenantal connotations are consequently *possible* but not *necessary* semantic resonances of the phrase δικαιοσύνη Θεοῦ."[19] In fact, Campbell asserts, "In the immediate

16. Chapter 12, p. 202.

17. Ibid., emphasis mine.

18. Cf., e.g., Ps 98:2LXX, where the God who rules as the one sitting amidst the cherubim on high is the great God who is exalted by all peoples as the God "in Zion" on earth, his characteristic covenant-location.

19. Campbell, *Deliverance*, 700, emphasis his.

location of 1:16–17, and its particular allusion to Psalm 98, I see nothing that activates such specific resonances explicitly."[20]

However, in Psalm 97:3LXX God makes known his righteousness before the peoples by mightily saving his people not because he is a "king," but as a result of the fact that God "remembered his mercy to Jacob and his truth to the house of Israel" (ἐμνήσθη τοῦ ἐλέους αὐτοῦ τῷ Ιακωβ καὶ τῆς ἀληθείας αὐτοῦ τῷ οἴκῳ Ισραηλ). Far from being merely "possible," the collocation of the motifs of "remembrance," "mercy and truth" (cf. the typical covenant formula for describing God, הנומאו דסח[21]), "Jacob," and "the house of Israel" is overwhelmingly covenantal. What obligates God is not the fact that he is a king *per se*, but the fact that he is King *over Israel* as a result of his own covenant-creating and covenant-sustaining actions in fulfillment of his promises to the patriarchs. It is not kingship *qua* kingship, but the king's role in the covenant that provides the key explanatory concept canonically for Paul's understanding of righteousness. God

20. Ibid., 701.

21. Contra Campbell, the reference to "his steadfast love and faithfulness" (ותנומאו ודסח) in Ps 98:3 is a reference to God's response to his covenant commitments or promises; cf. Gen 24:27 (covenant promise to Abraham); Gen 32:10 (covenant promises to Jacob over Esau); Exod 34:6 (basic covenant declaration); 2 Sam 2:6; Isa 16:5 (steadfast love, faithfulness, righteousness as coordinate concepts); Mic 7:20 (in reverse order, with reference in context both to Exod 34:6 and to God's faithfulness and steadfast love to Jacob and Abraham); Ps 25:10 (the Lord shows steadfast love and faithfulness to those who keep his covenant!); Ps 40:10–11 (God's righteousness, faithfulness, salvation, steadfast love [LXX: ἔλεος!], and truthfulness are all used synonymously in the context of keeping the covenant Torah); Ps 88:11 (they are not found in the grave or Abbadon!); Ps 89:2–3 [ET: 89:1–2] (in the context of an explicit reference of God's covenant to David); Ps 89:25, 34, 50 [ET: 89:24, 33, 49] (in the context of God's keeping his steadfast love in 89:29 [ET: 89:28], used synonymously with keeping the covenant to David); Ps 92:3 [ET: 92:2] (in a song for the Sabbath); Ps 100:5 (to his covenant people as his "sheep," cf. Num 27:17; 2 Sam 24:17//1 Chr 21:17, with king David, the former sheep herder now watching over the people); 1 Kgs 22:17//2 Chr 18:16; Pss 74:1; 78:52; 95:7; 119:176; Isa 53:6; Jer 23:1; 50:6; Ezek 34:2–31; Mic 2:12; Zech 10:2; 11:7, 11; Mark 6:34//Matt 9:36; John 10:4–27; 21:16–17; Heb 13:20; 1 Pet 2:25. Cf. דסח in the context of keeping the covenant in references to Exod 34:6 in Num 14:18; Deut 5:9–10; Jer 32:18; Joel 2:13; Jonah 4:2; Ps 103:8; 145:8; Neh 9:17; and דסח used alone in Deut 7:9, 12; 1 Kgs 8:23; Ps 106:45; Dan 9:4; Neh 1:5; 9:32; 2 Chr 6:14; 2 Sam 22:51, with its reference to praise among the nations for God's salvation of the king, David, and all his descendants (cf. Ps 18:50); 1 Kgs 3:6; Isa 54:10 and 55:3, used with an explicit reference to covenant; Isa 63:7, with reference to the house of Israel; Jer 9:24, in the context of God's righteousness to those of the circumcision, with uncircumcised hearts; Jer 33:11, with its contextual reference to keeping the promises of the covenant to David; and note esp. that Ps 61:7 speaks of the enthronement of God's king, with a prayer for God's steadfast love and truthfulness over him; cf. Ps 89:15.

is not simply a divine King, he is *Israel's* King because of the covenant he has enacted based on his acts of deliverance as recounted in the historical prologues of the covenant texts. It is this covenant-commitment that is the ground for Israel's appeal to YHWH for help.

The biblical material is unique in this regard. The Scriptures are the only ancient texts in which the concept of covenant was applied directly to a deity in relationship to his people; everywhere else it is used only of earthly kings.[22] To look to God as King is itself thus an inherently *covenantal* act. This ancient covenant framework also explains why, as Campbell rightly observes, that in the world of Israel the role of king and judge were united in one person. A covenantal notion of righteousness, with its forensic implications, is therefore integral to the righteousness of God expressed in his apocalyptic acts of deliverance. As Psalm 98/97LXX declares, God acts as King covenantally to deliver his people in accord with his righteous judgments in regard both to his people and to those who oppress them. In view of God's covenant promise to Abraham to bless those who, like Abraham, honor him as King by their faith in him (Gen 12:1–3, etc.), God may even decide that those called to be his people may not always be his people; likewise, the Gentiles who formerly oppressed God's people may be incorporated into them (cf. Rom 2:23–29 in relationship to Rom 4:11–12, 16–17 and Rom 9:24–26; 10:11–13).

The (Un)Conditionality of the Covenant

The diminishing of covenant as a key explanatory concept for Paul's theology of divine kingship and, hence, of the righteousness of God in Paul's thought, seems to lead Campbell to lapse into the same kind of natural theology that he rightly rejects as part of the traditional justification paradigm. The sinner and the sinful nation do not appeal to God's righteousness for help because they are sinners *qua* sinners and God is a King *per se*, banking on the fact that it is naturally "right" for God, as such, to help.[23] Biblically speaking and by definition, people have no inherent claim on God's mercy. This is made clear by Psalm 143/142:2LXX,

---

22. For a most helpful discussion of the comparative nature and function of covenant in the ANE and within the Pentateuch, see now Walton, *Ancient Near Eastern Thought*, 287–301, esp. his corresponding emphasis on the differences between the abstraction "law" within a legal system and the Torah of covenant stipulations.

23. Chapter 12, p. 202.

which Campbell again helpfully points out is quoted in Galatians 2:16 and Romans 3:20.[24] Here too the sinner's appeal for mercy is based on the fact that God's specific covenant acts and concomitant commitments (the "promises" of God) make the God of Abraham the King of this *particular* sinful nation, so that God's reputation is inextricably bound up with this people unlike all others. As the psalmist emphasizes, he cries for help and mercy because he is *God's* slave (Ps 142:2: καὶ εἰσέλθῃς εἰς κρίσιν μετὰ τοῦ δούλου σου) and can therefore appeal to *God's* righteousness, which is again paralleled to *God's* "truthfulness," which is the LXX's rendering of covenant faithfulness. In Psalm 142:1, ἐν τῇ ἀληθείᾳ σου [דבאמנת] parallels ἐν τῇ δικαιοσύνῃ σου, which again anticipates its covenant corollary, God's חסד/ἔλεος, in 142:8. In short, in the words of Psalm 142:10, the sinner confidently calls upon God to teach him to do God's will "because you are my God" (ὁ θεὸς μου). For as the parallel within Psalm 142:11 itself makes clear, God's righteousness is explicitly defined as God's concern for his own "name" as "Lord," so that the maintaining of which by answering the psalmist's cry is in essential accord with God's truthfulness. This divine righteousness, rather than contradicting the sinner's plea for mercy, can therefore be the basis for the sinner's appeal.

Psalm 143 is part of a larger canonical motif, in which God's righteousness is expressed in his never-changing commitment to remain faithful or "true" to his covenant commitments. These commitments entail helping those who humbly rely on God alone as their King, here expressed in the prayer of Psalm 142:1LXX.[25] God's own reputation is consequently at stake when his people take these promises seriously and look to him for help (Ps 142:9); not to help those who depend on him would consequently call his own righteousness into question. Preventing this from happening is therefore an essential aspect of God's "obligated righteousness" as Israel's King.[26] Conversely, God is not committed to

24. Chapter 12, p. 203.

25. I.e., what it means for YHWH to "do righteousness" (cf. Jer 9:23) is that "Yahweh is a God who acts true to himself and preserves proper order in the world," Scullion, "Righteousness," *ABD* 5:728. Cf. e.g., Gen 18:19; 38:26; Exod 23:7; Lev 19:36; Deut 16:18; 33:11; 2 Sam 8:15; 1 Kgs 8:23; Pss 23:3; 37:6; 72:1–2; 106:2–3; 119:7, 62, 75, 138; 143:2; Prov 17:5; Isa 1:26–7; 5:16; 9:6–7; 28:17; 33:5; 43:9, 26; 48:1; 56:1; 58:2; Ezek 3:16–21; 18:5, 19, 22, 27; 33:14, 16; 45:10; etc. God's righteousness encompasses us individually, as well as the cosmos (cf. Pss 33:4–6; 89:11–17). For the single OT use of the exact expression, "the righteousness of God" (צדקת יהוה/δικαιοσύνη κύριος), see Deut 33:21.

26. For the glory of God, i.e., acting "for the sake of his name," as the basis and goal

help those who do not trust in him. Seen in this covenant light, the unconditional acts of the divine King lead inextricably to a response of faith on the part of his people. This corresponds to Paul's own purpose as an apostle of Jesus Christ of bringing about the "obedience of faith among all the Gentiles on behalf of (God's) name" (Rom 1:5).[27]

Thus, contra Campbell, there is a *conditionality* of faith's obedience, which is albeit motivated, engendered, and *sustained* within a covenant relationship by God's own presence and power as King.[28] The ground

---

of God's action to save and to judge as the expression of his righteousness, see e.g., Exod 7:3–5; 9:14–16; 14:4; 1 Sam 12:22; 2 Sam 7:23; Pss 25:11; 79:9; 106:8; Isa 43:6–7, 21, 25; 44:23; 46:13; 48:9–11; 49:3; Jer 13:11; 14:7, 9, 20–21; 33:8–9; Ezek 20:9, 14, 22, 44; 36:20–32. I owe the insight that God's righteousness consists in God's commitment to maintain his "glory" or reputation as the sovereign, free Lord to Piper, *The Justification of God*, 81–101.

27. In unpacking the meaning of faith for Paul the reference to παντὶ τῷ πιστεύοντι in Rom 1:16 should not be read apart from the "obedience of faith" (ὑπακοὴ πίστεως) in Rom 1:5. Campbell's stress on the organic unity of being-activity is again helpful here. As another example of this differentiated, organic unity, the genitive πίστεως in Rom 1:5 is best construed not as an epexegetical genitive, in which obedience is redefined as faith (as in much Lutheran theology), or even as a genitive of source, in which faith leads to obedience as a second step entailing a distinct entity and response (as in much Reformed theology). Rather, its meaning correlates with the use of the middle voice in Gal 5:3, where faith's expression in love is the fulfillment of the law (Gal 5:14; see below). In the same way, in Rom 1:5 faith itself is expressed in obedience. Thus, since in the genitive construction of Rom 1:5 obedience is the lead noun incorporating faith as its descriptor, when Paul repeats his purpose as an apostle in Rom 15:16–18 he can do so in terms of bringing about obedience among the Gentiles without mentioning faith at all.

28. See Campbell, *Deliverance*, 862–64, 890, where Campbell convincingly links Gal 5:5 with Gal 3:11 and reads Gal 3:12 as a reference to eschatological life, but then limits the reference of πίστις in 3:12 solely to Christ's death and resurrection, though he takes Gal 5:5 to refer to the faith of Christians: in Gal 5:5, the Galatians are not being called "to have faith and hope in terms of their own pious resources; rather . . . to live in the unshakeable and irresistible faith and hope *that Christ has already established for them*—The Galatians' faith is resourced from elsewhere, and its end, in the glories of life at the eschaton, is already certain, *as long as they do not forcefully abandon this location*" (ibid., 891, second emphasis mine, pointing to Campbell's own version of the "conditional" soteriology he critiques). Compare esp. ibid., 101–4, 108, 116, 163–64, 179, 617, 705, 975 n. 13 and 712–13, 817–21 on faith as a "marker of salvation," rather than "a solitary condition" in "fulfillment of a contractual condition," with Campbell's portrayals of Paul's soteriology, which "continually creates room for the human rejection of God's constitutive initiative" (ibid., 161) based on human freedom (ibid., 162, cf. 908). Rather than this call to perseverance leading to anxiety, however, believers can await God's deliverance in hope, "completely assured of that event as the Spirit involves them in *Christ's* fidelity" (ibid., 892, emphasis his). Paul's gospel therefore "provides

clause in Psalm 142:10 that the Lord is the psalmist's God (ὅτι σὺ εἶ ὁ θεός μου), so that the psalmist is God's servant (142:2), is matched by the ground clause in 142:8 that the psalmist hopes/trusts in God (ὅτι ἐπὶ σοὶ ἤλπισα; cf. טחתיב כי־בך). In other words, he has taken refuge in God alone, having stretched out his hands to the Lord as one whose soul is like a waterless land (Ps 142:6, 9).

So regarding Paul's theology proper, I would reverse Campbell's emphasis that "the discourse of kingship is primary, dictating the shape of any covenant in play."[29] As an apostle of the Messiah, Paul conceives of himself as a servant of the new covenant (2 Cor 3:5-6), who then develops his argument in 2 Corinthians 3 in explicitly new covenant/old covenant terms. Second Corinthians 3 thus functions as a hinge between Galatians and Romans, picking up Paul's "allegory" in Galatians 4:21-31, which is based on this same two covenant structure, and preparing the way for Paul's use of Scripture in key fulfillment passages such as Romans 1:4, 9-11, 16-17; 4:1-25 and chapters 9-11.

From this same covenant perspective, Paul's passing on of the seminal tradition concerning the gospel as the fulfillment of Scripture in 1 Corinthians 15:1-5 must be held together with his previous reference to the tradition of the new covenant embodied in the Lord's Supper in 1 Corinthians 11:23-26. Strikingly, this earliest tradition of the gospel includes a strong conditionality at its heart (1 Cor 15:1[30]), just as the Lord's Supper passage supports why it is that the Corinthian disregard for one another (i.e., their lack of love as the greatest) is breaking the (new) covenant stipulations to such a degree that their "celebration" is no longer even to be considered the Lord's Supper (1 Cor 11:20-21). Hence, having profaned the body of the Lord, some are being judged with death (1 Cor 11:27-30).

---

real eschatological security, in Christ and the Spirit—so 5:5—and real ethical efficacy, from the same sources—so 5:6" (ibid., 892). Hence, as with the more traditional view, Campbell posits that believers can have assurance, since their faith and its ethical expression are God's apocalyptic work by the Spirit (cf. ibid., 892). Indeed, for Paul, the faith of the Christian is just as much a divine, apocalyptic act as the Christ-event and power of the Spirit that brings it about.

29. Campbell, *Deliverance*, 15 n. 11.

30. 1 Cor 15:1-2: Now I would remind you, brethren, in what terms I preached to you the gospel, which you received, in which you stand, 2 by which you are saved, if you hold it fast—unless you believed in vain (εἰ κατέχετε ἐκτὸς εἰ μὴ εἰκῇ ἐπιστεύσατε) (RSV).

The role these texts play in Paul's theology should not be minimized: the conditionality of the gospel must be maintained, but we must make equally sure that we distinguish between a pre-election/redemption conditionality, which is rejected by Paul, and all of Scripture, and a post-election/redemption conditionality, which is at the heart of the covenant structure. The covenant structure moves from the unconditional covenant prologue to the conditions of the covenant stipulations to the resultant covenant blessings and curses, a structure that is central to all of Scripture.[31]

The Apocalyptic Covenant

Again, the un-conditionality of God's gracious acts as King and the conditionality of his people's response of faith are not in conflict within a covenant relationship; the former *both* creates *and* sustains (not merely calls for!) the latter.[32] The covenant relationship between God and his people is not legalistic at its inception, nor is it a synergistic contract in its continuation. Every aspect of the covenant is apocalyptic, since the covenant relationship is wholly dependent on God invading and continuing to invade the believers' lives to deliver them (Phil 1:6). As Campbell himself has insightfully pointed out in *Deliverance*, this emphasis counters so much of the "new perspective," which has simply shifted legalism from "getting in" to "staying in," thereby creating a synergism between God and humanity.[33] But all legalism and synergism in relationship to God is

31. I have tried to map out the nature of this covenant structure throughout the canon in, "The Covenant Relationship," 20–65. For this same pattern in the Petrine tradition, see my "The (Un)Conditionality of Salvation," 240–62.

32. It is unclear in what way, for Campbell, faith functions "more as a *marker* of salvation than a solitary *condition*; it is a marker of participation in the faithful and resurrected Christ, which thereby implicitly *guarantees* for the believer a future participation in the resurrection that Christ has already achieved" (*Deliverance*, 817, emphasis his). The functional difference between a "marker" and a "condition" is not clear. Thus, for example, for Campbell "faith" is brought about by God, his Word, and the Spirit, and mediated by his messengers, but not caused by them (ibid., 819), so that faith "stems from participation in the faithful (Christ)" and is evidence and "*a marker of divine involvement, not the fulfillment of a contractual condition*" (ibid., 820, emphasis his). Such contrasts work only if, by a "condition," one always means a "contractual" condition rather than a covenant stipulation.

33. As Campbell points out (*Deliverance*, 103) Sanders' view simply shifts "legalism" to keeping the covenant, rather than entering into the covenant. So there is not a great deal that separates covenantal nomism from legalism "in strictly theoretical

to be rejected, including any "optimistic nomistic proto-Pelagianism" by Pauline opponents who argued that transgressions could be overcome by disciplined pursuits of the mind.[34]

In order to avoid slipping back into any kind of synergism in describing Paul's apostolic goal of creating covenant keepers, the determinative, apocalyptic (!) role of the Spirit must be kept in view. Campbell too emphasizes this creative, elective, liberating role of the Spirit as that which creates the new life of faith.[35] It is therefore surprising that at the same time Campbell questions what he calls Calvinism's "unaccountable privileging of faith" on the grounds that it attributes salvation directly to God, so that "no saving criterion is now necessary at all. God simply saves individuals at the requisite point."[36] Surely for Calvinism, as for Camp-

---

terms." For Sanders, the giving of covenant in the *past* only establishes the "possibility of salvation," i.e., establishing the covenant is "a moment of divine, if contractually limited generosity" (ibid., 103). With covenantal nomism legalism still exists in the *present and future*, in which salvation is dependent on fulfilling the conditions and evaluating individual performance of them in the present and future. "In short, it seems that the essential theoretical differences between covenantal nomism and legalism have effectively collapsed," since both are contractual (conditional) (ibid., 104).

34. Chapter 12, p. 205.

35. See Campbell, *Deliverance*, 64, where it is stressed that the Spirit inaugurates humanity's rescue from Sin and Death and accompanies it along its agonizing way to the final consummation of redemption (Rom 8:23–27). Moreover, salvation is "*fundamentally transformational*," from termination to reconstitution (Rom 6:1–11; 7:1–4; ibid., 64, emphasis mine). It is the Spirit who effects this transformation with reference to Christ. "In Christ" or its close equivalent thus summarizes this process of transformation (6:4, 8, 11, 23; 8:1, 9–11, 39; opposite sense perhaps in 7:5; 8:8, 9; ibid., 64), which entails an important ethical dimension (6:19, 22–23; ibid., 65). "*That is, a transformation of the ethical capacity of humanity seems intrinsic to the entire salvific process; it is part of the event of grace* (6:15, 23)" (ibid., 65, emphasis mine). Hence, soteriology is a "holistic process that extends far beyond mere corroboration" (ibid., 66). Indeed, "the saving transformation of the human being through participation in Christ in the Spirit *is* simultaneously an ethical transformation. Ethics merely denotes the behavioral aspect of this overarching process" (ibid., 83, emphasis his). "The unconditional, revelatory, transformational, and liberational aspects of this event mean that it is appropriately described as 'apocalyptic'" (ibid., 66). "An 'apocalyptic' approach to Paul emphasizes the revelatory and hence unconditional nature of the soteriology" (ibid., 903). For Campbell, therefore, it is important to see in Paul's argument that "the fidelity of Christ" mirrors "the fidelity of the Christian," since "Christians are faithful because they are being molded by the Spirit into the likeness of the faithful Christ" (ibid., 527).

36. Campbell, *Deliverance*, 59 (emphasis removed). As he queries, why in the Calvinist version of justification theory is faith necessary to be saved, when it is part of the Christian's overall transformation as those who are saved? "Since there is no condition

bell, faith is privileged and essential since it is the essential, salvific work of the Spirit; neither can exist without the other. How these two points fit together in Campbell's view remains unclear.

Here the tandem emphasis of 1 Corinthians 6:11 on both Jesus and the Spirit is significant: "But you were washed, you were sanctified, you were justified in the name of the Lord Jesus Christ (cf. Rom 3:24–6 in anticipation of Rom 5:9) and in the Spirit of our God (cf. Rom 8:1–4?)."[37] The presence of the Spirit is not just a divine, apocalyptic invasion of this world that rescues those baptized into Christ from sin negatively (Rom 6:1–14); positively, the Spirit is also the causative, new-creation source of Torah-keeping as fulfilled in love (Rom 2:29; 7:6; 8:3–6, 11–14; 14:17). There is "no [judgment of the] law" against the "fruit of the Spirit" precisely because the latter keeps the law (cf. Gal 5:22–23 with Gal 5:14, 16, 18). This keeping of the law by the Spirit is part and parcel of God's apocalyptic deliverance from the power of this present, evil age (Gal 1:4). God's grace through Christ includes the gift of being delivered both from the penalty of sin, i.e., from its curse (Gal 3:13), and from the power of sin, i.e., from its works of the flesh (Gal 5:19–21; Rom 8:13). The Spirit makes alive (2 Cor 3:6; Rom 7:6; Gal 5:25) and brings life and peace (Rom 8:6) because it submits to God's law and hence pleases God, which the flesh cannot do (Rom 8:7–9).

Within this paradigm for reading Paul, there is no need to construe δικαιόω in Romans 2:13 differently than in Romans 6:7, since in both cases it is an indicative-performative speech act (cf. 19). As such, it both evaluates *and* effects that the life of the righteous is justified and hence freed from the claims and consequences of sin both personally and forensically. For as Romans 2:25–29 makes clear in anticipation of Romans 8:4, the righteous are not condemned precisely because, by Christ and through the power of the Spirit of Christ, they keep the just requirements of the law. Paul emphasizes that it is not the possession of the law or the attempt to keep it in one's own strength that counts, but actually

---

for salvation, what is faith doing in the argument?" (ibid., 59). Indeed, "if . . . the Calvinist variant's construal of Justification cannot give a plausible account of the role of faith in Paul's argument, then its prospects are hopeless" (ibid., 59).

37. For an insightful treatment of the doctrine of justification that argues for the need to incorporate within its focus on forgiveness based on the cross of Christ the transformative, eschatological, and cosmic role of the Spirit in redemption as the inauguration of God's final righteousness and justice (thus replacing the need for an abstract notion of the imputation of Christ's merit), see Macchia, "Justification through New Creation," 202–17.

keeping the law by the power of the Spirit (cf. the reference to keeping τὰ δικαιώματα τοῦ νόμου in Romans 2:25 with keeping τὸ δικαίωμα in Romans 8:4). In *Deliverance*, Campbell seems to agree with this reading of Romans 2:25–29 as summarized in the letter/Spirit contrast of 2:29,[38] though in the end he opts for a participationist reading that is "law-free."[39] But in Romans 2:26 the uncircumcision of the Gentile who keeps the law is reckoned as circumcision (εἰς περιτομὴν λογισθήσεται), just as in Romans 4:5, 9 his faith is reckoned as righteousness (λογίζεται ἡ πίστις αὐτοῦ εἰς δικαιοσύνην), while in Romans 6:16 it is obedience that leads to (is reckoned as?) righteousness (ὑπακοῆς εἰς δικαιοσύνην). The conceptual-theological link between keeping the law, faith, and obedience in Romans 2, 4, and 6 seems clear. In the same way, the letter/Spirit contrast from Romans 2:27–29 is repeated in Romans 7:5–6. Paul's soteriology thus appears closest to that of the radical, monergistic nomism seen in many of the Qumran documents.[40]

38. As he puts it, *Deliverance*, 569–70:
Circumcision remains largely what it is within the Jewish propaganda literature—a symbol. And, as with all symbols, without the underlying reality—which must necessarily be grounded in divine action for Paul—it is empty. Consequently, Paul's cryptic criticism here is fundamentally realistic. The heart, as a metaphor for humanity's ethical condition, cannot be "circumcised" by any *literal* surgery . . . or by literalism per se. . . . To change human nature and its ethical workings requires divine involvement through the Spirit of creation. . . . Paul holds that only participation in Christ's death and resurrection, through the divine Spirit, can change the sinful ontology of humanity—for both Jew and pagan. . . . Hence, the ethical inadequacy of the Teacher's gospel is for Paul grounded in its ontological incapacity, which is rooted in turn in an inadequate evaluation of the work of Christ and the Spirit in the Christian life.

39. "The resurrected ethical condition in Christ, undergirded by the Spirit (and symbolized in baptism) is law-free in the sense of not taking its primary ethical orientation from God's written commands in Scripture (a posture that Paul accuses . . . of being deceptive and death dealing)" (Campbell, *Deliverance*, 607). So Paul lays out "a distinctive ethical system informed by participation in Christ through the Spirit . . . the inauguration of the resurrection of the Christian into a distinctively law-free praxis" (ibid.).

40. Campbell, *Deliverance*, 108, sees Qumran's soteriology as unconditional due to its emphasis on election and its attributing all actions to the "Spirit of Light" unconditionally. There are thus four types of soteriologies for Campbell: 1) Justification legalism; 2) Covenantal nomistic legalism; 3) Eschatological-Participationism; 4) and Qumran, which is "overwhelmingly nomistic" (ibid., 116), but according to Alexander is "an unconditional soteriology" that is "qualitatively different from either legalism or covenant nomism" (ibid., 118). Cf. 1023 n. 22, where in response to the "perfectionist

Another Paradigm

Campbell declares that "we know well by now that Paul is utterly opposed to any account of salvation—that is, to any gospel—couched in these terms," that is, in large measure in the terms I have just suggested! Such a gospel, in Campbell's view, "is simply wrong all the way across and all the way down."[41] I am not convinced, however, since it is Paul's fear of Christ's retributive judgment (2 Cor 5:10) that drives him to beg the Corinthians to be reconciled to God based on the cross of Christ (2 Cor 5:11, 18–20). Second Corinthians 5:10–20 corroborates the equally Pauline Romans 2:5–16, which is also based on Paul's awareness of the day of the Lord, "when God judges the hidden things of people according to (his) gospel through Christ Jesus" (Rom 2:16). For the same cross that brings forgiveness also creates the new, eschatological life of the new creation that lives for Christ in anticipation of that day of judgment (2 Cor 5:15, 17, 21; 6:1–2).

Hence, for Paul, rather than being a Jew or Gentile in accordance with the identities of the old covenant of the old age, what matters in the new age of the new covenant is the new creation brought about by Christ (2 Cor 5:17). Paul's programmatic statement in 2 Corinthians 5:17 summarizes the previous themes associated with the new creation, in particular, the parallels between Galatians 5:14, 6:15 and 1 Corinthians 7:19:

Gal 5:6a	οὔτε περιτομή τι ἰσχύει
	οὔτε ἀκροβυστία
Gal 6:15a	οὔτε περιτομή τί ἐστιν
	οὔτε ἀκροβυστία
1 Cor 7:19a	ἡ περιτομὴ οὐδέν ἐστιν
	καὶ ἡ ἀκροβυστία οὐδέν ἐστιν
Gal 5:6b	ἀλλὰ πίστις δι᾽ ἀγάπης ἐνεργουμένη

axiom" of Justification theory, Campbell sees that Qumran plays a key role in understanding the demands of the law in that in Qumran the Jewish language of perfection "is invariably counterbalanced by compensatory mechanisms—means of atonement and restoration, and also direct ethical assistance toward perfection. At Qumran, the covenanters—at least in some texts—were elected to salvation, and assisted in perfect law observance by the Spirit of Light, thereby overcoming the evil inclination." Campbell points out that the absence of these "mechanisms" is what creates difficulties for Justification theory (*Deliverance*, 1023n.22).

41. Chapter 12, p. 210.

Gal 6:15b   ἀλλὰ καινὴ κτίσις

1 Cor 7:19b   ἀλλὰ τήρησις ἐντολῶν θεοῦ[23]

As these parallels demonstrate, Paul's statement concerning the "new creation" in Galatians 6:15 is sandwiched between the mutually interpretive parallels of Galatians 5:6, on the one hand, and 1 Corinthians 7:19, on the other. For Paul, what now counts in the new, eschatological era is no longer one's identity under the old covenant as circumcised and uncircumcised. What now "exists" (cf. 1 Cor 7:19a) is the "new creation," which is equated with "faith working out with regard to itself through love" (Gal 5:6),[43] which in turn can be framed in terms of "keeping the commandments of God" (1 Cor 7:19).[44] Here too we see God's apocalyptic work of establishing the new creation decoded in terms of the realities of the new covenant—God's unconditional grace creating the keeping of

42. The interpretive parallel between these contrasts was first set forth simply in my *The God of Promise and the Life of Faith*, 196.

43. The force of ἐνεργέω in the middle is difficult to render in English, since it indicates that the faith that works is also impacted by its activity, being "directly and personally involved in the process," so Taylor, "Deponency and Greek Lexicography," 174. Betz, *Galatians*, 263 n. 97, suggests for its translation, "become effective," "come to expression," pointing to the "fruit of the Spirit" in 5:22–23 as its referent. Campbell, *Deliverance*, 887, renders it as faith being "active in relation to itself—putting itself into effect" . . . by means of 'love.'" On the necessary embodiment of dispositions such as "faith" in one's way of life, individually and communally, see now Thiselton, *Hermeneutics of Doctrine*, 19–61, and its application to the Pauline "justification by faith," 347–54. For the working out of other Christian dispositions, see 2 Cor 1:6 (comfort in endurance); 1 Thess 2:13 (the word of God in believers); Col 1:29 (Christ's ἐνέργεια in Paul's life); Eph 3:20 (God's power in believers); Rom 7:5 for its counter-point in terms of the "passions of sins" (τὰ παθήματα τῶν ἁμαρτιῶν) working out (ἐνηργεῖτο) in one's life in the "flesh" (σάρξ); and 2 Cor 4:12 for both death and life working out (ἐνεργεῖται) in one's life. As Betz, *Galatians*, 264, thus rightly concludes, it is impossible for Paul to separate faith and love into "theory" and "practice."

44. For the conviction that "a comparison of the second members in the three passages is instructive," see already Burton, *Galatians*, 356. Burton, 356, sees πίστις and ἀγάπη in Gal 5:6 as "purely ethical terms, descriptive of the fundamental moral attitude of the Christian," while "keeping the commandments" in 1 Cor 7:19 is "a more external characterization of the Christian life and more formal." Over against both, "new creation" in Gal 6:15 is "less definite as to the moral character of the new life than either of the other expressions," though it "directs attention to the radical change involved rather than to the external expression or the moral quality of the life thus produced." The deposit of these contrasts in 2 Cor 5:17 demonstrates, however, that such contrasts are only apparent.

the covenant conditions. In *Deliverance*, Campbell himself makes this point in regard to the conditionality expressed in Galatians 5:5, which sets up these passages.[45]

The Way Forward

Of course, in offering this response I am simply matching one paradigmatic reading of Paul against another. In the end, then, Campbell's work can be evaluated only by reading both the whole and its parts from a counter-direction to see which one fits better overall. One of the great values of Campbell's work is that it forces one to do just that, instead of simply taking old answers for granted.

I have learned a great deal from Campbell's encyclopedic, often brilliant and insightful work. I am not yet convinced, however, by his radical solution to the problem of how to map out the move in Paul's theology from Romans 1–4 to 5–8. But I am convinced that we should not read Paul "forward" theologically. Campbell is right that justification by faith for Paul was not conceived to be the result of turning, out of despair, from one's independent, failed attempt to live a moral life, usually based on some kind of natural theology, to God's revelatory, "law-free," salvific gospel. I also agree with Campbell's critique of the means of salvation within the justification paradigm, whose inherent legalism can only be solved by an imputed righteousness.

My own reading sits between the traditional view and Campbell's re-reading. I propose that the way to combat importing "Western contractualism" into our reading of Paul, while at the same time preserving the coherence of Paul's letters, is not to replace a contractual view of the divine-human relationship with an exclusively apocalyptic, participatory eschatology. Rather, we should recover the biblical category of an apocalyptically understood, thoroughly monergistic, yet conditional covenant relationship between God and his people, and through this covenant relationship, between God and his world (cf. Rom 8:18–25 with Ps 97:7–8).

---

45. See above, 221 n. 28.

Douglas Campbell's Response to Scott Hafemann

There is much to affirm and even applaud in Scott's learned essay, from which I learned a great deal. But it is important to recognize that it is, in the end of the day, a salvation-historical stealth attack! As such, it inaugurates a fascinating conversation that I will only be able to make some regrettably brief remarks in response to here. (The position he represents so ably here ultimately requires a detailed consideration, which I hope to supply in due course.)

To redescribe the situation in broad brush strokes that are hopefully not without some accuracy: in *Deliverance* I identify and try to subvert a rather individualistic interpretative discourse in relation to Paul that I view as rooted exegetically in Romans 1–4—the Justification discourse. Scott, however, really represents another major Pauline interpretative discourse, namely, a salvation-historical approach. Hence, he is clearly in sympathy with a certain amount that I am suggesting, but then is not so sure about other aspects of the participatory and apocalyptic discourse that I go on to affirm. However, *Deliverance* does not position itself especially clearly with respect to Scott's concerns and those who share them, in part, because any engagement between participatory and salvation-historical accounts of Paul must do detailed work on Romans 9–11, whereas an engagement with the justification paradigm only needs to address parts of 9:30—10:17 (and so on). In short, the detailed conversation between apocalyptic and salvation-historical advocates in relation to Paul has yet to happen (at least as far as I am concerned). A few gestures toward the shape of that future conversation will have to suffice here.

I appreciate Scott's suggestions that covenantal resonances are in play in Psalm 98, that is, more than I allowed, and hence arguably in the allusion by Romans 1:17 to this text. However, I wonder if the scriptural echo provides a sufficiently firm and overt textual basis from which to insert what amounts to a grand OT narrative of covenantalism into Paul's subsequent arguments in Romans. My reading suggests that the echoed psalm of kingship provides a semantic possibility for the phrase δικαιοσύνη Θεοῦ that then informs Paul's argument quite directly, albeit in a limited fashion; in this Psalm at this moment God is acting like a king in an executive action of deliverance. Hence, I suggest interpreting the phrase in these terms; this is what it *means* as illuminated semantically by this intertext. And a christological construal of the associated πίστις

Ἰησοῦ Χριστοῦ genitives and associated phrases (see 1:17b; 3:22, 25, 26), i.e., in terms of the faithfulness of Christ, then invites Paul's auditors to understand it further in explicitly christological terms.[46] The right activity of God here is in fact the deliverance of God that has been definitively revealed in the life, death, and resurrection of Christ. This is its concrete reference point. So the pressure of interpretation actually runs backward in 1:17 and any associated texts (i.e., from Paul's point of view) *from* the Christ event *to* his interpretation of a scriptural text.

If these points are clear then I need to ask to what extent Scott is actually overtly justified in textual terms to go beyond them to his rather more panoramic assertions. His compelling narrative is arguably a fundamentally historicizing and canonical exercise that is somewhat inappropriate for Paul himself. (It is, of course, deeply congenial to modern scholars concerned to interpret the canon constructively and appropriately!) And I fear that its persistent advocacy will generate a number of problems in due course, although now is not the time to explore those in detail.[47] But if I am resisting some of Scott's assertions here I would suggest that at other points what is required is only clarification.

Scott highlights several instances in my interpretations of what he calls conditionality, thereby really suggesting that conditionality cannot be repudiated in toto (that is, outside a theological schema committed to what we might call causal or "hard" predestination, which both Scott and I do not endorse). Even I apparently lapse into conditionality periodically, he implies, while repudiating the harsh form found in Justification Theory. And a covenantal account of the OT consequently needs to retain a degree of conditionality as well, defining this carefully. Correlative to this is a particular notion of judgment, which opens up a more accommodating position in turn in relation to some of the texts in Romans 1–3, that I have more difficulty with. And a clarification here should prove helpful; although I suspect that my views have developed on this issue since *Deliverance* was written, the manuscript being completed at the end

---

46. See my essay "The Faithfulness of Jesus Christ," 57–71.

47. I worry, among other things, that it will still become involved in a foundationalist and negative construction of the Other, leading to problems in relation to mission and the construction of Judaism. I worry that it will override the implicit operation of Nicene categories within Paul's thinking. And I worry that its broad historical claims are ultimately fragile; that is, it presupposes a coherent and successful account of the OT data when many OT analysts would either offer equally powerful but different accounts or would dispute this very possibility.

of 2007. So Scott should not be chided for missing this material, which was probably not present in *Deliverance* to the degree that it now probably would be.

Scott is really assuming with this line of criticism that any human responsiveness or agency, which are operative in most narratives of human ethics and accountability, must entail ultimately a contractual or conditional situation. So when he detects affirmations of Christian agency or responsiveness in my account of Paul he goes on to assume conditional and contractual entailments. However, this is to commit what one might call the great liberal sin, namely, the assumption that human freedom is best articulated in terms of human choice and hence can only be articulated ultimately in arrangements that are conditional and contractual. To preserve any notion of human freedom, human will must be affirmed and human choice expected. This is not a christological account of agency.

As Barth, among others, leaning on the work of Maximus the Confessor, emphasizes tirelessly,[48] human agency is best understood in terms of perfect obedience and *correspondence* to divine promptings and leadings—musical analogies often being very helpful for grasping this situation, whereas spatial conceptualizations, beloved of modernity, tend to distort it.[49] Perfect freedom is found in perfect obedience, as voices in songs sung freely correspond and directly harmonize with the tune, the conductor, and the rest of the choir. Conversely, to will or to choose to turn away from this relationship of correspondence is to struggle against the appropriate order of things—to cut against the grain—and to plunge into self-destructive sin (in the terms of the foregoing analogy, to disrupt and destroy the choral performance). Consequently *will* and *choice* are actually domestications of human *sin!* And this will all be judged by God, and implacably (although in a certain sort of way). Humanity will also be held constantly accountable.

These realizations generate in turn a particular account of the covenant. This arrangement describes how the principal component within the relationship between God and humanity, presaged in the relationship between God and Israel, is unconditional election and ongoing commitment by God to the group covenanted to. Moreover, everything is provided by the covenanting God. As a covenant with humanity/Israel,

48. See esp. *CD* III/1, III/2, and IV/2.

49. See here now helpfully Jeremy Begbie, "Room of One's Own?"

however, a response of perfect obedience to the relational expectations of the covenant is necessary. Of course, that response has generally been anything except perfectly obedient, entailing ongoing rescue operations by the covenantal God, and ongoing education into the destructiveness and stupidity of sin. But the covenant expects human responsiveness, although conceived of strictly in terms of correlative obedience.

The important implications in this brief explication for the interpretative stances of both Scott and I are that both his covenantal and my participatory emphases can wholeheartedly together affirm human freedom and responsiveness, and human accountability in turn, while resisting any further explanation of these dynamics in terms of will and choice, these being the further articulations that necessarily unleash a destructive conditionality and contractualism. And one further positive result flowing from this is the ability to affirm that God's covenant is thick with the appropriate ethical expectations but not conditional upon them; it is unconditional, eternal, and *unbreakable*, as any commitment by a fundamentally loving God should be. But these emphases in no way reduce or elide divine judgment and human accountability, or even freedom; rather, these secondary dynamics are explicable within this basic framework (i.e., in a way that has theological integrity and does not lapse ultimately into infralapsarianism or other acute theological problems). Indeed, all these dynamics are *strengthened* by them. (No accountability is more powerful or acute than covenantally generated accountability.)

In short then, I suggest that an appropriate understanding of agency in terms of correspondence—ultimately, of course, in christological terms—speaks to Scott's identification of frequent emphases in my work on the human responsiveness operative through Christ; these do not entail contractualism in any shape or form. And it also assists *his* account of the covenant, as that is articulated by so much of the OT— although, I would suggest again, as that is definitively revealed, articulated, and fulfilled, by Christ. Indeed, to be truly free and responsive to God is necessarily to resist any articulation of these notions by conditionality or contractualism, the latter being the conspicuous conceits of modernity and, even worse, ultimately corrupting of true and authentic relationships. And I am of course grateful to Scott for prompting me to deepen these claims implicit in my earlier work here, and also for his corrections in relation to some of Paul's invocations of covenantal material.

14

Campbell's Faith

Advancing the Pistis Christou Debate

Chris Tilling

A. Introduction

Campbell's work on Paul's πίστις/πιστεύω language represents some of the most exegetically innovative and insightful work in *Deliverance*. Yet it is also the case that his arguments have not always been understood by his reviewers, and his key exegetical moves have largely been ignored. We will now survey some of his central arguments before briefly considering some potential objections.

B. Campbell's Interpretive Strategy

I have regularly lamented the fact that the hardback version of *Deliverance* was published using endnotes (rather than footnotes), and this has no doubt meant that even those who have read the whole book may not have mustered the willpower to also enjoy some of the gold in those (often extensive) endnotes. Yet one of those, hidden away on a page with a four digit number, helpfully summarizes Campbell's approach to engaging the πίστις Χριστοῦ debate. Following the suggestion of Richard Hays,[1] Campbell maintains that progress in this debate can only be made "as the larger shape of Paul's argument is simultaneously introduced and addressed."[2] In other words, Campbell's arguments at this point need to be understood in terms of his construal of wider themes relating to Paul's soteriological vision. It will be necessary to overview what this looks like in practice in the following, and likewise to judge his success in this light.

C. Campbell's General Position

Campbell is very sensitive to the range of semantic possibilities in translating Paul's πιστ- terms. Building on his earlier work, he reminds his readers that it can signify "belief," "trust," and "faithfulness/fidelity" (the latter, connoting a passage of time and some kind of duress, was also the most common usage in both the Septuagint and Josephus).[3] This analysis links with his work on the story of Jesus in Romans and Galatians,[4] a story that involved a trajectory of descent (sent by the Father, suffering and dying, etc.) and a trajectory of ascent (resurrection through the Spirit of God to the right hand of God, as "firstborn among many brothers," etc.).[5] What is more, Paul could allude to this story *metonymically*, which is to say, a single motif could evoke the entire narrative (so Paul's language of "obedience," "blood," "cross"). His not uncommon conclusion: "the claim that the phrase 'the fidelity of Christ' could denote Jesus' entire passion more broadly is quite consistent with Paul's usual practice."[6] Πίστις as "fidelity" indeed corresponds well with the downward and martyrological trajectory of Paul's Christ-story (here he references the Maccabean martyrdom stories), and just as the "faith" of martyrs runs "the full semantic gamut of πίστις—they believe, they trust, and they are faithful to the point of death"—so too does a christological reading of πίστις in Paul.

1. Hays, "Πίστις and Pauline Christology," 35–60.
2. Campbell, *Deliverance*, 1096 n. 40.
3. Campbell, *Quest*, 178–207.
4. Campbell, "The Story of Jesus," 97–124.
5. See ibid., 108. It is worth pointing out that this narrative is found *within* Paul's letters, unlike other narratives (concerning land, exile, and restoration) about which Paul is not explicit.
6. Campbell, *Deliverance*, 611.

This "raises the possibility that πίστις Χριστοῦ *could* denote the 'belief' (i.e., conviction) or 'trust' rather than the 'faithfulness' of Christ."[7]

Paul's language is also to be understood in terms of the intertextual dynamics in his letters. Genesis 15:6, Isaiah 28:16b, and, most importantly, Habakkuk 2:4, explain both the distribution and relative importance of πιστ- language in key texts. This latter text in Habakkuk is particularly significant given its role in Paul's argumentation in Galatians and Romans, and Campbell provides numerous reasons to make a christological reading plausible.[8] He leans on Moody Smith's significant arguments that strongly maintain that the ἐκ πίστεως phrase, in Romans 1:17, functions not adjectivally but adverbially, modifying the verb "to live."[9] This suggests the text indicates it is "by means of his faithfulness to the point of death he [i.e., the righteous one spoke of here] will live."[10]

But why does Campbell's reading include the phrase "by means of" here? The answer to this question involves recognition of a key argument in his repertoire. He has long argued that the only possible semantic overlap in the (not infrequent) parallel use of the prepositions διά and ἐκ, in relation to πίστις, is to understand them as functioning *instrumentally*.[11] This means that ἐκ πίστεως is best translated as "*by means of* πίστις." After all, faith "responds to that prior disclosure as an act of affirmation" and is not "the act of disclosure itself."[12] It follows that ἐκ πίστεως should be translated as "by means of the faithfulness [of Christ]," as metaleptically or metonymically denoting Christ's loving self-sacrifice on the cross.[13] And this corresponds neatly with the fact that the Habakkuk

7. Ibid., 1093 n. 20, italics mine.

8. E.g., δίκαιος is a christological title in other parts of the NT. Paul regularly uses arthrous titles to denote Christ, etc. Prepared by the work of Heliso (*Pistis and the Righteous One*), I was favorably disposed towards a christological reading by some arguments relayed in Daniel Kirk's thesis on Romans, namely those concerning the connections between Romans 1:2–4 and 1:17 (Kirk, *Unlocking Romans*, 44–49), a strong argument also deployed in *Deliverance*. See also the various contributions of Kirk's doctoral supervisor, Richard Hays, on this, especially "Apocalyptic Hermeneutics," 119–42, to be noted later.

9. See Campbell, *Deliverance*, 1094–95 n. 26.

10. Ibid., 613.

11. Most recently, in the respect see Campbell, "Faithfulness," 57–71. See also Campbell, *Deliverance*, 379.

12. Campbell, "Faithfulness," 68, italics suppressed.

13. Matlock has disputed Campbell's reasoning at this point in his JSNT review, but given Campbell's response, his objections require greater substantiation. I particularly look forward to Matlock's contributions to the ongoing debate.

citation in Romans 1:17 is preceded by the phrase ἐκ πίστεως εἰς πίστιν, which in turn further supports a christological construal of ἐκ πίστεως, such that δικαιοσύνη θεοῦ is revealed by means of [Christ's] faithfulness for [Christian] faith ("as the goal or end of this process of disclosure").[14]

At this point it is worth responding to another misunderstanding of Campbell's thesis, one that suggests Campbell's work neglects the human element of "faith" in Paul. For it needs to be noted that the consequence of this understanding of ἐκ πίστεως means that human "faith," for Paul, "echoes the fidelity of Christ himself." "Christians possess 'faith,'" Campbell explains, "because they participate in the faithful Christ."[15] In other words, his understanding of "faith" language in Paul does not categorically make human "faith" irrelevant. Has he really been so misunderstood by critics, or am I constructing a straw man? Mark Seifrid, to cite an example, has countered Campbell's objection to making "'faith' a condition of salvation" by arguing that "unless human beings are to be regarded as nothing more than blocks of wood or stone, some accounting of human response to the Gospel has to be rendered."[16] Moo also suggests that Campbell's point must be that "any significant role for human faith in the experience of God's righteousness introduces a 'voluntarism' that fundamentally contradicts . . . God's righteousness as an unconditional act."[17]

But as even this short summary makes clear, there is an overt emphasis on human agency in responsive terms in Campbell, one grounded in Christ's fidelity and, as Campbell also notes, the Spirit's enabling power.[18] The key issue for Campbell is that faith *not* be understood, as the theoretical logic of a conventional reading of Romans 1–4 arguably demands, as the *condition* for salvation. Faith is certainly mandatory as part of a full response to God's grace, something, to cite Campbell, that is "necessary if final life or salvation is to be reached."[19] What is more, he also notes that Christian life begins "in some relation to a certain act of

14. Campbell, *Deliverance*, 379.

15. Ibid., 618. And tied into his broader arguments, this πίστις, which is "clearly a marker of salvation for Paul in Romans," indicates the inclusive and unconditional nature of the redemption in Christ, over against the restrictive gospel of the Teachers.

16. Seifrid, "*The Deliverance of God*," 309.

17. Moo, "*The Deliverance of God*," 149.

18. See, e.g., Campbell, *Deliverance*, 67–69.

19. Ibid., 68.

submission to a form of teaching."[20] But these aspects of faith cannot be spoken of without also speaking of the Spirit's enabling and the fidelity of Christ. I think Campbell would basically accept James Torrance's language as a good summary of the Pauline sentiment, at this point:

> Participation is what *we* do—we pray, we repent, we believe, we worship—but only in the sense of participating in what *Christ* has done and is doing. In this way, faith and repentance and prayer are *not conditions* of grace, but the gift of the Spirit of sonship who so unites us with Christ in his communion with the Father that we might have a ground for rejoicing in God.[21]

One must thus turn the inquest back on Moo and Seifrid at this point and ask where they have obtained the connotations of their notions of faith. Campbell's analysis of the link between Justification Theory, Western liberal anthropology, and modern philosophical individualism in chapter 9 of *Deliverance* may be particularly useful at this stage.

In terms of Campbell's general position, it remains to say that his objection that "faith" in Paul be understood as a condition of salvation takes us to the heart of his theological and exegetical endeavors. Understood as a *condition*, it corresponds to the foundationalist, Arian, contractual theological vision, one not only contradictory to orthodox Christian doctrine, but, and because of this, also damaging to Christian faith and life. Among other things, it has the potential to undermine Christian assurance by locating the basis for Christian life not in the gracious activity of God in Christ towards "sinners," but in the (always faltering and imperfect) response of humans (provoking anxious questions such as "Have I believed *enough* or believed *sincerely* enough?"). This pastoral dynamic, so beautifully captured in the James Torrance articles that inspired much of Campbell's work,[22] are also central to Paul's burdens in Romans. There, Paul emphasizes the unconditional nature of the love of God, a love demonstrated precisely for God's "enemies," for the "ungodly," for "sinners," as Romans 5 explains; a love, therefore, that does not regard the state of the one loved or the human fulfillment of any conditions, but is an expression of God's sheer generosity and graciousness. If Alan Torrance is right when he claims that the "universal tendency of human pride is to

---

20. Ibid., 67.

21. Torrance, "The Contribution of McLeod Campbell," 310.

22. See particularly Torrance, "Covenant and Contract," 51–76 and "The Contribution of McLeod Campbell," both reprinted in the two appendices of this book.

want to turn God's covenant of grace into a contract,"[23] then this love is as scandalous and difficult to grasp today as it was in the Rome of Paul's day. Campbell's exegetical endeavors are to be understood in light of these concerns.[24]

D. The Faith of Abraham in Romans 4

Campbell has thus much to say against contractual notions of faith, and his treatment of Abraham in Romans 4 is a good example of his argumentative strategy. Is Abraham an example of Paul's "insistence that righteousness can be attained only through faith" (to cite Moo)?[25] Romans 4 describes Abraham's faith in personal terms, as "trust" (cf. 4:5), and the text also assumes that this trust extends over a period of time (4:18–21), thus suggesting a translation of πίστις as "faithfulness," which does not cohere neatly with the logic of contractual theology, in which faith is the easier criterion to obtain righteousness. To underscore the point, Campbell notes that Abraham's faith is also conceived in this chapter as "positively superhuman," involving "a fourteen-year journey of unwavering trust, flying in the face of overt biological realities . . . described by Paul as being flawless, with no doubt, no wavering, and no anxiety."[26] Furthermore, the object of Abraham's trust is, in this text, God. And if that is the case, how does this passage correspond to the righteousness of God manifested διὰ πίστεως Ἰησοῦ Χριστοῦ, if understood anthropocentrically?

Positively, Campbell's project seeks to show that an unconditional and christological understanding of πίστις better corresponds with the Pauline evidence.[27] To exhibit the ways in which he positively constructs his arguments in *Deliverance*, we will now turn to his understanding of πίστις in Galatians.

23. Torrance, "The Theological Grounds for Advocating Forgiveness and Reconciliation in the Sociopolitical Realm," 48.

24. Some, of course, may thus charge Campbell that he has allowed a theological agenda to dictate his exegesis, rather than allowing exegesis to *serve* theology.

25. Moo, *The Epistle to the Romans*, 255.

26. Campbell, *Deliverance*, 389.

27. Campbell's language of over- and underdeterminations is deployed at such points.

E. Πίστις Χριστοῦ and Galatians

As noted above, many of Campbell's exegetical moves have yet to be seriously engaged by his reviewers. Because, for Campbell, Galatians is "all about 'faith,'"[28] his work on this letter will serve as an excellent example of the kind of exegetical strategies (not to mention flair and vigor) he employs. In a nutshell, Campbell will argue that important material in 2:15–21 is ambiguous. It is indeed more likely to correspond with his own christological and apocalyptic reading, rather than an anthropocentric one, but real clarity is found in 3:15–29, which strongly suggests the correctness of his overall approach. To outline his engagement with Galatians, we will begin with his analysis of 2:15–21, before turning to his analysis of material in Galatians 3, and finally the rest of Galatians.

Galatians 2:15–21

Although this text is undoubtedly important, Paul's argument is brief and concise.[29] Yet there is data in this passage that could be used to support a prospective and conditional soteriology.[30] Depending on how one understands the conjunction ἵνα[31] and the meaning of the genitive construction, this could be translated as "we believed in Christ Jesus *so that* we might be justified through faith in Christ."[32] This is certainly a possible translation, and could thus demonstrate faith's appropriative and conditional function with respect to justification.

So how does Campbell engage this material? He understands the ἵνα conjunction in explanatory terms ("we believed *concerning*"), which links together with a number of contextual clues, not least the usual practice of Paul (and Koine Greek generally) to understand an accusative prepositional construction (here εἰς Χριστὸν Ἰησοῦν) as indicating "the

---

28. Ibid., 838.

29. It should first be noticed that δικαιο- and πίστ- terminology is virtually absent from Paul's biographical arguments in 1:11—2:14, a fact, Campbell points out, embarrassing the expectations of readings that gain theoretical coherence from JT-related commitments.

30. Gal 2:16 ἡμεῖς εἰς Χριστὸν Ἰησοῦν ἐπιστεύσαμεν, ἵνα δικαιωθῶμεν ἐκ πίστεως Χριστοῦ.

31. I.e., here in purposive terms.

32. See ibid., 840.

thing about which certain beliefs are held."[33] Together with a subjective construal of πίστεως Χριστοῦ,[34] these (plausible) judgments facilitate a reading of the whole passage in ways that resist conditionality and prospective theological dynamics. Together with an exceptive understanding of ἐὰν μή (in 2:16a), which corresponds with the meaning it always has in Paul (so Andrew Das),[35] this leads to a retrospective reading of the logic of the whole text,[36] which thereby also sidesteps the theoretical and therefore argumentative level problems associated with the prospective reading.

For Campbell, 2:20 functions as a confirmation of his reading.[37] A subjective construal of πίστις in metaleptic[38] terms coheres with the associated loving self-sacrifice: Paul lives "by the faithfulness of the Son of God who loved me by giving himself for me" (so Michael Gorman's attractive translation).[39]

Galatians 3:1–14

The most important issue in verses 1–5 of Galatians 3 revolves around the interpretation of the following phrase: "Did you receive the Spirit by doing the works of the law or ἢ ξ ἀκοῆς πίστεως?" (3:2, 5). Campbell spends some time justifying the translation "the proclamation of fidelity" (in the sense of the righteous and faithful one),[40] against the common

---

33. Ibid.

34. I admit the problems associated in describing the debate in terms of subjective and objective genitive interpretations (see esp. the essays by Porter & Pitts and Seifrid in Bird and Sprinkle, *The Faith of Jesus Christ*), and so have tended to have avoided it in this paper. I am not, however, convinced that much is lost if one does use the terminology of obj/subj gen.

35. Campbell, *Deliverance*, 1147 n. 32.

36. The verse operates, then, as follows: While doing A (i.e., works), B arrived and effected transformation, therefore transformation is effected—and we trust and believe it—in relation to B and not A.

37. And not 2:21, which alone, he argues, does not necessarily evidence the retrospective logic Sanders saw.

38. Metalepsis is a figure of speech in which one thing is referred to by something else which is only remotely associated with it. One can also speak, here, of metonymy, where the association is not remote but closer.

39. Gorman, *Inhabiting the Cruciform God*, 58–60.

40. Campbell, *Deliverance*, 853–56.

"believing what you heard."[41] Once again, the matter is not about human agency, nor about faith as a condition. Rather, and coherent with the context, faith is understood in revelatory terms, as a gift of the Spirit. (I note that although the new NIV is to be congratulated for at least adding the subjective construal of πίστις Χριστοῦ in a footnote in 2:16, they do not offer these translation possibilities consistently, omitting alternatives to an objective reading in 2:20, and in 3:2, 5.)

3:6–14 is yet again a condensed passage, slightly ambiguous in its use of non-annotated scriptural citations. But Campbell works through the text, paying close attention to argumentative dynamics and lexical and syntactical possibilities, to show that Paul's argument is retrospective in nature. Christ's faithfulness leads to life, and *therefore* it is not found through works. Certainly, Campbell frames his arguments tentatively. He concedes that this subsection can be construed in terms of JT, or in the ways urged by Dunn or Watson. The most decisive evidence for Campbell's view comes, rather, from the following verses, namely 3:15–29.

Galatians 3:15–29

Rather ironically, as Campbell notes, scholars have often made up their mind concerning πίστις Χριστοῦ by the time they get to this passage.[42] It is ironic because it is in these verses that we find the clearest evidence to adjudicate on the whole debate. Here is "fairly decisive evidence," Campbell claims, "in favor of the rhetorical and apocalyptic reading that I'm advocating in relation to Paul's Justification texts more generally, and will, in addition, lend further confidence to our judgements reached earlier in relation to the more ambiguous texts."[43]

The first step in his argument is to note that this passage contains a sequence of five singular instances of πίστις, which are introduced by a genitive construction in 3:22 (ἐκ πίστεως Ἰησοῦ Χριστοῦ). Second, πίστις is linked in this section to the motif of "coming" or "arriving." Third, before this sequence of associations, Paul speaks of the "seed" (3:16 [x3],

---

41. See now, also de Boer, *Galatians*, 173–77.

42. The resultant scholarly rhetoric can be illuminating, and in this respect Campbell refers to the shaky argumentation in Moisés Silva's article in the second volume of *Justification and Variegated Nomism* (230–47), and the comments in Campbell, *Deliverance*, 1157–58 n. 99.

43. Ibid., 867.

19), which is likewise associated with the motif of "coming" (3:19). This suggests that the seed, in 3:16, should be associated with the πίστις. Fourth, both this "seed" and the πίστις are correlated to another motif in this passage, namely "promise" (3:16, 19 and 29 link the "seed" to the "promise"; 3:22 links the "promise" to πίστις).

In view of this clear evidence, Campbell then proposes five reasons for understanding this chain of motifs with reference to Christ. First, the "seed" is singular for one simple reason: it refers to Christ.[44] Second, 3:22, instead of breaking this tightly packed chain of christological motifs by speaking of a human faith in Christ, and given the link to the faith of Abraham in 3:6, rather indicates that the πίστεως Ἰησοῦ Χριστοῦ is best understood as Christ's faithfulness, with God as the (implicit) object of the participle, πιστεύουσιν (as was explicitly the case for Abraham). Third, the first nine "links" in this chain of motifs are all singular. If Paul meant to refer to the many followers of Christ, he would have indicated this with plural constructions, as was his normal practice. Fourth, understanding πίστις in christological terms accounts for the "singular event of *arrival and liberation* that the text speaks of."[45] Fifth, the parallelism between the two temporal εἰς phrases in 3:23 and 3:24 means that εἰς . . . πίστιν and εἰς Χριστόν must be synonymous. Together, these five points strongly point to "the identification of this chain of motifs and phrases through Galatians 3:15–29 with Christ, and hence [. . .] imply the identification of Christ with the motif of πίστις throughout as well."[46]

Having tackled Barry Matlock's case, that the P46 reading of Galatians 3:26 points to an objective genitive understanding of πίστις Χριστοῦ, Campbell instead goes on the offensive. 3:15–29 presents numerous problems for the anthropological reading of πίστις. The only other way to understand this passage in anthropological terms is to claim that the *possibility* of (Christian) faith arrived with Christ. However, to make this case one must insert a number of elided motifs into the text as Paul does not explicitly speak of "possibility" in this context. What is more, this suggestion indeed seems to be falsified in the text, not only given the link to Abraham (if the possibility arrived first after Christ, what about 3:8?), but also because of the emphasis on the singularity, and revelatory

---

44. Despite his valuable insights on this passage, N. T. Wright has to perform some exegetical gymnastics when he backs away from this identification. See Wright, *The Climax of the Covenant*, 162–68.

45. Campbell, *Deliverance*, 874, italics mine.

46. Ibid., 875.

function, of πίστις. The anthropocentric interpretation requires more emphasis on plurality and appropriative motifs, which is precisely what the text does *not* offer.

Finally, as Paul cited Habakkuk 2:4 in Galatians 3:11, and as ἐκ πίστεως language is repeated in 3:12 and picked up in 3:22, this passage thus confirms Campbell's claim that Paul's πίστις language works intertextually, with reference to Habakkuk, and does so christologically. To cite Campbell at some length, Galatians 3:22–26 in context means that:

> [Paul] deploys this text to affirm his own account of the centrality of the Christ event in soteriological and eschatological terms, and also to contradict any system, putatively justified by Scripture, that nevertheless locates the achievement of an eschatological life in relation to something else, like a law observance (whether this is alternative or merely additional to Christ). These judgments apply particularly to any use of the phrase ἐκ πίστεως, the closely allied phrase διὰ πίστεως . . . and any singular instances of πίστις in the immediate context.[47]

With this impressive case for the christological reading out of the way, material in 2:15–21 and 3:1–5 falls into place. All Campbell must do now is explore any final possible challenges in Galatians, but the likelihood that anything minor could overthrow his reading is now looking more and more unlikely.

The Rest of Galatians

Building on the work of Hung-Sik Choi,[48] Campbell argues that material in Galatians 5:5–6 should also be understood christologically. This is supported by the fact that the opposing, positive term over against the circumcised and uncircumcised state is always, in Galatians, Christ himself and not a human disposition. Furthermore, and especially given the link with the Spirit (also found in 3:1–5), Paul is not exhorting the Galatians "to have faith and hope in terms of their own pious resources." Rather, Paul "reminds them to live in the unshakable and irresistible faith and hope *that Christ has already established for them*."[49] This pneumatological and christologically based logic coheres well with the verb used in 5:5.

47. Ibid., 882.
48. Choi, "ΠΙΣΤΙΣ in Galatians 5:5–6," 467–90.
49. Campbell, *Deliverance*, 891.

They "do not need to 'work' (that is, in insecurity and anxiety) but only to 'wait.'"[50] As de Boer recently wrote in relation to this verse: "Christ, his faith, his love, his Spirit—these, not the law, provide the basis for the hoped-for justification."[51]

Galatians 1:23 speaks of εὐαγγελίζεται τὴν πίστιν (NRSV: "proclaiming the faith"). Campbell here suggests what he calls an equally "plausible" reading of this passage, which points out that an understanding of "faith" here, as that which Christians believe, would be an anachronism for Paul. For Paul it is rather an *activity* of Christians, Christ, or God. However, I am not sure that τὴν πίστιν is comfortably translated as "the faithful one," so perhaps better would be "the faith," implying an elision "of the Son of God," reflecting 2:20, or "of Jesus Christ," anticipating 2:16?[52] Possibly 2 Corinthians 13:5 would strengthen Campbell's case, a passage he has not made much use of in *Deliverance*. There, Paul exhorts the Corinthians: "Examine yourselves [to see] whether you are in the faith [ἐν τῇ πίστει]. Test yourselves. Do you not realize that Jesus Christ is in you [Ἰησοῦς Χριστὸς ἐν ὑμῖν]? Unless you fail the test."[53] Some, desiring to avoid collapsing "in the faith" into "the life of Christ in the believer," do not emphasize the parallelism of the passage.[54] Indeed, Barnett goes as far as to argue that "in the faith" is propositional and thus should be seen "in contrast" to the experiential "Christ Jesus is in you"![55] Harris argues that "the faith" in 13:5 likely does not denote "personal trust in Christ" given that the context emphasizes "the need for proper Christian conduct." For Harris, then, πίστις here is about proper Christian conduct that accords with Christian doctrine.[56] But it remains clear that the presence of Christ

---

50. Ibid., 892.

51. De Boer, *Galatians*, 319.

52. And while admitting the danger of anachronism, I tend to think that the distinctions Campbell presses could generate problems, and in this respect I refer to Bultmann's stellar essay, "The Object of Theology," in his little book *What is Theology?* "The *fides qua creditur* can only be understood in relation to the *fides quae creditur*, otherwise it has no object and is not what it is" (Rudolf Bultmann, *What is Theology?*, 49).

53. My translation.

54. Thrall, *The Second Epistle to the Corinthians Vol. 2*, 888.

55. Barnett, *The Second Epistle to the Corinthians*, 608.

56. Harris, *The Second Epistle to the Corinthians*, 920.

is paralleled with being "in the faith,"[57] so a christological interpretation of Galatians 1:23 is not entirely unlikely.[58]

Campbell, in *Deliverance*, perhaps questionably considered himself on surer ground when turning to address Galatians 6:10. Instead of translating τοὺς οἰκείους τῆς πίστεως as the households of faith, it can, he suggested, be understood as "the households belonging to the faithful one (i.e., Christ)."[59]

Faith and Galatians in Summary

If Galatians is indeed "all about faith," then Campbell's vigorous and sometimes brilliant exegetical moves lead one to understand πίστις christologically. Certainly, he has made a good case for a christological and apocalyptic reading of Galatians 2:15–21; 3:1–5; 5:5–6; and 6:10. However, he admits that these texts can be read in different ways. The jewel in his crown, the passage that makes a christological reading of πίστις the most plausible, is 3:15-29 (especially vv. 22–26). This fairly decisive passage thus gives his more ambiguous arguments more leverage.

F. Two Objections

The first objection I want to note, although not particularly important and certainly not decisive, is listed here as it is probably one that many *Deliverance* readers may consider at some stage. Some may argue that Campbell is simply too extreme in his treatment of πίστις language! Cannot both objective and subjective interpretations be in play? If not in the individual instances of πίστις Χριστοῦ phrases (as some have argued), why can't Paul, to take Galatians as an example, mean "Christ's faithfulness" in 3:22–26, and "faith in Christ" in 2:16, or at least 1:23?

Campbell may respond: "I have no difficulty ascribing different senses to these serried signifiers, but those reasons do need to be supplied; in their absence, it seems prima facie that the *same* notion is

---

57. This is noted by, e.g., Wendland, *Die Briefe an die Korinther*, 257; Barrett, *The Second Epistle to the Corinthians*, 338; Zeilinger, *Krieg und Friede in Korinth*, 138–39.

58. See also Stegman, *The Character of Jesus*, 360.

59. Campbell, *Deliverance*, 894. Cf. Rom 1:6 (κλητοὶ Ἰησοῦ Χριστοῦ, well rendered as "called to belong to Jesus Christ"); 8:9; 16:10–11; 1 Cor 1:12; 3:4; 3:23; 15:23; 2 Cor 10:7; Gal 3:29; 5:24.

being discussed throughout."[60] For those who may still object that this all sounds too extreme, he has another retort:

> [I]t is worth noting that an insidious false metaphor can operate within such an objection—a metaphor of quantity. . . . If interpretations can be placed on a spectrum, the sober and moderate exegete should presumably prefer the "middle" way between the "radical" and "extreme" interpretations operating on the edges of the putative standard distribution of readings.[61]

And he continues to describe how this metaphor is problematic (and, not unlike Tom Wright, he applies it to the example of a debate between flat and round earth theories![62]). Not only does the metaphor encourage a false account of the disposition of readings, Campbell's strategy throughout has remained sensitive to interpretive paradigms. It will thus not do to merge together semantic possibilities when there is a serious clash at other levels in the task of reading (argumentative, theoretical, and so on).

A second, more important objection is voiced with clarity by Francis Watson. (In numerous articles, Barry Matlock has also made particularly valuable contributions to this debate, disputing Campbell at different points, and had we space we would canvas some of those arguments, at least as they relate to Matlock's analysis of the structure of Galatians 2:16. But as Campbell has already engaged fairly extensively with Matlock's arguments in *Deliverance*—once again, in those valuable endnotes![63]— I will restrict myself to analysis of Watson's proposal.) Watson argues, in agreement with Campbell, that Paul's "by faith of Christ" language derives from Habakkuk 2:4. However, contra Campbell, he argues that the verse was not understood christologically by Paul. Not only is there "no non-Pauline evidence that this text was read christologically, as a reference to 'the Righteous One'," but Paul uses it *as he found it*, as an "assertion about a generic individual (the one-who-is-righteous-by-faith) rather than about Christ."[64] He thus criticizes Campbell for drawing from Habakkuk only ἐκ πίστεως, and not also δίκαιος ἐκ πίστεως.[65] Given the

60. Ibid., 1158 n. 101.

61. Ibid., 1165 n. 148.

62. Wright, *Justification*, 19–27.

63. See especially Campbell, *Deliverance*, chapter 17, but also 1145–46, and 1158 (which ably engages with Matlock's analysis of Gal 3).

64. Watson, "By Faith (of Christ)," 149.

65. Ibid., 149 n. 6.

centrality of Paul's association of πίστις language with Habakkuk 2:4, this could prove to be a crucial argument for an anthropocentric interpretation of πίστις Χριστοῦ (and Watson, I should add, also wants to maintain that *anthropocentric* readings do not immediately imply the faith is then a "condition," nor merely a mental disposition).[66] So he asks whether Paul, in citing Habakkuk, finds "one sense-unit in ὁ δίκαιος and another in ἐκ πίστεως ζήσεται? Or does he construe ὁ δίκαιος ἐκ πίστεως ζήσεται as a single sense-unit and treat ζήσεται as an absolute, without object or adverbial qualification?" In other words, Watson continues, "does ἐκ πίστεως point back to δίκαιος or forward to ζήσεται?"[67] His analysis proposes the following: Paul never associates ἐκ πίστεως with life, "yet it is *repeatedly* associated with righteousness or being made righteous."[68] This means, Watson presses, that "there is no evidence that Paul found the assertion that 'the Righteous One will live by faith' in Habakkuk, in contrast to overwhelming evidence that he read there that 'the-one-who-is-righteous-by-faith will live.'"[69]

What to say to this? More generally, many will perhaps want to know how much hangs on the subjective reading pursued in *Deliverance*. If we take the road of Watson and Matlock, are we bound over to an incoherent Paul? However, although I do not claim to see matters as clearly as either Campbell or Watson on these issues, I want, to finish, to at least offer a few suggestions to prompt discussion on some of Watson's specific arguments.

First, Watson has not made use of the important Moody Smith article, noted above. He thus misses that all the extant Jewish texts read Habakkuk 2:4 with an adverbial interpretation, which speaks for a christological interpretation in context in Romans. Second, Campbell could, of course, point to the positive evidence he has already gathered for a christological reading of Paul's use of the ἐκ πίστεως phrase, not least in Galatians 3:22 where it is deployed in the context of the developing chain of motifs until 3:26, as summarized above. What is more, reference can be made to Romans 1:17 as the first explicit OT citation following 1:2–4, where the gospel is "promised beforehand through his prophets in the Holy Scriptures" περὶ τοῦ υἱοῦ αὐτοῦ, a Son who is also then described

66. See e.g., ibid., 163.
67. Ibid., 159.
68. Ibid., 160.
69. Ibid., 161.

in terms of his "resurrection from the dead" (linking hands with the Habakkuk 2:4 verb, ζάω[70]). Third, although Watson's astute theological sense does not let him down when he denies that "faith" be understood in conditional and merely cognitive terms, Campbell, however, may argue that this must be demonstrated—not simply claimed—as a coherent deduction from an anthropocentric reading (for example, how obvious would it be that ἵνα δικαιωθῶμεν ἐκ πίστεως Χριστοῦ in Galatians 2:16 be understood in an objective and unconditional sense if the key phrase be read in Watson's terms?). Fourth, Watson must also tackle the strong arguments for an understanding of ὁ δίκαιος as referring to Jesus. Richard Hays, for example, has made the case particularly convincing in a couple of publications.[71] Fifth, although Watson's impressive learning and grasp of Paul's use of the OT will remain a vital voice in the continuing debates, key premises in his argument can be challenged, or at least qualified. For example, it is not true that "faith," or even the exact phrase ἐκ πίστεως, is never correlated with "life" (see, e.g., Rom 4:16–17; 6:8). A christological reading of Habakkuk 2:4 is also arguably not unknown in non-Pauline material. Hebrews 10:37–39 can and has been read christologically.[72] The combination of these points, it seems to me, make Watson's claims regarding ὁ δίκαιος ἐκ πίστεως ζήσεται less than decisive.[73]

70. See Hays, *The Conversion of the Imagination*, 140–41.

71. See ibid., 138–40; Hays, *The Faith of Jesus Christ*, 156–61. See also Strobel, *Untersuchungen zum eschatologischen Verzögerungsproblem*, for evidence that Hab 2:2–4 receives a messianic interpretation in the LXX.

72. See the analysis in Campbell, *Deliverance*, 614.

73. One could also challenge Watson's portrayal of Paul's use of the OT (here, Habakkuk) and Campbell has already undertaken the task of showing potential problems at a general level in his explicit engagement with Watson in chapter 12 of *Deliverance*. I for one remain unpersuaded that Watson's canonical hermeneutical approach best explains Paul's general use of Scripture (see ibid., 417–31). Daniel Kirk also disputes Watson's reasoning on different grounds (see Kirk, *Unlocking Romans*, 48). I would suggest that Paul's use of OT themes in, for example, 1 Corinthians 10:1–10, 22 is evidence that Paul's thinking was structured not simply according to the textual demands of canonical shape, but more according to OT themes surrounding the YHWH-Israel relation. Paul's Scripture-reading hermeneutic was thus neither christocentric, nor ecclesiological, but involved reading in such a way that would illumine the Christ-Christian *communal relation*. (For what it is worth, I suspect that a christologically controlled "Bultmannian" hermeneutic, with canonical-shape concerns playing a subordinate role, has much to say for itself, but that is for another day).

G. Conclusion

In conclusion, we must return to the point made at the start regarding Campbell's interpretative strategy. Progress can only be made in this debate, he argues, in so far "as the larger shape of Paul's argument is simultaneously introduced and addressed."[74] If Campbell is now also to be judged according to this criterion, even though the πίστις Χριστοῦ debate is far from over, I suggest that it will be difficult to deny that his work represents the most integrated set of detailed, theologically aware, and exegetically vigorous proposals to date.

---

74. Campbell, *Deliverance*, 1096 n. 40.

Douglas Campbell's Response to Chris Tilling

I am grateful to Chris again for his painstaking summary of my views on this particular question, which are otherwise somewhat buried in the latter portions and endnotes of *Deliverance*. I do continue to regard the evidence in Galatians 3:15–29 as among the most decisive concerning the probable meaning of Paul's debated πίστις Ἰησοῦ Χριστοῦ phrases, and look forward to some engagement with its construal by other interpreters of Galatians in due course. I would perhaps only want to add here that I think that my suggestions made in *Deliverance* concerning 1:23 and 6:10 are a little weak and should now be nuanced.

I would now more confidently exclude the evidence of the Pastorals from consideration, locating them in the middle of the second century, from which place they illuminate nicely the anachronistic danger of positing too quickly that Paul is speaking of "the Faith" in 1:23, nomenclature the Pastorals are entirely comfortable with, although arguably one hundred years later.[75] This would be the only instance in Paul's extant writings in which he would write this, and it would have to be queried whether a creedal tradition existed during his day sufficiently developed to allow this sort of reference to "the central things we Christians believe in." That is, a heavy burden of proof rests on those who would suppose the existence of some sort of rule of faith at this time. Having said this, an overtly christological reference is difficult as well, suggesting recourse to one of the other attested lexicographical possibilities in 1:23 for πίστις. And I wonder if something of a word play is not possible at this point in which Paul suggests that "the one persecuting us then now proclaims the loyalty which then he was destroying" (ὁ διώκων ἡμᾶς ποτε νῦν εὐαγγελίζεται τὴν πίστιν ἥν ποτε ἐπόρθει).

Similarly, I would not interpret 6:10 as overtly and directly christological now—i.e., as "the households of the faithful one" (τοὺς οἰκείους τῆς πίστεως)—which probably stretches the Greek too far. (I did note, incidentally, that this translation was a paraphrase denoting the sense as against the letter of Paul's phrase.) I would speak instead of "the households characterized by fidelity [to him]." It is still important to take account of the singular πίστις following the plural "households" here, and to bear in mind that an anachronistic reference—whatever it actually means precisely—to "the households of the Faith" still seems unlikely. Moreover,

---

75. See chapter 6 in my *Framing Paul* (forthcoming).

ancient auditors would expect a personal reference in this location to the key figure to whom the households in question were affiliated, as, for example, to the households of the Sergii in Pisidian Antioch, or some such. A translation in terms of loyalty captures this singular personal reference.

These two readings in a certain sense then participate in the motif of Christian fidelity, which is spoken of directly in 5:22, more indirectly in 5:5–6, and then reprised more confessionally, in terms of its specific implicit content, in 2:16 and 3:22. The text of Galatians goes on to suggest elsewhere that this virtue was evident in Abraham (see Gen 15:6 in Gal 3:6), and—in its central, dominant explication—effected definitively by Christ (so according to my construal 2:16 [2x], 20; 3:2, 5, 7, 8, 9, 11, 12, 14, 22a, 23 [2x], 24, 25, 26). Hence I hope that it is clear here that "Christians" ought to possess faith, and strictly speaking in numerous respects, as one aspect of their appropriate response to God. They should believe certain things, trust in God, and act with unwavering fidelity and loyalty toward God and one another. But the center of gravity in Paul's discussion of "faith" in Galatians remains the definitive instance of faith who effected it in grueling, martyrological circumstances and thereby made it available to those who later participate in him (through the Spirit; see 5:5, 22), namely, Christ himself. Πίστις is then not a *condition* of participation in Christ but a *marker* that such participation is taking place. And this particular marker can also give assurance to any Christians anxious about whether their situation is Scripturally anticipated and attested over against other accounts of Christian existence and its ethics that are appealing to Scripture as well.

15

The Faith of Jesus Christ

An Evangelical Conundrum

CURTIS W. FREEMAN

I was sitting in a Greek exegesis course my sophomore year in college when we came to the construction ἐν πίστει ζῶ τῇ τοῦ υἱοῦ τοῦ θεοῦ (Gal 2:20). Our professor, Dr. Richard Cutter (of blessed memory), asked me how the genitive should be translated: "Was the apostle Paul saying he lived by faith *in* the Son of God (an objective genitive) or the faith *of* the Son of God (a subjective genitive)?" When I answered that it could be translated either way, he pressed me to say which one I thought was the best translation. A long and heated discussion ensued. In the end I remember saying something to the effect that though the grammar could go either way it only seemed to make theological sense as an objective construction: "faith *in* the son of God." The truth of the matter is, as a born-again evangelical Christian, I could not imagine what it might have meant theologically to think about living by the faith *of* Jesus Christ. I could, however, imagine what it meant to have faith *in* Jesus Christ.

My thinking has changed significantly since then. I read *The Faith of Jesus Christ* by Richard Hays, who argued that "Faith *in* Jesus Christ is not the most natural translation of πίστις Ἰησοῦ Χριστοῦ."[1] He convinced

1. Hays, *The Faith of Jesus Christ*, 162.

me of the strong exegetical and theological grounds for the subjective view. But long before then, Karl Barth had already shaped my theological imagination to think about Paul's gospel as the revelation of God's righteousness "through his faithfulness in Jesus Christ."[2] And following Barth, Thomas Torrance argued that Paul's radical theology presented "the incarnate faithfulness of God" in Jesus as the turning point of the world's salvation.[3] I had even begun to engage the theological tradition of orthodoxy that stressed the reality of God in Christ who "became what we are that we might become what he is."[4] So by the time I read *The Quest for Paul's Gospel* and *The Deliverance of God*, I was already predisposed to be inclined toward the subjective view of "the faith *of* Jesus Christ." Looking back on my college experience, I think I understand why evangelicals have such a hard time making sense of Campbell's account of "the faith *of* Jesus Christ" or his larger argument for "the deliverance of God" in Jesus Christ. The answer is simple, although it will no doubt be disputed. Evangelicals do not understand Campbell's argument because: (1) evangelical theology is functionally unitarian rather than Trinitarian, and (2) evangelical theology is crucicentric rather than incarnational.

(1) Evangelical Theology is Functionally Unitarian Rather than Trinitarian

It may come as a shock to make this point with evangelicals, but the fact of the matter is that evangelical theology is functionally unitarian, not Trinitarian. This is not to suggest that there is no important work on the Trinity being done by evangelical theologians. There is actually quite a lot.[5] But evangelical theology, and popular evangelical religion more specifically, is not Trinitarian. The Jesus piety of most evangelicals leans

2. Barth, *The Epistle to the Romans*, 6th ed., 91–99.

3. Torrance, "One Aspect of the Biblical Conception of Faith," 112.

4. The patristic doctrine of *theosis*, as classically stated by Athanasius, affirms: "[God] assumed humanity that we might become God," *On the Incarnation*, §54, 93.

5. A sample of some excellent work on the Trinity by evangelical theologians would surely include Volf, *After Our Likeness*; Grenz, *Rediscovering the Triune God*; *The Social God and the Relational Self*; and *The Named God and the Question of Being*; Olson and Hall, *The Trinity*; Parry, *Worshipping Trinity*; Fairbairn, *Life in the Trinity*; Holmes, *The Quest for the Trinity*; Johnson, *Rethinking the Trinity and Religious Pluralism*; Giles, *Jesus and The Father*; and *The Trinity & Subordinationism*; Erickson, *God in Three Persons*; and *Who's Tampering with the Trinity?*

toward what H. Richard Niebuhr once described as a unitarianism of the second person.[6] This unitarianism of evangelicals, however, is latent. It is not anti-Trinitarian, but it is not Trinitarian either. How can this be? In short, the doctrine of the Trinity is not clearly and succinctly stated as a whole in any one biblical text. And because evangelical theology is based on explicit biblical warrant, it is not clearly and explicitly Trinitarian. Jesus, however, is central to the biblical canon. Thus, evangelicalism is committed to a functional unitarianism in which the devotion and commitment to Jesus is central.

Once upon a time there was a single biblical text that clearly and explicitly stated the doctrine of the Trinity. The Johannine Comma reads: "For there are three that bear record in heaven, the Father, the Word, and the Holy Ghost: and these three are one" (1 John 5:7, KJV). Although Erasmus expressed doubts about the authenticity of the Comma, he still included it in his third edition of the *Textus Receptus* (1522).[7] And because the Comma was retained in both the Geneva Bible and the King James Version, evangelical Protestants in the English-speaking world frequently appealed to it as warrant for the Trinity throughout the sixteenth and seventeenth centuries. But in 1716 something changed. Richard Bentley, the Master of Trinity College Cambridge and the pre-eminent classicist of the day, announced that he intended to prepare a critical edition of the Greek New Testament and the Latin Vulgate. Bentley concluded that the Johannine Comma was a spurious interpolation, and though he never published his critical edition, his judgment put an end to the Comma as justification for Trinitarian doctrine.[8] Thus evangelicals deprived of a simple biblical warrant for the Trinity were left with a Jesus piety or with complicated rational arguments that rendered the Trinity more arcane.

Lacking a rich Trinitarian theology, contemporary evangelicals are at a loss to understand salvation through the faithfulness of Jesus Christ and the enabling power of the Holy Spirit. To put this in terms of Campbell's models, without a Trinitarian theology there is no Pneumatologically Participatory Martyrological Eschatology (PPME) in Paul's gospel.[9]

---

6. H. Richard Niebuhr actually identified three unitarianisms in Christianity (i.e., of the Father, the Son, and the Spirit), "The Doctrine of the Trinity and the Unity of the Church," 371–84.

7. Metzger, *The Text of the New Testament*, 2nd ed., 101.

8. Ellis, *Bentleii Critica Sacra*, 86; and *The Correspondence of Richard Bentley*, 2:529–31.

9. Campbell, *Quest*, 41.

And without an inchoate Pauline Trinitarian theology evangelicals are left with *just me and Jesus and God*; a unitarianism of the second person and an individualistic anthropology that construes the gospel in contractual terms. The upshot of this chastened biblicism is a functionally unitarian-contractual theology of salvation, where in the words of the nineteenth century Baptist preacher, Elder John Leland: "the preaching that has been most blessed of God, and most profitable to men, is the doctrine of sovereign grace in the salvation of souls, mixed with a little of what is called Arminianism,"[10] by which he meant "free will." In this diminished evangelical theology of a soteriological contract, the trick is to maintain a balance between a semi-pelagianism on the one hand, in which "If I do my part then God does God's part," and antinomianism on the other, that celebrates, "Free from the law / O happy condition / Sin all I want / And still get remission."

(2) Evangelical Theology is Crucicentric Rather than Incarnational

Evangelicals have historically defended the soteriological theology of satisfaction and penal substitution against moral and exemplary theories put forth by liberals. I do not want to overstate the case, so let me be clear: the incarnation does no theological work in evangelical theology. It only serves the functional purpose of getting Jesus to earth so he can die for our sins. I recently gave a lecture at an evangelical seminary where I asked them to consider how our understanding of the atonement might be enriched by a sustained conversation with the affirmation about Christ in the Nicene Creed that "for us humans and for our salvation he came down from the heavens and became incarnate from the Holy Spirit and the Virgin Mary."[11] One of the participants responding to this suggestion dismissed the value of the Nicene Creed, asserting that it contained no article on the doctrine of the atonement, which (he added) was a "real failure."[12] Such a view would have been news to the theologians of the

---

10. Leland, *Letter of Valediction on Leaving Virginia in 1791 in The Writings of John Leland*, 172.

11. Pelikan and Hotchkiss, *Creeds and Confession of Faith in the Christian Tradition*, 1:162–63.

12. DeVine, "Can the Church Emerge without or with Only the Nicene Creed?" 194.

ancient church, who understood that in Pauline theology, humanity, and indeed the entire cosmos, was redeemed through the incarnation. They saw in this new creation the cosmic reversal of the law of sin and death is the result of the fullness of Christ's life, not only in the sacrifice of his death. For example, in *On the Incarnation of the Word*, Athanasius of Alexandria contended that the salvation of the world was due to Christ the Word who became incarnate to restore the image of God in which humanity was made and from which all have fallen.[13]

Some of the harshest criticisms of crucicentric theology have come from within the ranks of evangelicals. Evangelical leader, Steve Chalke, went so far as to characterize penal substitution as "cosmic child abuse," which, he argued, stands in contradiction with the statement "God is love."[14] Evangelical theologian Stephen Holmes has offered a more constructive and nuanced defense of penal substitution for contemporary Christians.[15] Holmes appropriates a wide range of images and metaphors of atonement in the Bible. He deals responsibly with the issues of guilt transference, law and love, divine retribution, and redemptive violence. What he does not consider, however, is the biblical witness to the conviction that, in John Calvin's lovely phrase, "Christ has redeemed us . . . by the whole course of his obedience."[16] Yet Holmes is not alone in this omission. He shares this deficiency with other evangelicals for whom exclusive attention is given to the cross without considering the saving effects of the entire course of Christ's life, death, and resurrection.

Campbell argues that the focus on the cross alone in evangelical theology fails to be sufficiently biblical. He observes:

> The justification by faith perspective on Christ's work, while placing a satisfactory emphasis on the cross, evacuates his incarnation, much of his life, his resurrection, and his ascension, of all soteriological value. According to the justification by faith model, these aspects of Christ have no real part to play in the great drama by which God saves humanity, since the justification by faith account of that drama focuses solely on the cross. Indeed, the justification by faith model struggles to justify the

---

13. Athanasius, *On the Incarnation of the Word*, §13, 41.

14. Chalke and Mann, *The Lost Message of Jesus*, 182.

15. Holmes, *The Wondrous Cross*.

16. Calvin, *Institutes of the Christian Religion*, 2.16.5, 1:507.

inclusion of these other aspects of Christ's life and ministry within a full account of salvation at all![17]

Campbell further contends that any theology that seeks to do justice to Paul's gospel "understands Christ's atoning work as transformational, and . . . consequently encompasses his incarnation, life, death, resurrection, and glorification." In short, he concludes, "both Jesus' life and his death matter to our salvation, and we should not rest content with one without the other."[18] How could evangelicals, who place such a high value on Scripture, miss what seems to be such an obvious message in Scripture? Campbell's answer is simple: their commitment to a "Lutheran" account of justification by faith has occluded their vision to the narrative whole of the gospel.

Some readers may think Campbell has introduced a new criticism, but in fact he is repeating an argument that is quite old. Luther's Wittenberg colleague, Andreas Karlstadt, diverged from the teaching of the justification of sinners by grace through faith. He believed that God's grace would remake sinners and lead to a life of discipleship and obedience in which sin would be overcome. For Karlstadt sin was conquered through the "yieldedness" (*Gelassenheit*) of the Christian's will to God's will. This notion of *Gelassenheit* became central in Anabaptist theology and spirituality as believers were called to yield *inwardly* to the promptings of the Spirit of God and *outwardly* to the discipline of the community and the hostility of the world. The prime examples of yieldedness were the martyrs, who, through suffering discipleship, become mystically united with Christ and with one another in Christ.[19] Dietrich Bonhoeffer similarly diverged from the Lutheran doctrine of justification by describing a Christlike suffering that comes by bearing the sins and burdens of others. While Bonhoeffer was clear to note that "only the sufferings of Christ are a means of atonement," the Christian also "must bear the sins of others" and "be driven like a scapegoat from the gate of the city." Bonhoeffer continued that "he would certainly break down under this burden, but for the support of him who bore the sins of all," for "the passion of Christ strengthens him to overcome the sins of others by forgiving them."[20] Bonhoeffer and the Anabaptists thus anticipate, not only

17. Campbell, *Quest*, 168.
18. Campbell, *Deliverance*, 76.
19. Snyder, *Anabaptist History and Theology*, 26 and 89.
20. Bonhoeffer, *The Cost of Discipleship*, 98 and 100.

the pneumatological and participatory nature of the atonement, but its martyrological embodiment as well.

As a young Christian, my evangelical imagination had no place for living by the incarnate faithfulness of God in Jesus Christ. Yet as I have shown, I was not alone in my limited theological imagination. Evangelicalism has so objectified the atoning work of Christ in the cross and so abstracted Christ's redeeming work from all human participation that Christians have been reduced to the role of mere spectators. Why are evangelicals so puzzled by Douglas Campbell's analysis of Paul's gospel in *The Deliverance of God*? In sum, the root of the problem is *theological*, not grammatical. Is there any hope for evangelicals to understand Campbell? Yes, but only if they take two important steps: (1) evangelicals must begin to ask what it might mean to read the Scriptures (not just the writings of Paul) as the unfolding narrative of the triune God, and (2) they must begin to take seriously the whole course of Christ's life as the enactment of the story of the salvation of the world. Then, and only then, will they be in a position to begin to imagine what Douglas Campbell is saying. Otherwise the faith *of* Jesus Christ will remain an evangelical conundrum.

Douglas Campbell's Response to Curtis Freeman

To Curtis's delightful brief analysis of evangelical recalcitrance I would add only that I think that a powerful and rather sinister political and cultural dynamic can also be at work reinforcing the ongoing occupation of the evangelical imagination by the Justification discourse (and I touch on this in chapter 9 of *Deliverance*; more thorough and learned treatments can generally be found by Hauerwas). This discourse fits like a hand in a glove with modern liberal pretensions, and allows its privatized and individualized Christian subjects to participate in the modern world essentially without hindrance from the teachings and example of Jesus, etc. In my local context, for example, in North Carolina in the USA, many Christians can consequently live largely undisturbed by some of the most challenging and costly aspects of the gospel; they can live and act, that is, primarily as Americans, whether that means more specifically as Democrats, Republicans, or some other essentially godless variation. And the overall result of this, as Barth saw long ago, is a tragic cultural compromise. Evil is excused and the witness of the church is caught up in hypocrisies evident even to pagan outsiders (Rom 2:24). All of which is to say that the stakes are quite real and rather high when assessing this theological model—which is really no theology at all (Gal 1:6b–7a). We may not hold out much hope for the displacement of this sinister model by either my work or the work of others, but we should certainly pray for it—a suitable note perhaps on which to end all my responses.

APPENDIX A

Covenant or Contract?

A Study of the Theological Background of Worship in Seventeenth-Century Scotland[1]

JAMES B. TORRANCE

The Westminster *Directory for the Public Worship of God*, 1645, acknowledged by Presbyterian churches throughout the English-speaking world, emerged at a time of political controversy, when an attempt was made to achieve liturgical uniformity in England and Scotland, and therefore must be understood not only in terms of the theology that it embodies, but also in terms of the social and political revolution of which it was a kind of liturgical manifesto. The immediate context was that of a national struggle for freedom, a revolt from all forms of "catholic" authoritarianism (Charles I, Archbishop Laud, divine right of kings, the papacy, Erastianism, etc.) and a rising suspicion of anything that savored of imposed form and ritual.

---

1. ©1970 *Scottish Journal of Theology*. Originally published in *Scottish Journal of Theology* 23.1 (1970) 51–76. Reprinted with permission.

Research[2] has shown that the subsequent influence of the *Directory* is negligible. Apparently it failed to gain acceptance in England, and although it gained formal sanction in Scotland, it was in fact little used for the next two hundred years. For a variety of reasons, political, ecclesiastical, and theological, Scotland, especially after 1638 (the year of the National Covenant), was to become a land where any form of directorial authority was suspect. But if the *Directory* has had little direct influence on Scottish worship, the theology that lay behind the *Directory* has also been the theology that has profoundly influenced the worship of Scotland for the last three hundred years. The emphasis on freedom in worship and "free prayer" results in worship and prayer being "controlled," "directed" by the theology that lies behind them. The concern of this paper is to indicate certain basic features of Scottish theology (particularly of seventeenth-century theology), which have greatly molded our worship habits as well as the content of our preaching.

The Rise of Federal Theology

The seventeenth century marks the rise of so-called Federal Theology, which was to become the criterion of orthodoxy for the next two hundred years. In a number of significant ways it constituted a movement away from the older Scottish tradition of Knox, the Scots Confession, the pre-Westminster confessions as well as from the theology of Calvin himself. Indeed Scottish worship has been influenced by the intermingling of these two traditions the older Scottish, more Catholic tradition, and the more rationalistic federal scheme of the seventeenth century. The Westminster documents, which are the first reformed documents to enshrine

2. Cf. Frederick W. McNally, "The Westminster Directory." McNally has shown that although the composers' aim was to work only from biblical principles and to subordinate everything to the authority of the Bible, without any regard for tradition, nevertheless there are other influences. (1) The whole general approach is that of the *Genevan Scottish Book of Common Order*. (2) In certain details there is the influence of the *Anglican Book of Common Prayer*. (3) There is the unwritten tradition of English Puritanism, with its revolt from form, and Scottish Presbyterianism as modified by English Puritanism. McNally argues that the main influence of the *Directory* is seen after the middle of the nineteenth century, in those movements in Scotland that sought to recover and enrich the Reformed liturgical tradition, when scholars began to look again at the *Directory* and *Book of Common Order* as repositories of Reformed principles and usages of worship, i.e., in the numerous official and semi-official service books of the different Scottish churches of the last half century.

officially the federal scheme in a mild way, themselves bear witness to this intermingling.

Federal Theology is that form of theology that gave central place to the concept of *covenant* and that distinguished different covenants in God's relation to the world. On the one hand, it was recognized that the concept of covenant was a central one in both the Old and New Testaments. On the other hand, the word was also a significant one in Scottish and English sociopolitical thought, not least in the upheavals of the sixteenth, seventeenth, and eighteenth centuries. With the break up of feudalism, and the struggles for liberty, men made "bands" and "pacts" and "contracts" and "covenants" to defend their freedom and to preserve the rights of a people vis-à-vis their sovereign and the rights of a sovereign vis-à-vis his subjects. The Westminster Assembly met at a time when the whole nation was caught up in a struggle for freedom. The attempt of Charles I to impose uniformity of worship by the introduction of Laud's Liturgy in 1637 brought the response of the National Covenant in 1638. This was followed by the Solemn League and Covenant of 1643 with its counter-attempt to impose uniformity of presbyterian government and worship in Scotland, England, and Ireland. The same year marked the opening of the Westminster Assembly as a parliamentary commission to achieve these ends. It is significant that the *Directory for the Publick Worship of God* was officially described as "a part of the covenanted uniformity in religion betwixt the Churches of Christ in the kingdoms of Scotland, England and Ireland." The key word throughout was *Foedus*-"covenant." For the next hundred years we read about churches, congregations, and individuals like Thomas Boston, Ebenezer Erskine, and Adam Gib, making covenants with God. Innumerable books, pamphlets, and sermons were to appear on this subject, written by Dickson, Durham, Rutherford, George and Patrick Gillespie, and many others. The background of much theological controversy was the emerging sociopolitical philosophy of "social contract," "contract of government," "the rights of man," "natural law"—illuminated by the "light of reason" and given divine sanction by "revelation." This, as Perry Miller[3] has shown, was the philosophy of the many puritans who left these shores to get away from the "tyranny" of British kings and feudal overlords for the "free world" where they would

---

3. Miller, *The New England Mind: The Seventeenth Century*; Miller, *The New England Mind: From Colony to Province*; Miller, *The Life of the Mind in America: From the Revolution to the Civil War*; Miller and Johnson, *The Puritans*; Cf. Gough, *The Social Contract*, see chap. 7 "Puritanism and the Contract."

be free to worship God as they pleased and with whom they pleased and where no one would "tell" them.

If, on the one hand, this was the birth of modern democracy (and the so-called "American way of life"), it was, on the other hand, to have a profound influence on Protestant theology and worship. It provided a conceptual framework within which Reformed theology was to be recast (federal theology), but also provided a language of communication (virtually a "theology of politics") that could be readily grasped by the man in the street, in a land struggling for freedom. (It is also interesting to notice how the language of the market place and the rising mercantile society of the day created a language of communication, where preachers talked about "closing with the offer of Christ," etc.[4]) Fundamental, therefore, for our evaluation of the theology of the time is our scrutiny of the word "covenant" (*foedus*).

Covenant or Contract?

What do we mean by a covenant? Theologically speaking a covenant is a promise binding two people or two parties to love one another *unconditionally*. So the word was used of marriage in the English service book of 1549 and retained subsequently in the traditional forms of marriage service. A bride and bridegroom promise and covenant to love one another "for better for worse . . ." (i.e., unconditionally). Indeed the marriage service enshrines the fact that all true love and all true forgiveness are in fact unconditional, and there is no such thing as conditional love or conditional forgiveness.

It is precisely this that makes a covenant so different from a contract. A contract is a *legal* relationship in which two people or two parties bind themselves together on mutual *conditions* to effect some future result. It betokens a mutual bargain, a compact, a business deal, grounded on certain terms or conditions with some future state of affairs in mind. It takes the form, "If . . . if . . . then . . . ," as in the business world, etc.

No doubt in Scots law a covenant and a contract mean the same thing. So traditionally we have spoken about the "marriage contract" or of giving money to the church by a "deed of covenant," where we mean by legal contract. But theologically the two must be carefully distinguished.

4. Henderson, "The Idea of the Covenant in Scotland," 13.

In the Bible there are many kinds of covenant. For example, there are (a) *bilateral* covenants, as in the classical example between David and Jonathan, covenants between equals, as in marriage. Such a covenant is a *suntheke*; (b) *unilateral* covenants, as when in old Israel at the time of his coronation a king made a covenant for (rather than "with") his people, saying, "This is the kind of king I am going to be, and this is the kind of people you are going to be!" The classical example again is Rehoboam, where the people either said, "Amen" to it, or, "To your tents O Israel, we shall not have this man to reign over us!" Such a covenant is a *diatheke*. The important thing is that God's dealings with men in creation and in redemption—in grace—are those of covenant and not of contract. This was the heart of the rediscovery of the Reformation (and is also the thesis of Martin Buber's *Moses*[5]). Divine covenants have their source in the divine initiative, in the loving heart of God. God conceives of the covenant, God announces it. God confirms and establishes it and carries it through to fulfillment, and the motive is love. The form of the covenant is the indicative of grace—the promise, "I will be your God and you shall be my people." The word always used is *diatheke*.

For our evaluation of Federal theology we might summarize three things about the divine *diatheke*—which led the Reformers themselves to make use of the concept of covenant.

(a) *It is a covenant of grace.* It is not conditioned by anything in man, but is founded solely on the love of God. God has made a covenant for us in Christ (*kaine diatheke*)—nineteen hundred years before we were born. In Christ he has freely bound himself to man, and man to himself, in covenant love, revealing himself as the covenant-making God ("I will be your God and you shall be my people"), and providing *for us* one in Christ, who from our side, in our name, on our behalf, as our great High Priest, has made the one true response for us and for all men ("for us and for our children") and is our one true offering before God. So Calvin, Knox, the Scots Confession, and the older Scottish tradition understood God's covenant dealings with the world.

---

5. Martin Buber, *Moses*. Cf. 101ff: "The original meaning of *berith* is not 'contract' or 'agreement': that is, no conditions were originally stipulated therein, nor did any require to be stipulated—not a contract but an assumption into a life-relationship." Ibid., 103.

(b) *Nevertheless God's covenant of grace demands a response* from men—a response of faith and gratitude and love. But here the distinction between a bilateral and a unilateral covenant is important.

(i) Clearly in a bilateral covenant (*suntheke*) there can be no covenant without a response. So in marriage a man cannot make a covenant *for* his beloved. He has to wait until she says yes to his proposal before they can enter mutually into a two-way covenant. Such a covenant is open-ended and contingent upon the mutual response of both parties. This is not the nature of the New Covenant in Christ.

(ii) A unilateral covenant (*diatheke*) is quite different. God has made a covenant *for us* in Christ—the New Covenant "in my blood." But it still demands a response. On the contemporary political scene, Mr. Ian Smith and his colleagues declared U.D.I.[6] But although it was a unilateral declaration it demanded a response of acceptance or rejection by the British Government. So also with Rehoboam's covenant made for all Israel—it split the nation in two. So the New Covenant made by God for us in Christ demands the joyful, grateful, loving, "Amen" of the whole man— which worship is.

Two things must be held together on this understanding of grace in worship, (i) It is *unconditioned*—by any considerations of worth in man, i.e., it is *free*, (ii) It is *unconditional* in the claims it makes upon us, i.e., it is *costly*. No doubt Lutheranism stressed free grace, and puritan Calvinism stressed the costly claims of grace. But something goes wrong if we stress one at the expense of the other. If, as Bonhoeffer has urged, Lutheranism can sometimes turn free grace into cheap grace, Puritan Calvinism can sometimes turn costly grace into conditional grace.

(c) The sin of late Judaism—and it is the sin of the human heart in all ages—was to try to *turn God's covenant of grace into a contract*, with serious consequences for worship. In the Bible, the form of covenant (in both the Old and New Testaments) is such that the *indicatives of grace are always prior to the imperatives* of law and human obligation. "I have loved you, I have redeemed you . . . therefore, keep my commandments . . ." But Judaism turned it the other way round. "If you keep the law,

6 [Editor note: The author here refers to the unilateral declaration of independence declared by the cabinet of Rhodesia in November 1965, announcing that Rhodesia, previously a British territory, now considered itself an independent sovereign state.]

God will love you. If you keep the sabbath, the kingdom of God will come," etc. That is, the *imperatives are made prior to the indicatives.* The covenant has been turned into a contract, and God's grace made conditional on man's obedience. It is precisely against this inversion of the order of grace that Paul protests in Galatians 3:17–22. God made a covenant with Abraham, and although the law came 430 later (to spell out the obligations of grace) it did not suddenly introduce conditions of grace. It did not turn the covenant into a contract. To introduce conditions would be to break a promise. Love always brings its obligations. But the obligations of love are not the conditions of love. If this is true of human love, how much more of divine love. *The God of the Bible is a covenant-God not a contract-god,* and the worship appropriate to a covenant God is radically different from the worship appropriate to a contract-god. The one is a worship of joy and gratitude, the other can be a worship of fear and anxiety—a "yoke grievous to be borne."

The Relation between Forgiveness and Repentance

What happened in the history of Israel, has happened in the church in all ages. There is something in the human heart that makes men want to bargain with God. We see it in the story of the early medieval church, and also in the development of theology in seventeenth-century Scotland. As so often, the issue emerges most clearly when the church is most concerned about godly discipline and the relation between forgiveness and repentance. This was the focal point of the Reformation and was to become a burning issue in Scotland.

Already by the end of the second century, in the period of Tertullian, the church was struggling with the question of discipline. The New Testament had given certain guidance, as in Matthew 18:15–22, and in the Corinthian epistles—guidance based on the unconditional nature of forgiveness, which nevertheless demands unconditionally the response of repentance. The priority of forgiveness is seen in the fact that Christ died for us while we were yet sinners, and it is this word of the cross that leads a man to repentance. But the question emerged, "What about the man who has been excommunicated in the manner of Matthew 18:17, and who then apparently repents and seeks readmittance to the fellowship?" Here the natural thing seemed to be to say, that *if* the church was satisfied that he was truly repentant—*if* he was truly contrite, and confessed his sins and made due amends (*contritio, confessio, satisfactio*) *then* he could be forgiven and restored. This in embryo was the later sacrament of penance. But as Calvin argued in the *Institutes* Book 3, the basic fallacy here was to invert the evangelical order of grace and make repentance prior to forgiveness, whereas in the New Testament forgiveness is logically prior to repentance.

It was precisely with this issue in mind that some of the seventeenth-century divines made a distinction between: (a) *legal repentance*—where the form is "If you repent, you will be forgiven" ... "This do and thou shalt live!" and (b) *evangelical repentance*—where the form is "Christ has done this for you, therefore repent!"

This same problem that was the dividing point between the Church of Rome and the Reformers became a living issue in Scotland about 150 years after the Reformation, in the so-called "Marrow Controversy," which is most illuminating because it highlights some of the consequences of the rise of federal theology.

During the seventeenth century, a change began to take place in Scottish preaching where a subtle kind of legalism began to creep in. The Scottish preacher preached the law in such a way that his concern was to produce a conviction of sin and a fear of judgment, so that he could call upon the sinner to repent and renounce his sin so that he might receive the word of forgiveness and hear the comforts of the gospel. This pattern became so widespread that many divines felt that it was producing a doctrine of conditional grace that was foreign to the gospel. The presbytery of Auchterarder raised the issue when in 1717 it inserted the following clause as one of the articles for trials for licence: "I believe it is not sound or orthodox to teach that we must forsake sin in order to come to Christ and to be instated in covenant with God." This of course, as Thomas Boston commented at the time, was badly worded, and on the face of it sounded like a deliberate statement of irresponsible anti-nomianism—an encouragement to licentious living! One of the students refused to subscribe and appealed to the General Assembly in 1717. The Assembly supported his plea and condemned the presbytery, declaring the proposition to be "unsound and most detestable." This decision triggered off fierce controversy, significant because it brought to light the extent to which legalistic forms of preaching and worship, and a kind of legalistic moralism, had pervaded the church. Referring to this decision of the General Assembly, Ralph Erskine, preaching in his pulpit in Dunfermline, could say, "Some speak of forsaking sin in order to and before coming to Christ. But never will you forsake sin evangelically till once Christ come to you and you come to Him. When Christ comes into the temple, He drives out all the buyers and sellers. Therefore let Him come in and He will make the house clean."

Another person who sat in that General Assembly in 1717 and who strongly protested against the decision was the Rev. Thomas Boston of Simprin and Ettrick. Twenty years before, Boston had written in his diary—in a time of spiritual perplexity—"I had no great fondness for the doctrine of the conditionality of the Covenant of Grace."[7] He had felt that something was going wrong with Scottish preaching. In the course of his parish ministry he came across a copy of a book entitled *The Marrow of Modern Divinity* by a certain Edward Fisher, written in England in 1645. It was a book which re-affirmed the teaching of the Reformation about grace—in the manner of Luther's *Galatians*—and it was destined to exert a profound influence on Boston and many others. The central theme of the book was the distinction between legal repentance and evangelical repentance, arguing as Calvin had done, that forgiveness leads to true repentance. When you preach legal repentance, you are in fact appealing to the false motives of fear of hell and hope of heaven, and by a doctrine of conditional forgiveness destroying the grounds of Christian assurance, engendering the question, "Have I fulfilled the conditions . . . ?" When, however, you preach evangelical repentance you preach Christ and his cross and appeal to the motives of gratitude and joy, and the believer finds assurance of forgiveness in Christ.

Boston handed the book to some of his minister colleagues at the time of the Auchterarder controversy, and one of them, James Hog of Carnock, had it printed in Scotland (seventy years after its original publication in England). Once again enormous controversy was stirred up over this question, particularly in the Synod of Fife where Principal Hadow of St. Andrews denounced the book and published a tract called *The Antinomianism of the Marrow Detected*.

It is beyond the scope of this paper to enter into the details of "The Marrow Controversy"—which in itself is from beginning to end a most revealing commentary on Scottish theology.[8] But in 1720 the

---

7. Boston and Low, *A General Account of My Life*, 153. Cf. Brown, *Gospel Truth*, 139.

8. For a fuller account, cf. Brown, *Gospel Truth*; Macewen, *The Erskines*.

General Assembly (in what has subsequently been called the Black Act) condemned the book, prohibited ministers from recommending it, and enjoined ministers to warn their people against it.

The central issue of the whole controversy was whether repentance and faith and holiness are *conditions* of the covenant of grace. This the Marrow men denied and the General Assembly affirmed. Outstanding among the Marrow men were Thomas Boston, Ralph and Ebenezer Erskine, James Hog, Ralph Wardlaw, and others, who a few years later seceded from the Church of Scotland (with the exception of Boston, who died before the First Secession). The Secession was primarily over the vexed question of patronage, but there were deep-seated theological issues as well—issues that were to occasion constant controversy until John McLeod Campbell was to raise the same issues in a more thoroughgoing way a hundred years later and be condemned on similar grounds.

The basic concern of the Marrow men in spite of certain other tendencies in their thought was to get back to the theology of the Reformers and the older Scottish tradition. In a strange way the legalism and rationalism of the orthodoxy of Scottish Calvinism of the day was beginning to throw up its opposite in the form of Moderatism, perhaps not so much as a reaction against federal Calvinism but rather as a development from it.

The theological lesson that we learn from this whole period is that whenever a doctrine of conditional grace is taught, and the emphasis in worship and preaching begins to fall heavily on what *we* have to do—on *our* faith, *our* repentance, *our* need for humility and obedience—then the gospel of the grace of God, the joyful news of what God has done for us in Christ, begins to be pushed into the background, if not to disappear, and worship can become "a yoke grievous to be borne."

The question at once arises, *Where did this doctrine of conditional grace come from* in a Calvinistic land like Scotland? Different answers have been given. (1) Arminianism. This is unlikely to have had any significant influence in a church so committed to the theology of the Westminster Confession. (2) The influence of English puritanism in the form of the neonomianism of Richard Baxter and Daniel Williams (that Christ fulfilled the conditions of the old law for us but has imposed a new law, which must be fulfilled if we would obtain evangelical righteousness). The Marrow men certainly felt this was a powerful influence. (3) The influence of rationalism and the spirit of the age—the Age of Reason— which was to produce many attempts to synthesize natural and revealed theology. (The Marrow men felt that, in this direction, the Assembly had been too lenient in the Simson case in Glasgow.) (4) I suspect that the deepest reason lies in the rise of what we have come to call *federal theology.*

Features of Federal Theology

Federal theology, as indicated above, is that kind of theology that developed in the seventeenth century (in England and Holland as well as Scotland) and which distinguished different kinds of covenant, and made out of these a framework within which all theology is cast. In so doing, it was far more influenced by certain sociopolitical concepts of covenant than it probably ever realized. In particular it made a hard and fast distinction between the so-called covenant of works and the covenant of grace.

According to this scheme, God made Adam the child of nature, who could discern the laws of nature by the light of reason. On the basis of this, he entered into a covenant with him (the so-called covenant of works—or should we call it a "contract" between a sovereign and his subjects?) that if he obeyed the laws of nature (which are the laws of God) and fulfilled the conditions of the covenant, he would find eternal life. This is the *foedus naturae*—the contract of nature upon which all society is based. Adam as such is not a private individual but the federal head of the race. Thus when he disobeyed, he brought the curse not only upon himself, but on all for whom he contracted. But God in his sovereign grace does not destroy the human race, but elects out of the mass of fallen mankind a number for himself and makes a covenant of grace for them in Christ. This covenant of grace is already promised in the protevangelium of Genesis, announced by Abraham, reaffirmed at Sinai, and fulfilled in Christ. God by his Holy Spirit effectually calls the elect by his Spirit and brings them to saving faith by the instrumentality of Word and sacrament, the signs and seal of the covenant of grace.

This distinction between a covenant of works and a covenant of grace was unknown to Calvin and the Reformers—nor indeed would Calvin ever have taught it. The very distinction implies the confusion between a *covenant* and a *contract*—the one Latin word *foedus* meaning both and hence obscuring the distinction. So, as we have seen, in Scots law we talk about a "deed of covenant" and the "marriage contract." For Calvin, all God's dealings with men are those of grace, both in creation and in redemption. They flow from the loving heart of the Father. The two poles of his thought are grace and glory—from grace to glory. There has been only *one eternal covenant of grace*, promised in the Old Testament and fulfilled in Christ. "Old" and "New" do not mean two covenants but two forms of the one eternal covenant—the central theme of Book Two of the *Institutes*.

Zwingli was probably the first of the reformers to use the covenant concept in theology in 1526 in the defense of infant baptism. But still for Zwingli there is only one covenant. In 1534 Bullinger wrote a work on "The One Eternal Covenant and Testament of God." In 1584 we find Ursinus speaking of a *foedus naturae* and others begin to speak of a *foedus generale*. The first person in Scotland, so far as I know, to speak of a "covenant of works" was Robert Rollock, the first Principal of Edinburgh University, in 1596 in *Some Questions about the Covenant of God* and in 1597 in his *Treatise on Effectual Calling* where he speaks of "God's two covenants, both that of works and that of grace." The distinction had already been used in the immediately preceding years in England by Dudley Fenner, Perkins, and other puritans. From this time this distinction comes to be accepted and there emerges the federal scheme, which for 250 years was to become the standard of orthodoxy in Scotland.

In 1638, the year of the National Covenant, David Dickson expounded the theme before the General Assembly, having the year before written his *Therapeutica Sacra* (published in 1656). But David Dickson, like Samuel Rutherford, distinguished three covenants (or shall we again call them "contracts"?). (1) The *covenant of works* between God and Adam; (2) the *covenant of redemption* between the Father and the Son; and (3) the *covenant of grace* between God and man through Jesus Christ the Mediator. The formulation of each of these is thrown into contractual form. For example, the covenant of redemption means that from all eternity the Father has made a covenant (contract) with the Son that if the Son fulfills the conditions of the covenant (contract) of works for the elect, God will be gracious to the elect. Correspondingly, the covenant of grace is interpreted to mean that God makes a covenant (contract) for the elect that on the *condition* of faith and repentance they will receive the benefits of Christ's redemptive work (forgiveness, justification, sanctification, etc.). One can see at once the dangers of this contractual language. For example, (a) when applied to the doctrine of atonement, it implies that the Father has to be conditioned into being gracious—a view that Calvin, following Augustine, had vigorously rejected. Atonement flows from the grace of God. (b) As so interpreted, forgiveness is made conditional upon repentance. It was this latter view that brought the protest of the Marrow men. They were themselves federalists and did not adequately see that the legalism against which they were protesting grew in no small measure out of federalism itself. But they did see that part of the trouble was the distinction between the covenant of redemption and the covenant of grace—a distinction that they rejected in their reconstruction of the federal scheme, as in Boston's *Fourfold State*. Boston rightly argued that in the New Testament there is only the one covenant of grace made for us in Christ. This was clearly a return to Calvin and an attempt to interpret faith in non-contractual terms as "union with Christ." His weakness was that he still clung to the doctrine of a covenant of works, with its consequent restriction of the covenant of grace to the elect, although he struggled to do justice to the New Testament warrant that grace should be offered to all.

The threefold scheme was set out in a small pamphlet entitled *The Sum of Saving Knowledge* (written possibly by David Dickson and/or James Durham)—a work that was regularly bound in with copies of the Westminster Confession of Faith and the Larger and Shorter Catechisms, as though offering a summary of Westminster theology, and widely read all over Scotland. It specifically speaks of "covenant or contract" and argues that all three covenants were based on "conditions." The Westminster Confession of Faith, in sections vii and xiv, was the first reformed confession to teach the federal scheme, certainly in a mild way, distinguishing the two covenants of works and grace.

Similar advocates of federal theology had been emerging elsewhere, for example, Cocceius in Holland, John Preston, William Ames, John Ball in England, and in New England some eight works on federal theology appeared before 1650. In 1677 appeared a work that was to be widely read in Scotland, Witsius on the *The Economy of the Covenants*. As mentioned above, numerous volumes of sermons and books were to emerge expounding the theme of covenant. In the sociopolitical context of a nation struggling for freedom, this was a language that people understood, as possibly people today would understand the language of trade unions, civil rights, settlement of wage disputes, etc. It was a kind of "theology of politics" that provided a conceptual framework for communication of the gospel to the man in the pew, and by means of such terminology the gospel grasped the imagination of a covenanted nation. Through it the Scottish people became aware of the great central realities of the Bible and were gripped by the gospel of grace. Much of Scotland's best theological and devotional literature was to be couched in these terms. It was by reading the *Sum of Saving Knowledge* that Robert Murray McCheyne was converted, and copies of Boston's *Fourfold State* found their way into many homes throughout the land. To this day the writings of the Erskines are read and have even been recently reprinted in Holland.

But, as so often in the attempt to effect a synthesis between Christianity and culture in the interests of communication, the gospel itself was to suffer certain modifications in this framework, and contractual notions were to be introduced that were radically to change the preaching and worship habits of the Scottish church. With the deposition of Mary Queen of Scots, the question was raised and discussed—as by George Buchanan in his *De jure regni apud Scotos* (On the Rights of the Crown in Scotland)—as to the rights of a sovereign vis-à-vis the rights of the people, and how both could be safeguarded. Samuel Rutherford in his *Lex Rex* later argued that sovereign and people are bound by law. The concepts of "social contract" and "contract of government" were already emerging under the influence of medieval notions of natural law, and to receive later extensive development in the writings of John Locke, Rousseau, and others, and to exert a profound influence in New England. Theologians begin to speak about the "sovereignty of God," "the crown rights of the Redeemer," "the covenant of nature," "the rights of man," "closing with Christ," "contracting in marriage".

Evaluation of Federal Theology

What then are we to make of federal theology? On the positive side we can recognize the following features.

(1) It emerged out of a concern for biblical exegesis and a desire to see the fundamental unity of the Bible, and for this the notion of "covenant" was a coordinating hermeneutical principle. We see this particularly in Cocceius. The danger was that when an appeal was made to biblical authority, it was the Bible understood in terms of the federal scheme.

(2) There was a concern to discern the historical nature of revelation and see the movement of God in history—an anticipation of the notion

of *Heilsgeschichte*. So T. M. Lindsay[9] interpreted federal theology. But I think we can add two qualifying notes, (a) The earlier Scots Confession had already manifested a sense of God's dealings with Israel and the church in history and interpreted it in terms of the category of promise and fulfillment, which preserved better a christological understanding of grace and election than the later federal scheme, (b) The federal emphasis on the eternal decrees of God places the real moment of salvation beyond history and sees history as the arena for the execution of the decrees in a way that can detract from the more dynamic notion of God as actively at work within history.

(3) There is a dogmatic concern to have a carefully wrought out systematic presentation of Reformed thought—for example, over against the Roman theology of the Counter Reformation—and an attempt to recognize the importance of the teaching office of the church. The seventeenth century was to produce many catechisms.[10]

(4) The appeal to the concept of covenant may have also emerged out of an attempt to hold together divine predestination and human responsibility, the sovereignty of God and human activity, the rightful claims of God and the freedom of man. There may also have been a concern to safeguard a high doctrine predestination from antinomianism or laxity in morals.[11]

(5) As mentioned above, it provided a language of communication in terms of which the great doctrines of the faith were presented and gripped the imagination of many generations in the upheavals and political struggles of the Scottish nation, so that few nations were so deeply instructed and catechized in the gospel.

But on the *negative side there were great weaknesses.*

(1) First and foremost, the whole federal scheme is built upon the deep seated *confusion between a covenant and a contract*, a failure to recognize that the God and Father of our Lord Jesus Christ is a covenant-God and not a contract-god. A covenant brings its promises, its obligation, and

9. Lindsay, "The Covenant Theology," 521–38.

10. Mitchell, *Catechisms of the Second Reformation.*

11. Cf. the accusation of antinomianism levelled against the Marrow men, or such a later novel as Hogg, *Private Memoirs.*

indeed its warnings. But the obligations of grace are *not* conditions of grace, and it is false in Christian theology to articulate moral obligation in contractual terms (however much it may be necessary to safeguard the covenant of marriage by legal contract). Nearly all the definitions of a covenant in these theological writers are cast in contractual terms, for example, Ursinus says: "A covenant in general signifieth a mutual contract or agreement of two parties joined in the covenant, whereby is made a bond or obligation on certain conditions for the performance of giving or taking something with the addition of outward signs and tokens."[12] Samuel Rutherford in his Catechism describes the covenant of grace as "a contract of marriage" between Christ and the believer, and then goes on to speak of the conditions of the contract. This confusion between a covenant and a contract leads to the notion of conditional grace, which inverts the evangelical order of forgiveness and repentance, so that we hesitate in the name of Christ to proclaim absolution and free forgiveness of sins, or hesitate to believe that we are truly forgiven. So the Scottish mind has too often been torn by the question of assurance, which was to become such a point of issue in the Marrow controversy and lead McLeod Campbell in his pastoral concern for his flock at Rhu to break with the whole federal scheme—for which he was deposed by the General Assembly. It is significant that the question of assurance never assumed the same importance for Calvin with his stronger emphasis on the objectivity and unconditional nature of grace, although he too, in the language of the later Marrow men, saw that assurance is of the essence of faith in Christ.

(2) The federal scheme made a radical *dichotomy between the sphere of nature and the sphere of grace*, of natural law and the gospel, so that the mediatorial work of Christ is limited to the covenant of grace and the church, the sphere marked out by the covenant of grace. All men by nature stand related to God, the contracting Sovereign, as to a *Judge*, under natural law and exposed to the sanctions of law. Only the elect are related to God through Christ as Mediator. So the relationship between church and the world, church and state is no longer understood christologically, as by Calvin and Knox, but in terms of gospel and natural law. The influence of this on the doctrine of the church, "the two kingdoms," preaching,

---

12. Ursinus, *The Summe of Christian Religion*, 218, quoted in Murray, *The Covenant of Grace*.

intercessory prayer is inevitable, as we can see from the protests of Boston, the Erskines and, in a more radical way, by McLeod Campbell.

This separation between nature and grace amounts to a version to the pre-Reformation medieval view that *grace presupposes nature and grace perfects nature*—a departure from the great emphasis of the Reformation that nothing is prior to grace. An illustration of this is the interpretation of the Sabbath in Scotland. The Ten Commandments are a transcript, a re-publication of the law of nature, and the law of nature (including the law of the Sabbath) is the foundation of society and for the state consequently to violate the law of nature is to expose society to divine judgment. It is on similar grounds that certain defenses have been made elsewhere of racial discrimination and policies of segregation. God has made men by nature black and white. Grace does not destroy nature but conforms to nature, and so justification has been sought for the fact that black and white Christians should worship apart. Again such a doctrine of separation of nature and grace has been the ground of certain doctrines of "the spirituality of the church" where it has been argued the church is concerned with spiritual matters like the preaching of the gospel but civil matters like civil rights and race relations should be left to the state.[13]

(3) The federal scheme thrust up the doctrine of a *limited atonement*, that Christ only died for the elect—a doctrine or conclusion unknown to Calvin. It is beyond our scope here to trace the development of a doctrine that was to be regarded as orthodoxy for two hundred years and lead to McLeod Campbell's deposition for his rejection of it. But two comments can be made, (a) The doctrine implies a loss of the notion of Christ's headship over all creation, his solidarity with all men as the Head of the race, as in the theology of Ephesians and Colossians, or as expounded by Irenaeus, Athanasius, and the Cappadocians as well as by Calvin and such older Scottish divines as Boyd of Trochrig. The emphasis of doctrine is no longer on the incarnation, on Christ's solidarity with all men, but almost exclusively on his work on behalf of the elect, his passive obedience on the cross for the sins of believers, with whom he stands related,

13. Cf. the famous defense of slavery at the time of the American Civil War in the *Address by the General Assembly*—"To all the churches of Jesus Christ throughout the earth, unanimously adopted at their sessions in Augusta, Georgia, December 1861," signed by Palmer, Thornwell, and others. For an examination of this approach, see Thompson, *The Spirituality of the Church*.

not in terms of incarnational oneness but of *foedus*, of contract. The result was a loss of the older emphasis on "union with Christ our Head," which is replaced by a more judicial interpretation of faith. Boston saw this and sought valiantly to recover it within the federal scheme. He saw that this was particularly the result of distinguishing the covenant of redemption from the covenant of grace—a distinction he consequently rejected. We might well ask what happens to our understanding of Communion and the sacrament of the Lord's Supper if faith is interpreted in contractual terms rather than in terms of union with Christ? Does it not lead to that kind of "fencing of the table" that implies we may only come to the table and communicate *if* we have fulfilled certain conditions? Is this not precisely what we have witnessed in Scotland? Is there not the real danger here of turning the sacrament of the Lord's Supper into a sacrament of penance by making forgiveness and the benefits of redemption conditional on repentance and conversion and some great act of renunciation? (b) Limited atonement also means that you cannot say to all men unequivocally, "Christ died for you." But what you can say to all men is that "You are all under the law. You are all guilty and under judgment." What you can say to all men without exception is, "Repent!" Then, if in fact they repent, we can take that as evidence of election and grace, and then hold out the comforts of the gospel! It was in these terms that Principal Hadow attacked the Marrow men who held that Christ should be offered to all even if Christ did not die for all. But as the Marrow men saw, this approach made forgiveness conditional on repentance, gave priority to the preaching of law over the preaching of the gospel, and bred a deep lack of assurance in that it left people tortured by the question, "Am I one of the elect? Have I fulfilled the conditions of grace?" It also appealed to the motives of "fear of hell and hope of heaven," which, they said, was wrong. The one true motive is gratitude for grace. *It was such preaching that became preoccupied with sin and judgment and repentance and which laid such an emphasis on the element of self-examination in prayer*, with a loss of the notes of joy and peace and gratitude and praise for the forgiveness so freely given in Christ. Again perhaps no one saw this more clearly than John McLeod Campbell.

(4) The whole focus of attention moves away from *what Christ has done for us* and for all men, to *what we have to do* IF we would be (or know that we are) in covenant with God. For preaching, this means that the emphasis falls less on the indicatives of grace and more on the imperatives

of repentance, obedience, and faith. Baptism and the Lord's Supper are seen not so much as seals of the gospel, evangelical ordinances or "converting ordinances"—as interpreted by John Davidson of Prestonpans in the older tradition, an interpretation rejected by George Gillespie—but rather as seals of our faith, or seals of our repentance. Where this shift of emphasis occurs, then the sacraments become badges of *our* personal covenant, and the Lord's Table becomes the feast of the converted, of the penitent. With the emergence of this changed emphasis, the fencing of the tables and catechizing assume a different significance in the discipline of the church, as stressing the need for repentance and faith as conditions for coming to the table.

(5) The development of the federal scheme in Scotland and the historical situation in the seventeenth century produced an unhappy if not false distinction between the visible and invisible church, which lost sight of the passionate emphasis of the Scots Confession and the older Scottish tradition on the view that there is only one church, the body of Christ.[14] In the federal scheme, the invisible church comprises the elect, known only to God, whereas the visible church is the sphere of the penitent, who have made their "external covenant." The notion of a "covenanted nation" also pointed to the need to distinguish the church as known to God and the church as visible in the nation. On the one hand, it is true (as in the teaching of Samuel Rutherford) the concept of covenant held together the thought of the kingdom of God and the covenanted nation, the church visible and invisible—and was able to preserve the doctrine of the one church, so long as the nation was united in covenant. But with the fierce division between protesters and resolutioners in the covenanting period, and the Secessions of the eighteenth century, the visible church began to break up, with the loss of the sense of the one holy Catholic Church to which all the earlier divines (including the earlier federalists) held so firmly, and an increasing appeal was made to the distinction between the church visible and invisible. Baptism then becomes a badge of the visible church but not of the invisible church.

In each of these five negative evaluations of the federal scheme, we can see an impoverishment and restriction of the concept of grace— a shift of emphasis from what God has so freely and unconditionally done for all men in Christ, to a more subjective interest in what we have

14. Cf. Walker, *The Theology and Theologians of Scotland*; Macpherson, *The Doctrine of the Church in Scottish Theology*.

to do—to our need for repentance, personal covenanting, obedience, subjective grounds for assurance, closing with Christ, signing the covenants, keeping the Sabbath, a preoccupation with election and the outward evidences of election. One can well understand the emergence of the distinction between "evangelical preaching" and "legal preaching"— between "evangelical repentance" and "legal repentance"—in the concern to recover the centrality of Christ (as in McLeod Campbell's doctrine of the so-called "vicarious penitence of Christ"—a concern to recover Calvin's teaching that Christ has fulfilled for us all the obligations of grace). We can also see how these changes in theological emphasis can all too readily alter the whole content of worship where worship can become less and less a joyful, grateful, believing response to the objective realities of Christ and the gospel, to a more inward-looking subjective preoccupation with penitence and personal assurance of election.

The Impoverishment of Worship

There is no doubt that the covenanting period saw a sad impoverishment in the worship of the Church of Scotland, when developments took place that not only marked a movement, away from the older forms of Scottish worship, but also a movement away from the patterns of Reformed worship in other parts of Europe, so that the question must be asked how far the Scottish church of that time was really the guardian of "Reformed Worship."[15]

Apart from the more general considerations above, two other features lie behind this impoverishment, which can only be indicated in brief outline.

(1) The first is *the revolt from any kind of required liturgical form in the interest of freedom in worship*—with an emphasis on "free prayer" and the "freedom of the Spirit." Behind this we can discern the powerful influence of Brownism and English sectarianism and puritan Independency, which called for a modification, indeed an abandoning of certain features of worship that had prevailed since the Reformation in Scotland and which had been associated with the Genevan Scottish Book of Common Order. The General Assemblies each year between 1638 and 1645— between the time of the National Covenant (1638) and the Solemn League

15. Cf. Sprott, *The Worship of the Church.*

and Covenant (1643) and the formal endorsement of the *Westminster Directory for the Publick Worship of God* (1645)—were torn by the question of "innovations" into Scottish worship from Brownism and sectarianism. The records of these and subsequent Assemblies tell the story of a losing struggle to preserve the older forms of worship and stem the tide of ideas coming from English Independency. The central issues were the use of the Apostles' Creed in baptism and of the Lord's Prayer in public worship; the singing of the Gloria Patri at the end of the Psalms; the minister's habit of kneeling for personal devotions in the pulpit; the reading of Holy Scripture without an accompanying lecture or running commentary, and the widespread practice of having daily services in churches.

Henderson, Baillie, Calderwood and Blair, and others passionately pled for the retention of these practices. But with the rapid increase of puritan influence at a time of reaction against imposed Anglican forms of worship (following Laud's Liturgy of 1637) and with the avowed concern to reach agreement with English puritans in the interest of imposing uniformity of worship under the Solemn League and Covenant, concession after concession was made, if not with Assembly sanction, certainly in general practice. The Assembly accepted the resultant *Directory*, which was thus a compromise document. By request from Westminster it agreed to call on ministers to abandon personal devotions in the pulpit, but could not bring itself to legislate against the use of the Gloria Patri (which, however, from that time fell into desuetude). One by one the older Scottish practices were discontinued largely in concession to puritan pressures, both at the Westminster Assembly and afterwards. The Apostles' Creed was dropped from the baptismal service, but formally appended at the end of the Catechisms; the Lord's Prayer was gradually omitted from public worship (as another form of imposed prayer!) and was almost unused for public worship for two hundred years: daily services were largely discontinued; read prayers were replaced by "conceived" prayers; Holy Scripture was only read if accompanied by a lecture; and the taking up of the offering excluded from the actual service of worship. The following years, in the period of "rigid Presbyterianism" (1648–51) saw even more drastic modifications, such as the discontinuance of Holy Communion in the larger towns and in many country villages.[16] It was not celebrated for six years in Edinburgh, for five years in Glasgow, for nine in Stirling, and

16. Cf. ibid., 34.

for six in St. Andrews. In 1649 an attempt was even made to call upon the Assembly to prohibit the use of the Lord's Prayer in public worship.

The story is a sad one. No doubt, there was a genuine plea for the liberty of the spirit, but the changes were as much influenced by the emerging philosophy of self-determination, a concept of freedom that was interpreted to mean that we worship God as we please, when we please, and with whom we please, according to one's own individual conscience and personal interpretations of Holy Scripture. This was a far cry from Knox's contention that within the covenant of grace there is a prescribed way of response in Scripture where the church must take the form of a servant. Liturgical form was now interpreted as loss of freedom, and "protest" and "dissent" were regarded as the marks of godliness of those who were determined to stand fast in what they believed to be the liberty of the gospel.

When Episcopacy was restored in 1661, the first move of the bishops was to give instructions that "the reading of Scripture, the use of the Lord's Prayer and Gloria Patri, the repetition of the Creed at baptism, and (in some dioceses) that morning and evening daily prayer should be resumed."[17] The tragic irony is that these old Scottish Presbyterian usages were henceforth to be associated with Episcopacy or Anglican intrusion! Conversely, the more austere forms of worship, so influenced by English Brownism, were to be associated with the sufferings of the persecuted Covenanters and popularly regarded as the form of worship introduced by the Reformers!

(2) The other significant feature of Scottish theology of the seventeenth century that marked a departure from the older Reform was the loss of the doctrine of the continuing priesthood of Christ, without which it seems to me one cannot have an adequate theology of worship. Whatever else our worship is, it is our participation through the Spirit in the self-offering of Christ and the intercession of Christ. If there is one doctrine that more than any other characterized the theology of both Calvin and Knox, it was the doctrine of the sole priesthood of Christ within his church. It was in terms of this that they attacked the medieval concept of the priesthood, and interpreted prayer, communion, forgiveness, union with Christ, and the church as the body of Christ. The thought pervades the prayers of Calvin and is uppermost in Knox's interpretation of the sacrament of the Lord's Supper in the light of our Lord's high priestly

17. Ibid., 48–49.

prayer in John 17. Yet this very doctrine recedes in the theology of the so-called "second Reformation." This I think is in large measure due to the following reasons.

(a) The severe polarization between *what Christ did for us then*, once and for all, and *what we must do now*, in obedience, penitence, and faith, can have the effect of eclipsing what Jesus Christ is doing *now* as the Leader of our worship in his continuing ministry of drawing men to himself and uniting us with himself in his communion with the Father.

These two sharply contrasted poles were held together in federal theology by the concept of covenant. But where the shift of emphasis moved more and more to the subjective pole, the objective pole of the gospel steadily receded. The objective pole no doubt was acknowledged as an article of orthodox belief, but the real interest became the anthropocentric one—what *we* do! We see this in the eighteenth century, where the orthodox evangelicals are preoccupied with personal covenanting, and the Moderates with moral behavior, with their resulting radically different understandings of the church, the one moving toward a voluntarist doctrine of the gathered church, the other to a greater preoccupation with the question of the Establishment, but both with a meagre conception of the church as the body of Christ.

(b) The Reformers had stressed the threefold office of Christ as Prophet, Priest, and King, and this found due formulation in the Westminster Confession of Faith. But what about the *continuing* threefold office of Christ? The seventeenth century certainly emphasized that Christ is the *one King* and Head of his church—the crown rights of the Redeemer—against the papacy, Erastianism, and divine right of kings. This has always been high doctrine in Scotland, not least in the later patronage controversies. Christ was likewise the *one Prophet* in the church, whose voice is heard in the preaching of the Word and in the councils of the church. *But what about the sole priesthood of Christ?* Over against Rome, like Calvin, they continued to expound the once and for all work of Christ in these terms, but unlike Calvin—perhaps out of fear of Roman practices or of prelacy—they did not work out any doctrine of the continuing sole priesthood of Christ as the heart of the worship life of the church. But had they done so, would this not have been the best theological answer to the very prelacy they so much dreaded? Would they not have preserved a better balance within worship between preaching, prayer, and praise?

Has it not constantly been the tendency of Scottish Presbyterians ever since to emphasize the prophetic ministry of Christ at the expense of the priestly? Precisely because *our* ministry is a participation in *Christ's* ministry, this has led to our emphasizing our *prophetic* ministry at the expense of our *priestly*.

Lost Emphasis We Need to Recover

This paper has been primarily a study of seventeenth-century theology. But I think it can be seen that this was the theology that was to mold Scottish church life for the next two centuries and its influence is with us still. It seems to me, theologically speaking, if we are to have a theology of worship in the Reformed tradition, we need to recover the New Testament understanding of priesthood at different levels.

(a) We need a recovery of the doctrine of the sole priesthood of Christ, (as indicated above). Worship is not so much something that *we* do, but what *Christ is doing* and in which we are given to participate through the Spirit. He is the one Mediator of all communion between God and man, who unites us with himself in his communion with the Father as we sing our psalms and offer our prayer and praise and meet at the table "in the name of Christ." The great strength of the Church of Rome in her misguided way is that she preserves the sense of mystery and objectivity in worship by the profound belief that Christ is exercising his priestly ministry in the Mass. Presbyterian worship today is often far more Pelagian than anything in Rome, by its all too exclusive emphases on what *we do*.

(b) We need a recovery of the doctrine of the priestly ministry of the Spirit. Christ as the one Mediator alone represents God to man and man to God. The Spirit as the Spirit of Christ is *speaking Spirit* and *interceding Spirit* (Rom 8). As speaking Spirit he mediates God's Word to men and summons us to faith and obedience. As interceding Spirit, he lifts us up into heavenly places in Christ. He puts the prayer of Jesus into our lips—"Abba, Father." He intercedes for us, helping our infirmities. God draws near to us in Christ through the Spirit, and we are drawn near to God through the blood of Christ by the Spirit. Perhaps in Presbyterianism we have emphasized speaking Spirit at the expense of the interceding Spirit. At the heart of all worship lies the doctrine of the third person of the Trinity—that our ascended Lord, by his Spirit poured out upon his church at Pentecost, lifts us up into his life of praise and communion with the Father—so that we know we are "lifted out of ourselves" into an objective world of worship and praise and prayer in communion with all saints.

(c) We need a recovery of the doctrine of the corporate priesthood of the church where together with all the saints in the name of Christ we bear the joys and the needs and sorrows of the world on our hearts before God in our worship, and wherein the name of Christ we represent God *to* the world in mission and in *diaconia*—participating in this twofold way in the twofold mediatorial ministry of Christ.

(d) We need a recovery of the priestly work of the ministry to complement our prophetic ministry, if we would understand aright both our pastoral office of shepherding the flock and ministering Christ and his forgiveness to the flock and our office as leaders of worship—not in any Pelagian Roman sense, but in the Reformed sense of sharing by grace in the one ministry of Christ, who is the one true *Leitourgos* within his church—the one true Leader of our worship.

Appendix B

The Contribution of McLeod Campbell to Scottish Theology

JAMES B. TORRANCE[1]

John McLeod Campbell died one hundred years ago, in February 1872, and hence it is fitting that at this time we consider the contribution and insight of one of the greatest (if not the greatest) of our Scottish theologians—whose voice we need to hear again today.

I suppose he is most widely known because of the General Assembly proceedings against him on the charge of heresy, which led to his deposition from the ministry of the Church of Scotland in 1831, and because of his book *The Nature of Atonement* (1856), which, with Athanasius' *De Incarnatione* and Anselm's *Cur Deus Homo*, is one of the classics of all time on this doctrine.

He was born in 1800 in Argyllshire, the son of a minister, educated in Glasgow University and Divinity Hall, and in May 1825 was presented by the Duke of Argyll to the Parish of Rhu (Row) in Dumbartonshire, where he spent the next five years as devoted pastor and preacher. It was

1. ©1973 *Scottish Journal of Theology*. Originally published in *Scottish Journal of Theology* 26.3 (1973) 295–311. Reprinted with permission.

while he was there that objections were made to his teaching on assurance, leading to charges being brought against him, and found proven, first by the Presbytery of Dumbarton in March 1831, then by the Synod of Glasgow and Ayr in April 1831, and finally by the General Assembly in May 1831—resulting in his disposition from the holy ministry.

The charges against him declared that:

> the doctrine of universal atonement and pardon through the death of Christ, as also the doctrine that assurance is of the essence of faith and necessary for salvation are contrary to the Holy Scripture and to the Confession of faith approven by the General Assemblies of the Church of Scotland, and ratified by the law in the year sixteen hundred and ninety: and were moreover condemned by the fifth act of the General Assembly held in seventeen hundred and twenty, as being directly opposed to the Word of God, and to the Confession of the Faith and Catechisms of the Church of Scotland.[2]

That is, he was charged with teaching two doctrines, "universal atonement" and "assurance of faith"—doctrines that were said to be contrary to Holy Scripture, the Westminster Confession of Faith, and the Act of the General Assembly of 1720 (condemning the teaching of the book *The Marrow of Modern Divinity*).

What was it that led him to assert these two doctrines? In his *Reminiscences and Reflections* he tells us that it was in the first instance the *pastoral situation* in which he found himself, the attitudes of his people, and their understanding of the Christian gospel. Secondly, it was certain aspects of federal Calvinism, which had come to be the orthodox view of the church, but which he felt were a departure from the teaching of the New Testament. It was the first (the religious attitude of the people) that led him to scrutinize the kind of Calvinism that had molded their thinking. We cannot read Campbell's writings without being aware that here is a godly man with the heart of a pastor and an evangelical concern to instruct his flock in the gospel of grace. His theology is one hammered out on the anvil of the parish ministry.

One of the first things he discovered in Rhu was his people's lack of any kind of Christian assurance. Whereas the New Testament rings with the note of assurance, and the imperatives of the gospel flow from the apostles' understanding of the indicatives of the gospel, among his people

2. *Proceedings* 1, 1.

he found little evidence of peace and joy and confidence in God. The more he thought about this, the more he became convinced it was due to a "legal strain" in their thinking that led to a want of true religion in the land. Although his people professed belief in the gospel, in fact he says—

> I came to see that, in reality, whatever I preached they were only hearing a *demand on them to be*—not hearing the Divine Secret of the Gospel as to how to be—*that which they were called to be.* Of this they themselves had no suspicions; they said, and honestly, that they did not question Christ's power to save, neither did they doubt the freeness of the Gospel of Christ's willingness to save them: *all their doubts were as to themselves.*[3]

In other words, deep in their thinking was a *doctrine of conditional grace*—"only if we do this, and don't do that, can we come to the enjoyment of salvation."

> This meant, it was clear, that between them and the comfort of the consciousness of a personal possession of Christ as Saviour they were vaguely conscious of a something by which they were to make Christ their own—a *condition* proposed to them, the consciousness of compliance with which would introduce them to the enjoyment of salvation. This is something they attempted to speak of as *repentance, faith*, or *love,* or "being good enough," which last expression gave really the secret of their difficulty. Christ was to be the reward of some goodness—not "perfect" goodness but some goodness that would sustain a personal hope of acceptance in drawing near to him. In this mind, the gospel was practically a law, and the call to trust in Christ only an addition to the demand that the law makes—an additional duty added to the obligation to love God and to love man, not the secret of the power to love God and to love man. Seeing this clearly, my labour was to fix their attention on the love of God revealed in Christ, and to get them into the mental attitude of looking at God to learn his feelings towards them, not at themselves, to consider their feelings towards him.[4]

That is, he made it his concern to summon them to look away from themselves—to the love of God, that they might know him as Father and discover there is forgiveness in God, and that God's grace, which certainly lays costly unconditional claims upon us, is not conditioned by

3. McLeod Campbell, *Reminiscences and Reflections*, 132.
4. Ibid., 132–33.

considerations of worth and merit. Repentance, faith, and love, are not conditions of grace, but our *response* to grace, and the way to evoke that response is to hold out to men the love of the Father, the grace of the Lord Jesus Christ, and the promises of the Spirit—and this is the road to *assurance*.

The other thing that led to his people's lack of assurance and joy was the high Calvinist doctrine of election, and a double decree—the doctrine that Christ did not die for all men, but only for some, the elect. Deep down, his people were tortured by the question, "Yes, Christ died upon the cross to bring forgiveness, but did he die for *me*? Am *I* one of the elect? Have *I* any grounds for believing that God loves me?" Consequently, they looked inward to see if they could to discern the fruits of faith—"evidences" of the work of the Spirit. Hadn't Jesus said, "By their fruits you shall know them"? The Calvinist preachers had taught them to *repent* of their sins, and that only if they came under deep conviction of sin, and renounced them, could they have grounds for claiming the blessings of the gospel, and believing they were among the elect. In other words, the doctrine of limited atonement, ploughed into a legalism, and an inward looking attitude which cut away the possibility of finding the "assurance of faith":

> This led [me] directly to the closer consideration of the *extent of the atonement*, and the circumstances in which mankind had been placed by the shedding of the blood of Christ; and it soon appeared to me manifest that unless Christ had died *for all*, and unless the Gospel announces him as *the gift of God to every human being*, so that there remained nothing to be done to give the individual a title to rejoice in Christ as his own Saviour, there was no foundation in the record of God for the Assurance which I demanded, and which I saw to be essential to true holiness. The next step, therefore, was my teaching (as the subject matter of the Gospel) Universal Atonement and pardon through the blood of Christ.[5]

Campbell saw that fundamental to the whole issue was the doctrine of God. Instead of thinking of God as the Father, who loves all men, and who in Christ gives us the gift of sonship, and who freely forgives us through Jesus Christ, they thought of God as one whose love is conditioned by human repentance and faith, and whose forgiveness had to be

---

5. Ibid., 24.

purchased by the payment of the sufferings of Christ on behalf of the elect. "Instead of resting in the character of God as revealed in Christ, they looked upon the death of Christ as so much suffering—the purchase money of heaven to a certain number, to whom it infallibly secured heaven."[6]

McLeod Campbell was disturbed at the fierce opposition to this teaching, and the false misrepresentation of his view as universalism, antinomianism, etc. "Such opposition made more and more apparent to me the want of true religion in the land." There was a loss of the gospel of grace. His teaching about assurance and universal atonement, led him consequently into conflict with federal Calvinism—as expounded in a mild form in the Westminster Confession of Faith, and as widely preached and taught Scotland.

What then is Federal Calvinism, and what are the features in it which, for Campbell, obscure the New Testament meaning of grace?

Federal Calvinism developed at the end of the sixteenth and particularly in the seventeenth century in England and Scotland—as well as in Holland and New England. It is the form of theology that gave central place to the concept of *covenant*, and that distinguished different covenants in God's relation to the world, and made out of them a framework within which all theology is cast. In particular, it made a hard and fast distinction between the so-called *covenant of works* and the *covenant of grace*.

According to this scheme, God made Adam the child of nature, who could discern the laws of nature by the light of reason. On the basis of this, he entered into a covenant or contract with him (the so-called covenant of works) that if he obeyed the laws of nature (which are the laws of God) and fulfilled the conditions of the covenant, he would find eternal life. This is the *foedus naturae*—the contract of nature upon which all society is based. Adam as such is not a private individual but the federal head of the race. Thus, when he disobeyed, he brought the curse not only on himself, but all for whom he contracted. But God in his sovereign grace does not destroy the human race, but elects out of the mass of fallen mankind a number for himself and makes a covenant of grace for them in Christ. God then calls the elect by his Spirit and brings them to saving faith by the instrumentality of Word and sacrament, the signs and seals of the covenant of grace.

6. Ibid., 25.

This distinction between a covenant of works and a covenant of grace was unknown to Calvin and the Reformers—nor indeed would Calvin have ever taught it. For Calvin there has been only one *eternal covenant of grace* promised in the Old Testament and fulfilled in Christ. "Old" and "New" do not mean two covenants, but two forms of the one eternal covenant—"God has never made any other covenant than that which he made formerly with Abraham" (Calvin on Jer 31:31–35).

The first person to use the phrase a "covenant of works" in Scotland was Robert Rollock, the first Principal of Edinburgh University, in a work published in 1596. It had already been used in England by the English Puritan, Dudley Fenner, about 1585, and by William Perkins in 1590. The Westminster Confession of Faith (with the Larger and Shorter Catechism) was the first reformed Confession to embody the federal scheme.

It is beyond my scope in this paper to expand on the theme of the rise and development of federal theology—but let me single out those features of it that are significant for our discussion here, and which led McLeod Campbell to break with the scheme.

1. The whole federal scheme is built upon the deep-seated confusion between *covenant* and a *contract*.[7] Whereas a covenant (theologically speaking) is a promise in which two people or two parties bind themselves to *love* one another *unconditionally* (as in the marriage covenant), a contract is a *legal* relationship in which two parties bind themselves together on mutual *conditions*—as in business and political contracts. No doubt a covenant and a contract mean the same thing in Scots law (e.g., "Deed of Covenant") but in theology they must be carefully distinguished. The God of the Bible, the God and Father of our Lord Jesus Christ is a covenant-God, and not a contract-god. God's covenant brings its promises, its obligations, and its warnings. But the obligations of grace are *not* conditions of grace, and it is false in Christian theology to articulate moral obligation in contractual terms. It is no accident that with the rise of federal theology, the *question of assurance* became a highly problematic one, as in the Marrow controversy in the early eighteenth century, when Thomas Boston wrote in his diary, "I perceived I had no fondness for the doctrine of the conditionality of the covenant of grace." Indeed Boston set out to reinterpret the federal scheme to show that the covenant of grace is an unconditional covenant of love made for the elect in Christ. But he still held to the doctrine of the covenant of works made with Adam.

7. Cf. Torrance, "Covenant or Contract?"

2. The federal scheme made a *radical dichotomy between the sphere of nature and the scheme of grace*, of natural law and gospel. All men by nature stand related to God, the contracting Sovereign, as to a *Judge*, under natural law and exposed to the sanctions of law. Only the elect are related to God by grace through Christ the Mediator. The relationship between church and the world, church and state, is no longer understood christologically, as by Calvin and Knox, but in terms of gospel and natural law. This separation between nature and grace amounts to a reversion to the pre-Reformation medieval view that grace presupposes nature—and *grace perfects nature*—a departure from the great emphasis of the Reformation that nothing is prior to grace.

3. Consequently, the federal scheme, with the doctrine of a double decree thrust up the doctrine of a *limited atonement*, that Christ only died for the elect—a doctrine or a conclusion unknown to Calvin. The consequence of this doctrine is twofold. (a) The doctrine implies a loss of the notion of Christ's headship over all creation as Mediator, his solidarity with all men as the Head of the race, as in the theology of the Ephesians and Colossians or as expounded by Irenaeus, Athanasius, and the Cappadocian divines, as well as by Calvin. The emphasis in doctrine is no longer on the incarnation, on Christ's solidarity with all men, but almost exclusively on Christ's *work* on behalf of the elect, his passive obedience on the cross and satisfaction for the sins of believers, with whom he stands related, not in terms of incarnational oneness—but of *foedus*, contract. As a consequence, the older doctrine, which interpreted faith in terms of "union with Christ the Head" and "participation" in Christ, is replaced by a more judicial interpretation of faith, as Thomas Boston also saw. (b) Limited atonement also means that you cannot say to all men unequivocally that "Christ died for you." But what you can say to all men is, that "You are all under the law, you are all guilty and under judgment." What you can then say to all men without exception is "Repent!" Then, if in fact they do repent, we can take that as *evidence* of election and grace, and then held out the comforts of the gospel! It was in these terms that Principal Hadow of St. Andrews attacked the Marrowmen who held that Christ should be offered freely to all, even if Christ did not die for all. Christ is God's deed of gift to all mankind. But, as the Marrowmen saw, his approach made forgiveness conditional on repentance, gave priority to the preaching of the law over the preaching of the gospel, and bred a deep lack of assurance. When the Marrowmen said that, they were condemned in 1720,

and in 1831 the General Assembly interpreted McLeod Campbell's views as a reassertion of those condemned in 1720.

4. In the federal scheme, the focus of attention moves away from *what Christ has done for us* and for all men to *what we have to do IF we would be* (or know that we are) in covenant with God. For preaching this means that the emphasis falls less on the indicatives of grace and more on the imperatives of repentance, obedience, and faith. Baptism and the Lord's Supper are seen, not so much as seals of the gospel (as evangelical ordinances or "converting ordinances," as interpreted, for example, by John Davidson of Prestonpans in the older tradition, an interpretation rejected by George Gillespie)—but rather as seals of *our faith*, or seals of *our repentance*. Where the shift of emphasis occurs, then sacraments become badges of *our* personal covenant and the Lord's Table becomes a feast of the converted, of the penitent. With the emergence of this changed emphasis, the fencing of the table and catechizing assume a different significance in the discipline of the church, as stressing the need for repentance and faith as *conditions* for coming to the Lord's Table.

In each of these four negative evaluations of the federal scheme, we can see an impoverishment and restriction of the concept of grace—a shift of emphasis from what God has so freely and unconditionally done for all men in Christ, to a more *subjective* interest in what *we* have to do—to our need for repentance, personal covenanting, obedience, subjective grounds for assurance—a preoccupation with election and the *evidences* of election.

We can begin to see something of McLeod Campbell's concern to reinterpret in more biblical and New Testament terms the meaning of grace as the Father's gift of his Son to the world, who on behalf of all men in our humanity has fulfilled for us all God's holy requirements, and in whose vicarious life and intercession we are freely given to participate through the Holy Spirit.

We can also see how McLeod Campbell was led to see that here was one of the *root* causes of the lack of joy and assurance in Scottish religion. Let me summarize his critique of Calvinism on this score.

1. He saw that the doctrine of a "limited atonement" destroyed the gospel offer to all men, and undermined the basis of the assurance of faith. The Marrowmen a century before, in their concern to recover the doctrine of the assurance of faith, had seen that the New Testament gives us a

warrant to offer the gospel to *all* men—to preach all grace to all. But they still held to the doctrine of the limited atonement in the federal scheme. McLeod Campbell came to see that you can only offer the gospel to all men if indeed it *is* good news for all men—that Christ died for all. Only then can we have an adequate ground for rejoicing in God and calling on our people to rejoice in God.

2. As we have seen, the doctrine of election—as so expounded—turns our attention away from God and Jesus Christ to *ourselves,* to the question of "evidences" and the consideration of our own repentance and faith and holiness as grounds for inference that we might be among the elect.

3. McLeod Campbell saw—as in his discussion of the views of Owen and Jonathan Edwards in *The Nature of the Atonement*—that the doctrine of God was at stake. In the federal scheme, the justice of God is the essential attribute, and the love of God (or mercy of God) is an arbitrary attribute. All men are necessarily related to God as Judge in the framework of law, but only the elect are related to God by his love and mercy. The demands of justice must be met before God can be merciful and this he does by providing one in Jesus who satisfies the demands of justice on behalf of the elect, in virtue of which there is forgiveness and salvation for these in whose stead Christ died.

This McLeod Campbell rejected. God is love as truly as he is just, and God is related to all men as Father in love as well as in justice. He saw that the doctrine of a limited atonement cuts away the basis of our assertion that *God is love*. It is a fundamental axiom in Christian theology, that what God is towards us he is eternally and antecedently in himself. So the early church rejected Sabellianism. Because God reveals himself to man as Father, Son, and Holy Spirit, he is Father, Son, and Holy Spirit himself. The doctrine of limited atonement runs into the same problems. God is loving towards some men but not towards other men. If so, there is an arbitrariness in God we have no warrant for believing that God is love *in himself.* We are left asking, "Yes, the Bible says God loves the world—but doesn't that mean the elect of all nations? Does he love *me*? Perhaps God in himself in the secret counsels of eternity is different to me from what he appears to be towards the elect." Consequently, we have no grounds in the fatherly heart of God for peace and assurance and for rejoicing in God. But this Campbell was convinced we do have in teaching of the New

Testament. Jesus the true Son of the Father has declared to *all men*, the love of the Father.

4. The federal scheme, in its doctrine of atonement and penal substitution (as expounded there) inverts the biblical order of the relationship between forgiveness and atonement. In the teaching of the Bible, *there is forgiveness in God our Father* who loves his world, and because there is forgiveness he offers us a way of atonement and propitiation in Christ to cover our sins. In the federal scheme, that order is inverted. There can only be forgiveness of sins for the elect when atonement has been first made—and, because of the priority of retributive justice, there must be an equivalence of sufferings in Christ to the sufferings due as the just penalty for the sins of the elect, before forgiveness can be held out to the elect as the *reward* for the sufferings of Christ. In other words, the Father has to be conditioned into being gracious by the obedience and the satisfaction of the Son—a view that Calvin in the *Institutes*, following St. Augustine, had explicitly rejected. Atonement, Calvin argued, flows from the loving, forgiving heart of the Father.[8] (The extreme form of this kind of Calvinism comes in the three-fold federal scheme—taught by S. Rutherford, Dickson, and Durham, and expounded in *The Sum of Saving Knowledge*.)

5. The federal scheme, with its priority of justice over love, consequently (McLeod Campbell argued) gives priority to the *judicial over the filial*. It comes to the New Testament, to the study of theology, with a prior framework—a set of doctrines about the nature of God, the nature of justice, the need for the penalties of the law being met as a condition of forgiveness—with the result that the *filial* categories, the filial purposes of the Father for mankind, are, if not eclipsed, pushed into the background, in a way that is not true to the New Testament. In the Bible, God is the Father who created men to be sons, and in order to fulfill his filial purpose for mankind, sends his Son to become our brother, to make the Father known to men, to lead men to the Father, and to give us the Spirit of adoption, the Spirit of his Son, whereby we cry, "Abba Father." God's end for man is that through the Holy Spirit we might participate in the Son's communion with the Father—which worship is—but to secure that end—to accomplish it—he provides a way of atonement. So in theology, Campbell argues, we must not think of incarnation as simply the

8. Calvin, *Inst.* 2.xvi.4.

necessary means toward atonement (for the sins of the elect, as in the federal scheme); but rather think of the atonement as securing the ends of the incarnation—the Father's filial purposes for men.

Traditional doctrines of atonement, McLeod Campbell argues, have limited themselves to the retrospective aspect of atonement (dealing with our guilty past) and have not given adequate consideration to the *prospective* aspect—"bringing many sons to glory." He often quotes Galatians 4:4: "In the fullness of time, God sent forth his Son, born of a woman, made under the law, that he might redeem those who are under the law *that we might receive the adoption of sons*. And because you are sons, God has sent forth the Spirit of his Son into your hearts crying 'Abba Father.'" Consequently in *The Nature of the Atonement*, he takes care to balance both the retrospective and the prospective. Christ takes away our past sins in order that he might fulfill his purpose of sharing his sonship.

What then is the nature of the atonement that God has provided for us in the person of his Son to secure his filial purposes for mankind? Campbell sees that the question of the *extent* of the atonement is bound up with the question of *nature of* the atonement. The doctrine of a limited atonement unfolded from certain views of its nature. So universal atonement, as he understands it, unfolds from a view of its nature.

The *twin* categories in terms of which he expounded its nature are (1) the *Father-Son relationship*, which we see in Jesus Christ, in whom the Eternal Son of God has become incarnate in time, and into whose communion with the Father we are called to participate by the Spirit in receiving eternal life; and (2) the *vicarious humanity of Jesus Christ*, in whom and through whom we come to know the Father and who in our name and on our behalf, in leading us to the Father, made the one true response to the Father in his whole life of filial obedience as well as in his sufferings and death upon the cross.

The coming of Jesus Christ is at once the coming of *God as God* and at the same time, the coming of *God as man* in our humanity. We do not know God as God apart from the humanity of Jesus Christ. But in the humanity of Jesus Christ, we come to know God. We come to know the Father, in the person of the incarnate Son. So McLeod Campbell focuses our attention, in a decidedly devotional and moving way on the whole history of the human Jesus. Jesus Christ has a double ministry of representing God to man, and representing man to God. There is a God-manward movement in Jesus Christ. God (and the kingdom of God) came in Jesus

Christ. But there is also a man-Godward movement (in worship, communion, prayer, loving trust, obedience, and in the self-offering of Jesus on behalf of the sins of the world). In Campbell's language, Christ deals with men on behalf of the Father, in making the Father and his loving judgments known to men; and Christ deals with the Father on behalf of men in a life of perfect acknowledgement and obedient submission to the loving judgment of God. It is in this latter context that McLeod Campbell made his famous statement about Jesus making "a perfect Amen in humanity to the judgment of God on the sin of man" and expounds what has come to be known (and which has been so often misunderstood) as the doctrine of *vicarious penitence.*[9]

What Was His Teaching about Vicarious Penitence?

To understand it aright, it seems to me we must see it:

1. First, in the total context of his understanding of the *vicarious humanity* of Jesus Christ—of the Son's oneness of mind with the Father's holy yet loving condemnation of our sins;

2. Secondly, against the background of Scottish theology and federal Calvinism. John Calvin, in the *Institutes* (Book Three) in his critique of the medieval sacrament of penance drew a distinction between *legal* repentance and *evangelical* repentance. *Legal* repentance said, "Repent, and if you repent, you will be forgiven!" This made the imperative prior to the indicative and made forgiveness conditional upon an adequate repentance. So the medieval world said that *if* the sinner is truly contrite, if he confesses his sins and makes due amends (*contritio, confessio, satisfactio*) then he may be forgiven and restored. This was the root of much of the medieval doctrine of merit. Calvin argued that this inverted the evangelical order of grace, and made repentance prior to forgiveness, whereas in the New Testament *forgiveness is logically prior to repentance. Evangelical repentance*, consequently, takes the form "Christ has borne your sins on the cross, therefore repent!" That is, repentance, Calvin argues, is our response to grace, not a condition of grace.

This same question became a living issue in Scotland 150 years after the Reformation, in the so-called "Marrow controversy," which is most

---

9. McLeod Campbell, *Nature of the Atonement*, chapter 6.

illuminating because it highlights some of the consequences of the rise of federal theology.

During the seventeenth century, a change began to take place in Scottish preaching, where a subtle kind of legalism began to creep in. The Scottish preacher preached the law in such a way that his concern was to produce a conviction of sin and fear of judgment, so that he could call upon the sinner to repent and renounce his sin that he might receive the word of forgiveness and hear the comforts of the gospel. This pattern became so widespread that many divines (Thomas Boston, Ralph and Ebenezer Erskine, Hog of Carnock, and others) began to see that it was producing a doctrine of conditional grace that was foreign to the gospel. But when they sought to bring the matter out into the open—appealing to this very distinction between legal and evangelical repentance as expounded in a puritan work called *The Marrow of Modern Divinity* (Edward Fisher, 1645), they ended by being condemned by the General Assembly of 1720—for teaching on these grounds, that *assurance is of the essence of faith.*

What did Calvin and the Marrowmen mean by saying that "forgiveness is logically prior to repentance"? Let me use an illustration. Suppose I had the misfortune to have a quarrel with someone, and the result was that we became estranged from one another. Then suppose after some time I came to my friend sincerely seeking reconciliation and said to him, "I forgive you!," it would be clear that this would be not only a word of *love*, it would be a word of *condemnation* for I would be clearly implying that he was the guilty party! How would he react? His immediate reaction would probably be one of indignation, for, sensing the element of judgment in my words, he might reject my word of forgiveness by refusing to *submit to the verdict of guilt implied in it.* He would be impenitent—there would be no "change of heart" towards me. But suppose on subsequent reflection, he comes back and says "I am sorry. I was quite wrong." That would mean, in accepting my approach of love and forgiveness, he would in the very act be submitting to the verdict of guilty. There would be a change of mind—an act of penitence on his part.

The good news of the gospel is that there is forgiveness with God, and he has spoken his word of forgiveness in Christ on the cross—a word of love to mankind, and yet also a word of judgment. But that word summons from us a response of faith and penitence. In accepting the forgiveness of the cross, we not only accept the gift of love, but in the very act know we are submitting to the verdict of guilty—acknowledging that it was our sins that put Christ on the cross. Before the cross, we know we are unconditionally summoned to renounce the sins for which Christ died. That is, God's forgiveness is logically prior to our repentance. It is the goodness of God that leads us to repentance. We might symbolize this in the following way.

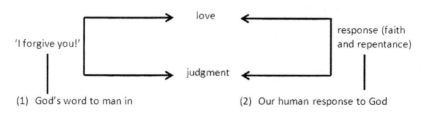

John McLeod Campbell grasped very vividly the significance of this understanding of forgiveness for his pastoral situation, but carried it further than the Marrowmen, working it out in terms of Christ's vicarious humanity.

1. On the one hand, God *has spoken* this word of forgiveness (of love and judgment) to the world in Jesus Christ. So Jesus Christ lived a life of real *oneness of mind with the Father*, when in the course of his whole life on earth, he made the Father's love and the Father's holy condemnation of sin known to men. That in itself meant suffering, and in the sufferings of Jesus, we see the sufferings of the Father, in *his dealings with men on behalf of the Father*.

2. But Jesus Christ does not merely represent God to men in bringing God's word of forgiveness to men (dealing with men on behalf of the Father). He also represents *men to God*, and *deals with the Father on behalf of men*—as our great High Priest, our Intercessor. So as man, his whole life of sonship is a perfect *response on our behalf to the Father*, as the well-beloved Son in whom the Father is well pleased—a response that is at once one of perfect trust in the Father's love and at the same time one of *perfect submission on our behalf to the verdict of guilty* (yet "without any personal consciousness of sin").

> That oneness with the Father, which towards man took the form
> of condemnation of sin, would in the Son's dealing with the

> Father in relation to our sins, take the form of a perfect confession of our sins. This confession as to its own nature must have been *a perfect Amen in humanity to the judgment of God on the sin of men.* ... He responds (to the divine wrath) with a perfect response—a response from the depths of that divine humanity—and *in that perfect response He absorbs it.* For that response has all the elements of a perfect repentance in humanity for all the sins of man—a perfect sorrow—a perfect contrition—all the elements of such a repentance, and that in absolute perfection, all—*excepting the personal consciousness of sin;*—and by that perfect response in Amen to the mind of God in relation to sin is the wrath of God rightly met, and that is accorded to divine justice which is its due, and could alone satisfy it.[10]

Very movingly, McLeod Campbell interprets the once and for all vicarious humanity of Christ and the continuing vicarious humanity of Christ under the category of *prayer*, seeing the whole ministry of Jesus in dealing with the Father on behalf of men in these terms, presenting us to the Father as God's dear children.

Does the vicarious response of Jesus Christ offered to the Father on our behalf then eliminate the need for a response on our part? Not at all. Conversely, it gives us a basis for a joyful response of praise and gratitude and trust and love—a basis for worship, where our response is the gift of participating by the Spirit in the Son's self-offering on our behalf to the Father. When we realize that Christ bore our sins in his own body on the tree and submitted *for us* to the verdict of guilty, *then* we know we are unconditionally summoned to personal repentance and faith.

Participation is consequently a key word in McLeod Campbell's theology. The Son of God has participated in our humanity, that through the Spirit we might participate in his Sonship and communion with the Father. Participation is what *we* do—we pray, we repent, we believe, we worship—but only in the sense of participating in what *Christ* has done and is doing. In this way, faith and repentance and prayer are *not conditions* of grace, but the gift of the Spirit of sonship who so unites us with Christ in his communion with the Father that we might have a ground for rejoicing in God.

We can see therefore how McLeod Campbell develops the concept of "evangelical repentance" as expounded by Calvin and the Marrowmen, and interprets it in terms of Christ's vicarious humanity—of his

10. McLeod Campbell, *Nature of Atonement*, 135–36.

twofold mission of representing God to men and men to God—in order to eliminate any notion of conditional grace, and interpret the gospel in New Testament terms as good news for all in the gift of Jesus Christ to the world. One of his favorite tests is "God has given to us eternal life, and this life is in his Son. He who has the Son has life; and he who has not the Son has not life" (1 John 5:11–12).

We might therefore expand the above model to summarize McLeod Campbell's understanding of atonement and vicarious penitence, in those terms.

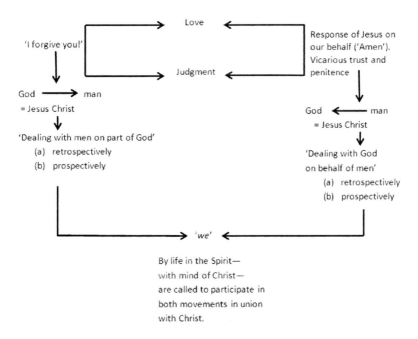

Thus, if following Calvin and Marrowmen, he interprets "evangelical repentance" to mean "forgiveness, therefore repentance" (and NOT "repentance, therefore forgiveness"), in terms of his doctrine of atonement he sees with Augustine and Calvin that the order is "forgiveness, therefore atonement" (and NOT "atonement, therefore forgiveness," as in certain types of Western penal satisfaction theories). In his own language, the filial is prior to the judicial, NOT the judicial prior to the filial.

Bibiography

Adamantius. *Dialogue on the True Faith in God: De Recta in Deum Fide.* Translated by Robert A. Pretty. Leuven: Peeters, 1997.

Anatolios, Khaled. *Athanasius: The Coherence of His Thought.* London: Routledge, 1998.

———. *Retrieving Nicaea: The Development and Meaning of Trinitarian Doctrine.* Grand Rapids: Baker Academic, 2011.

Anselm of Canterbury. *The Major Works.* Edited by Brian Davies and G. R. Evans. Oxford: Oxford University Press, 2008.

Athanasius. *On the Incarnation.* Crestwood, NY: St. Vladimir's, 1944.

Austin, J. L. *How to Do Things with Words.* Cambridge: Harvard University Press, 1962.

Ayres, Lewis. *Nicaea and Its Legacy: An Approach to Fourth-Century Trinitarian Theology.* Oxford: Oxford University Press, 2004.

Baldwin, Barry. *Studies in Lucian.* Toronto: Hakkert, 1973.

Barclay, John M. G. *Jews in the Mediterranean Diaspora: From Alexander to Trajan (323 BCE–117 CE).* Edinburgh: T. & T. Clark, 1996.

———. "Mirror-Reading a Polemical Letter: Galatians as a Test Case." *Journal for the Study of the New Testament* 31 (1987) 73–93.

Barker, Margaret. *The Great Angel: A Study of Israel's Second God.* London: SPCK, 1992.

———. "The High Priest and the Worship of Jesus." In *The Jewish Roots of Christological Monotheism,* edited by C. C. Newman, J. R. Davila, and G. S. Lewis, 93–111. Leiden: Brill, 1999.

Barnett, Paul. *The Second Epistle to the Corinthians.* Grand Rapids: Eerdmans, 1997.

Barr, James. *The Semantics of Biblical Language.* Oxford: Oxford University Press, 1961.

Barrett, C. K. *The Second Epistle to the Corinthians.* London: Black, 1973.

Barth, Karl. *Church Dogmatics.* 4 vols. in 13 parts. Edited by T. F. Torrance and G. W. Bromiley. Edinburgh: T. & T. Clark, 1956–77.

———. *The Epistle to the Romans.* 6th ed. London: Oxford University Press, 1977.

———. *God Here and Now.* With a new introduction by George Hunsinger. Routledge Classics. London: Routledge, 1964.

———. *The Humanity of God.* Richmond, VA: John Knox, 1960.

———. "No!" (1934) In *Natural Theology,* edited by G. Bromiley and translated by P. Fraenkel, 67–128. London: Centenary, 1946.

Basil of Caesarea. *Against Eunomius.* Translated by M. DelCogliano and A. Radde-Gallwitz. In *The Fathers of the Church* 122. Washington, DC: Catholic University of America Press, 2009.

Bassler, Jouette M. "God in the NT." In *The Anchor Bible Dictionary,* edited by David Noel Freedman, 2:1049–55. New York: Doubleday, 1992.

Bauckham, Richard. "Biblical Theology and the Problems of Monotheism." In *Out of Egypt: Biblical Theology and Biblical Interpretation*, edited by Craig Bartholomew, Mary Healy, Karl Möller, and Robin Parry, 187–232. Milton Keynes, UK: Paternoster, 2004.

———. *God Crucified: Monotheism and Christology in the New Testament.* Carlisle, UK: Paternoster, 1998.

———. *God and the Crisis of Freedom: Biblical and Contemporary Perspectives.* Louisville: Westminster John Knox, 2002.

———. *Jesus and the God of Israel.* Milton Keynes, UK: Paternoster, 2008.

———. "The Worship of Jesus in Apocalyptic Christianity." *New Testament Studies* 27 (1981) 322–41.

Bauman, Richard. "Verbal Art as Performance." *American Anthropologist* 77 (1975) 290–311.

Baur, Ferdinand Christian. *Paul the Apostle of Jesus Christ: His Life and Works, His Epistles and Teachings.* 2nd ed. 1845. Reprint. London: Williams and Norgate, 2003.

Beeley, Christopher A. *Gregory of Nazianzus on the Trinity and the Knowledge of God: In Your Light We Shall See Light.* New Haven, CT: Yale University Press, 2008.

Begbie, Jeremy S. "Room of One's Own? Music, Theology and Freedom." In *Music, Modernity and God: Essays in Listening.* Oxford: Oxford University Press, Forthcoming 2014.

———. *Theology, Music, and Time.* Cambridge Studies in Christian Doctrine. Cambridge: Cambridge University Press, 2000.

Behr, John. *The Nicene Faith*, vol. 1 Crestwood, NY: Saint Vladimir's, 2004.

Beilby, James K., and Paul R. Eddy, editors. *Justification: Five Views.* Spectrum Multiview Books. Downers Grove, IL: InterVarsity Academic, 2011.

Beker, J. Christiaan. *Paul the Apostle: The Triumph of God in Life and Thought.* Philadelphia: Fortress, 1980.

———. *Paul the Apostle: The Triumph of God in Life and Thought.* 2nd ed. Philadelphia: Fortress, 1984.

Bentley, Richard. *Bentleii Critica Sacra.* Edited by Arthur Ayers Ellis. Cambridge: Deighton, Bell, and Co., 1862.

———. *The Correspondence of Richard Bentley, D.D.*, 2 vols. London: John Murray, 1842.

Betz, Hans Dieter. *Galatians: A Commentary on Paul's Letter to the Churches in Galatia.* Hermeneia. Philadelphia: Fortress, 1979.

Bird, Michael F., and James G. Crossley. *How Did Christianity Begin? A Believer and Non-Believer Examine the Evidence.* London: SPCK, 2008.

Bird, Michael F., and Preston M. Sprinkle, editors. *The Faith of Jesus Christ: Exegetical, Biblical, and Theological Studies.* Milton Keynes, UK: Paternoster, 2010.

Blondell, Ruby. *The Play of Character in Plato's Dialogues.* Cambridge: Cambridge University Press, 2005.

Boegehold, Alan L. *When a Gesture Was Expected: A Selection of Examples from Archaic and Classical Greek Literature.* Princeton: Princeton University Press, 1999.

Bonhoeffer, Dietrich. *The Cost of Discipleship.* New York: Macmillan, 1976.

Boston, Thomas, and George D. Low. *A General Account of My Life.* Edinburgh: Hodder and Stoughton, 1908.

Bousset, Wilhelm. *Kyrios Christos: A History of Belief in Christ from the Beginnings of Christianity to Irenaeus.* 1970. Reprint. Waco, TX: Baylor University Press, 2013.

Bowler, Kate. *Blessed: A History of the American Prosperity Gospel.* Oxford: Oxford University Press, 2013.

Boyarin, Daniel. *Border Lines: The Partition of Judaeo-Christianity.* Divinations: Rereading Late Ancient Religion. Philadelphia: University of Pennsylvania Press, 2004.

Braund, Susan H. *Beyond Anger: A Study of Juvenal's Third Book of Satires.* Cambridge Classical Studies. Cambridge: Cambridge University Press, 1988.

Braund, Susanna Morton. *The Roman Satirists and Their Masks.* London: British Classical, 1996.

Brown, Alexander. *The Cross and Human Transformation.* Minneapolis: Fortress, 1995.

Brown, John. *Gospel Truth Stated and Vindicated.* Glasgow: Blackie, Fullarton, 1831.

Bruce, F. F. *The Epistle to the Galatians: A Commentary on the Greek Text.* New International Greek Testament Commentary. Grand Rapids: Eerdmans, 1982.

Brueggemann, Walter. *Theology of the Old Testament: Testimony, Dispute, Advocacy.* Minneapolis: Fortress, 1998.

Bruun, Christer. "Water for Roman Brothels: Cicero 'Cael.' 34." *Phoneix* 51.3 (1997) 364–73.

Buber, Martin. *Moses.* London: East and West Library, 1946.

Buckley, Michael J. *At the Origins of Modern Atheism.* New Haven, CT: Yale University Press, 1987.

Bultmann, Rudolf. *What is Theology?* Edited by Eberhard Jüngel and Klaus W. Müller. Translated by Roy A. Harrisville. Fortress Texts in Modern Theology. Minneapolis: Fortress, 1997.

Burton, Ernest de Witt. *A Critical and Exegetical Commentary on the Epistle to the Galatians.* International Critical Commentary. Edinburgh: T. & T. Clark, 1920.

Busch, Eberhard. *Karl Barth: His Life from Letters and Autobiographical Texts.* Translated by J. Bowden. Philadelphia: Fortress, 1976.

Calvin, John. *Commentaries on the Book of the Prophet Jeremiah and the Lamentations.* Vol. 4. Translated and edited by John Owen. Edinburgh: Calvin Translation Society, 1854.

———. *Institutes of the Christian Religion,* 2 vols. Philadelphia: Westminster, 1960.

Campbell, Douglas. "An Attempt to be Understood: A Response to the Concerns of Matlock and Macaskill with *The Deliverance of God.*" *Journal for the Study of the New Testament* 34 (2011) 162–208.

———. *The Deliverance of God: An Apocalyptic Rereading of Justification in Paul.* Grand Rapids: Eerdmans, 2009.

———. "An Echo of Scripture in Paul, and Its Implications." In *The Word Leaps the Gap: Essays on Scripture and Theology in Honor of Richard B. Hays,* edited by J. R. Wagner, C. K. Rowe, and A. K. Grieb, 367–391. Grand Rapids: Eerdmans, 2008.

———. *The End of Religion: A Theological Reading of Romans.* Grand Rapids: Eerdmans, Forthcoming.

———. "An Evangelical Paul: A Response to Francis Watson's *Paul and the Hermeneutics of Faith.*" *Journal for the Study of the New Testament* 28.3 (2006) 337–51.

———. "The Faithfulness of Jesus Christ in Romans 3:22." In *The Faith of Jesus Christ: Exegetical, Biblical, and Theological Studies,* edited by Michael F. Bird and Preston M. Sprinkle, 57–71. Milton Keynes, UK: Paternoster, 2009.

———. *Framing Paul: An Epistolary Account*. Grand Rapids: Eerdmans, Forthcoming 2014.

———. "Is Tom Right? An Extended Review of N. T. Wright's Justification: God's Plan and Paul's Vision." *Scottish Journal of Theology* 65.3 (2012) 323–45.

———. "Paul's Apocalyptic Politics." *Pro Ecclesia* 22.2 (2013) 129–52.

———. *The Quest for Paul's Gospel*. London: T. & T. Clark, 2005.

———. "The Story of Jesus in Romans and Galatians." In *Narrative Dynamics in Paul: A Critical Assessment*, edited by B. W. Longenecker, 97–124. Louisville: Westminster John Knox, 2002.

———. "What Is at Stake in the Reading of Romans 1–3?: An Elliptical Response to the Concerns of Gorman and Tilling." *Journal for the Study of Paul and His Letters* 1 (2011) 113–37.

Campbell, John McLeod. *The Nature of Atonement and Its Relation to Remission of Sins and Eternal Life*. 4th ed. London: James Clarke, 1959.

———. *Reminiscences and Reflections, Referring to His Early Ministry in the Parish of Row, 1825–31*. Edited, with an introductory narrative by his son, Donald Campbell. London: Macmillan and Co., 1873.

Capes, David B. *Old Testament Yahweh Texts in Paul's Christology*. Tübingen: Mohr Siebeck, 1992.

Carter, J. Kameron. *Race: A Theological Account*. Oxford: Oxford University Press, 2008.

Casey, Maurice. *From Jewish Prophet to Gentile God: The Origins and Development of New Testament Christology*. Cambridge: James Clarke, 1991.

———. "Monotheism, Worship and Christological Developments in the Pauline Churches." In *The Jewish Roots of Christological Monotheism*, edited by C. C. Newman, J. R. Davila, and G. S. Lewis, 214–33. Leiden: Brill, 1999.

Chalke, Steve, and Alan Mann. *The Lost Message of Jesus*. Grand Rapids: Zondervan, 2003.

Chester, Andrew. *Messiah and Exaltation: Jewish Messianic and Visionary Traditions and New Testament Christology*. Wissenschaftliche Untersuchungen Zum Neuen Testament. Tübingen: Mohr Siebeck, 2007.

Choi, Hung-Sik. "ΠΙΣΤΙΣ in Galatians 5:5–6: Neglected Evidence for the Faithfulness of Christ." *Journal of Biblical Literature* 124.3 (2005) 467–90.

Clay, Diskin. *Platonic Questions: Dialogues with the Silent Philosopher*. University Park, PA: Pennsylvania State University Press, 2000.

Cousar, Charles B. "Major Book Review." *Interpretation* 64 (2010) 414–16.

Cranfield, C. E. B. *A Critical and Exegetical Commentary on the Epistle to the Romans*. International Critical Commentary. 1974. Reprint. London: T. & T. Clark, 2003.

Cremer, Hermann. *Paulinische Rechtfertigungslehre im Zusammenhange ihrer geschichtlichen Voraussetzungen*. Gütersloh: Bertelsmann, 1900.

Crossley, James G. *Reading the New Testament: Contemporary Approaches*. London: Routledge, 2010.

Cyril of Alexandria. *Commentary on the Gospel according to S John*. 2 Vols. Translated by Philip E. Pusey and Thomas Randell. Oxford: J. Parker, 1874, 1885.

———. *Cyrilli archiepiscopi Alexandrini in D. Joannis Evangelium*. 3 vols. Edited by Philip E. Pusey. Oxford: Clarendon, 1873.

De Boer, Martinus C. *The Defeat of Death: Apocalyptic Eschatology in 1 Corinthians 15 and Romans 5*. Journal for the Study of the New Testament. Supplement Series 22. Sheffield, UK: JSOT, 1988.

———. "Paul and Apocalyptic Eschatology." In *The Encyclopedia of Apocalypticism, Vol. 1: The Origins of Apocalypticism in Judaism and Christianity*, edited by J. J. Collins, 345–83. New York: Continuum, 1998.

———. "Paul, Theologian of God's Apocalypse." *Interpretation* 56 (2002) 21–33.

Daube, David. *The New Testament and Rabbinic Judaism*. London: Athlone, 1956.

Deddo, Gary W. *Karl Barth's Theology of Relations: Trinitarian, Christological, and Human: Towards an Ethic of the Family*. New York: Lang, 1999.

Deissmann, A. *Saint Paul: A Study in Social and Religious History*. London: Hodder & Stoughton, 1912.

Derrida, Jacques. *Of Grammatology*. Baltimore, MD: Johns Hopkins University Press, 1976.

Dibelius, Martin. *Geisterwelt im Glauben des Paulus*. Göttingen: Vandenhoeck und Reuprecht, 1909.

Dunn, James D. G. *The Christ and the Spirit: Collected Essays of James D. G. Dunn*. Grand Rapids: Eerdmans, 1998.

———. *Christology in the Making: A New Testament Inquiry into the Origins of the Doctrine of the Incarnation*. London: SCM, 1989.

———. *Did the First Christians Worship Jesus?: The New Testament Evidence*. London: SPCK, 2010.

———. *The Theology of Paul the Apostle*. Grand Rapids: Eerdmans, 1998.

———. "Was Christianity a Monotheistic Faith from the Beginning?" 1982. Reprinted in *The Christ and the Spirit: Christology*, 315–44. Edinburgh: T. & T. Clark, 1998.

———. "When Was Jesus First Worshipped? In Dialogue with Larry Hurtado's *Lord Jesus Christ: Devotion to Jesus in the Earliest Christianity*." *Expository Times* 116.6 (2005) 193–96.

Eco, Umberto. *A Theory of Semiotics*. Bloomington, IN: Indiana University Press, 1976.

Eichrodt, Walther. *Theology of the Old Testament. Vol. 1.* Translated by J. A. Baker. Philadelphia: Westminster John Knox, 1961.

Eisenbaum, Pamela. *Paul Was Not a Christian: The Original Message of a Misunderstood Apostle*. New York: HarperOne, 2009.

Elliott, Neil. *The Arrogance of Nations: Reading Romans in the Shadow of Empire*. Paul in Critical Contexts. Minneapolis: Fortress, 2008.

Erickson, Millard J. *God in Three Persons: A Contemporary Interpretation of the Trinity*. Grand Rapids: Baker, 1995.

———. *Who's Tampering with the Trinity?: An Assessment of the Subordination Debate*. Grand Rapids: Kregel, 2009.

Eriksson, Anders. *Traditions as Rhetorical Proof: Pauline Argumentation in 1 Corinthians*. Stockholm: Almqvist & Wiksell, 1998.

Esler, Philip. *Conflict and Identity in Romans*. Minneapolis: Augsburg Fortress, 2003.

Evans, G. R. *The Language and Logic of the Bible: The Road to Reformation*. Cambridge: Cambridge University Press, 1985.

Fairbairn, Donald. *Life in the Trinity: An Introduction to Theology with the Help of the Church Fathers*. Downers Grove, IL: InterVarsity, 2009.

Farmer, W. R. et al., editors. *Christian History and Interpretation: Studies Presented to John Knox*. Cambridge: Cambridge University Press, 1967.

Fatehi, Mehrdad. *The Spirit's Relation to the Risen Lord in Paul: An Examination of Its Christological Implications*. Tübingen: Mohr Siebeck, 2000.

Fee, Gordon D. *The First Epistle to the Corinthians*. New International Commentary on the New Testament. Grand Rapids: Eerdmans, 1987.

———. *Pauline Christology: An Exegetical-Theological Study*. Peabody, MA: Hendrickson, 2007.

Finney, Charles G. *Memoirs of Rev. Charles G. Finney*. New York: Barnes, 1876.

Fitzmyer, Joseph A. *First Corinthians*. Anchor Bible. New Haven, CT: Yale University Press, 2008.

Forde, Gerhard O. *The Captivation of the Will: Luther vs. Erasmus on Freedom and Bondage*. Edited by Paul Rorem. Lutheran Quarterly Books. Grand Rapids: Eerdmans, 2005.

———. *Justification by Faith: A Matter of Death and Life*. Philadelphia: Fortress, 1982.

Forsyth, P. T. *God the Holy Father*. 1897. Reprint. London: Independent, 1957.

Fotopoulos, John. *Food Offered to Idols in Roman Corinth: A Social-Rhetorical Reconsideration of 1 Corinthians 8:1—11:1*. Tübingen: Mohr Siebeck, 2003.

Frankenmölle, H. *Das Taufverständnis des Paulus: Taufe, Tod und Auferstehung nach Röm 6*. Stuttgarter Bibelstudien 47. Suttgart: Katholisches Bibelwerk, 1970.

Fredriksen, Paula. "Mandatory Retirement: Ideas in the Study of Christian Origins Whose Time Has Come to Go." In *Israel's God and Rebecca's Children: Essays in Honor of Larry W. Hurtado and Alan F. Segal*, edited by David B. Capes, April DeConick, Helen Bond, and Troy Miller, 25–38. Waco, TX: Baylor, 2007.

Gadamer, Hans-Georg. *Philosophical Hermeneutics*. Translated by David Linge. 1976. Reprint. Berkeley: University of California Press, 2008.

———. *Truth and Method*. Translated by Joel Weinsheimer and Donald G. Marshall. 1960. Reprint. London: Bloomsbury Academic, 2004.

Gardiner, Alan H. *Egyptian Hieratic Texts. Series I: Literary Texts of the New Kingdom. Part I, the Papyrus Anastasi I and the Papyrus Koller, together with the parallel texts*. Leipzig: Hinrichs, 1911.

Garland, David E. *1 Corinthians*. Grand Rapids: Baker, 2003.

Gaventa, Beverly Roberts. "The Cosmic Power of Sin in Paul's Letter to the Romans." In *Our Mother Saint Paul*, 125–36. Louisville: Westminster John Knox, 2007.

———. "'For the Glory of God': Learning the Future of the Church from Paul." In *Calvin Today: Reformed Theology and the Future of the Church*, edited by M. Welker, M. Weinrich, and U. Möller, 6–14. London: T. & T. Clark, 2011.

———. "From Toxic Speech to the Redemption of Doxology in Paul's Letter to the Romans." In *The Word Leaps the Gap: Essays on Scripture and Theology in Honor of Richard B. Hays*, edited by J. R. Wagner, C. K. Rowe, and A. K. Grieb, 392–408. Grand Rapids: Eerdmans, 2008.

———. "God Handed Them Over." 2005. Reprinted in *Our Mother Saint Paul*, 113–23. Louisville: Westminster John Knox, 2007.

———. "Interpreting the Death of Jesus Apocalyptically: Reconsidering Romans 8:32." In *Jesus and Paul Reconnected: Fresh Pathways into an Old Debate*, edited by T. D. Still, 125–45. Grand Rapids: Eerdmans, 2007.

———. "Maternal Imagery in Its Cosmic and Apocalyptic Context." In *Our Mother Saint Paul*, 79–84. Louisville: Westminster John Knox, 2007.

———. "'Neither Height nor Depth': Cosmos and Soteriology in Paul's Letter to the Romans." In *Apocalyptic and the Future of Theology: With and Beyond J. Louis Martyn*, edited by J. B. Davis and D. Harink, 185–201. Eugene, OR: Cascade, 2012.

———. *Our Mother Saint Paul*. Louisville: Westminster John Knox, 2007.

———. "Paul and the Roman Believers." In *The Blackwell Companion to Paul*, edited by Stephen Westerholm, 93–107. Malden, MA: Wiley-Blackwell, 2011.

———. "Rescue Mission: A Review of *Deliverance of God: An Apocalyptic Rereading of Justification in Paul* by Douglas A. Campbell." *Christian Century* 127 (2010) 36–37.

———. "The Rhetoric of Violence and the God of Peace in Paul's Letter to the Romans." In *The Armor of Light*, forthcoming.

———. "'To Preach the Gospel': Romans 1,15 and the Purposes of Romans." In *The Letter to the Romans*, edited by U. Schnelle, 179–95. Bibliotheca Ephemeridum Theologicarum Lovaniensium 226. Leuven: Peeters, 2009.

Gäckle, Volker. *Die Starken und die Schwachen in Korinth und in Rom: Zu Herkunft und Funktion der Antithese in 1 Kor 8,1—11,1 und Röm 14,1—15,13*. Tübingen: Mohr Siebeck, 2005.

George, Timothy, editor. *Evangelicals and Nicene Faith: Reclaiming the Apostolic Witness*. Grand Rapids: Baker Academic, 2011.

Genette, Gérard. *Palimpsests*. Translated by Channa Newman and Claude Donbinsky. 1982. Reprint. Lincoln, NE: University of Nebraska Press, 1997.

Giblin, Charles H. "Three Monotheistic Texts in Paul." *Catholic Biblical Quarterly* 37 (1975) 527–47.

Gorman, Michael. "Douglas Campbell's *The Deliverance of God*: A Review by a Friendly Critic." *Journal for the Study of Paul and His Letters* 1 (2011) 99–107.

———. *Inhabiting the Cruciform God: Kenosis, Justification, and Theosis in Paul's Narrative Soteriology*. Grand Rapids: Eerdmans, 2009.

Gorringe, Timothy. *God's Just Vengeance: Crime, Violence, and the Rhetoric of Salvation*. Cambridge: Cambridge University Press, 1996.

Gough, John W. *The Social Contract: A Critical Study of Its Development*. Oxford: Clarendon, 1936.

Graber, Jennifer. *The Furnace of Affliction: Prisons & Religion in Antebellum America*. Chapel Hill, NC: University of North Carolina Press, 2011.

Grace Communion International. "Statement of Beliefs." Online: http://www.gci.org/aboutus/beliefs. Accessed 10th December 2011.

———. "You're Included—Douglas Campbell: Our Participation with Christ." Interview at http://www.gci.org/yi/campbell97. Accessed 10th December 2011.

Gregory of Nazianzus. *Oration* 28. Translated by L. Wickham in *On God and Christ*. Crestwood, NY: St. Vladimir's Seminary Press, 2002.

Grenz, Stanley J. *The Named God and the Question of Being: A Trinitarian Theo-Ontology*. Louisville: Westminster John Knox, 2005.

———. *Rediscovering the Triune God: The Trinity in Contemporary Theology*. Minneapolis: Fortress, 2004.

———. *The Social God and the Relational Self: A Trinitarian Theology of the Imago Dei*. Louisville: Westminster John Knox, 2001.

Griffith-Jones, Robin. "'Keep up your Transformation in the Renewal of the Mind': Romans as a Therapeutic Letter." In *Experientia II*, edited by Rodney Werline, 137–60. Atlanta: SBL, 2012.

Grillmeier, Aloys. *From the Apostolic Age to Chalcedon (451)*. Vol. 1 of *Christ in Christian Tradition*. 2nd ed. Translated by John Bowden. Atlanta: John Knox, 1975.

Giles, Kevin. *Jesus and The Father: Modern Evangelicals Reinvent the Doctrine of the Trinity*. Grand Rapids: Zondervan, 2006.

————. *The Trinity & Subordinationism: The Doctrine of God & the Contemporary Gender Debate.* Downers Grove, IL: InterVarsity, 2002.

Gunton, Colin E. *A Brief Theology of Revelation.* London: T. & T. Clark, 1995.

————. *Enlightenment and Alienation: An Essay Towards a Trinitarian Theology.* Grand Rapids: Eerdmans, 1985.

Hafemann, Scott. "The Covenant Relationship." In *Central Themes in Biblical Theology: Mapping Unity in Diversity,* edited by Scott J. Hafemann and Paul R. House, 20–65. Grand Rapids: Baker, 2007.

————. *The God of Promise and the Life of Faith.* Wheaton: Crossway, 2001.

————. "'The 'Righteousness of God': An Introduction to the Theological and Historical Foundation of Peter Stuhlmacher's *Biblical Theology of the New Testament.*" In *How to do Biblical Theology,* edited by Peter Stuhlmacher, xv–xli. Princeton Theological Monograph Series 38. Allison Park, PA: Pickwick, 1995.

————. "The (Un)Conditionality of Salvation: The Theological Logic of 2 Peter 1:8–10a." In *Getting "Saved": The Whole Story of Salvation in the New Testament,* edited by Charles H. Talbert and Jason A. Whitlark, 240–62. Grand Rapids: Eerdmans, 2011.

Hanson, R. P. C. *The Search for the Christian Doctrine of God.* London: T. & T. Clark, 1988.

Harink, Douglas. *Paul among the Postliberals: Pauline Theology beyond Christendom and Modernity.* Grand Rapids: Brazos, 2003.

————. "Time and Politics in Four Commentaries on Romans." In *Paul, Philosophy, and the Theopolitical Vision: Critical Engagements with Agamben, Badiou, Žižek and Others,* edited by Douglas Harinck, 282–312. Theopolitical Vision. Eugene, OR: Cascade, 2010.

Harris, Murray J. *The Second Epistle to the Corinthians.* New International Greek Testament Commentary. Grand Rapids: Eerdmans, 2005.

Harris, William V. *Ancient Literacy.* Cambridge: Harvard University Press, 1989.

Hart, David Bentley. *Atheist Delusions: The Christian Revolution and Its Fashionable Enemies.* New Haven, CT : Yale University Press, 2009.

Hartwig, Charlotte, and Gerd Theissen. "Die Korinthische Gemeinde als Nebenadressat des Romerbriefs. Eigentextreferenzen des Paulus und kommunikativer Kontext des längsten Paulusbriefes." *Novum Testamentum* 46 (2004) 229–52.

Harvey, A. E. *Jesus and the Constraints of History.* London: Duckworth, 1982.

Harvey, Lincoln. "The Double *Homoousion*: Forming the Content of Gunton's Theology." In *The Theology of Colin Gunton,* edited by Lincoln Harvey, 86–99. London: T. & T. Clark, 2010.

Hatch, Nathan. *The Democratization of American Christianity.* New Haven, CT: Yale University Press, 1991.

Hauerwas, Stanley. *After Christendom? How the Church Is to Behave If Freedom, Justice, and a Christian Nation Are Bad Ideas.* Nashville: Abingdon, 1991.

————. "Seeing Darkness, Hearing Silence: Augustine's Account of Evil." In *Working with Words: On Learning to Speak Christian.* Eugene, OR: Cascade, 2011.

Hauerwas, Stanley, and William H. Willimon. *Where Resident Aliens Live: Exercises for Christian Practice.* Nashville: Abingdon, 1996.

Hays, Richard B. *Echoes of Scripture in the Letters of Paul.* New Haven. CT: Yale University Press, 1989.

————. *The Faith of Jesus Christ: An Investigation of the Narrative Substructure of Galatians 3:1—4:11*. Chicago: Scholars, 1983.

————. "Πίστις and Pauline Christology: What Is at Stake?" In *Pauline Theology, Volume 4. Looking Back, Pressing On*, edited by David M. Hay, E. Elizabeth Johnson, 35–60. Atlanta: Scholars, 1997.

Head, Peter M. "Letter Carriers in the Ancient Jewish Epistolary Material." In *Jewish and Christian Scripture as Artifact and Canon*, edited by Craig A. Evans and H. Daniel Zacharias, 203–19. Library of Second Temple Studies. London: T. & T. Clark, 2009.

————. "Named Letter-Carriers among the Oxyrhynchus Papyri." *Journal for the Study of the New Testament* 31 (2009) 279–99.

Healy, Mary. "Knowledge of the Mystery: A Study of Pauline Epistemology." In *The Bible and Epistemology*, edited by Mary Healy and Robin Parry, 134–57. Milton Keynes, UK: Paternoster, 2007.

Heidegger, Martin. *Being and Time*. Translated by John Macquarrie and Edward Robinson. Oxford: Blackwell, 1962.

Heliso, Desta. *Pistis and the Righteous One: A Study of Romans 1:17 against the Background of Scripture and Second Temple Jewish Literature*. WUNT II. Tübingen: Mohr Siebeck, 2007.

Henderson, George D. "The Idea of the Covenant in Scotland." *Evangelical Quarterly* 27.1 (1955) 2–14.

Heron, Alasdair I. C. "*Homoousios* with the Father." In *Incarnation: Ecumenical Studies in the Nicene-Constantinopolitan Creed A.D. 381*, edited by T. F. Torrance, 58–87. Edinburgh: Handsel, 1981.

Hilborn, David, editor. *The Nature of Hell*. Carlisle, UK: Paternoster, 2000.

Hofius, Otfried. "'Einer ist Gott—Einer ist Herr': Erwägungen zu Struktur und Aussage des Bekenntnisses 1.Kor 8,6." In *Eschatologie und Schöpfung: Festschrift für Erich Gräßer zum siebzigsten Geburtstag*, edited by Martin Evang, Erich Gräßer, Helmut Merklein, and Michael Wolter, 95–108. Berlin: de Gruyter, 1997.

Hogg, James. *The Private Memoirs and Confessions of a Justified Sinner*. New York: Grove, 1959.

Holmes, Stephen R. *The Quest for the Trinity: The Doctrine of God in Scripture, History, and Modernity*. Downers Grove, IL: InterVarsity, 2012.

————. *The Wondrous Cross: Atonement and Penal Substitution in the Bible and History*. Milton Keynes, UK: Paternoster, 2007.

Hunter, A. M. *P. T. Forsyth: Per Crucem ad Lucem*. London: SCM, 1974.

Hurtado, Larry W. *How on Earth Did Jesus Become a God?* Grand Rapids: Eerdmans, 2005.

————. *Lord Jesus Christ: Devotion to Jesus in Earliest Christianity*. Grand Rapids: Eerdmans, 2003.

Instone-Brewer, David. *Traditions of the Rabbis in the Era of the New Testament, Vol. 1*. Grand Rapids: Eerdmans, 2004.

Jaffee, Martin S. *Torah in the Mouth: Writing and Oral Tradition in Palestinian Judaism, 200 BCE-400 CE*. Oxford: Oxford University Press, 2001.

Jennings, Willie James. *The Christian Imagination: Theology and the Origins of Race*. New Haven, CT: Yale University Press, 2010.

Jenson, Robert W. *Ezekiel*. Brazos Theological Commentary on the Bible. Grand Rapids: Brazos, 2009.

Jipp, Joshua W. "Douglas Campbell's Apocalyptic, Rhetorical Paul: Review Article." *Horizons in Biblical Theology* 32.2 (2010) 183–97.

Johnson, Keith E. *Rethinking the Trinity and Religious Pluralism: An Augustinian Assessment.* Downers Grove, IL: InterVarsity, 2011.

Johnson, William A. *Readers and Reading Culture in the High Roman Empire: A Study of Elite Communities.* Oxford: Oxford University Press, 2010.

———. "Toward a Sociology of Reading in Classical Antiquity." *American Journal of Philology* 121 (2000) 593–627.

Jüngel, Eberhard. *The Doctrine of the Trinity.* Translated by Horton Harris. Edinburgh: Scottish Academic, 1976.

———. *Gottes Sein ist im Werden: Verantwortliche Rede vom Sein Gottes bei Karl Barth: Ein Paraphrase.* Tübingen: Mohr, 1976.

———. *Paulus und Jesus: Eine Untersuchung zur Präzisierung der Frage nach dem Ursprung der Christologie.* Tübingen: Mohr Siebeck, 2004.

Kahn, Charles H. *Plato and the Socratic Dialogue. The Philosophical Use of a Literary Form.* Cambridge: Cambridge University Press, 1996.

Kahneman, Daniel. *Thinking, Fast and Slow.* New York: Farrar, Straus & Giroux, 2011.

Käsemann, Ernst. *Paulinische Perspektiven.* Tübingen: Mohr, 1969.

Kearns, C. "The Interpretation of Romans 6, 7." Vol. 1: *Studiorum Paulinorum congressus internationalis catholicus 1961.* Analecta Biblica 17–18. Rome: Pontifical Biblical Institute Press, 1963.

Kennedy, George Alexander, editor. *Progymnasmata: Greek Textbooks of Prose Composition and Rhetoric.* Atlanta: Society of Biblical Literature, 2003.

Kerr, Nathan R. *Christ, History and Apocalyptic: The Politics of Christian Mission.* London: SCM, 2008.

Kirk, J. R. Daniel. *Unlocking Romans: Resurrection and the Justification of God.* Grand Rapids: Eerdmans, 2008.

Klauck, H.-J. and Daniel P. Bailey. *Ancient Letters and the New Testament: A Guide to Context and Exegesis.* 1998. Reprint. Waco, TX: Baylor University Press, 2006.

Kolb, Robert. "Contemporary Lutheran Understandings of the Doctrine of Justification: A Selective Glimpse." In *Justification: What's at Stake in the Current Debates,* edited by Mark Husbands and Daniel Treier, 153–76. Downers Grove, IL: InterVarsity, 2004.

Koonz, Claudia. *The Nazi Conscience.* Cambridge: Harvard University Press, 2003.

LaCugna, Catherine M. *God for Us: The Trinity and Christian Life.* San Francisco: HarperSanFrancisco, 1991.

Lakoff, George. *Whose Freedom? The Battle over America's Most Important Idea.* New York: Farrar, Straus and Giroux, 2006.

Lampe, Peter. *From Paul to Valentinus: Christians at Rome in the First Two Centuries.* Translated by Michael Steinhauser. 1989. Reprint. Minneapolis: Fortress, 2003.

Lash, Nicholas. *Believing Three Ways in One God: A Reading of the Apostles' Creed.* South Bend, IN: University of Notre Dame Press, 1993.

Leigh, Matthew. "The Pro Caelio and Comedy." *Classical Philosophy* 99.4 (2004) 300–35.

Leithart, Peter J. *Athanasius.* Foundations of Theological Exegesis and Christian Spirituality. Grand Rapids: Baker Academic, 2011.

Leland, John. *Letter of Valediction on Leaving Virginia in 1791 in The Writings of John Leland.* Edited by L. F. Greene. New York: Arno, 1969.

Lindsay, Thomas M. "The Covenant Theology." *The British and Foreign Evangelical Review* 28 (July 1879) 521–38.

Logan, James Samuel. *Good Punishment? Christian Moral Practice and U.S. Imprisonment.* Grand Rapids: Eerdmans, 2008.

Lohse, B. *Martin Luther: An Introduction to His Life and Work.* Edinburgh: T. & T. Clark, 1986.

Longenecker, Richard N. *Introducing Romans: Critical Issues in Paul's Most Famous Letter.* Grand Rapids: Eerdmans, 2011.

Luther, Martin. *A Commentary on St. Paul's Epistle to the Galatians.* Translated by Philip S. Watson. 1535. Reprint. London: Clarke, 1953.

Lyotard, Jean-François. *The Post-Modern Condition: A Report on Knowledge.* Manchester: University of Manchester Press, 1984.

Macaskill, Grant. "Review Article: *The Deliverance of God.*" *Journal for the Study of the New Testament* 34 (2011) 150–61.

Macchia, Frank D. "Justification through New Creation: The Holy Spirit and the Doctrine by Which the Church Stands or Falls." *Theology Today* 58 (2001) 202–17.

MacDonald, Nathan. *Deuteronomy and the Meaning of "Monotheism."* Tübingen: Mohr Siebeck, 2003.

Macewen, Alexander R. *The Erskines.* London: Oliphant, Anderson, & Ferrier, 1900.

MacIntyre, Alasdair C. *Three Rival Versions of Moral Enquiry: Encyclopaedia, Genealogy, and Tradition.* Notre Dame: University of Notre Dame Press, 1990.

———. *Whose Justice? Which Rationality?* Notre Dame: University of Notre Dame Press, 1988.

Macpherson, John. *The Doctrine of the Church in Scottish Theology: The Sixth Series of the Chalmers Lectures.* Edinburgh: Macniven & Wallace, 1903.

Malherbe, Abraham J. *Ancient Epistolary Theorists.* SBL Sources for Biblical Study 19. Atlanta: Scholars, 1988.

Martin, Dale B. *Pedagogy of the Bible: An Analysis and Proposal.* Louisville: Westminster John Knox, 2008.

Martyn, J. Louis. "Epistemology at the Turn of the Ages: 2 Corinthians 5.16." In *Theological Issues in the Letters of Paul*, 89–110. 1967. Reprint. Edinburgh: T. & T. Clark, 1997.

———. *Galatians: A New Translation with Introduction and Commentary.* Anchor Bible 33A. New York: Doubleday, 1997.

Matlock, Barry. "Zeal for Paul But Not according to Knowledge: Douglas Campbell's War on 'Justification theory.'" *Journal for the Study of the New Testament* 34 (2011) 115–49.

McGrath, Alister E. *Iustitia Dei: A History of the Christian Doctrine of Justification.* 3rd ed. Cambridge: Cambridge University Press, 2005.

McGrath, James F. *The Only True God: Early Christian Monotheism in Its Jewish Context.* Urbana, IL: University of Illinois Press, 2009.

McNally, Frederick W. "The Westminster Directory: Its Origin and Significance." PhD thesis, University of Edinburgh, 1958.

Metzger, Bruce Manning. *The Text of the New Testament.* 2nd ed. New York: Oxford University Press, 1968.

Meyer, Paul W. "The Worm at the Core of the Apple: Exegetical Reflections on Romans 7." In *The Conversation Continues: Studies in Paul and John in Honor of J. Louis*

Martyn, edited by R. T. Fortna and B. R. Gaventa, 62–84. Nashville: Abingdon, 1990.

Miller, Perry. *The Life of the Mind in America: From the Revolution to the Civil War*. New York: Harcourt, Brace & World, 1965.

———. *The New England Mind: From Colony to Province*. Cambridge: Harvard University Press, 1953.

———. *The New England Mind: The Seventeenth Century*. New York: Macmillan, 1939.

Perry Miller and Thomas Herbert Johnson. *The Puritans*. New York: Harper & Row, 1963.

Mitchell, Alexander F. *Catechisms of the Second Reformation: With Historical Introduction and Biographical Notices*. London: Nesbit, 1886.

Moltmann, Jürgen. *The Trinity and the Kingdom: The Doctrine of God*. Minneapolis: Fortress, 1981.

Moo, Douglas J. "The Deliverance of God: An Apocalyptic Rereading of Justification in Paul by Douglas A. Campbell." Review Article, *Journal of the Evangelical Theological Society* 53.1, (2010) 143–50.

———. *The Epistle to the Romans*. New International Commentary on the New Testament. Grand Rapids: Eerdmans, 1996.

Moule, C. F. D. *The Origin of Christology*. Cambridge: Cambridge University Press, 1977.

Moxnes, Halvor. *Theology in Conflict: Studies in Paul's Understanding of God in Romans*. Leiden: Brill, 1980.

Munzinger, André. *Discerning the Spirits: Theological and Ethical Hermeneutics in Paul*. Cambridge: Cambridge University Press, 2007.

Murray, John. *The Covenant of Grace: A Biblico-Theological Study*. London: Tyndale, 1953.

Neyrey, J. *Render to God: New Testament Understandings of the Divine*. Minneapolis: Fortress, 2004.

Nicholson, Suzanne. *Dynamic Oneness: The Significance and Flexibility of Paul's One-God Language*. Eugene, OR: Pickwick, 2010.

Niebuhr, H. Richard. "The Doctrine of the Trinity and the Unity of the Church." *Theology Today* 3 (1946) 371–84.

Olson, Roger E., and Christopher A. Hall. *The Trinity*. Grand Rapids: Eerdmans, 2002.

Origen. *Commentary on the Epistle to the Romans*. Books 6–10. Fathers of the Church 104. Translated by Thomas P. Scheck. Washington, DC: Catholic University of America Press, 2002.

———. *Der Römerbriefkommentar des Origenes: Kritische Ausgabe der Übersetzung Rufins*. 3 vols. Vetus Latina Die Reste der altlateinischen Bible Aus der Geschichte der Lateinischen Bibel 16, 33, 34. Edited by Caroline P. Hammond Bammel. Freiburg in Breisgau: Herder, 1990.

Ostmeyer, Karl-Heinrich. *Kommunikation mit Gott und Christus: Sprache und Theologie des Gebetes im Neuen Testament*. Tübingen: Mohr Siebeck, 2006.

Parker, T. H. L. *Calvin's Doctrine of the Knowledge of God*. Grand Rapids: Eerdmans, 1959.

Parry, Robin A. *Worshipping Trinity: Coming Back to the Heart of Worship*. 2nd ed. Eugene, OR: Cascade, 2012.

Parry, Robin, and Mary Healy, editors. *The Bible and Epistemology: Biblical Soundings on the Knowledge of God*. Milton Keynes, UK: Paternoster, 2007.

Pearsall, Judy, and William R. Trumble, editors. *The Oxford English Reference Dictionary.* Oxford: Oxford University Press, 1995.

Pelikan, Jaroslav, and Valerie Hotchkiss, editors. *Creeds and Confession of Faith in the Christian Tradition.* 4 vols. New Haven, CT: Yale University Press, 2004.

Pettersen, Alwyn. *Athanasius.* London: Geoffrey Chapman, 1995.

Piper, John. *The Justification of God: An Exegetical and Theological Study of Romans 9:1–23.* Grand Rapids: Baker, 1983.

Pitts, Andrew. "Philosophical and Epistolary Contexts for Pauline Paraenesis." In *Paul and the Ancient Letter Form.* Edited by Stanley Porter. Leiden: Brill, 2010.

Placher, William C. *The Domestication of Transcendence: How Modern Thinking about God Went Wrong.* Louisville: Westminster John Knox, 1996.

Plato. *The Republic.* Translated by R. E. Allen. New Haven, CT: Yale University Press, 2006.

Polanyi, Michael. *Personal Knowledge: Towards a Post-Critical Philosophy.* Chicago: University of Chicago Press, 1974.

———. *The Tacit Dimension.* Chicago: University of Chicago Press, 1966.

Porter, Stanley E. *Verbal Aspect in the Greek of the New Testament: With Reference to Tense and Mood.* Studies in Biblical Greek 1; New York: Lang, 1989.

Radford Ruether, Rosemary. *Faith and Fratricide: The Theological Roots of Anti-Semitism.* New York: Seabury, 1974.

Rae, Murray A. *History and Hermeneutics.* London: T. & T. Clark, 2005.

Räisänen, Heikki. *Paul and the Law.* Wissenschaftliche Untersuchungen zum Neuen Testament 29. Tübingen: Mohr Siebeck, 1983.

Richard, E. *Jesus: One and Many: The Christological Concept of New Testament Authors.* Wilmington, DE: Glazier, 1988.

Riesebrodt, Martin. *The Promise of Salvation: A Theory of Religion.* Chicago: University of Chicago Press, 2010.

Rose, Margaret A. *Paraody: Ancient, Modern, and Post-Modern.* Cambridge: Cambridge University Press, 1993.

Roukema, Riemer. *The Diversity of Laws in Origen's Commentary on Romans.* Amsterdam: Free University Press, 1988.

Rowe, C. Kavin. "Biblical Pressure and Trinitarian Hermeneutics." *Pro Ecclesia* 11 (2002) 295–312.

———. "For Future Generations: Worshipping Jesus and the Integration of the Theological Disciplines." *Pro Ecclesia* 17.2 (2008) 186–209.

———. "The Grammar of Life: The Areopagus Speech and Pagan Tradition." *New Testament Studies* 97 (2011) 31–50.

———. *World Upside Down: Reading Acts in the Graeco-Roman Age.* Oxford: Oxford University Press, 2009.

Royse, James R. *Scribal Habits in Early Greek New Testament Papyri.* Leiden: Brill, 2008.

Saenger, Paul Henry. *Space between Words: The Origins of Silent Reading.* Figurae: Reading Medieval Culture. Stanford, CA: Stanford University Press, 1997.

Sanders, E. P. *Paul, the Law, and the Jewish People.* Philadelphia: Fortress, 1983.

———. *Paul and Palestinian Judaism: A Comparison of Patterns of Religion.* Philadelphia: Fortress, 1977.

———. *Paul: A Very Short Introduction.* Oxford: University Press, 1991.

Sandnes, Karl Olav. *Belly and the Body in the Pauline Epistles.* Society for New Testament Studies Monograph Series 120. Cambridge: Cambridge University Press, 2002.

Schnabel, Eckhard J. *Der erste Brief des Paulus an die Korinther.* Wuppertal: Brockhaus, 2006.

Schnelle, Udo. *Paulus: Leben und Denken.* Berlin: de Gruyter, 2003.

Schrage, Wolfgang. *Der erste Brief an die Korinther (2).* Zürich: Benziger, 1995.

————. *Unterwegs zur Einzigkeit und Einheit Gottes: zum "Monotheismus" des Paulus und seiner alttestamentlich-frühjüdischen Tradition.* Neukirchen-Vluyn: Neukirchener Verlag, 2002.

Schreiner, Thomas R. *Galatians.* Zondervan Exegetical Commentary on the New Testament. Grand Rapids: Zondervan, 2010.

————. "Review: *The Deliverance of God: An Apocalyptic Rereading of Justification in Paul.*" *Bulletin for Biblical Research* 20 (2010) 289–90.

————. *Romans.* Grand Rapids: Baker, 1998.

Schwöbel, Christoph. *Gott in Beziehung: Studien Zur Dogmatik.* Tübingen: Mohr Siebeck, 2002.

Scott, Ian W. *Implicit Epistemology in the Letters of Paul: Story, Experience and the Spirit.* Tübingen: Mohr Siebeck, 2006.

Scott, James C. *Domination and the Arts of Resistance: Hidden Transcripts.* New Haven, CT: Yale University Press, 1990.

Scroggs, Robin. "Romans 6:7: *Ho gar apothanōn dedikaiōtai apo tēs hamartias.*" *New Testament Studies* 10 (1963) 104–8.

Scullion, J. J., and John Reumann. "Righteousness." *Anchor Bible Dictionary,* edited by David Noel Freedman, 5:724–73. New York: Doubleday, 1992.

Searle, John R. *Speech Acts: An Essay in the Philosophy of Language.* London: Cambridge University Press, 1969.

Seifrid, Mark. "Book Review: Douglas Atchison Campbell. *The Deliverance of God: An Apocalyptic Rereading of Justification in Paul.*" *Themelios* 35 (2010) 307–9.

————. "The Narrative of Scripture and Justification by Faith: A Still Fresher Reading of Paul." Presented to a *Symposium on Exegetical Theology,* Concordia Theological Seminary, Fort Wayne, IN, 2006.

Sellers, R. V. *Two Ancient Christologies: A Study in the Christological Thought of the Schools of Alexandria and Antioch in the Early History of Christian Doctrine.* London: SPCK, 1940.

Seneca. *Moral and Political Essays.* Translated by John M. Cooper and J. F. Procopé. Cambridge: Cambridge University Press, 1995.

Sidanius, Jim, and Felicia Pratto. *Social Dominance.* Cambridge: Cambridge University Press, 1999.

Silva, Moisés. "Faith Versus Works of Law in Galatians." In *Justification and Variegated Nomism, Vol. II, The Paradoxes of Paul,* edited by D. A. Carson, P. T. O'Brien, and M. A. Seifrid, 230–47. Wissenschaftliche Untersuchungen zum Neuen Testamentum II.181. Tübingen: Mohr Siebeck, 2004.

Smith, Christian, and Melina Lundquist Denton. *Soul Searching: The Religious and Spiritual Lives of American Teenagers.* Oxford: Oxford University Press, 2009.

Smith, Warren. *Christian Grace and Pagan Virtue: The Theological Foundation of Ambrose's Ethics.* Oxford: Oxford University Press, 2011.

Snyder, C. Arnold. *Anabaptist History and Theology: An Introduction.* Kitchener, Ontario: Pandora, 1995.

Sprott, George W. *The Worship of the Church of Scotland During the Covenanting Period, 1638-1661.* Edinburgh: Blackwood & Son, 1893.

Stegman, Thomas. *The Character of Jesus: The Linchpin to Paul's Argument in 2 Corinthians*. Rome: Editrice Pontifico Istituto Biblico, 2005.

Stendahl, Krister. *Final Account: Paul's Letter to the Romans*. Minneapolis: Fortress, 1995.

———. *Paul among Jews and Gentiles, and other Essays*. Philadelphia: Fortress, 1976.

Stowers, Stanley Kent. "Apostrophe, *Prosōpopoieia*, and Paul's Rhetorical Education." In *Early Christianity and Classical Culture: Comparative Studies in Honor of Abraham J. Malherbe*, edited by John T. Fitzgerald and L. Michael White. Novum Testamentum Supplements 110. Leiden: Brill, 2003.

———. *A Rereading of Romans: Justice, Jews, and Gentiles*. New Haven, CT: Yale University Press, 1994.

———. "Romans 7:7-25 as a Speech-in-Character (*Prosōpopoieia*)." In *Paul in His Hellenistic Context*, edited by T. Engberg-Pedersen, 180–202. Minneapolis: Fortress, 1995.

Strachey, Lytton. *Eminent Victorians*. New York: Continuum, 2002.

Strobel, August. *Untersuchungen zum eschatologischen Verzögerungsproblem: auf Grund der spätjüdisch-urchristlichen Geschichte von Habakuk 2,2 ff*. Leiden: Brill, 1961

Sumney, Jerry L. *Identifying Paul's Opponents: The Question of Method in 2 Corinthians*. Journal for the Study of the Old Testament Supplements 40. Sheffield, UK: Sheffield Academic, 1990.

Tanner, K. "Kingdom Come: The Trinity and Politics." *The Princeton Seminary Bulletin* 28.2 (2007) 129–45.

Taylor, Bernard A. "Deponency and Greek Lexicography." In *Biblical Greek Language and Lexicography: FS Frederick W. Danker*, edited by Bernard A. Taylor et al., 167–76. Grand Rapids: Eerdmans, 2004.

Thielicke, Helmut. *The Evangelical Faith. Volume 1: Prolegomena*. Grand Rapids: Eerdmans, 1974.

Thiselton, Anthony C. *The First Epistle to the Corinthians*. New International Greek Testament Commentary. Grand Rapids: Eerdmans, 2000.

———. *First Corinthians: A Shorter Exegetical and Pastoral Commentary*. Grand Rapids: Eerdmans, 2006.

———. *Hermeneutics of Doctrine*. Grand Rapids: Eerdmans, 2007.

———. "Human Being, Relationality, and Time in Hebrews, 1 Corinthians, and Western Traditions." *Ex Auditu* 13 (1997) 76–95.

Thompson, Ernest Trice. *The Spirituality of the Church: A Distinctive Doctrine of the Presbyterian Church in the United States*. Richmond, VA: John Knox, 1961.

Thrall, Margaret E. *The Second Epistle to the Corinthians Vol. 1*. London: T. & T. Clark, 2004.

———. *The Second Epistle to the Corinthians Vol. 2*. London: T. & T. Clark, 2004.

Thyen, H. *Studien zur Sündenvergebung in Neuen Testament und seinen alttestamentlichen und jüdischen Voraussetzungen*. Forschungen zur Religion und Literatur des Alten und Neuen Testaments 96. Göttingen: Vandenhoeck & Ruprecht, 1970.

Tilley, Terrence W. *The Disciples' Jesus: Christology as Reconciling Practice*. Maryknoll, NY: Orbis, 2008.

Tilling, Chris. "The Deliverance of God, and of Paul?" *Journal for the Study of Paul and His Letters* 1 (2011) 85–101.

————. "Ephesians and Christology." In *Christ, Spirit and the Church: Essays in Honour of Max Turner*, edited by Volker Rabens, Howard I. Marshall, and Cornelis Bennema, 177–97. Grand Rapids: Eerdmans, 2011.

————. *Paul's Divine Christology*. Wissenschaftliche Untersuchungen zum Neuen Testamentum II. Tübingen: Mohr Siebeck, 2012.

Tolstoy, Leo. *Anna Karenina*. Translated by Constance Garnett. 1877. Reprint. New York: Random House, 1993.

Torrance, Alan J. "Can the Truth Be Learned? Redressing the 'Theologistic Fallacy' in Modern Biblical Scholarship." In *Scripture's Doctrine and Theology's Bible: How the New Testament Shapes Christian Dogmatics*, edited by Markus Bockmuehl and Alan J. Torrance, 143–63. Grand Rapids: Baker Academic, 2008.

————. "Is Love the Essence of God?" In *Nothing Greater, Nothing Better: Theological Essays on the Love of God*, edited by Kevin J. Vanhoozer, 114–37. Grand Rapids: Eerdmans, 2001.

————. *Persons in Communion: An Essay on Trinitarian Description and Human Participation, with Special Reference to Volume One of Karl Barth's Church Dogmatics*. Edinburgh: T. & T. Clark, 1996.

————. "The Theological Grounds for Advocating Forgiveness and Reconciliation in the Sociopolitical Realm." In *The Politics of Past Evil*, edited by Daniel Philpott, 65–121. South Bend, IN: Notre Dame University Press, 2006.

Torrance, James B. "Contribution of McLeod Campbell to Scottish Theology." *Scottish Journal of Theology* 26 (1973) 295–311.

————. "Covenant or Contract: A Study of the Theological Background of Worship in Seventeenth-Century Scotland." *Scottish Journal of Theology* 23 (1970) 51–76.

Torrance, Thomas F. "Athanasius: A Study in the Foundations of Classical Theology." In *Theology in Reconciliation: Essays Towards Evangelical and Catholic Unity in East and West*, 215–66. London: Geoffrey Chapman, 1975.

————. "The Doctrine of the Holy Trinity according to St Athanasius." *Australasian Theological Review* 71 (1989) 395–405.

————. "Karl Barth and the Latin Heresy." *Scottish Journal of Theology* 39 (1986) 461–82.

————. "One Aspect of the Biblical Conception of Faith." *Expository Times* 68.4 (1957) 111–14.

————. "Spiritus Creator: A Consideration of the Teaching of St. Athanasius and St. Basil." In *Theology in Reconstruction*, 209–28. Edinburgh: T. & T. Clark, 1965.

Travis, Stephen H. *Christ and the Judgment of God: The Limits of Divine Retribution in New Testament Thought*. 2nd ed. Milton Keynes, UK: Paternoster, 2009.

Troeltsch, Ernst. *Die Absolutheit des Christentums und die Religionsgeschichte*. 1912. Reprint. Berlin: de Gruyter, 1998.

————. *The Christian Faith*. Translated by Garrett E. Paul. Minneapolis: Fortress, 1991.

————. *Religion in History*. Translated by James Luther Adams and Walter E. Bense. Minneapolis: Fortress, 1991.

Turner, Max. "'Trinitarian' Pneumatology in the New Testament?—Towards an Explanation of the Worship of Jesus." *Asbury Theological Journal* 58.1 (2003) 167–86.

Ursinus, Zacharias. *The Summe of Christian Religion*. Translated by Henry Parry. Oxford: Barnes, 1601.

Volf, Miroslav. *After Our Likeness: The Church as the Image of the Trinity.* Grand Rapids: Eerdmans, 1998.

Von Rad, Gerhard. *Old Testament Theology. Volume 1.* 1957. Reprint. London: SCM, 1975.

Vriezen, Th. C. *An Outline of Old Testament Theology.* 2nd rev. ed. Newton, MA: Branford, 1970.

Waaler, Erik. *The Shema and the First Commandment in First Corinthians: An Intertextual Approach to Paul's Re-Reading of Deuteronomy.* Tübingen: Mohr Siebeck, 2008.

Wacker, Grant. *Augustus H. Strong and the Dilemma of Historical Consciousness.* Macon, GA: Mercer University Press, 1985

Walker, James. *The Theology and Theologians of Scotland: Chiefly of the Seventeenth and Eighteenth Centuries.* 2nd ed. Edinburgh: T. & T. Clark, 1888.

Walton, John. *Ancient Near Eastern Thought and the Old Testament: Introducing the Conceptual World of the Hebrew Bible.* Grand Rapids: Baker, 2006.

Watson, Francis. "Book Review: Douglas Campbell, *The Deliverance of God: An Apocalyptic Rereading of Justification in Paul.*" *Early Christianity* 1.1 (2010) 179–85.

———. "By Faith (of Christ): An Exegetical Dilemma and Its Scriptural Solution." In *The Faith of Jesus Christ: Exegetical, Biblical, and Theological Studies*, edited by Michael F. Bird and Preston M. Sprinkle, 147–63. Milton Keynes, UK: Paternoster, 2009.

———. *Paul and the Hermeneutics of Faith.* London: T. & T. Clark, 2004.

———. *Paul, Judaism, and the Gentiles: A Sociological Approach.* Society for New Testament Studies Monograph Series 56. Cambridge: Cambridge University Press, 1986.

———. *Text and Truth: Redefining Biblical Theology.* Edinburgh: T. & T. Clark, 1997.

Watson, Janet, editor. *Speaking Volumes: Orality and Literacy in the Greek and Roman World.* Leiden: Brill, 2001.

Watts, John D. W. *Isaiah 34–66.* Word Biblical Commentary. Waco, TX: Word, 1987.

Watts, Michael. *The Philosophy of Heidegger.* Durham, NC: Acumen, 2011.

Welborn, L. L. *Paul, the Fool of Christ: A Study of 1 Corinthians 1–4 in the Comic-Philosophic Tradition.* Journal for the Study of the New Testament Supplement Series 293. London: T. & T. Clark, 2005.

Wendland, Heinz-Dietrich. *Die Briefe an die Korinther.* 1932. Reprint. Göttingen: Vandenhoeck & Ruprecht, 1972.

Wengert, Timothy J. *Law and Gospel: Philip Melanchthon's Debate with John Agricola of Eisleben over Poenitentia.* Edited by R. A. Muller. Texts & Studies in Reformation and Post-Reformation Thought. Grand Rapids: Baker, 1997.

Westerholm, Stephen. *Perspectives Old and New on Paul: The "Lutheran" Paul and His Critics.* Grand Rapids: Eerdmans, 2004

The Whole Proceedings before the Presbytery of Dumbarton, and Synod of Glasgow and Ayr, in the case of the Rev. John McLeod Campbell, Minister of Row. Including the Libel, Answers to the Libel, Evidences, and Speeches. Edinburgh: Waugh & Innes, and J. Lindsay & Co., 1831.

Wilken, Robert Louis. *The Spirit of Early Christian Thought: Seeking the Face of God.* New Haven, CT: Yale University Press, 2003.

Williams, Rowan. *Arius: Heresy and Tradition.* Rev. ed. Grand Rapids: Eerdmans, 2001.

Wolfson, Harry Austryn. *The Philosophy of the Kalam*. Cambridge: Harvard University Press, 1976.

Woolf, Greg. "Literacy." In *The Cambridge Ancient History, Volume 11, The High Empire, A.D. 70–192*, 2nd ed, edited by A. K. Bowman, P. Garnsey, and D. Rathbone, 875–97. Cambridge: Cambridge University Press, 2008.

Woyke, Johannes. "Das Bekenntnis zum einzig allwirksamen Gott und Herrn und die Dämonisierung von Fremdkulten: Monolatrischer und polylatrischer Monotheismus in 1. Korinther 8 und 10." In *Gruppenreligionen im römischen Reich. Sozialformen, Grenzziehungen und Leistungen*, edited by J. Rüpke, 87–112. Tübingen: Mohr Siebeck, 2007.

———. *Götter, "Götzen", Götterbilder: Aspekte einer paulinischen "Theologie der Religionen."* Berlin: de Gruyter, 2005.

Wrede, William. *Paul*. Translated by Edward Lummis. 1908. Reprint. Eugene, OR: Wipf & Stock, 2001.

Wright, N. T. *The Climax of the Covenant: Christ and the Law in Pauline Theology*. Edinburgh: T. & T. Clark, 1991.

———. "Coming Home to St. Paul? Reading Romans a Hundred Years after Charles Gore." *Scottish Journal of Theology* 55.4 (2002) 392–407.

———. *The Resurrection of the Son of God*. Christian Origins and the Question of God 3. Minneapolis: Fortress, 2003.

Wright, Tom. *Justification: God's Plan and Paul's Vision*. London: SPCK, 2009.

Yeago, David S. "The New Testament and the Nicene Dogma: A Contribution to the Recovery of Theological Exegesis." *Pro Ecclesia* 3 (1994) 152–64.

Yinger, Kent L. *The New Perspective on Paul: An Introduction*. Eugene, OR: Cascade, 2011.

Zeilinger, Franz. *Krieg und Friede in Korinth: Kommentar zum 2. Korintherbrief des Apostels Paulus. Band 1: Der Kampfbrief, Der Versöhnungsbrief, Der Bettelbrief*. Köln: Böhlau, 1992.

Zellentin, Holger M. *Rabbinic Parodies of Jewish and Christian Literature*. Tübingen: Mohr Siebeck, 2011.

Zizioulas, J. D. *Being as Communion: Studies in Personhood and the Church*. Crestwood, NY: St. Vladimir's Seminary Press, 1985.

Ancient Sources Index

~

NEW TESTAMENT

∼

CLASSICAL

Modern Author Index

Subject Index

CPSIA information can be obtained
at www.ICGtesting.com
Printed in the USA
LVOW12*2308171216
517781LV00004B/20/P